FrontPage 98

The Cram Sheet

This Cram Sheet contains the distilled, key facts about FrontPage 98. Review this information last thing before you enter the test room, paying special attention to those areas where you feel you need the most review. You can transfer any of these facts from your head onto a blank sheet of paper before beginning the exam.

ANALYZING BUSINESS REQUIREMENTS

1. Know browser support for FrontPage features (see Table 10.1).
2. Match graphics, speed, and non-standard components with browser/client/connection speed.
3. SSL is the only protection for passwords during authentication.
4. Ease of maintenance means either few manual pages or use of a database for large or quickly expanding sites.
5. Compare hardware and software capabilities with requirements defined by target audience, bandwidth, multimedia capabilities, security, maintenance/administration, and performance.

TECHNICAL ARCHITECTURE

6. Know Web server support for FrontPage features (see Table 13.1).
7. Always include Text options for graphical elements and navigational controls. The Image Properties dialog box offers this option.
8. When you're in the Navigation View, you can right-click and bring up the Web Settings. On the Advanced tab, you can set the language for the validation scripts.
9. User registration forces users to register before they are granted access. It does not provide security.

CONCEPTUAL AND LOGICAL DESIGN

10. The Tasks View is used to assign actions to multiple site administrators.
11. When using frames, an existing frame can be split by using the Split Frame command. You can also hold down the Ctrl button while dragging and dropping a frame pane edge.
12. Use include or scheduled include components for HTML or images that are the same throughout a site but that may change or be updated.
13. Use sub-Webs to divide a site into manageable sections, each assigned to a different administrator, each having different access permissions, and/or each having a different type of content.

48. Common items, such as phone numbers and addresses, can be defined on the Parameters tab of the Web Settings dialog box. Once changed, all references to the defined item are automatically updated through the use of the Substitution component.

49. The Configuration tab of the Web Settings dialog box allows you to change the Web's name and title.

50. To include or exclude files in Search, add or remove them from the _private directory. This does not alter layout or navigation.

51. File types are associated with editors on the Configure Editors tab of the Options dialog box.

52. You can be informed automatically when Web site components, such as scheduled include page and scheduled image, are out of date by selecting the Warn When Included Components Are Out Of Date checkbox on the General tab of the Options dialog box.

MANAGING ACCESS TO A FRONTPAGE 98 WEB SITE

53. Security settings on sub-Webs do not need to be the same as the root or other sub-Webs.

54. Multiple users and computers can be defined at various levels of access to a root or sub-Web through the dialog box Tools|Permissions.

55. Author privileges are required to create, modify, and delete pages in a FrontPage Web.

56. Admin privileges are required to create, modify, and delete entire FrontPage Webs.

57. To grant creation privileges to multiple groups without overlapping, use multiple sub-Webs and assign a single sub-Web to each group.

58. Admin, author, and browser privileges are granted on a user or group basis.

Certification Insider™ Press

23. FrontPage 98 includes its own Web server for local testing; thus a separate Web server is not necessary for development of Web sites.

CREATING USER SERVICES

24. The Navigation View is used to create a site navigation scheme.
25. The names of the navigation buttons are defined or reset to defaults on the Navigation tab of the Web Settings dialog box.
26. A form element is changed by editing its properties, such as the selections in an option list.
27. Validation scripts fail when the submitted criteria fail to meet the restrictions.
28. User input to a form can be sent via email, saved to a file, or displayed in a frame pane using a WebBot.
29. Hidden fields can be used to submit information unseen by the user, such as a form name.
30. A channel definition requires a source directory. Logging of usage information is optional.
31. To include a background sound for both Netscape Navigator and Internet Explorer, you must use JavaScript to determine the browser type and issue the correct markup code.
32. For Web sites interacting with a SQL database, a DSN must be defined and used with ASP.
33. The Database Region wizard is used to configure the interaction between a database and a Web site. It requires the DSN, the name and password to access the database, and the proper SQL query string.
34. If ASP is not used, IDC can be used to interact with a database. This requires an IDC file and an HTX file.
35. ASP files must be stored in a directory where at least script permission is set.

TESTING A FRONTPAGE 98 WEB SITE

36. Web sites can be viewed in multiple browsers using the Preview In Browser command from FrontPage Editor.
37. The Preview In Browser dialog box offers you four selections of window sizes to simulate various display resolutions.
38. The FrontPage Editor offers several views of a Web page: Normal, HTML, and basic Preview. Forms pages have two additional views: No Frames and Frames Page HTML.

PUBLISHING A FRONTPAGE 98 WEB SITE

39. FrontPage can publish through a proxy server. You must define the proxy server on the Proxies tab of the Options dialog box. Proxies are listed by IP address or NetBIOS name followed by their port address (for example, Proxy1:81).
40. You can use FTP to publish Webs sites to servers that do not have FrontPage Server Extensions installed.
41. When publishing a Web site, you can publish only the changed files or all files.

MANAGING A FRONTPAGE 98 WEB SITE

42. Office 97 documents can be included as pages in a FrontPage Web site.
43. All of the files created by a single user can be found in the All Files View.
44. The Navigation View offers you the capability to add pages to the navigation structure, to move pages from one level to another in the navigation, and to change a page's title.
45. The Hyperlink Status View is used to determine if links are broken.
46. The Hyperlinks View only shows the relationship between internal documents. It does not highlight broken links.
47. Spellchecking a site can be set to appear as an item in the Tasks View.

DESIGNING A USER INTERFACE AND USER SERVICES

14. Using FrontPage's navigation tools is better than relying on your own manual design. The built-in navigation controls are automatically updated, which results in less administrative overhead.

15. Themes help create a consistent look to a Web site. Individual sub-Webs and even pages can conform to the entire site's theme or support a different or variant theme.

16. Themes can include the following: Vivid Colors, Active Graphics, and/or Background Image.

17. Include user feedback and interface features in Web sites. These include:
    - Discussion sections
    - Email forms
    - FAQs
    - Bug reports
    - Suggestions
    - Search

18. The important Corporate Web wizard components include:
    - Selection of main pages/sections
    - Home page and "What's New?" topics
    - Number of products and number of services and elements for each Product page and Service page
    - Feedback form elements and how to store feedback information (text or HTML format)
    - Table of contents options
    - Page banner and page footer elements
    - The Under Construction icon (for incomplete pages)
    - Company info (name, one-word nickname, and street address)
    - More company info (telephone number, fax number, Webmaster's email address, and general info email address)
    - Web themes

19. Common borders maintain consistency throughout a site. They are turned on and off through the Tools|Shared Borders dialog box.

ESTABLISHING THE DEVELOPMENT ENVIRONMENT

20. Server Extensions must be used for most FrontPage WebBot components.

21. The FrontPage components:
    - Comment
    - Confirmation field
    - Hit counter
    - Include page
    - Insert HTML
    - Page banner
    - Scheduled image
    - Scheduled include page
    - Substitution
    - Hover buttons
    - Banner ad manager
    - Marquee
    - Search form
    - Video
    - Timestamps
    - Table of contents
    - Navigation bar
    - User registration

22. FrontPage Server Extensions provide the following:
    - Multiuser authoring, which allows multiple users to work on the same Web site simultaneously
    - Remote authoring via FrontPage, which allows users to connect and write directly to the Web server over the Internet
    - Form handling for the custom forms that can be added via FrontPage
    - Support for discussion Webs, which is closely related to multiuser authoring
    - Full-text indexing, which allows users to search the Web site when the proper HTML search forms are available
    - Support for FrontPage hit counters

EXAM CRAM™

FrontPage 98

Microsoft Certified Solution Developer

Ed Tittel, Kurt Hudson, James Michael Stewart

MCSD/MCP+SB FrontPage 98 Exam Cram

The Coriolis Group, Inc.
An International Thomson Publishing Company
14455 N. Hayden Road, Suite 220
Scottsdale, Arizona 85260-

602/483-0192
FAX 602/483-0193
http://www.coriolis.com

Library of Congress Cataloging-in-Publication Data
Tittel, Ed.

MCSD/MCP+SB FrontPage 98 exam cram / by Ed Tittel, Kurt Hudson, and James Michael Stewart.

p. cm.

Includes index.

ISBN 1-57610-398-6

1. Electronic data processing personnel--Certification. 2. Microsoft software--Examinations--Study guides. 3. Microsoft FrontPage. I. Hudson, Kurt. II. Stewart, James Michael. III. Title.
QA76.3.T57365 1999
005.7'2--dc21 98-45353
CIP

Printed in the United States of America
10 9 8 7 6 5 4 3 2 1

Publisher
Keith Weiskamp

Acquisitions Editor
Shari Jo Hehr

Marketing Specialist
Cynthia Caldwell

Project Editor
Jeff Kellum

Technical Editor
Gary Clarke

Production Coordinator
Meg E. Turecek

Cover Design
Anthony Stock

Layout Design
April Nielsen

CORIOLIS

an International Thomson Publishing company

Albany, NY • Belmont, CA • Bonn • Boston • Cincinnati • Detroit • Johannesburg • London • Madrid
Melbourne • Mexico City • New York • Paris • Singapore • Tokyo • Toronto • Washington

14455 North Hayden, Suite 220 • Scottsdale, Arizona 85260

The Smartest Way To Get Certified ™

Thank you for purchasing one of our innovative certification study guides, just one of the many members of the Coriolis family of certification products.

Certification Insider Press™ was created in late 1997 by The Coriolis Group to help professionals like you obtain certification and advance your career. Achieving certification involves a major commitment and a great deal of hard work. To help you reach your goals, we've listened to others like you, and have designed our entire product line around you and the way you like to study, learn, and master challenging subjects. Our approach is the *Smartest Way to Get Certified.*

In less than a year, Coriolis has published over one million copies of our highly popular *Exam Cram*, *Exam Prep*, and *On Site* guides. Our *Exam Cram* series, specifically written to help you pass an exam, are the number one certification self-study guides in the industry. They are the perfect complement to any study plan you have, as well as to the rest of the Certification Insider Press series: *Exam Prep*—comprehensive study guides designed to help you thoroughly learn and master certification topics, and *On Site*—guides that really show you how to apply your skills and knowledge on the job.

Our commitment to you is to ensure that all of the certification study guides we develop help you save time and frustration. Each one provides unique study tips and techniques, memory joggers, custom quizzes, insight about test taking, practical problems to solve, real-world examples, and much more.

We'd like to hear from you. Help us continue to provide the very best certification study materials possible. Write us or email us at **craminfo@coriolis.com** and let us know how our books have helped you study, or tell us about new features that you'd like us to add. If you send us a story about how an *Exam Cram*, *Exam Prep*, or *On Site* guide has helped you, and we use it in one of our books, we'll send you an official Coriolis shirt for your efforts.

Good luck with your certification exam and your career. Thank you for allowing us to help you achieve your goals.

Keith Weiskamp

Keith Weiskamp
Publisher, Certification Insider Press

About The Authors

Ed Tittel

Ed Tittel has worked on more than 70 computer books, including numerous titles for the *Exam Cram* and *Exam Prep* series for Certification Insider Press, for which he is also the Series Editor. When he's not hunched over a keyboard, one hand in a Resource Kit, the other on the telephone, he tries to run the show at LANWrights, Inc., a small training and consulting firm in beautiful Austin, TX. In his copious spare time, Ed is also a member of the program committee for NetWorld + Interop, where he walks the distributed systems beat. When he's not working, Ed likes to shoot pool, drink wine, and mess around with his rambunctious Labrador retriever, Blackie. You can contact Ed by email at **etittel@lanw.com** or through his Web page at **www.lanw.com/staff/etbio.htm**.

Kurt Hudson

Kurt Hudson is a technical author, trainer, and consultant in the field of networking and computer-related technologies. For the past seven years, he has focused his energy on learning and teaching technical skills. He has written several training manuals and books for government and private industry on topics ranging from inventory control to network administration.

Kurt first started working with computer technology in the U.S. Air Force, where he served as a Korean linguist, production controller, and trainer. While still in the Air Force, Kurt also earned a Master's degree in Management from Troy State University, in Alabama. After an honorable discharge from the Air Force, Kurt went to work for several civilian companies, including Unisys and Productivity Point International.

James Michael Stewart

James Michael Stewart is a full-time writer focusing on Windows NT and Internet topics. Most recently, he has worked on several titles in the *Exam Cram* series, including *MCSE NT Server 4 Exam Cram, MCSE NT Workstation 4 Exam Cram, MCSE NT Server 4 in the Enterprise Exam Cram, MCSE Windows 95 Exam Cram, MCSE IIS 4 Exam Cram*, and *MCSE Proxy Server 2*

Exam Cram. Additionally, he has co-authored the *Hip Pocket Guide to HTML 4* (1998) and the *Intranet Bible* (1997). Michael has written articles for numerous print and online publications, including C|Net, *Computer Currents*, *InfoWorld*, *Windows NT* magazine, and *Datamation*. He is also a regular speaker at NetWorld + Interop, and has taught at WNTIS and NT SANS.

Michael has for many years been developing Windows NT 4 MCSE-level courseware and training materials, including both print and online publication as well as classroom presentation of NT training materials. He has been an MCSE since 1997, with a focus on Windows NT 4.

You can reach Michael by email at **michael@lanw.com** or through his Web pages at **www.lanw.com/jmsbio.htm** or **www.impactonline.com**.

Acknowledgments

Ed Tittel

I'm starting to learn that writing a book is a lot like architecting a building. In some weird sense, the thing belongs to you, and even has your name on it. But it involves the work of so many people that it doesn't seem fair to take too much of the credit for oneself. With that in mind, I'd like to start by thanking my stellar co-authors, including those named on the front cover—James Michael Stewart and Kurt Hudson, who did the bulk of the work—but also Natanya Pitts-Moultis and John Cook, who contributed one very important chapter apiece to this book as well. While I'm at it, I'd like to thank our sterling Technical Editor, Gary Clarke, without whose painstaking contributions this book wouldn't be anywhere near as complete or correct.

Next, my most fervent thanks go to the terrific team of editors and project managers at LANWrights. They deserve much of the credit for this tome, especially Dawn Rader, our Managing Editor, and Mary Burmeister, our "editor-in-waiting." Finally, there's the whole crew at Coriolis who made this book possible, in all the departments from sales and marketing, to editorial, to production, and so forth. We're especially grateful to Paula Kmetz, the Managing Editor, who worked extra hard with us on this book to streamline the process for everybody, and to Jeff Kellum, our Project Editor, who is truly wonderful to work with. Also, thanks must go to Meg Turecek, the Production Coordinator, and Anthony Stock, the Cover Designer, for their hard work on this project. As always, there are far too many people to mention by name, but please accept our thanks anyway, even if you don't get to see your name in lights, so to speak.

I've saved the best thanks for last: First, to Keith Weiskamp, the Publisher at Coriolis, for taking this concept further and faster than I ever thought it could go; thanks for teaching me how to stretch my boundaries. Second, to Shari Jo Hehr, our Acquisition Editor, for making deal-making easy and fun. Third, to Carole McClendon, our agent, for keeping us so very busy and engaged. And finally, to Mom and Dad, for making the whole thing possible. Thanks alone are not enough, but that's all I have to give...for now!

Kurt Hudson

I would like to thank Dawn Rader and Ed Tittel for bringing me into the writing business. I also want to thank Ed, Dawn, James Michael Stewart, and Mary Burmeister for the help they have provided along the way.

James Michael Stewart

Thanks to my boss and co-author, Ed Tittel, for including me in this book series. To my parents, Dave and Sue, you are the best parents a guy could every have. To Mark, every moment you are away, I learn how valuable friendship is. To HERbert, well it's just you and me again. And finally, as always, to Elvis—I see that you like to travel in style. Your airplanes have a bar (although you don't drink, *wink*, *wink*), an entertainment center, and a bed for those post-fried-banana-sandwich naps.

Contents At A Glance

Table Of Contents

Introduction

Welcome to the *MCSD/MCP+SB FrontPage 98 Exam Cram*! This book aims to help you get ready to take—and pass—the Microsoft certification test numbered 70-055, "Designing and Implementing Web Sites with Microsoft FrontPage 98." This introduction explains Microsoft's certification programs in general and talks about how the *Exam Cram* series can help you prepare for Microsoft's certification exams.

Exam Cram books help you understand and appreciate the subjects and materials you need to pass Microsoft certification exams. *Exam Cram* books are aimed strictly at test preparation and review. They do not teach you everything you need to know about a topic (such as the ins and outs of managing a Web site or all the nitty-gritty details involved in using FrontPage Editor and FrontPage Explorer). Instead, we (the authors) present and dissect the questions and problems we've found that you're likely to encounter on a test. We've worked from Microsoft's own training materials, preparation guides, and tests, as well as from a battery of third-party test preparation tools. Our aim is to bring together as much information as possible about Microsoft certification exams.

Nevertheless, to completely prepare yourself for any Microsoft test, we recommend that you begin your studies with some classroom training, or that you pick up and read one of the many study guides available. We also strongly recommend that you install, configure, and fool around with the software or environment that you'll be tested on, because nothing beats hands-on experience and familiarity when it comes to understanding the questions you're likely to encounter on a certification test. Book learning is essential, but hands-on experience is the best teacher of all.

The Microsoft Certified Professional (MCP) Program

The MCP program currently includes seven separate tracks, each of which boasts its own special acronym (as a would-be certificant, you need to have a high tolerance for alphabet soup of all kinds):

- **MCP (Microsoft Certified Professional)** This is the least prestigious of all the certification tracks from Microsoft. Passing any of the major Microsoft exams (except the Networking Essentials exam) qualifies an individual for MCP credentials. Individuals can demonstrate proficiency with additional Microsoft products by passing additional certification exams.
- **MCP+I (Microsoft Certified Professional + Internet)** This midlevel certification is attained by completing three core exams: Windows NT Server 4, TCP/IP, and Internet Information Server (3 or 4).
- **MCP+SB (Microsoft Certified Professional + Site Building)** This certification program is designed for individuals who are planning, building, managing, and maintaining Web sites. Individuals with the MCP+SB credential will have demonstrated the ability to develop Web sites that include multimedia and searchable content and Web sites that connect to and communicate with a back-end database. It requires passing two of the following three exams: "Designing and Implementing Commerce Solutions with Microsoft Site Server 3.0, Commerce Edition," "Designing and Implementing Web Sites with Microsoft FrontPage 98," and "Designing and Implementing Web Solutions with Microsoft Visual InterDev 6.0." This book is devoted to the FrontPage 98 exam in this series. Table 1 shows the requirements for the MCP+SB certification.
- **MCSD (Microsoft Certified Solution Developer)** The MCSD credential reflects the skills required to create multitier, distributed, and COM-based solutions, in addition to desktop and Internet applications, using new technologies. To obtain an MCSD, an individual must demonstrate the ability to analyze and interpret user requirements; select and integrate products, platforms, tools, and technologies; design and implement code; customize applications; and perform necessary software tests and quality assurance operations.

  To become an MCSD, you must pass a total of four exams: three core exams (available spring 1999) and one elective exam. The required core exam is "Analyzing Requirements and Defining Solution Architectures."

Table 1 MCP+SB requirements.

Choose 2	
➤ **Exam 70-055**	Designing and Implementing Web Sites with Microsoft FrontPage 98
Exam 70-057	Designing and Implementing Commerce Solutions with Microsoft Site Server 3.0, Commerce Edition
Exam 70-152	Designing and Implementing Web Solutions with Microsoft Visual InterDev 6.0

Each candidate must also choose one of these two desktop applications exams—"Designing and Implementing Desktop Applications with Microsoft Visual C++ 6.0" or "Designing and Implementing Desktop Applications with Microsoft Visual Basic 6.0"—plus one of these two distributed application exams—"Designing and Implementing Distributed Applications with Microsoft Visual C++ 6.0" or "Designing and Implementing Distributed Applications with Microsoft Visual Basic 6.0."

Elective exams cover specific Microsoft applications and languages, including Visual Basic, C++, the Microsoft Foundation Classes, Access, SQL Server, Excel, and more, including FrontPage, the subject of this book. If you're on your way to becoming an MCSD and have already taken some exams, visit **www.microsoft.com/train_cert/** for information about how to proceed with your MCSD certification under this new track. Table 2 shows the requirements for the MCSD certification.

- **MCSE (Microsoft Certified Systems Engineer)** Anyone who has a current MCSE is warranted to possess a high level of expertise with Windows NT (version 3.51 or 4) and other Microsoft operating systems and products. This credential is designed to prepare individuals to plan, implement, maintain, and support information systems and networks built around Microsoft Windows NT and its BackOffice family of products.

  To obtain an MCSE, an individual must pass four core operating system exams, plus two elective exams. The operating system exams require individuals to demonstrate competence with desktop and server operating systems and with networking components.

  You must pass at least two Windows NT-related exams to obtain an MCSE: "Implementing and Supporting Microsoft Windows NT Server" (version 3.51 or 4) and "Implementing and Supporting Microsoft Windows NT Server in the Enterprise" (version 3.51 or 4). These tests are intended to indicate an individual's knowledge of Windows NT in smaller, simpler networks and in larger, more complex, and heterogeneous networks, respectively.

  You must pass two additional tests as well. These tests relate to networking and desktop operating systems. At present, the networking requirement can be satisfied only by passing the Networking Essentials test. The desktop operating system test can be satisfied by passing a Windows 95, Windows NT Workstation (the version must match whichever core NT curriculum you are pursuing), or Windows 98 test.

  The two remaining exams are elective exams. An elective exam may fall in any number of subject or product areas, primarily BackOffice components. These include tests on Internet (IE) 4, SQL Server, IIS, SNA

Table 2 MCSD requirements*.

Core

Choose 1 from the desktop applications development group	
Exam 70-016	Designing and Implementing Desktop Applications with Microsoft Visual C++ 6.0
Exam 70-176	Designing and Implementing Desktop Applications with Microsoft Visual Basic 6.0
Choose 1 from the distributed applications development group	
Exam 70-015	Designing and Implementing Distributed Applications with Microsoft Visual C++ 6.0
Exam 70-175	Designing and Implementing Distributed Applications with Microsoft Visual Basic 6.0
This solution architecture exam is required	
Exam 70-100	Analyzing Requirements and Defining Solution Architectures

Elective

Choose 1 from this group	
Exam 70-015	Designing and Implementing Distributed Applications with Microsoft Visual C++ 6.0
Exam 70-016	Designing and Implementing Desktop Applications with Microsoft Visual C++ 6.0
Exam 70-029	Designing and Implementing Databases with Microsoft SQL Server 7.0
Exam 70-024	Developing Applications with C++ Using the Microsoft Foundation Class Library
Exam 70-025	Implementing OLE in Microsoft Foundation Class Applications
Exam 70-055	Designing and Implementing Web Sites with Microsoft FrontPage 98
Exam 70-057	Designing and Implementing Commerce Solutions with Microsoft Site Server 3.0, Commerce Edition
Exam 70-165 **Exam 70-175** **Exam 70-176**	Developing Applications with Microsoft Visual Basic 5.0 **OR** Designing and Implementing Distributed Applications with Microsoft Visual Basic 6.0 **OR** Designing and Implementing Desktop Applications with Microsoft Visual Basic 6.0
Exam 70-069	Application Development with Microsoft Access for Windows 95 and the Microsoft Access Developer's Toolkit
Exam 70-091	Designing and Implementing Solutions with Microsoft Office 2000 and Microsoft Visual Basic for Applications
Exam 70-152	Designing and Implementing Web Solutions with Microsoft Visual InterDev 6.0

* This is not a complete listing—you can still be tested on some earlier versions of these products. However, we have tried to include the most recent versions so that you may test on these versions and thus be certified longer. We have not included any tests that are scheduled to be retired.

The MCSD program is being expanded to include FoxPro and Visual J++. However, these tests are not yet available and no test numbers have been assigned.

Core exams that can also be used as elective exams can be counted only once toward certification. The same test cannot be used as both a core and elective exam.

Server, Exchange Server, Systems Management Server, and the like. However, it's also possible to test out on electives by taking advanced networking tests such as "Internetworking with Microsoft TCP/IP on Microsoft Windows NT" (but here again, the version of Windows NT involved must match the version for the core requirements taken).

Whatever mix of tests is completed toward MCSE certification, individuals must pass six tests to meet the MCSE requirements. It's not uncommon for the entire process to take a year or so, and many individuals find that they must take a test more than once to pass. Our primary goal with the *Exam Cram* series is to make it possible, given proper study and preparation, to pass all Microsoft certification tests on the first try.

- **MCSE+Internet (Microsoft Certified Systems Engineer + Internet)** This is a newer Microsoft certification and focuses not just on Microsoft operating systems, but also on Microsoft's Internet servers and TCP/IP.

  To obtain this certification, an individual must pass seven core exams, plus two elective exams. The core exams include not only the server operating systems (NT Server and Server in the Enterprise) and a desktop operating system (Windows 95, Windows 98, or Windows NT Workstation), but also include Networking Essentials, TCP/IP, IIS, and the Internet Explorer Administration Kit (IEAK).

  The two remaining exams are electives. These elective exams can be in any of four product areas: SQL Server, SNA Server, Exchange Server, and Proxy Server.

- **MCT (Microsoft Certified Trainer)** Microsoft Certified Trainers are individuals deemed able to deliver elements of the official Microsoft curriculum based on technical knowledge and instructional ability. Therefore, it's necessary for an individual seeking MCT credentials (which are granted on a course-by-course basis) to pass the related certification exam for a course and to take the official Microsoft training on the subject, as well as to demonstrate an ability to teach.

  This latter criterion may be satisfied by proving that one has already attained training certification from Novell, Banyan, Lotus, the Santa Cruz Operation, or Cisco, or by taking a Microsoft-sanctioned workshop on instruction. Microsoft makes it clear that MCTs are important cogs in the Microsoft training channels. Instructors must be MCTs before Microsoft will allow them to teach in any of its official training channels, including Microsoft's affiliated Authorized Technical Education Centers (ATECs), Authorized Academic Training Programs (AATPs), and the Microsoft Online Institute (MOLI).

Certification is an ongoing activity. Once a Microsoft product becomes obsolete, MCPs typically have 12 to 18 months in which to recertify on current product versions. (If individuals do not recertify within the specified time period, their certification becomes invalid.) Because technology keeps changing and new products continually supplant old ones, this should come as no surprise.

The best place to keep tabs on the MCP program and its various certifications is on the Microsoft Web site. The current root URL for the MCP program is at **www.microsoft.com/mcp/**. However, Microsoft's Web site changes frequently, so if this URL doesn't work, try using the search tool on Microsoft's site with either "MCP" or the quoted phrase "Microsoft Certified Professional program" as the search string. This will help you find the latest and most accurate information about the company's certification programs.

Taking A Certification Exam

Alas, testing is not free. Each computer-based MCP exam costs $100, and if you do not pass, you may retest for an additional $100 for each additional try. In the United States and Canada, tests are administered by Sylvan Prometric and Virtual University Enterprises (VUE). Here's how you can contact them:

- **Sylvan Prometric** You can sign up for a test through the company's Web site at **www.slspro.com/**. You can also register by phone at 800-755-3926 (within the United States or Canada) or at 410-843-8000 (outside the United States and Canada).
- **Virtual University Enterprises** You can sign up for a test or get the phone numbers for local testing centers through the Web page at **www.microsoft.com/train_cert/mcp/vue_info.htm**.

To sign up for a test, you must possess a valid credit card or contact either company for mailing instructions to send it a check (in the United States). Only when payment is verified, or a check has cleared, can you actually register for a test.

To schedule an exam, call Sylvan or VUE, or sign up online at least one day in advance. To cancel or reschedule an exam, you must call by 7 P.M. (Pacific time) the day before the scheduled test (or you may be charged, even if you don't appear to take the test). When you want to schedule a test, have the following information ready:

- Your name, organization, and mailing address.
- Your Microsoft test ID. (Inside the United States, this is your Social Security number; citizens of other nations should call ahead to find out what type of identification number is required to register for a test.)

- The name and number of the exam you wish to take.
- A method of payment. (As we've already mentioned, a credit card is the most convenient method, but alternate means can be arranged in advance, if necessary.)

Once you sign up for a test, you'll be informed as to when and where the test is scheduled. Try to arrive at least 15 minutes early. You must supply two forms of identification to be admitted into the testing room—one of which must be a photo ID.

All exams are completely "closed book." In fact, you will not be permitted to take anything with you into the testing area. However, you will be furnished with a blank sheet of paper and a pen. We suggest that you immediately write down on that sheet of paper all the information you've memorized for the test.

In *Exam Cram* books, this information appears on The Cram Sheet inside the front of each book. You'll have some time to compose yourself, record this information, and even take a sample orientation exam before you must begin the real thing. We suggest you take the orientation test before taking your first exam, but because they're all more or less identical in layout, behavior, and controls, you probably won't need to do this more than once.

When you complete a Microsoft certification exam, the software will tell you whether you've passed or failed. All tests are scored on a basis of 1,000 points, and results are broken into several topic areas. Even if you fail, we suggest you ask for—and keep—the detailed report that the test administrator should print for you. You can use this report to help you prepare for another go-around, if needed.

If you need to retake an exam, you'll have to call Sylvan Prometric or VUE, schedule a new test date, and pay another $100. Microsoft has the following policy regarding failed tests: The first time you fail a test, you are able to retake the test the next day. However, if you fail a second time, you must wait 14 days before retaking that test.

Tracking MCP Status

As soon as you pass any Microsoft exam (other than Networking Essentials), you'll attain Microsoft Certified Professional (MCP) status. Microsoft also generates transcripts that indicate which exams you have passed and your corresponding test scores. You can order a transcript by email at any time by sending an email addressed to **mcp@msprograms.com**. You can also obtain a copy of your transcript by downloading the latest version of the MCT guide from the Web site and consulting the section titled "Key Contacts" for a list of telephone numbers and related contacts.

Once you pass the necessary set of exams (one for MCP, two for MCP+SB, or four for MCSD), you'll be certified. Official certification normally takes anywhere from four to six weeks, so don't expect to get your credentials overnight. When the package for a qualified certification arrives, it includes a Welcome Kit that contains a number of elements:

- An MCP+SB or MCSD certificate, suitable for framing, along with a Professional Program Membership card and lapel pin.
- A license to use the MCP logo, thereby allowing you to use the logo in advertisements, promotions, and documents, as well as on letterhead, business cards, and so on. Along with the license comes an MCP logo sheet, which includes camera-ready artwork. (Note that before using any of the artwork, individuals must sign and return a licensing agreement that indicates they'll abide by its terms and conditions.)
- A subscription to *Microsoft Certified Professional Magazine*, which provides ongoing data about testing and certification activities, requirements, and changes to the program.
- A one-year subscription to the Microsoft Beta Evaluation program. This subscription will get you all beta products from Microsoft for the next year. (This does not include developer products. You must join the MSDN program or become an MCSD to qualify for developer beta products. To join the MSDN program, go to **http://sdn.microsoft.com/developer/join/**.)

Many people believe that the benefits of MCP certification go well beyond the perks that Microsoft provides to newly anointed members of this elite group. We're starting to see more job listings that request or require applicants to have an MCP, MCP+SB, MCSD, and so on, and many individuals who complete the program can qualify for increases in pay and/or responsibility. As an official recognition of hard work and broad knowledge, one of the MCP credentials is a badge of honor in many IT organizations.

How To Prepare For An Exam

Preparing for any Microsoft product-related test (including FrontPage 98) requires that you obtain and study materials designed to provide comprehensive information about the product and its capabilities, plus Web site design and maintenance techniques, that will appear on the specific exam for which you are preparing. The following list of materials will help you study and prepare:

- The FrontPage 98 product CD-ROM includes comprehensive online documentation and related materials; it should be a primary resource when you are preparing for the test.

- Microsoft Press offers titles on FrontPage 98. Visit **http://mspress.microsoft.com/findabook/list/subject_MF.htm** for a complete list of its offerings. The more advanced titles will help you learn FrontPage 98.
- The Microsoft TechNet CD-ROM delivers numerous electronic titles on FrontPage 98. Its offerings include Product Manuals, Product Facts, the FrontPage 98 Server Extensions Resource Kit, Technical Notes, Tips and Techniques, Tools and Utilities, and information on how to access the Seminars Online training materials for FrontPage 98. A subscription to TechNet costs $299 per year but is well worth the price. Visit **www.microsoft.com/technet/** and check out the information under the "TechNet Subscription" menu entry for more details.
- Find, download, and use the exam prep materials, practice tests, and self-assessment exams on the Microsoft Training And Certification Download page (**www.microsoft.com/train_cert/download/downld.htm**).

In addition, you'll probably find any or all of the following materials useful in your quest for FrontPage 98 expertise:

- **Microsoft Training Kits** Although there's no training kit currently available from Microsoft Press for FrontPage 98, many other topics have such kits. It's worthwhile to check to see if Microsoft has come out with anything by the time you need this information.
- **Study Guides** Several publishers—including Certification Insider Press—offer learning materials necessary to pass the tests. The Certification Insider Press series includes:
  - **The *Exam Cram* series** These books give you information about the material you need to know to pass the tests.
  - **The *Exam Prep* series** These books provide a greater level of detail than the *Exam Cram* books.

  Note: *There currently is no* Exam Prep *book for FrontPage available.*
- **Classroom Training** ATECs, AATPs, MOLI, and unlicensed third-party training companies (such as Wave Technologies, American Research Group, Learning Tree, Data-Tech, and others) all offer classroom training on FrontPage 98. These companies aim to help prepare Web administrators to run Windows-based Web sites and to pass the FrontPage test. Although such training runs upwards of $350 per day in class, most of the individuals lucky enough to partake (including your humble authors, who've even taught such courses) find them to be quite worthwhile.

- **Other Publications** You'll find direct references to other publications and resources in this text, but there's no shortage of materials available about FrontPage 98. To help you sift through some of the publications out there, we end each chapter with a "Need To Know More?" section that provides pointers to more complete and exhaustive resources covering the chapter's information. This should give you an idea of where we think you should look for further discussion.

By far, this set of required and recommended materials represents a nonpareil collection of sources and resources for FrontPage 98 and related topics. We anticipate that you'll find that this book belongs in this company. In the section that follows, we explain how this book works, and we give you some good reasons why this book counts as a member of the required and recommended materials list.

About This Book

Each topical *Exam Cram* chapter follows a regular structure, along with graphical cues about important or useful information. Here's the structure of a typical chapter:

- **Opening Hotlists** Each chapter begins with a list of the terms, tools, and techniques that you must learn and understand before you can be fully conversant with that chapter's subject matter. We follow the hotlists with one or two introductory paragraphs to set the stage for the rest of the chapter.

- **Topical Coverage** After the opening hotlists, each chapter covers a series of topics related to the chapter's subject title. Throughout this section, we highlight topics or concepts likely to appear on a test using a special Study Alert layout, like this:

> This is what a Study Alert looks like. Normally, a Study Alert stresses concepts, terms, software, or activities that are likely to relate to one or more certification test questions. For that reason, we think any information found offset in Study Alert format is worthy of unusual attentiveness on your part. Indeed, most of the information that appears on The Cram Sheet appears as Study Alerts within the text.

Pay close attention to material flagged as a Study Alert; although all the information in this book pertains to what you need to know to pass the exam, we flag certain items that are really important. You'll find what appears in the meat of each chapter to be worth knowing, too, when preparing for the test. Because this book's material is very condensed, we recommend that you use this book along with other resources to achieve the maximum benefit.

In addition to the Study Alerts, we have provided tips that will help you build a better foundation for FrontPage knowledge. Although the information may not be on the exam, it's certainly related and will help you become a better test-taker.

> **TIP** This is how tips are formatted. Keep your eyes open for these, and you'll become a FrontPage 98 guru in no time!

- **Practice Questions** Although we talk about test questions and topics throughout each chapter, this section presents a series of mock test questions and explanations of both correct and incorrect answers. We also try to point out especially tricky questions by using a special icon, like this:

  Ordinarily, this icon flags the presence of a particularly devious inquiry, if not an outright trick question. Trick questions are calculated to be answered incorrectly if not read more than once—and carefully at that. Although they're not ubiquitous, such questions make regular appearances on the Microsoft exams. That's why we say exam questions are as much about reading comprehension as they are about knowing your material inside out and backwards.

- **Details And Resources** Every chapter ends with a section titled "Need To Know More?". These sections provide direct pointers to Microsoft and third-party resources offering more details on the chapter's subject. In addition, these sections try to rank or at least rate the quality and thoroughness of the topic's coverage by each resource. If you find a resource you like in this collection, use it, but don't feel compelled to use all the resources. On the other hand, we recommend only resources we use on a regular basis, so none of our recommendations will be a waste of your time or money (but purchasing them all at once probably represents an expense that many network administrators and would-be MCP+SBs or MCSDs might find hard to justify).

The bulk of the book follows this chapter structure slavishly, but there are a few other elements we'd like to point out. Chapter 15 is a sample test that provides a good review of the material presented throughout the book to ensure you're ready for the exam. Chapter 16 is an answer key to the sample test that appears in Chapter 15. Additionally, you'll find a glossary that explains terms and an index that you can use to track down terms as they appear in the text.

Finally, the tear-out Cram Sheet attached next to the inside front cover of this *Exam Cram* book represents a condensed and compiled collection of facts, figures, and tips that we think you should memorize before taking the test. Because you can dump this information out of your head onto a piece of paper before taking the exam, you can master this information by brute force—you need to remember it only long enough to write it down when you walk into the test room. You might even want to look at it in the car or in the lobby of the testing center just before you walk in to take the test.

How To Use This Book

If you're prepping for a first-time test, we've structured the topics in this book to build on one another. Therefore, some topics in later chapters make more sense after you've read earlier chapters. That's why we suggest you read this book from front to back for your initial test preparation. If you need to brush up on a topic or you have to bone up for a second try, use the index or table of contents to go straight to the topics and questions that you need to study. Beyond helping you prepare for the test, we think you'll find this book useful as a tightly focused reference to some of the most important aspects of FrontPage 98.

Given all the book's elements and its specialized focus, we've tried to create a tool that will help you prepare for—and pass—Microsoft Exam 70-055, "Designing and Implementing Web Sites with Microsoft FrontPage 98." Please share your feedback on the book with us, especially if you have ideas about how we can improve it for future test-takers. We'll consider everything you say carefully, and we'll respond to all suggestions.

Please send your questions or comments to us at **craminfo@coriolis.com** or to our series editor, Ed Tittel, via email at **etittel@lanw.com**. He coordinates our efforts and ensures that all questions get answered. Please remember to include the title of the book in your message; otherwise, we'll be forced to guess which book you're writing about. And we don't like to guess—we want to *know*! Also, be sure to check out the Web pages at **www.certificationinsider.com** and **www.lanw.com/examcram**, where you'll find information updates, commentary, and certification information.

Thanks, and enjoy the book!

1

Microsoft Certification Exams

Terms you'll need to understand:

- √ Radio button
- √ Checkbox
- √ Exhibit
- √ Multiple-choice question formats
- √ Careful reading
- √ Process of elimination
- √ Adaptive tests
- √ Fixed-length tests
- √ Simulations

Techniques you'll need to master:

- √ Preparing to take a certification exam
- √ Practicing (to make perfect)
- √ Making the best use of the testing software
- √ Budgeting your time
- √ Saving the hardest questions until last
- √ Guessing (as a last resort)

Exam taking is not something that most people anticipate eagerly, no matter how well prepared they may be. In most cases, familiarity helps offset test anxiety. In plain English, this means you probably won't be as nervous when you take your fourth or fifth Microsoft certification exam as you'll be when you take your first one.

Whether it's your first exam or your tenth, understanding the details of exam taking (how much time to spend on questions, the environment you'll be in, and so on) and the exam software will help you concentrate on the material rather than on the setting. Likewise, mastering a few basic exam-taking skills should help you recognize—and perhaps even outfox—some of the tricks and snares you're bound to find in some of the exam questions.

This chapter, besides explaining the exam environment and software, describes some proven exam-taking strategies that you should be able to use to your advantage.

The Exam Situation

When you arrive at the testing center where you scheduled your exam, you'll need to sign in with an exam coordinator. He or she will ask you to show two forms of identification, one of which must be a photo ID. After you've signed in and your time slot arrives, you'll be asked to deposit any books, bags, or other items you brought with you. Then, you'll be escorted into a closed room. Typically, the room will be furnished with anywhere from one to half a dozen computers, and each workstation will be separated from the others by dividers designed to keep you from seeing what's happening on someone else's computer.

You'll be furnished with a pen or pencil and a blank sheet of paper, or, in some cases, an erasable plastic sheet and an erasable pen. You're allowed to write down anything you want on both sides of this sheet. Before the exam, you should memorize as much of the material that appears on The Cram Sheet (in the front of this book) as you can, so you can write that information on the blank sheet as soon as you are seated in front of the computer. You can refer to your rendition of The Cram Sheet anytime you like during the test, but you'll have to surrender the sheet when you leave the room.

Most test rooms feature a wall with a large picture window. This permits the exam coordinator to monitor the room, to prevent exam-takers from talking to one another, and to observe anything out of the ordinary that might go on. The exam coordinator will have preloaded the appropriate Microsoft certification exam—for this book, that's Exam 70-055—and you'll be permitted to start as soon as you're seated in front of the computer.

All Microsoft certification exams allow a certain maximum amount of time in which to complete your work (this time is indicated on the exam by an onscreen counter/clock, so you can check the time remaining whenever you like). The fixed-length FrontPage 98 exam consists of 72 randomly selected questions. You may take up to 105 minutes to complete the exam.

All Microsoft certification exams are computer generated and use a multiple-choice format. Although this may sound quite simple, the questions are constructed not only to check your mastery of basic facts and figures of FrontPage 98 and related Web tools and technologies, but they also require you to evaluate one or more sets of circumstances or requirements. Often, you'll be asked to give more than one answer to a question. Likewise, you might be asked to select the best or most effective solution to a problem from a range of choices, all of which technically are correct. Taking an exam is quite an adventure, and it involves real thinking. This book shows you what to expect and how to deal with the potential problems, puzzles, and predicaments.

Some Microsoft exams employ more advanced testing capabilities than might immediately meet the eye. Although the questions that appear are still multiple choice, the logic that drives them is more complex than older Microsoft tests, which use a fixed sequence of questions (called a *fixed-length* computerized exam). Other exams employ a sophisticated user interface (which Microsoft calls a *simulation*) to test your knowledge of the software and systems under consideration in a more or less "live" environment that behaves just like the original.

For upcoming exams, Microsoft is turning to a well-known technique, called *adaptive testing*, to establish a test-taker's level of knowledge and product competence. These exams look the same as fixed-length exams, but an adaptive exam discovers the level of difficulty at and below which an individual test-taker can correctly answer questions. At the same time, Microsoft is in the process of converting all its older fixed-length exams into adaptive exams as well.

Test-takers with differing levels of knowledge or ability therefore see different sets of questions; individuals with high levels of knowledge or ability are presented with a smaller set of more difficult questions, whereas individuals with lower levels of knowledge are presented with a larger set of easier questions. Both individuals may answer the same percentage of questions correctly, but the test-taker with a higher knowledge or ability level will score higher because his or her questions are worth more.

Also, the lower-level test-taker will probably answer more questions than his or her more knowledgeable colleague. This explains why adaptive tests use ranges of values to define the number of questions and the amount of time it takes to complete the test.

Adaptive tests work by evaluating the test-taker's most recent answer. A correct answer leads to a more difficult question (and the test software's estimate of the test-taker's knowledge and ability level is raised). An incorrect answer leads to a less difficult question (and the test software's estimate of the test-taker's knowledge and ability level is lowered). This process continues until the test targets the test-taker's true ability level. The exam ends when the test-taker's level of accuracy meets a statistically acceptable value (in other words, when his or her performance demonstrates an acceptable level of knowledge and ability) or when the maximum number of items has been presented (in which case, the test-taker is almost certain to fail).

Microsoft tests come in one form or the other—either they're fixed-length or they're adaptive. Therefore, you must take the test in whichever form it appears—you can't choose one form over another. However, if anything, it pays off even more to prepare thoroughly for an adaptive exam than for a fixed-length one: The penalties for answering incorrectly are built into the test itself on an adaptive exam, whereas the layout remains the same for a fixed-length test, no matter how many questions you answer incorrectly.

> The biggest difference between an adaptive test and a fixed-length test is that, on a fixed-length test, you can revisit questions after you've read them over one or more times. On an adaptive test, you must answer the question when it's presented, and you'll have no opportunities to revisit that question thereafter. As of this writing, the FrontPage 98 exam is a fixed-length exam, but this can change at any time. Therefore, you must prepare as if it were an adaptive exam to ensure the best possible results.

In the section that follows, you'll learn more about what Microsoft test questions look like and how they must be answered.

Exam Layout And Design

Some exam questions require you to select a single answer, whereas others ask you to select multiple correct answers. The following multiple-choice question requires you to select a single correct answer. Following the question is a brief summary of each potential answer and why it is either right or wrong.

Question 1

To reflect the release of a new product, you want to replace the string "Mark I" with the string "Mark II" across your entire Web site, which contains over 100 documents altogether. Of the following options, which one is the best way to complete this activity?

- ❍ a. FrontPage Editor: Edit|Find And Replace|Match Whole Word Only|All Pages
- ❍ b. FrontPage Explorer: Edit|Find And Replace|Match Whole Word Only|All Pages
- ❍ c. FrontPage Explorer: Tools|Find And Replace|All Pages
- ❍ d. FrontPage Explorer: Edit|Find And Replace|All Pages

Answer c is correct. FrontPage Explorer is the tool of choice for editing entire Web sites, whereas FrontPage Editor is best for editing single documents. It's also possible to eliminate two of the four choices because they include the "Match Whole Word Only" criterion, which does not apply to a phrase with an embedded space such as "Mark I" or "Mark II". Either the use of this criterion, or the wrong tool, is what disqualifies the other answers from further consideration.

This sample question format corresponds closely to the Microsoft certification exam format—the only difference on the exam is that questions are not followed by answer keys. To select an answer, position the cursor over the radio button next to the answer. Then, click on the mouse button to select the answer.

Let's examine a question that requires choosing multiple answers. This type of question provides checkboxes rather than radio buttons for marking all appropriate selections.

Question 2

Which of the following design criteria should you consider when analyzing requirements for a Web site? [Check all correct answers]

- ❑ a. The message and communication goals that drive the Web site
- ❑ b. The browser or browsers that the site's primary audience members will use
- ❑ c. The level of security and access controls that the site will require
- ❑ d. The technologies you plan to use to build this site

The correct answers to this question are a, b, and c. The purpose and goals that drive a site, browser issues, and the site's security needs and access controls all represent aspects that help to determine a Web site's requirements. Answer d is incorrect because you should choose specific technologies to build your site as a direct outcome of your analysis of a Web site's requirements, not as a part of the requirements themselves.

For this type of question, more than one answer may be required. As far as the authors can tell (and Microsoft won't comment), such questions are scored as wrong unless all the required selections are chosen. In other words, a partially correct answer does not result in partial credit when the test is scored. For Question 2, you have to check the boxes next to items a, b, and c to obtain credit for a correct answer. Notice that picking the right answers also means knowing why the other answers are wrong.

Although these two basic types of questions can appear in many forms, they constitute the foundation on which all the Microsoft certification exam questions rest. More complex questions include so-called *exhibits*, which are usually screenshots of various FrontPage 98 tools or utilities. For some of these questions, you'll be asked to make a selection by clicking on a checkbox or radio button on the screenshot itself. For others, you'll be expected to use the information displayed therein to guide your answer to the question. Familiarity with the underlying tool or utility is your key to choosing the correct answer(s).

Other questions involving exhibits use charts or network diagrams to help document a workplace scenario that you'll be asked to troubleshoot or configure. Careful attention to such exhibits is the key to success. Be prepared to toggle frequently between the exhibit and the question as you work.

Recognizing Your Exam Type: Fixed-Length Or Adaptive

When you begin your exam, the software will tell you the test is adaptive, if in fact the version you're taking is presented as an adaptive test. If your introductory materials fail to mention this, you're probably taking a fixed-length test. However, when you look at your first question, you'll be able to tell for sure: If it includes a checkbox that lets you mark the question (for later return and review) you'll know you're taking a fixed-length test, because adaptive test questions can be visited (and answered) only once, and they include no such checkbox.

The Fixed-Length Exam Strategy

A well-known principle when taking fixed-length exams is to first read over the entire exam from start to finish while answering only those questions you feel absolutely sure of. On subsequent passes, you can dive into more complex questions more deeply, knowing how many such questions you have left. On adaptive tests, you get only one shot at the question, which is why preparation is so crucial for such tests.

Fortunately, the Microsoft exam software for fixed-length tests makes the multiple-visit approach easy to implement. At the top-left corner of each question is a checkbox that permits you to mark that question for a later visit. (Note that marking questions makes review easier, but you can return to any question if you're willing to click on the Forward or Back buttons repeatedly.) As you read each question, if you answer only those you're sure of and mark for review those that you're not sure of, you can keep working through a decreasing list of questions as you answer the trickier ones in order.

There's at least one potential benefit to reading the exam over completely before answering the trickier questions: Sometimes, information supplied in later questions will shed more light on earlier questions. Other times, information you read in later questions might jog your memory about FrontPage 98 facts, figures, or behavior that also will help with earlier questions. Either way, you'll come out ahead if you defer those questions about which you're not absolutely sure.

Here are some question-handling strategies that apply only to fixed-length tests. Use them if you have the chance:

- When returning to a question after your initial read-through, read every word again—otherwise, your mind can fall quickly into a rut. Sometimes, revisiting a question after turning your attention elsewhere lets you see something you missed, but the strong tendency is to see what you've seen before. Try to avoid that tendency at all costs.
- If you return to a question more than twice, try to articulate to yourself what you don't understand about the question, why the answers don't appear to make sense, or what appears to be missing. If you chew on the subject for awhile, your subconscious might provide the details that are lacking, or you might notice a "trick" that will point to the right answer.

As you work your way through the exam, another counter that Microsoft thankfully provides will come in handy—the number of questions completed and questions outstanding. For fixed-length tests, it's wise to budget your time by making sure that you've completed one-quarter of the questions one-quarter of the way through the exam period (or the first 18 questions in the first 26 minutes) and three-quarters of the questions three-quarters of the way through (54 questions in the first 78 minutes).

If you're not finished when 100 minutes have elapsed, use the last 5 minutes to guess your way through the remaining questions. Remember, guessing is potentially more valuable than not answering, because blank answers are always wrong, but a guess may turn out to be right. If you don't have a clue about any of the remaining questions, pick answers at random, or choose all a's, b's, and so on. The important thing is to submit an exam for scoring that has an answer for every question.

At the very end of your exam period, you're better off guessing than leaving questions unanswered.

The Adaptive Exam Strategy

If there's one principle that applies to taking an adaptive test, it could be summed up as "Get it right the first time." You cannot elect to skip a question and move on to the next one when taking an adaptive test, because the testing software uses your answer to the current question to select whatever question it plans to present to you next. Also, you cannot return to a question once you've moved on, because the software gives you only one chance to answer the question.

When you answer a question correctly, you are presented with a more difficult question next to help the software gauge your level of skill and ability. When you answer a question incorrectly, you are presented with a less difficult question, and the software lowers its current estimate of your skill and ability. This continues until the program settles into a reasonably accurate estimate of what you know and can do, and it takes you through somewhere between 25 and 35 questions, on average, as you complete the test.

The good news is that if you know your stuff, you'll probably finish most adaptive tests in 30 minutes or so. The bad news is that you must really, really know your stuff to do your best on an adaptive test. That's because some questions are so convoluted, complex, or hard to follow that you're bound to miss one or two, at a minimum, even if you do know your stuff. Therefore, the more you know, the better you'll do on an adaptive test, even accounting for the occasionally weird or unfathomable question that appears on these exams.

TIP

As of this writing, Microsoft has not advertised which tests are strictly adaptive. You'll be best served by preparing for the exam as if it were adaptive. That way, you should be prepared to pass no matter what kind of test you take (that is, fixed-length or adaptive). If you do end up taking a fixed-length test, remember our tips from the preceding section. They should help you improve on what you could do on an adaptive test.

If you encounter a question on an adaptive test that you can't answer, you must guess an answer. Because of the way the software works, you may have to suffer for your guess on the next question if you guess right, because you'll get a more difficult question next.

Exam-Taking Basics

The most important advice about taking any exam is this: Read each question carefully. Some questions are deliberately ambiguous, some use double negatives, and others use terminology in incredibly precise ways. The authors have taken numerous exams—both practice and live—and in nearly every one have missed at least one question because they didn't read it closely or carefully enough.

Here are some suggestions on how to deal with the tendency to jump to an answer too quickly:

- Make sure you read every word in the question. If you find yourself jumping ahead impatiently, go back and start over.
- As you read, try to restate the question in your own terms. If you can do this, you should be able to pick the correct answer(s) much more easily.

Above all, try to deal with each question by thinking through what you know about FrontPage 98 as well as Web document and site design—the characteristics, behaviors, facts, and figures involved. By reviewing what you know (and what you've written down on your information sheet), you'll often recall or understand things sufficiently to determine the answer to the question.

Question-Handling Strategies

Based on exams we have taken, some interesting trends have become apparent. For those questions that take only a single answer, usually two or three of the answers will be obviously incorrect, and two of the answers will be plausible—of course, only one can be correct. Unless the answer leaps out at you (if it does, reread the question to look for a trick; sometimes those are the ones you're most likely to get wrong), begin the process of answering by eliminating those answers that are most obviously wrong.

Things to look for in obviously wrong answers include spurious menu choices or utility names, nonexistent software options, and terminology you've never seen. If you've done your homework for an exam, no valid information should be completely new to you. In that case, unfamiliar or bizarre terminology probably indicates a totally bogus answer.

Numerous questions assume that the default behavior of a particular utility is in effect. If you know the defaults and understand what they mean, this knowledge will help you cut through many Gordian knots.

Mastering The Inner Game

In the final analysis, knowledge breeds confidence, and confidence breeds success. If you study the materials in this book carefully and review all the practice questions at the end of each chapter, you should become aware of those areas where additional learning and study are required.

Next, follow up by reading some or all of the materials recommended in the "Need To Know More?" section at the end of each chapter. The idea is to become familiar enough with the concepts and situations you find in the sample questions that you can reason your way through similar situations on a real exam. If you know the material, you have every right to be confident that you can pass the exam.

After you've worked your way through the book, take the practice exam in Chapter 15. This will provide a reality check and help you identify areas to study further. Make sure you follow up and review materials related to questions you miss on the practice exam before scheduling a real exam. Only when you've covered all the ground and feel comfortable with the whole scope of the practice exam should you take a real one.

TIP

If you take the practice exam and don't score at least 75 percent correct, you'll want to practice further. Though one is not available for FrontPage 98 yet, Microsoft usually provides free Personal Exam Prep (PEP) exams and the self-assessment exams from the Microsoft Certified Professional Web site's download page (its location appears in the next section). If you're more ambitious or better funded, you might want to purchase a practice exam from a third-party vendor.

Armed with the information in this book and with the determination to augment your knowledge, you should be able to pass the certification exam. However, you need to work at it, or you'll spend the exam fee more than once before you finally pass. If you prepare seriously, you should do well. Good luck!

Additional Resources

A good source of information about Microsoft certification exams comes from Microsoft itself. Because its products and technologies—and the exams that go with them—change frequently, the best place to go for exam-related information is online.

If you haven't already visited the Microsoft Certified Professional site, do so right now. The MCP home page resides at **www.microsoft.com/mcp/** (see Figure 1.1).

Note: This page might not be there by the time you read this, or it might have been replaced by something new and different, because things change regularly on the Microsoft site. Should this happen, please read the sidebar later in this chapter titled "Coping With Change On The Web."

The menu options in the left column of this site point to the most important sources of information in the MCP pages. Here's what to check out:

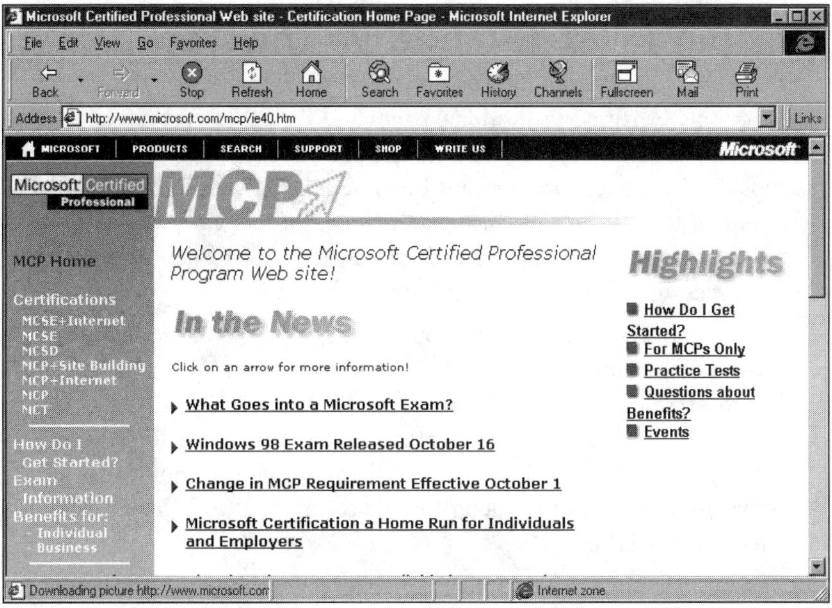

Figure 1.1 The Microsoft Certified Professional Web site.

- **Certifications** Use this menu entry to pick whichever certification program you want to read about.
- **Find Exam** Use this menu entry to pull up a search tool that lets you list all Microsoft exams and locate all exams relevant to any Microsoft certification (MCP, MCP+SB, MCSD, and so on) or those exams that cover a particular product. This tool is quite useful not only to examine the options but also to obtain specific exam preparation information, because each exam has its own associated preparation guide.
- **Downloads** Use this menu entry to find a list of the files and practice exams that Microsoft makes available to the public. These include several items worth downloading, especially the Certification Update, the Personal Exam Prep (PEP) exams, various assessment exams, and a general exam study guide. Try to make time to peruse these materials before taking your first exam.

These are just the high points of what's available in the Microsoft Certified Professional pages. As you browse through them—and we strongly recommend that you do—you'll probably find other informational tidbits mentioned that are every bit as interesting and compelling.

Coping With Change On The Web

Sooner or later, all the information we've shared with you about the Microsoft Certified Professional pages and the other Web-based resources mentioned throughout the rest of this book will go stale or be replaced by newer information. In some cases, the URLs you find here might lead you to their replacements; in other cases, the URLs will go nowhere, leaving you with the dreaded "404 File not found" error message. When that happens, don't give up.

You can always find what you want on the Web if you're willing to invest some time and energy. Most large or complex Web sites—and Microsoft's qualifies on both counts—offer a search engine. On all of Microsoft's Web pages, a Search button appears along the top edge of the page. As long as you can get to Microsoft's site (it should stay at **www.microsoft.com** for a long time), use this tool to help you find what you need.

The more focused you can make a search request, the more likely the results will include information you want. For example, search for the string "training and certification" to produce a lot of data about the subject in general, but if you're looking for a preparation guide for Exam 70-055, "Designing and Implementing Web Sites with Microsoft FrontPage 98," you'll be more likely to get there quickly if you use a search string similar to the following:

```
"Exam 70-055" AND "preparation guide"
```

Likewise, if you want to find the Training and Certification downloads, try a search string such as this:

```
"training and certification" AND "download page"
```

Finally, feel free to use general search tools—such as **www.search.com**, **www.altavista.com**, and **www.excite.com**—to look for related information. Although Microsoft offers great information about its certification exams online, there are plenty of third-party sources of information and assistance that need not follow Microsoft's party line. Therefore, if you can't find something where the book says it lives, start looking around. If worse comes to worst, you can email us. We just might have a clue.

2

Introduction To Microsoft FrontPage 98

Terms you'll need to understand:

- √ FrontPage 98
- √ Image Composer
- √ Personal Web Server
- √ FrontPage Server Extensions

Techniques you'll need to master:

- √ Understanding the components of FrontPage 98
- √ Understanding the features of FrontPage 98
- √ Integrating FrontPage 98 into a Web publishing environment
- √ Installing FrontPage 98
- √ Using FrontPage 98 with Office 97

FrontPage 98 is a multipurpose Web site authoring and administration utility from Microsoft. When used in conjunction with other Microsoft desktop, BackOffice, and operating system products, FrontPage can streamline development of Web environments of any size and complexity. In this chapter, the basics of FrontPage 98 are discussed, as well as an overview of FrontPage 98 installation.

FrontPage 98: Explored And Explained

The Internet is a fertile field for the development of new technologies. Many significant technology changes and advances now center on and around the Web. HTML (Hypertext Markup Language) and simple graphics are no longer "all you need to know" when creating a Web presence. Dynamic HTML, Cascading Style Sheets, Java, scripting, CGI, plug-ins, MIME, and proprietary markup are just a few of the Web technologies every Web author eventually encounters. Fortunately, you don't need to be an expert in every one of these technologies to use them on your Web site. Microsoft's FrontPage 98 confers the benefits of new technologies without requiring you to master all the complex details.

Simply put, FrontPage 98 (shown in Figure 2.1) is a Web site creation and management tool. FrontPage 98 is a full-featured WYSIWYG (What You See Is What You Get) Web editor that may be used to either create a new Web

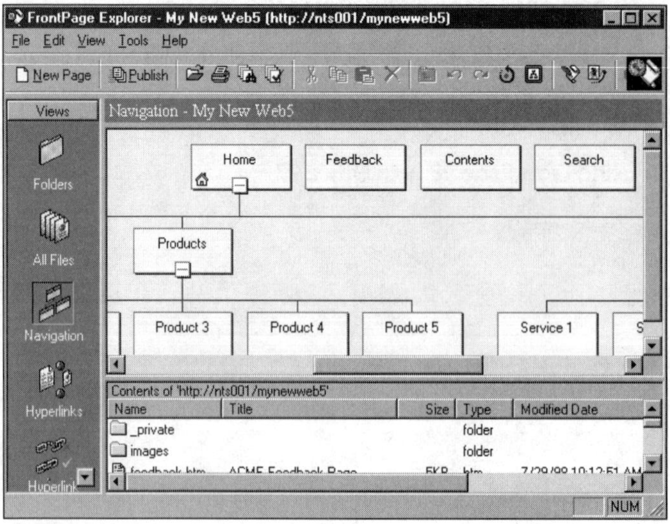

Figure 2.1 The Navigation View of FrontPage 98.

site from scratch or modify existing Web site documents. The authoring environment of FrontPage 98 is not limited to manipulating standard HTML. It can be used to control site access, automate content creation, test new compositions, integrate advanced Internet technologies, and even create push channels. Beyond site creation, FrontPage 98 may be used to publish your creations to a Web server, to allow multiple authors to work together, and to administer the Web remotely.

FrontPage 98 was designed with a specific purpose in mind: to grant nonprogrammers the ability to create and manage professional-looking Web sites. For the most part, Microsoft has accomplished this purpose. FrontPage is easy to use, uses an intuitive graphical interface and layout, offers a wide range of wizards, and automates many complex tasks.

FrontPage 98 is not a monolithic tool; instead, it represents a composite product that incorporates several tools. Its two primary components are FrontPage Explorer and FrontPage Editor. FrontPage Explorer is a complete site management utility that allows you to administer Web documents on a file, folder, or site basis. FrontPage Editor is an individual page composer in which any Web document may be created or modified. Other FrontPage 98 components include:

- **Microsoft Image Composer 1.5** This tool is used to create and edit graphics files for Web publication.
- **Microsoft Personal Web Server 1.5** This is a Windows 95 version of the popular Internet Information Server (IIS) for Windows NT Server. Personal Web Server (PWS) is a Web server that may be used to test your creations before you publish them for broader access or to host a personal Web site from your desktop. Note that Windows NT Workstation and Windows 98 include versions of PWS that are also based on IIS for the same purposes.
- **FrontPage 98 Server Extensions** These Web server add-ons enable some of the more advanced features found in FrontPage 98. These are covered in Chapter 13.
- **Microsoft Internet Explorer 3.02** This is Microsoft's popular Web browser. Although 3.02 was the version of this browser available at the time of FrontPage's release, the current version of Internet Explorer (at the time of this book's writing) is Internet Explorer (IE) 4.01. We recommend using IE 4.01 instead of IE 3.02.

By integrating these tools, FrontPage 98 offers a reasonably complete solution for developing, deploying, and maintaining one or more Web sites.

FrontPage 98 Features And Functions

FrontPage 98's features and functions are numerous and far ranging. You don't need to memorize all of them, but familiarity with these capabilities will help you use the product and study for the exam. These features and functions are covered briefly in this section and in more detail throughout the book.

FrontPage 98's features and functions can be categorized into three main groups: Web site creation, content and site structure management, and product integration.

Web Site Creation

With FrontPage 98, professional-looking, content-rich, engaging Web sites may easily be created by Internet novices and experienced Webmasters alike. The program's capabilities along these lines include the following elements:

- **Navigation bars** Generate navigational controls for Web pages with just a few deft mouse clicks. Consistent navigation based on the site's structure is automatically maintained by FrontPage 98.
- **Table creation** Create and manipulate complex tables quickly using FrontPage Editor. With drag-and-drop editing, tables can be created with pixel-level precision.
- **Frames control** FrontPage's WYSIWYG drag-and-drop frame editing simplifies the sometimes daunting task of creating a well-crafted frame-based site.
- **FrontPage components** Add precompiled CGI scripts included with FrontPage to a Web site to add significant functionality to your Web pages, including text searches, a page hit counter, threaded discussion groups, automated forms input handling, and more.
- **Import existing Web sites** You can easily import existing Web sites created using other tools or by hand into FrontPage. Once these sites are imported, all of FrontPage's features can be applied to such legacy sites. Web sites can be imported from a local hard drive or from a location elsewhere on the Web (through a URL).
- **Performance estimates** FrontPage automatically computes the download time for Web documents. This feature helps you maintain an interesting but responsive site, and it lets users decide whether to download files based on time estimates.

- **Templates and wizards** Templates support quick creation of several documents or Web sites using the same layout and design. Wizards perform complex operations or configuration tasks, yet prompt users for site- or page-specific details. Both of these tools simplify the overall Web site creation process.
- **Themes** FrontPage includes collections of backgrounds, bullets, banners, hyperlinks, and navigation bars called *themes*. The more than 50 design schemes can establish the look and feel for an entire Web site or for individual Web documents.
- **Shared borders** Multiple pages can now share the same headers and/or footers to improve consistency across an entire Web site.
- **Hover buttons** Hover buttons are Java applets included with FrontPage that can animate button activity. Hover buttons can change color, shape, image, and text, and they require no programming skills to use.
- **Banner Ad Manager** Banner Ad Manager is used to rotate a set of graphics (like those advertisements you've seen all over the Web) with or without transition effects.
- **Support for TWAIN devices and digital cameras** The use of scanners and digital cameras adds a rich source for potential graphics to Web authoring.
- **Java applets and ActiveX controls** Support for Java and ActiveX permits Web applications to interact with your Web site. FrontPage supports both of these technologies to permit you to integrate external applications and services into your Web sites.
- **Database integration** FrontPage 98 can use Active Server Pages (ASP) and the Database Region wizard to incorporate ODBC-compliant database data into Web sites. This is a significant topic to consider when you are preparing for the test; it's covered in more detail in Chapter 12.
- **Dynamic HTML** Support for Dynamic HTML grants you the ability to add life to otherwise static content, without requiring the use of Java, ActiveX, or other programming technologies.
- **Page transitions** FrontPage 98 can use page transitions (the page dissolving, washing away effect) when you're navigating between documents. Most of these effects are quite similar to transitions available between slides in Microsoft PowerPoint presentations.
- **Push channels** Using FrontPage's CDF wizard, you can transform your Web site into a push channel, or you can add push content to an existing

site. With push channels enabled, your users will be informed automatically whenever your content changes.

- **Cascading Style Sheets (CSS)** FrontPage's support for Cascading Style Sheets (CSS) provides you with complete type, color, positioning, and display controls.
- **Secure Sockets Layer (SSL) security** The Secure Sockets Layer (SSL) can be used to establish a degree of communications security between clients and servers. SSL is not included with FrontPage 98, but its use within the FrontPage environment is supported.

Across all these facilities, we hope that it's obvious that Microsoft tried to include a broad range of capabilities, tools, and utilities in the Web content creation part of FrontPage 98. Even prior to its acquisition by Microsoft in 1995, FrontPage had a reputation as a "best of breed" Web development and management tool. Microsoft has not stinted on the product since then, and this reputation remains well deserved.

Content And Site Structure Management

Management responsibilities increase as the size and complexity of Web sites increase. Most Web sites of any consequence are difficult to manage by hand, especially if content changes frequently. With FrontPage 98, most of the routine management and maintenance tasks associated with a Web site are automated or may be eliminated altogether. The following FrontPage components assist in the efforts that must go into maintaining a Web site once the content has been created and published (which most experts recognize consumes as much as 90 percent of the work and time involved):

- **Views** The FrontPage Explorer offers several views that give you various perspectives on a site's layout, organization, and design. Each view offers unique controls and management capabilities.
- **Print** FrontPage makes it possible to print a Web site layout without diagramming it manually.
- **Check hyperlinks** FrontPage can check for the existence of links between site pages within a single Web site and also verify links to external Web sites in various views.
- **Orphans** FrontPage can identify and remove orphaned files quickly to help keep the storage footprint of your Web site at a minimum. *Orphans* are files in a Web directory to which no link is currently attached.
- **Find and replace** FrontPage permits sections of text to be altered easily throughout an entire Web site via the Cross-Web find and replace tool.

- **Spelling** FrontPage can spellcheck all pages on your site.
- **One-click publishing** If your site runs on a Web server that supports FrontPage Server Extensions, you can upload all changes with a single mouse click.
- **Multiple author support** Using FrontPage, several authors can work on a Web site simultaneously without causing file or version conflicts.
- **Permissions** FrontPage controls user access to content on a Web site, folder, or document basis. Its unique access levels include administrators, authors, and browsers, each with different privileges and permissions.
- **Visual SourceSafe** FrontPage is compatible with Microsoft Visual SourceSafe. This tool is an advanced security and version control utility that uses file check-in and check-out mechanisms to manage documents, code, graphics, and other Web site components.

Using the diverse collection of utilities, capabilities, and facilities, FrontPage 98 offers strong functionality when it comes to managing and maintaining an existing Web site—from performing across-the-board updates or integrity checks, to one-click publishing of an entire site update.

Product Integration

One key selling point for FrontPage 98 is its ability to integrate with existing Microsoft product environments. Its layout, controls, and interface are also quite similar to those of Microsoft Office. As a result, you can apply existing skills, thus reducing training time. However, the benefits of integration within FrontPage go beyond human convenience:

- **Shared tools** The clip art, spellchecker, find and replace, and thesaurus components of FrontPage 98 are the same as those in Office 97. Therefore, information is shared and disk space is conserved.
- **File converters** Office 97 documents can be added to Web sites using the built-in document converters for the native Office 97 file formats.
- **Cross-platform support** Office 97 and FrontPage users from Windows 95, Windows NT Workstation, and Macintosh computers can work together without suffering from platform difference.
- **Internet Explorer (IE) 4** FrontPage 98 supports most of the features found in IE 4. In addition, the IE 4 HTML Editor and FrontPage 98 Editor share a common interface.
- **Remote administration** FrontPage 98 Server Extensions enable remote administration of Web sites located anywhere.

- **Web server support** Support for Unix and Windows NT-based Web servers includes Apache 1.2 and Netscape Enterprise 3 Unix Web servers, as well as Netscape Enterprise 3 and Microsoft Internet Information Server (IIS) 4 Web servers for Windows NT.
- **Internet Information Server (IIS)** Tight integration with IIS helps exploit the performance gains that the ISAPI DLL can deliver (this code runs in the same process space as IIS itself), rather than using only extensions based on Common Gateway Interface (CGI). CGIs run in separate process spaces and are therefore slower and more resource consumptive.
- **Index Server** Integrated support for Index Server expands the searching capabilities of FrontPage-created Web sites.
- **Database** FrontPage 98 includes several specific components that add database integration and interaction to Web sites. These permit all kinds of external data repositories to be queried, reported on, or manipulated from within Web pages.

For those developers already using Microsoft products to create content, FrontPage 98 makes it extremely simple to convert and incorporate such content, regardless of the platform used to create it. Likewise, for those working in a Windows NT-based environment—especially those using IIS—FrontPage makes it easy to leverage that environment's programming interfaces, Web extension technologies, and services.

FrontPage As Part Of An Overall Internet, Intranet, Or Extranet Solution

FrontPage 98 is a great tool for individual Web authors as well as enterprises with complex network and publishing environments. The features of FrontPage that relate to creation and maintenance of Web sites can apply to nearly every conceivable Web publishing environment.

For individuals, FrontPage can serve as an elegant authoring tool. Newly created Web sites can be completely tested and previewed before public consumption. With a dedicated Internet connection, FrontPage can even act as a Web server using Personal Web Server (PWS).

For enterprises, FrontPage is more than just a development utility; it is also a groupware product and an integrated management system. FrontPage can tie together SQL servers and Access databases, support fully encrypted secure transmissions with SSL, support multiple redundant Web servers, and allow several authors to work simultaneously on a single set of materials without causing version conflicts. FrontPage may also be configured easily to operate over a proxy server or behind a firewall.

The flexibility offered by FrontPage enables an operator inside or outside a corporate LAN to manage Web servers within an intranet, on the Internet, or anywhere on an extranet. With access to IIS 4, Index Server, Visual SourceSafe, and other Microsoft products, FrontPage 98 can provide the means to control, access, and maintain your entire Web publishing system centrally and universally.

> *Note: These and other issues involving FrontPage 98 in complex publishing environments, including evaluating the security, performance, maintenance, and scalability of a Web, are discussed in Chapter 14.*

Hardware And Software Requirements

Before you install FrontPage 98, you should know the hardware and software requirements for this utility and its components. The system requirements for the basic FrontPage 98 utility are as follows:

- An Intel 486 computer or better.
- 16MB of RAM on Windows 95 or Windows 98; 32MB of RAM on Windows NT.
- 32MB of hard drive space.
- A CD-ROM drive.
- A VGA 256-color video card and compatible monitor or better.
- A mouse or other pointing device.
- Windows 95 or later; Windows NT Workstation 4 or later; Windows NT Server 4 or later (previous versions of these operating systems are not compatible with FrontPage 98).
- Internet access is required to use any of the program's Internet features. FrontPage 98 may be used without Internet access; however, even if Internet access is not available, TCP/IP must be present on the local machine.

If you install the additional components included on the distribution CD-ROM, you'll need additional hard drive space:

- IE 3.02 requires 11MB of additional space.

- Microsoft Personal Web Server (PWS) for Windows 95 requires 1MB of additional disk space.
- Microsoft PWS for Windows 98 requires 10MB (minimal install), 25MB (typical install), or 52.6MB (full install) of disk space.
- Microsoft PWS for Windows NT Workstation requires 10MB of additional disk space.
- The Web Publishing wizard requires 1MB of additional space.
- Internet Mail And News requires 2MB of additional space.

Microsoft Image Composer has more stringent requirements than FrontPage 98 and other components. To use Microsoft Image Composer, your system must meet the following system requirements:

- An Intel 486DX66 CPU or better
- 28 to 44MB of additional hard drive space

You may also use a Windows-compatible drawing tablet and a TWAIN-compatible scanner or digital camera with Microsoft Image Composer.

Overview: Installing FrontPage

The installation process for FrontPage 98 is similar to that for most other Microsoft products. It's controlled by an installation wizard that prompts you for the desired configuration settings as needed. Before starting the installation process, you must perform the following tasks:

- Verify that your computer system meets the minimum requirements.
- Save all your work.
- Close all applications and terminate any virus-checking programs that may be active.

Installing FrontPage 98 involves the following steps:

1. Insert the FrontPage 98 distribution CD-ROM into your CD-ROM drive.
2. The autorun component on the CD-ROM should launch the FrontPage installation interface. If not, use the Start|Run command to execute the SETUP.EXE file located in the root directory of the CD-ROM.
3. Click on the Install FrontPage 98 selection from the installation interface.
4. The setup wizard launches and displays the Welcome screen. Click on Next.

5. Provide your name and company name in the text fields on the FrontPage Registration page. Then, click on Next. Click on Yes to confirm your name and company name.
6. Enter the 11-digit CD-ROM key from the back of the CD-ROM case. Click on OK.
7. Read the license agreement. Click on Yes.
8. The Setup Type page is displayed. You're given two options: Typical and Custom. The Typical option automatically installs the client software, PWS, and Server Extensions. The Custom option allows you to select which components are installed. Select Custom.
9. Verify that the Destination Directory points to the location where you want the main FrontPage files installed (typically the default is satisfactory). Click on Next.
10. Select the items from the Components list for the setup wizard to install. Select everything but Additional Clipart. Once these are selected, click on Next.
11. Select the directory in which the Web sites created and managed by FrontPage will be stored locally. Click on Next.
12. The setup wizard installs all the necessary files and sets system configurations for FrontPage.
13. After all of the necessary files are copied, the setup wizard prompts you for the name and password to use to control access to the FrontPage Web root. Be sure to take notice of capitalization, because FrontPage is case-sensitive. For example, "Admin" and "admin" are two different user names for FrontPage (this is unlike standard NT/95 security). Click on OK.
14. The Setup Complete page is displayed. Click on Finish.
15. FrontPage Explorer is automatically launched. A message appears stating that a TCP/IP examination will occur. Click on OK. If TCP/IP is configured properly, a message will display your local computer name. Click on OK. If TCP/IP is not configured properly, you must exit FrontPage and correct the problem.
16. The Getting Started dialog box appears. This interface is used to open an existing Web site or launch the wizard for creating a new Web site. Click on Cancel.
17. Exit FrontPage (File|Exit).

18. You should see the FrontPage installation interface again. Notice that two other installation links are present: Image Composer and Internet Explorer. If you already have IE 3.02 or greater installed, do not install IE again. The installation of Image Composer is covered in Chapter 9. Click on Exit.

Integrating FrontPage With Office 97

Microsoft Office 97 is a desktop productivity suite for the PC. It includes Word, Excel, PowerPoint, and Access. Word is a professional word processor. Excel is a macro-capable spreadsheet. PowerPoint is a multimedia presentation tool. Access is a relational database. FrontPage can include documents or data from each of these applications in your Web sites.

The integration of FrontPage 98 with Office 97 extends to the following features:

- Using the same icons in Views as those used in Windows Explorer
- Verifying and repairing links in Office 97 documents
- Cutting and pasting document sections from Office 97 into FrontPage
- Dragging and dropping document sections or whole documents from Office 97 into FrontPage
- Using a shared spellchecker and thesaurus
- Sharing the same look and feel

Additionally, even without converting Office 97 documents into standard Web formats (which FrontPage can do automatically), you can include Office 97 documents as-is into Web sites. Microsoft offers helper applications called *Office viewers* that can be associated with Office file extensions. This enables Web visitors to view Office 97 documents without requiring them to own Office 97. You can download these viewers from or point Web site visitors to **www.microsoft.com/office/office/viewers.asp**.

For more information about Office 97, visit the Microsoft Web site at **www.microsoft.com/office/**.

FrontPage 98 Prerequisites

The FrontPage 98 certification exam and this study guide assume you have knowledge of or experience with the following:

- Using HTML to create Web pages
- Using multimedia in a Web document (graphics, video, sound, Java applets, ActiveX controls, and so on)
- Using scripts (CGI, client side, server side, Java, JavaScript, VBScript, and so on)
- Publishing Web sites (HTTP and FTP)
- Hosting and maintaining a Web server
- Using security, databases, Dynamic HTML, Cascading Style Sheets, firewalls, and proxies

In this book, we assume you're familiar with the HTML authoring and Web server publishing processes. This means that when we discuss tables, frames, buttons, forms, and other common HTML elements, we won't cover the markup tags and the attributes involved in any detail. Instead, we just discuss the capabilities and controls offered by FrontPage to deal with these markup tags.

You don't need to be a Web expert to start using FrontPage 98. In fact, you don't even need to know what HTML is to create an interesting Web site. However, you may find the certification exam difficult if you don't know basic Web concepts. We recommend that you learn as much about these technologies as you can.

Additional HTML Resources

You can pass the exam without being an expert in any of these items. But the more experience and familiarity you have with them, the more likely it is that you'll understand the scenarios and questions on the test. If you're a Web novice, we highly recommend that you take the time to understand Web publishing before tackling the FrontPage 98 certification exam. The following books can help you understand Web publishing in general:

- *Dynamic HTML Black Book*. Natanya Pitts-Moultis, C.C. Sanders, and Ramesh Chandak. The Coriolis Group. Scottsdale, AZ, 1998. List price: $49.99. ISBN: 1-57610-188-6.
- *HTML Style Sheets Design Guide*. Natanya Pitts, Ed Tittel, and Stephen N. James. The Coriolis Group. Scottsdale, AZ, 1997. List price: $39.99. ISBN: 1-57610-211-4.

- *Microsoft Dynamic HTML EXplorer*. James Meade, David Crowder, and Rhonda Crowder. The Coriolis Group. Scottsdale, AZ, 1998. List price: $39.99. ISBN 1-56604-798-6.
- *HTML Publishing on the Internet, Second Edition*. Brent Heslop and David Holzgang. The Coriolis Group. Scottsdale, AZ, 1998. List price: $39.99. ISBN 1-56604-625-4.

Practice Questions

Question 1

FrontPage 98 is a full-featured WYSIWYG Web editor. What other features does FrontPage 98 include? [Check all correct answers]

- ❑ a. Personal Web hosting
- ❑ b. Push channels
- ❑ c. E-commerce shopping cart
- ❑ d. Database integration

FrontPage 98 can be used to host (serve) personal Web sites, offer push channels, and provide database integration. Therefore, answers a, b, and d are correct. FrontPage 98 does not include an e-commerce shopping cart system, but it can be used to maintain a Web site that employs such a system. Therefore, answer c is incorrect.

Question 2

FrontPage Editor is used to examine and manipulate Web sites as a whole, whereas FrontPage Explorer is used to create and alter individual Web documents.

- ❍ a. True
- ❍ b. False

This is a false statement. Therefore, answer b is correct. FrontPage Explorer is used to examine and manipulate Web sites as a whole, whereas FrontPage Editor is used to create and alter individual Web documents.

Question 3

FrontPage Editor includes an automatic performance estimate that computes the average download time for the document being edited.

- ❍ a. True
- ❍ b. False

This is a true statement. Therefore, answer a is correct.

Question 4

FrontPage 98 is more than just a Web site creation tool. Which of the following components included with FrontPage 98 add other features and functions? [Check all correct answers]

- ❑ a. Index Server 2
- ❑ b. Server Extensions
- ❑ c. Internet Information Server 4
- ❑ d. Personal Web Server 1.5
- ❑ e. Transaction Server 2
- ❑ f. Image Composer 1.5
- ❑ g. Internet Explorer 4.01

FrontPage 98 includes Server Extensions, Personal Web Server 1.5, and Image Composer 1.5. Therefore, answers b, d, and f are correct. Index Server 2, IIS 4, and Transaction Server 2 are part of the Windows NT 4 Option Pack and not part of FrontPage 98, even though these products can be used by FrontPage Webs. Therefore, answers a, c, and e are incorrect. FrontPage includes Internet Explorer 3.02 not 4.01. Therefore, answer g is incorrect.

Question 5

Which of the following devices may be used with FrontPage 98? [Check all correct answers]

- ❑ a. Audio card microphone
- ❑ b. Digital camera
- ❑ c. Virtual reality goggles
- ❑ d. TWAIN-compliant scanners
- ❑ e. Thumbprint pads

FrontPage 98 includes native support for digital cameras and TWAIN-compliant scanners. Therefore, answers b and d are correct. FrontPage 98 does not include native support for microphones, VR goggles, or thumbprint pads. Therefore, answers a, c, and e are incorrect.

Question 6

Which of the following Web technologies are directly supported in FrontPage 98 Editor? [Check all correct answers]

- ❑ a. Dynamic HTML
- ❑ b. XML
- ❑ c. Cascading Style Sheets
- ❑ d. Client-side Java applets

The FrontPage Editor supports Dynamic HTML, CSS, and client-side Java applets. Therefore answers a, c, and d are correct. XML is not currently supported by FrontPage. Therefore, answer b is incorrect.

Question 7

Which feature of FrontPage 98 is useful to help keep the overall size of Web folders to a minimum?

- ❍ a. Cross-Web find and replace
- ❍ b. Spellchecker and thesaurus
- ❍ c. Locate orphans
- ❍ d. Multiauthor support

The ability to locate orphans helps keep Web folders to a minimal size. Therefore, answer c is correct. The other options are not related to a Web site's size. Therefore, answers a, b, and d are incorrect.

Question 8

Web sites created with FrontPage 98 can be edited only by the original author on the original computer platform.

- ❍ a. True
- ❍ b. False

This is a false statement. Therefore, answer b is correct. FrontPage 98 Webs can be edited by anyone granted administrator or author privileges to the site. In addition, authorized users can operate from Windows 95, Windows 98, Windows NT, or a Macintosh computer using FrontPage 98 without difficulty.

Question 9

Which of the following is not a minimal requirement for installing FrontPage 98 and all its optional components on Windows NT?

- ❍ a. An Intel 486 CPU
- ❍ b. 32MB of RAM
- ❍ c. 101MB of hard drive space
- ❍ d. Internet access

Internet access is not a minimal requirement (only TCP/IP is required). Therefore, answer d is correct. Many would assume that because FrontPage is an Internet-related tool, Internet access is a requirement, and therein lies the trick to this question. FrontPage requires an Intel 486 CPU or better and at least 32MB of RAM on Windows NT. If all optional components are installed, 101MB of hard drive space is required (32 + 11 + 1 + 10 + 1 + 2 + 44). Therefore, answers a, b, and c are incorrect.

Question 10

Which of the following features are associated with FrontPage 98 and Office 97 integration? [Check all correct answers]

- ❑ a. Spellchecking
- ❑ b. Link verification
- ❑ c. One-click publishing
- ❑ d. Drag-and-drop documents

Spellchecking, link verification, and drag-and-drop documents are all features associated with Office 97 integration. Therefore, answers a, b, and d are correct. One-click publishing is a feature of FrontPage 98 but is not associated with Office 97 integration. Therefore, answer c is incorrect.

Need To Know More?

Karlins, David and Stephanie Cottrell. *Teach Yourself Microsoft FrontPage 98 in a Week, Second Edition*, Sams.net Publishing, Indianapolis, IN, 1998. ISBN 1-57521-350-8. Chapter 1 includes a brief but cogent overview of FrontPage 98. An excellent beginner's book.

Lehto, Kerry A. and W. Brett Polonsky. *Official Microsoft FrontPage 98 Book*, Microsoft Press, Redmond, WA, 1997. ISBN 1-57231-629-2. Chapter 1 provides a good overview of FrontPage 98.

Matthews, Martin S. and Erik B. Poulsen. *FrontPage 98: The Complete Reference*, Osborne McGraw-Hill, Berkeley, CA, 1998. ISBN 0-07-882394-3. Chapter 2 includes a detailed guided tour of FrontPage; a great place to start learning about this software package.

Stanek, William R., et al. *Microsoft FrontPage 98 Unleashed*, Sams.net Publishing, Indianapolis, IN, 1998. ISBN 1-57521-349-4. Chapter 1 provides an overview of FrontPage 98.

Tauber, Daniel and Brenda Kienan. *Mastering Microsoft FrontPage 98*, Sybex, Alameda, CA, 1998. ISBN 0-7821-2144-6. Chapter 1 provides an overview of FrontPage 98 and FrontPage Explorer. Appendix A covers the installation of FrontPage 98.

Microsoft TechNet. Useful overview information about FrontPage 98 is included in the following documents: "Product Overview MS FrontPage 98 for Windows," "MS FrontPage 98 Datasheet," and "MS FrontPage 98 Reviewer's Guide."

The official FrontPage Web site hosted by Microsoft can be found at **www.microsoft.com/frontpage/**. It offers overview information about this product.

3

Creating And Managing Webs With FrontPage Explorer

Terms you'll need to understand:

- √ FrontPage Explorer
- √ Views: Folders, All Files, Navigation, Hyperlinks, Hyperlink Status, Themes, and Tasks
- √ Importing
- √ Publishing
- √ Root Webs
- √ Sub-Webs
- √ Browse access
- √ Author access
- √ Administer access

Techniques you'll need to master:

- √ Using the FrontPage Explorer
- √ Creating and modifying Web sites
- √ Managing Web sites
- √ Publishing Web sites

FrontPage 98 is comprised of two tools: FrontPage Explorer and FrontPage Editor. Both of these tools need to be mastered to use FrontPage effectively to create and manage Web sites. This chapter covers FrontPage Explorer; Chapter 4 discusses FrontPage Editor.

FrontPage Explorer: An Overview

FrontPage Explorer is the primary interface to FrontPage. It's also where most organizational and administrative tasks are performed. FrontPage Explorer is the point from which all FrontPage-related activity starts—in fact, Editor and Image Composer are launched and accessed from FrontPage Explorer. Therefore, a thorough understanding and familiarity with FrontPage Explorer is essential.

FrontPage Explorer is launched from the Start menu. FrontPage Explorer is located in Start|Programs|Microsoft FrontPage, by default. When FrontPage Explorer is launched for the first time, you'll encounter the Getting Started dialog box, shown in Figure 3.1. Select the radio button that reads Open An Existing FrontPage Web; then select the entry that reads Personal Web (Local) and click on the OK button. The Personal Web (Local) entry is created automatically when FrontPage 98 is installed. Once this option is selected, you'll be prompted to provide the administrator's user name and password for this site. Once you obtain access to the site, its details are loaded into FrontPage and then you can use FrontPage Explorer.

> *Note: To use FrontPage, you must have Personal Web Server installed locally or have access to a Web server with FrontPage Server Extensions installed that's accessible over your network or through a proxy server.*

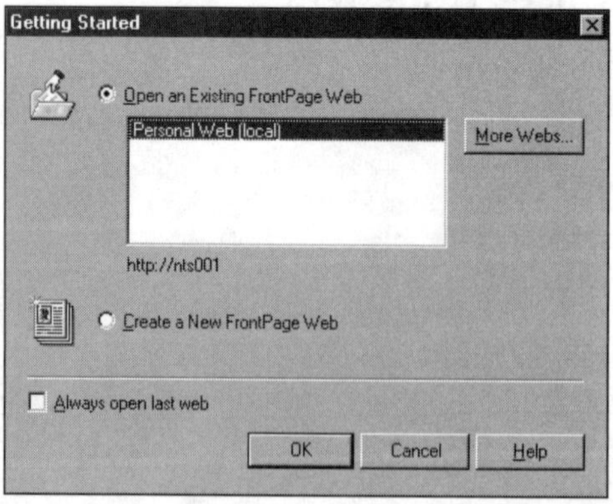

Figure 3.1 The Getting Started dialog box of FrontPage 98.

FrontPage Explorer is divided into several areas: a menu bar, a toolbar, the Views toolbar, and the main window. The menu bar, toolbar, and main window are common elements that appear in nearly every Windows-based application. The Views toolbar is an element borrowed from Outlook and is used to switch between views. FrontPage Explorer's main window uses different layouts and display schemes, depending on which view is selected. In the following sections, you'll explore the numerous views and menus found in FrontPage Explorer.

Utilizing The Different Explorer Views

FrontPage Explorer uses seven views to offer administrators various perspectives on the Web sites they manage, as well as a variety of ways to exercise administrative control over those sites. Within FrontPage Explorer, a *view* is simply a way to look at a Web site. Each view offers a different perspective and a different set of operational controls, which, when used in conjunction with one another, greatly simplify Web management tasks.

Each view has its own content-specific pop-up menu, which can be accessed by right-clicking on it. All the commands that appear in these pop-up menus are also available in the menu bar and are detailed in the "Menu Bar Commands" section later in this chapter. A different list of commands appears in these menus, depending on which view is selected and what type of object is beneath your cursor.

In addition to a custom right-click pop-up menu, each view has its own uniquely configured toolbar. These toolbars offer single-click access to many of the most commonly used commands in each view. Position your cursor over any button on the toolbar to reveal its associated tooltip, or the name of the associated button or command. Remember that all commands that appear as buttons on the toolbar also appear on the menu bar.

No matter which view is active in FrontPage Explorer, you can always launch FrontPage Editor by double-clicking on any file. This launches Editor and loads the selected document, ready to be edited. The seven FrontPage Explorer views are detailed in the following sections.

Folders View

The Folders View, shown in Figure 3.2, displays a list of all folders and files contained within the current Web site. All folders appear in the left-hand pane of the main window. All subfolders and files appear in the right-hand pane of the main window. This view is useful when you need to locate a single file somewhere in your Web site's file hierarchy.

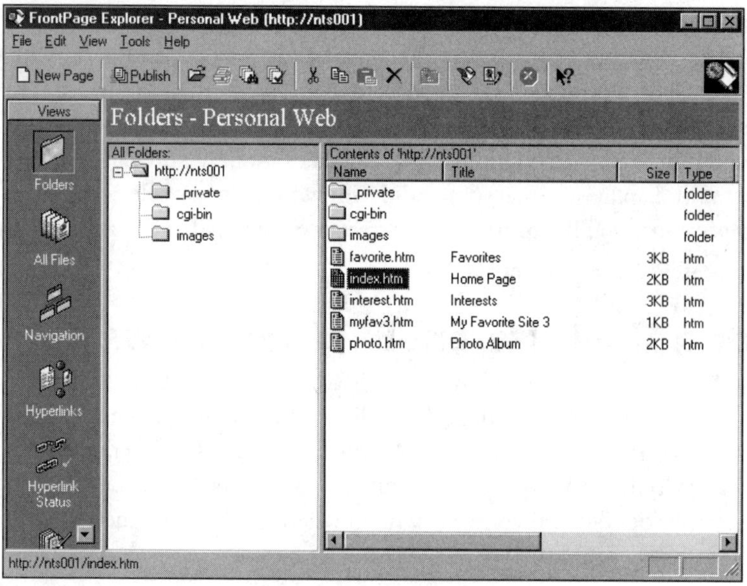

Figure 3.2 FrontPage Explorer's Folders View.

Beyond looking almost exactly like the Windows NT Explorer, the Folders View and All Files View (discussed in the next section) operate in much the same way. For example, you can double-click on any column to sort the files and folders by that column. You can also resize the columns, right-click on an object to examine its properties and related commands, and so forth. If you're familiar with NT Explorer, you'll feel right at home in the Folders View in FrontPage Explorer.

All Files View

The All Files View, shown in Figure 3.3, displays a list of all the files contained within the selected Web site. This view does not list folders per se; instead, folder information is included as another column of information for the files that appear in this view. Also, note that this view indicates whether a file is an orphan. An *orphan* is a file not referenced by any other document in a Web site that appears within the site's directory structure. This view is also useful when you are looking through all the files in a Web site at once.

Navigation View

The Navigation View is depicted in Figure 3.4. It's the default view for new sites created using FrontPage. The Navigation View's main window is divided into two areas: the Navigation pane and the Contents pane. The Navigation pane is the top pane; it displays a graphical representation of the links between

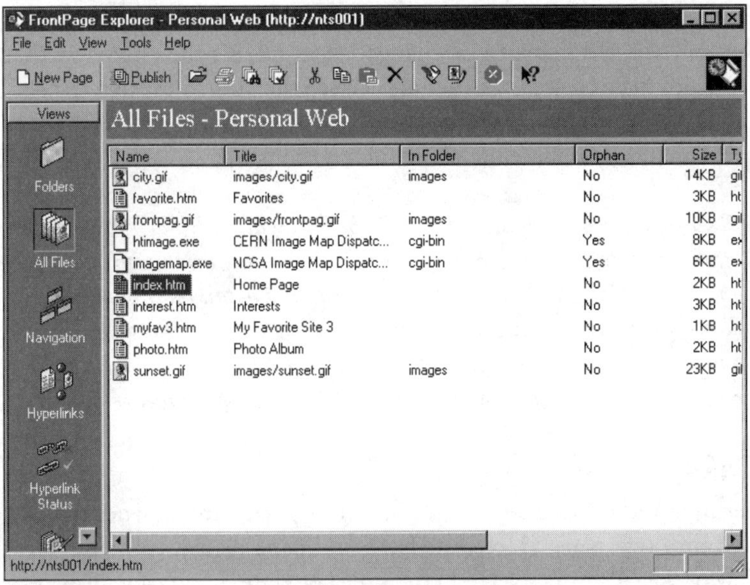

Figure 3.3 FrontPage Explorer's All Files View.

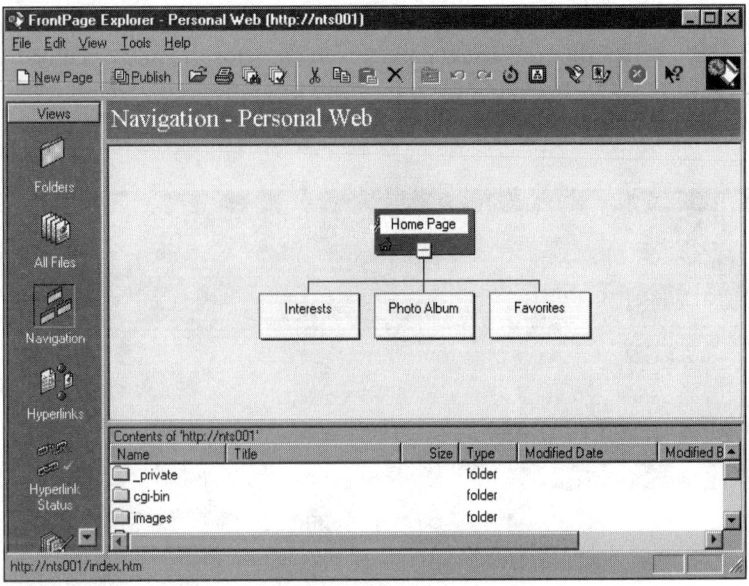

Figure 3.4 FrontPage Explorer's Navigation View.

pages. The Contents pane is the bottom pane; it displays all files and folders referenced in the currently selected Web site. This view can be useful if you want to create a quick overview of the layout and structure of your Web site as a whole.

The Natigation View is unique in a number of ways. First, it is the only view that allows only the file name to be changed. Second, it's the only view that allows new pages to be created with an implicit relationship to the parent page. When "child" pages are created this way, the Navigation Bar WebBots in other pages are automatically updated to show this relationship.

> *Note: Some of the page representations on the Navigation View feature a small square with a plus or minus sign inside. This convention is used throughout FrontPage Explorer and indicates that a detail level may be expanded (plus sign) or contracted (minus sign) by double-clicking on any icon that contains a plus or minus sign. Use this feature to drill down into portions of a Web site or to climb higher in a Web site's object hierarchy.*

Hyperlinks View

The Hyperlinks View appears in Figure 3.5. It displays a main window that's also divided into two panes. Here, the left-hand pane displays a hierarchical outline view of the currently selected Web site. The right-hand pane displays a graphical view of the Web site using a linked set of objects with lines between them to indicate how documents and other objects are connected to one another. The arrows that point from one object to another indicate a link or embedding (the object that the arrow points from contains the link or embedding; the object that the arrow points to is linked or embedded). Detail levels in both panes may be expanded or contracted by double-clicking on the plus or

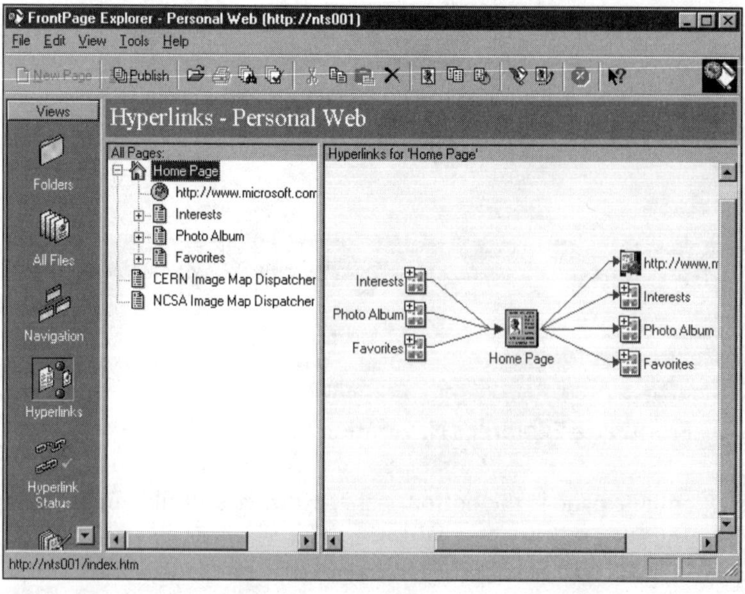

Figure 3.5 FrontPage Explorer's Hyperlinks View.

minus signs for the objects that contain them. The Hyperlinks View is useful when examining a Web site to determine how it's "interlinked."

Hyperlink Status View

The Hyperlink Status View, shown in Figure 3.6, displays the status of links to internal and external resources within a Web site. Green circles indicate verified links with OK status when they're displayed (verified links are not displayed by default; the assumption is that most links will be working and that only unknown or bad links should be shown). Yellow circles denote unchecked links with Unknown status. Red circles flag bad links with Broken status. This view is useful for helping administrators maintain Web sites with a minimum of questionable or broken links.

Themes View

The Themes View is shown in Figure 3.7. This view may be used to assign or alter a FrontPage theme for a Web site. A *theme* is simply a collection of graphics, background images, and color schemes used to give a Web site a consistent look and feel. FrontPage 98 includes over 50 predefined themes that are ready to use within this view.

Tasks View

The Tasks View, shown in Figure 3.8, is a multiuser to-do list. Action items are added to the task list and assigned a priority level. Tasks created from other

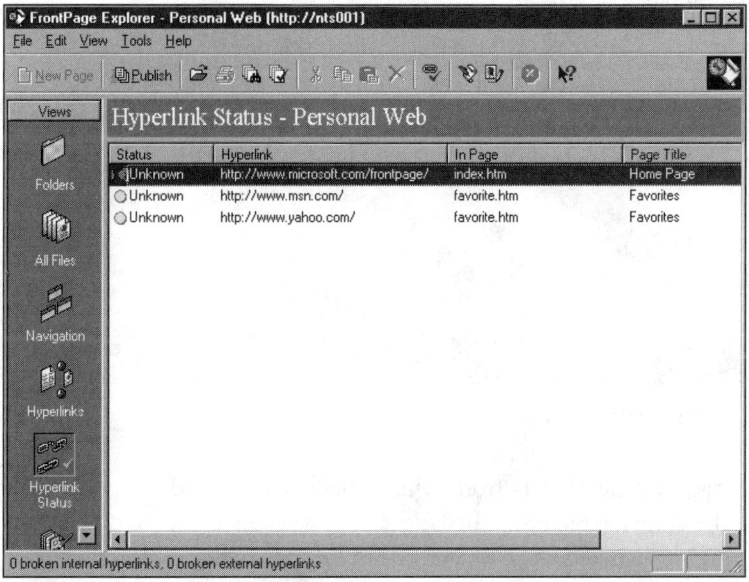

Figure 3.6 FrontPage Explorer's Hyperlink Status View.

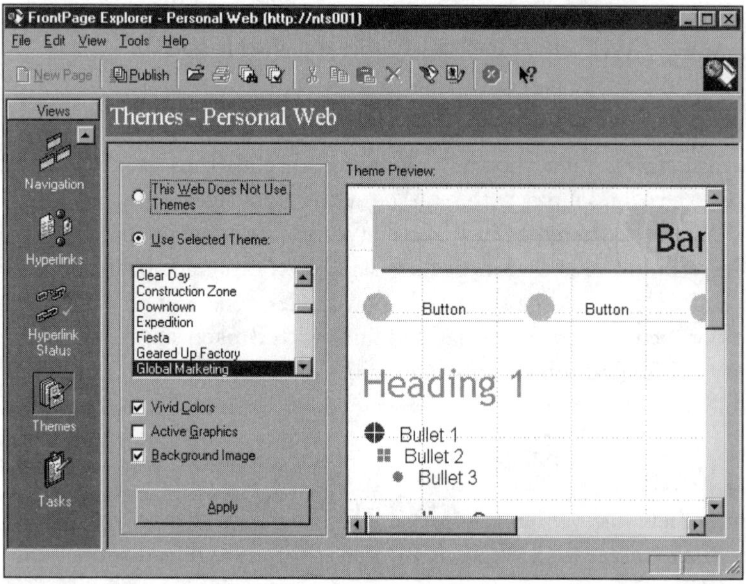

Figure 3.7 FrontPage Explorer's Themes View.

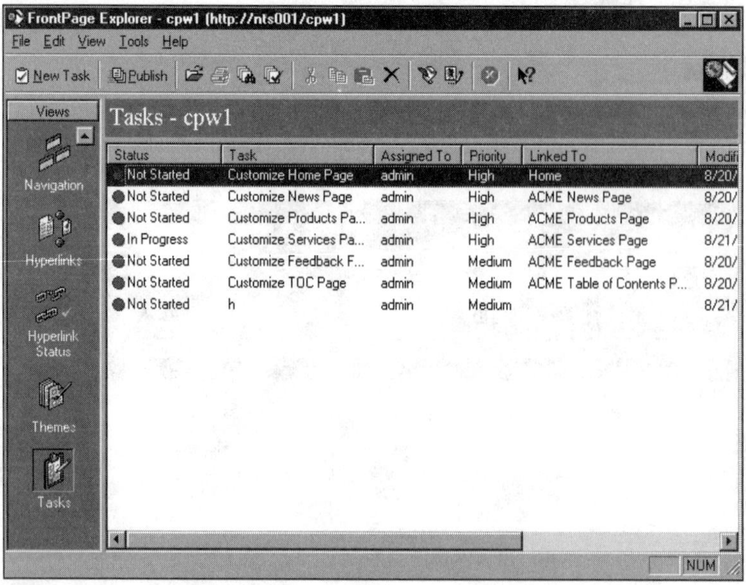

Figure 3.8 FrontPage Explorer's Tasks View.

views link back to the objects from which they were created. Uncompleted tasks take the status value named Not Started, whereas completed tasks are labeled Complete. Linked tasks are marked In Progress when you edit a linked object and answer "no" to the "Mark task as completed?" query when you save your changes. This tool helps to keep track of active tasks in the FrontPage environment and can also report on their status of completion.

Menu Bar Commands

FrontPage Explorer's menu bar contains five drop-down menus: File, Edit, View, Tools, and Help. For the most part, these menus are consistent in every view, but not all commands are enabled for every view. The Help menu is a standard Windows Help environment and is not discussed in any further detail (we assume you already know how to use the Windows Help facility). The other menu hierarchies are discussed in the following sections.

File Menu

The File menu contains the following commands:

- **New|Page** Creates a new Web document inside the currently selected or active folder.
- **New|Task** Creates a new task. If an object is selected, that object is linked to the task.
- **New|Folder** Creates a new folder inside the currently selected or active folder.
- **New|FrontPage Web** Opens the New FrontPage Web dialog box used to create new Web sites from scratch manually or with a wizard.
- **Open FrontPage Web** Opens an existing site.
- **Close FrontPage Web** Closes the currently active site.
- **Publish FrontPage Web** Publishes the current Web site to a Web server.
- **Delete FrontPage Web** Removes a Web site from a Web server.
- **Import** Imports objects from a folder or Web site.
- **Export** Exports individual files to a local disk drive.
- **Page Setup** Defines the print parameters.
- **Print Preview** Displays the output on screen that will appear on paper if printed.
- **Print Navigation View** Prints the Navigation View.

Note: Inside FrontPage Explorer, you can only print from within the Navigation View.

- **Exit** Exits FrontPage. If any unsaved work is present, you are prompted to save or discard it.

Edit Menu

The Edit menu contains the following commands:

- **Undo** Retracts the last change made.
- **Redo** Reapplies the last retracted (undone) change.
- **Cut** Moves the selected object(s) into the Clipboard.
- **Copy** Copies the selected object(s) into the Clipboard.
- **Paste** Pastes a copy of the Clipboard's contents to a new location.
- **Select All** Highlights all possible objects within the current pane.
- **Open** Opens the selected object with the default viewer/editor.
- **Open With** Opens the selected object with an alternate viewer/editor that you must select from a list of known editors.
- **Delete** Removes the selected object(s).
- **Rename** Changes the name of the selected object with a new name you provide.
- **Do Task** Opens the object linked to a task with the editor associated with the object's type.
- **Mark Task Complete** Sets the status of a task to Complete.
- **Properties** Opens the Properties dialog box for the selected object.

The Properties dialog box displays information about the selected object. A directory object's Properties dialog box, shown in Figure 3.9, displays the directory name, type, location (path), how many objects it contains, and whether scripts and programs may be executed within it. A file object's Properties dialog box displays the name, title, type, size, location, creation date, creator, modified data, modifier, and comments. For some file types, such as graphics files, the title may be changed to something a bit more descriptive than its file name (the default title for graphics).

View Menu

The View menu contains a command to switch to each of the seven views plus a Refresh command to update whatever content is displayed. Additional commands may appear in the View menu when a particular view is selected, as follows:

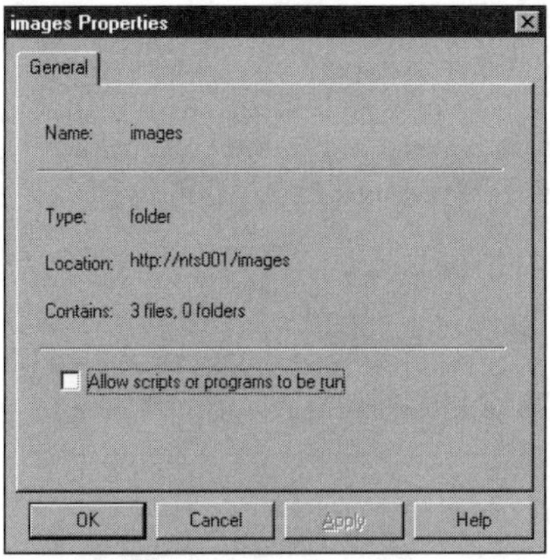

Figure 3.9 The directory (folder) object's Properties dialog box.

- **Expand All (Navigation View)** Reveals all of the detail visible in the Navigation pane.
- **Rotate (Navigation View)** Rotates the Navigation pane display from a top-to-bottom format to a left-to-right format.
- **Size To Fit (Navigation View)** Contracts the details (that is, it displays smaller page representations with truncated titles) of a Web site so the site's layout fits within the Navigation pane.
- **Hyperlinks To Images (Hyperlinks View)** Adds links to images in the display.
- **Repeated Hyperlinks (Hyperlinks View)** Shows every link, even repeated links from the same page.
- **Hyperlinks Inside Page (Hyperlinks View)** Shows self-referential links.
- **Show All Hyperlinks (Hyperlink Status View)** Shows all hyperlinks or only those that are not okay.
- **Task History (Tasks View)** Shows all tasks or just those not yet completed.

Tools Menu

The Tools menu contains the following commands:

- **Spelling** Checks the spelling of all pages or just the selected pages. A task can be created for each page with misspelled words.
- **Find** Searches all or selected pages for a specific string of characters or keywords.

- **Replace** Searches and replaces a specific string of characters or keywords in all or selected pages.
- **Recalculate Hyperlinks** Instructs FrontPage to retest and confirm all internal hyperlinks. This command does not check external links.
- **Verify Hyperlinks** Verifies all external hyperlinks.
- **Shared Borders** Defines what borders will be shared by Web pages.
- **Define Channel** Defines a CDF (Channel Definition Format) file for the current Web site.
- **Show FrontPage Editor** Launches FrontPage Editor.
- **Show Image Editor** Launches Image Composer.
- **Web Settings** Opens the FrontPage Web Settings dialog box. (Details are covered in the "Modifying Web Settings" section later in this chapter.)
- **Permissions** Opens the Permissions dialog box. (Details are covered in the "Setting Web Permissions" section later in this chapter.)
- **Change Password** Changes the current administrator's/author's password.
- **Options** Opens the Options dialog box. (Details are covered in the "Setting Web Options" section later in this chapter.)

Creating Web Sites

The FrontPage Explorer is the primary tool used to create and manage Web sites as a whole. The content and structure of individual pages is manipulated with the FrontPage Editor (the topic of Chapter 4). A *Web site* is a collection of HTML documents and graphics with a scattering of sound files, scripts, and other multimedia or programming components that, when linked together, create a cohesive presentation of content on a specific topic.

Within FrontPage Explorer, new Web sites may be created using one of three methods:

- Creating an entire Web site from scratch
- Creating a Web site using a wizard and templates
- Importing an existing Web site and incorporating root Webs and sub-Webs

Creating A Web Site From Scratch

Creating a new Web site from scratch places the burden of structure, navigation, and design solely on your shoulders. Prior to the introduction of FrontPage and similar Web authoring tools, all Web sites were built from scratch. Many Webmasters still prefer this method because it gives them complete control instead of their having to rely on a tool or being restricted by a tool's capabilities. Starting a new Web site from scratch involves the following list of menu selections and commands:

1. Issue the File|New|FrontPage Web command from the menu bar.
2. On the New FrontPage Web dialog box, select the From Wizard Or Template radio button (see Figure 3.10).
3. Locate and select Empty Web from the list of wizards and templates. (Note that Empty Web is a template.)
4. Choose a title for the new Web.
5. Click on OK.

FrontPage then creates a new root on the Web server with two subdirectories: images and _private. This Web root is otherwise empty and contains no Web documents or other objects. From this point on, you must create new pages manually, define the structure of the site, define navigation aids, and manage the site's layout. (Note that all these functions are described later in this chapter or in other chapters in this book.)

A related new Web creation process is the One Page Web selection on the New FrontPage Web dialog box. This selection creates a single content-free document, called the Home Page, with the file name of INDEX.HTM. Otherwise, it's exactly the same as the Empty Web template.

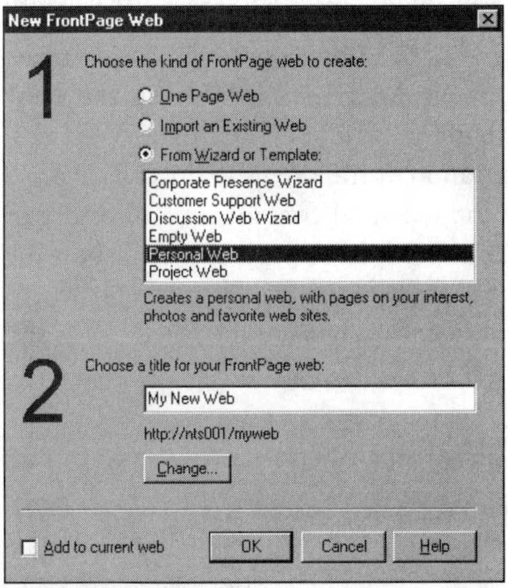

Figure 3.10 The New FrontPage Web dialog box.

Creating Wizards And Templates

Creating a new Web site using a wizard or template is quite simple. A *wizard* is a "smart" tool that builds a Web site based on your input to specific prompts. A *template* is a cookie-cutter layout tool you can customize for your own purposes. You only need to follow the steps defined for scratch creation, but instead of selecting Empty Web, select one of the following wizards or templates:

- **Corporate Presence wizard** Builds a Web site suitable for a small company.
- **Customer Support Web template** Creates a Web site that may be used to offer customers online help or technical support.
- **Discussion Web wizard** Builds a Web site suitable for hosting Web-based discussion groups.
- **Personal Web template** Creates a Web site that may be customized as your own personal site to offer information about your interests, hobbies, photos, or whatever.
- **Project Web template** Creates a Web site suitable for managing project development and direction.

Detailed discussion of the use of wizards and templates appears in Chapter 5.

Importing

Creating a new FrontPage Web by importing an existing Web site brings legacy sites under FrontPage's management and allows the enhanced capabilities found in FrontPage and Server Extensions to be incorporated into your existing creations.

Starting the import process is the same as the other methods already mentioned; however, you must select Import An Existing Web on the New FrontPage Web dialog box. In response to this selection, the Import Web wizard appears and prompts you for the location of the Web site (local hard drive or Internet site). You can import just the top-level contents of a directory or everything within its subfolders. You're offered the opportunity to inspect the list of files to be imported, and you may exclude individual files you don't want. After FrontPage completes the import, you can manage the legacy Web site just as if it originated within FrontPage.

Root Webs And Sub-Webs

FrontPage is able to manage multiple Web sites hosted from a single Web server. The primary Web site on a Web server is known as the *root Web*. This is the Web site in which documents reside in the top-most directory of the Web.

In other words, when the URL for the Web server is issued, such as **http://nts001/**, the root Web appears in the browser for that URL. A *sub-Web* is a self-contained Web site that exists inside a folder beneath the main root directory. A sub-Web may be accessed by adding its folder name to the root Web URL, as in **http://nts001/personal/**. FrontPage can manage an unlimited number of sub-Webs, but only a single root Web may exist on any one Web server.

Modifying Web Sites

Altering a Web site involves adding and removing pages. These actions can be performed from the Folders, All Files, or Navigation Views. However, before any action can be taken against a Web site, the Web site must be loaded into FrontPage.

An existing Web site can be opened using the File|Open FrontPage Web command or by clicking on the Open FrontPage Web toolbar button. Either action displays the Getting Started dialog box (shown earlier in Figure 3.1), which is also displayed when FrontPage is initially launched. All known Web sites are listed in this dialog box.

You may access other Web sites by clicking on the More Webs button. This opens another dialog box in which you can specify the server name or drive path for other existing Webs. Any FrontPage-created Web sites found in whatever alternate location you provide will be displayed. Select a site from either dialog box and then click on OK.

Clicking on the New Page button on the toolbar or issuing the File|New|Page command from the menu bar creates a new blank Web document. The location for insertion of this new document depends on the selected context. If an existing document is selected in a files listing, the new document is added to the same folder. If an object is selected in the graphical navigational view, the new document is added in the same folder and placed as a navigational child object. If a folder is selected, the new document is added into the selected folder. The file name of the new document will be NEWPAGE#.HTM (where # is replaced by a numeral) if other HTML documents exist in the folder, or INDEX.HTM if it's the only HTML document in the currently selected folder.

Removing existing pages or objects is just as simple as creating them. Locate and select the objects in the Folders, All Files, or Navigation Views and then click on the Delete button on the toolbar, select Edit|Delete from the menu bar, or press the Delete key on your keyboard. You'll be prompted to confirm or cancel the deletion. If you select an object displayed in the graphical pane of the Navigation View, you'll be prompted whether to remove the document from the navigation bars or to remove it from the site entirely.

A Web site can be deleted. However, once a Web site is deleted, it cannot be recovered (assuming you did not make a backup using a non-FrontPage utility). To delete a Web site, you must first open it in FrontPage. Once it's open, issue the File|Delete FrontPage Web command from the menu bar. You'll be prompted to confirm the deletion of the Web.

Managing Web Sites

Managing Web sites involves three main activities: modifying Web settings, setting access permissions, and setting Web options. These are discussed in the following sections.

Modifying Web Settings

The menu bar command Tools|Web Settings reveals the five-tabbed FrontPage Web Settings dialog box. This dialog box is used to define several parameters that apply to a Web site as a whole. The significant items for each tab are as follows:

- **Parameters** Defines variables to be used by your Webs. For example, you can define a variable named FaxNumber that's your actual fax machine number. This variable can be used within any page by inserting a Substitution component in the FrontPage Editor. Changes made to variables are automatically reflected in all the pages that reference those variables.
- **Configuration** Changes the Web's name and title. This tab also displays information about the Web, including Web server URL, Server Extensions version, server version, IP address, and proxy server address (if used).
- **Advanced** Sets the image map style, sets the validation script language, and hides/displays documents in hidden directories. It also displays the recalculation status of the Web site (that is, if page dependencies and indexes are out of date).
- **Language** Defines the language to be used by FrontPage Server Extensions for messages such as errors and the type of HTML encoding scheme to be used (in other words, this defines the character set for your computer).
- **Navigation** Defines the names of the four standard navigation bar controls used by FrontPage (that is, Home Page, Parent Page, Previous Page, and Next Page).

Setting Access Permissions

Controlling who can visit your site and who can make modifications to your content is important. FrontPage offers direct control over content access from both browsing and authoring perspectives.

Setting Web Permissions

The menu bar command Tools|Permissions reveals the tabbed Permissions dialog box. This dialog box is used to set Web site access parameters. When you're working with a root Web, the dialog box has only two tabs: Users and Computers. When you're working with a sub-Web, an additional tab named Settings appears. The three tabs are discussed here:

- **Users** Defines specific user names and passwords to grant administrative, author, and/or browse access. User names are not pulled from NT security. The list of users is a unique list of users not managed by the User Manager For Domains. You can select to allow anonymous browsing access (under this setting, everyone has browse access) or named user access only (under this setting, only registered users have browse access).
- **Computers** Defines a single computer or group of computers (by IP address) that can host users who can administer, author, and/or browse.
- **Settings** Sets the permissions of the sub-Web as unique to themselves or to use the same permissions as the root Web. The default for all sub-Webs is to assume the permissions of the root Web.

Here are the three access levels used by FrontPage:

- **Browse** Access to view the Web site with a Web browser.
- **Author** Access to create, modify, and delete pages in a FrontPage Web. Also includes browse access.
- **Administer** Access to create, delete, and manage FrontPage Webs. Also includes browse and author access.

When defining security for a Web site, keep one important item in mind: The access permissions set through FrontPage apply only to Web servers that use FrontPage Server Extensions. Web sites hosted by Web servers that do not use FrontPage Server Extensions or Web sites that reside on file systems on another machine are not subject to FrontPage permission settings. Access permissions for such sites must be maintained manually through the local file system or through the administrative utilities for whatever Web server may be in use.

Using SSL

FrontPage 98 includes support for the Secure Sockets Layer (SSL). *SSL* is an encryption scheme used to protect the communications between clients and servers. All such communications between the participants are fully encrypted. This offers a high level of security against Internet "wire tapping." FrontPage does not include SSL, but it includes support for SSL when communicating with a Web server with SSL installed and configured.

The SSL support feature is enabled during the initial creation of a new Web site. On the New FrontPage Web dialog box, once you've defined the title for the new Web, click on the Change button below the Web server URL. This reveals the Change Location dialog box in which you can change the URL for the Web server and a checkbox that requires the use of SSL for all connections with the Web server. After you click on OK on the Change Location dialog box and on the New FrontPage Web dialog box, the wizard attempts to communicate with the Web server using SSL. If an error message appears stating that port 443 does not exist on the server, the Web server is not properly configured for SSL communications. If an error message does not appear, FrontPage is using SSL successfully.

Each time you define access parameters for FrontPage to communicate with a new Web server, you can indicate whether to use SSL by selecting the checkbox below the URL field.

Setting Web Options

The menu bar command Tools|Options reveals the Options dialog box. This three-tabbed dialog box manages FrontPage-specific parameters and settings. Several significant items occur in each tab:

- **General** Sets the options to display the Getting Started dialog box, toolbar, status bar, and theme application, as well as issues warnings for expired components and old indexes.
- **Proxies** Defines proxy servers to use as access points to Web servers hosted outside the local network across firewalls or other network obstructions or security barriers. A *proxy server* simply defines the network pathway FrontPage must use to communicate with the Web server.
- **Configure Editors** Defines the default editors to be used to modify files based on their extensions. When you double-click on an object within FrontPage, the defined editor is launched to manage editing or modifying that object.

Publishing A Web Site

FrontPage 98 manages or modifies a Web site directly. This means that FrontPage uses a Web server, whether remotely or locally, to host all its Web sites. FrontPage does not "store" a Web site in any other form or location other than on a Web server. If a Web server is not present locally, the FrontPage Personal Web Server can be installed to support FrontPage Webs. When a Web site is created using the New FrontPage Web dialog box, you're instructing a creation wizard where to create the Web site by defining a Web server and a directory in which to install the new Web. When you open a Web site to modify it, you're opening it from a Web server.

In most cases, you'll use FrontPage on a workstation computer using the FrontPage Personal Web Server to host your Webs locally as you develop them. Once they're complete, you'll move the Web to your production Web server located somewhere on your network or outside your network through a proxy server. The process of moving a finished Web site to a production location is called *publishing*.

Publishing is used only when the Web server used to create a Web site is not the same Web server used to host the Web site for public or general consumption. This often occurs in businesses that want to work with a Web site extensively in-house before releasing it to the public. However, publishing a Web site means you must move the site from an internal location to an external one. Publishing can simply be used to make a duplicate copy of a Web site on another Web server.

FrontPage Explorer offers three methods or processes for moving a completed or modified Web site to another Web server: one-click publishing, multisite publishing, and FTP publishing. The first time a Web site is published, you must provide the URL for a path on a Web server. The Publish FrontPage Web dialog box appears the first time publishing is launched either from the Publish toolbar button or the File|Publish FrontPage Web command from the menu bar. This dialog box includes a field for the URL path and a checkbox to use SSL communications.

> *Note: If you don't already have access to a Web server to host your Web, the Publish FrontPage Web dialog box has a button used to access a Microsoft-hosted Web site that offers information about FrontPage Server Extensions supporting Web services.*

After a Web site has been published once, the Publish button on the toolbar acts as a one-click publishing tool. *One-click publishing* means the Web site is updated using the defined Web server URL(s) without any further prompts.

To change the Web server or add additional Web servers to the publishing process, use the menu bar File|Publish FrontPage Web command. The Publish dialog box lists all the Web servers defined to receive content updates for this Web. A checkbox labeled Publish Changed Pages Only sets FrontPage to upload the new objects only (instead of the entire site) to reduce publishing time. Clicking on the More Webs button opens the Publish FrontPage Web dialog box where another Web server can be defined.

> *Note: FrontPage can only publish to one Web server at a time. To perform multiuse publishing, each Web server must be individually selected from the Publish FrontPage Web dialog box.*

When a Web server is defined on the Publish FrontPage Web dialog box that does not use Server Extensions (or if the proprietary transfer method fails), the Publish wizard will prompt you for FTP information. If the Web server can be accessed by FTP, you can provide a domain name, path, user name, and password so that the Publish wizard can send the files via FTP. Once FTP publishing is defined, each time a Web site is published, the wizard automatically uses the stored FTP parameters to upload content changes.

Practice Questions

Question 1

Which view should you use to check external hyperlinks?

- ❍ a. All Files
- ❍ b. Navigation
- ❍ c. Hyperlinks
- ❍ d. Hyperlink Status

The Hyperlink Status View is used to check external hyperlinks. Therefore, answer d is correct. The All Files and Navigation Views do not check hyperlinks at all. Therefore, answers a and b are incorrect. The Hyperlinks View is only used to check internal document linkage. Therefore, answer c is incorrect.

Question 2

When a Web site is checked for spelling errors, all mistakes must be corrected as they are found.

- ❍ a. True
- ❍ b. False

This is a false statement. Therefore, answer b is correct. The Spelling wizard can create tasks for each document that contains spelling errors instead of prompting for immediate correction.

Question 3

You need to create a Web site to offer visitors technical documentation and help regarding a product sold by your organization. Which wizard or template should you use to aid in the creation of such a Web site?

- ❍ a. Corporate Presence wizard
- ❍ b. Discussion Web wizard
- ❍ c. Customer Support Web template
- ❍ d. Project Web template

The Customer Support Web template is the best solution for creating a technical documentation and help Web site. Therefore, answer c is correct. The Corporate Presence wizard offers too many objects that are not useful for the particular focus of this Web site. Therefore, answer a is incorrect. The Discussion Web wizard creates a Web site useful for discussion groups, but it does not lend itself to distributing documentation. Therefore, answer b is incorrect. The Project Web template is too simplistic and unfocused for the purpose of this Web. Therefore, answer d is incorrect.

Question 4

FrontPage maintains a local compressed database copy of every object published to a Web server. Therefore, if you delete a Web site, it can be restored at a later time without losing any files or other information.

- ❍ a. True
- ❍ b. False

This is a false statement. Therefore, answer b is correct. FrontPage does not maintain a separate backup of Web sites. If a Web site is deleted, it's lost forever (unless you've created a backup using other means).

Question 5

You've created a new Web site using the Corporate Presence wizard. Your organization has no need for the Download section of the created site. How can you remove this section of the wizard-created Web site without introducing broken links or leaving orphaned files? [Check all correct answers]

- ❑ a. Use the Folders View and delete all the files with a file name or title containing the word Download.
- ❑ b. Use the Navigation View and delete the section from the Navigation pane.
- ❑ c. Use the All Files View and delete all files listed as orphans.
- ❑ d. Use the Hyperlink Status View to locate hyperlinks from the Download section.

Using the Navigation and All Files Views comprises the best solution to this problem. Therefore, answers b and c are correct. The Folders View does not remove deleted documents from the navigation bars. Therefore, answer a is incorrect. The Hyperlink Status View will not indicate any broken links if the Navigation View is used to delete the Download section, thus making this view useless. If you use the All Files or the Folders View to delete the documents, the Hyperlink Status View will display the broken links, which will need to be repaired manually one at a time using the Editor. This is a long and difficult process that could be avoided by using the correct action, as stated in answer b. Therefore, answer d is incorrect.

Question 6

By default, sub-Webs assume the access permission settings of the root Web.

❍ a. True

❍ b. False

This is a true statement. Therefore, answer a is correct.

Question 7

Trick! question

Your business network is designed so no traffic flows in or out of the network to the Internet unless it passes through a firewall. You're assigned the task of using FrontPage to update the corporate Web site and to take advantage of the Server Extensions features. Your workstation is located inside the network. The Web server is located on the other side of the firewall. What's the best option to complete this task without violating security?

❍ a. Use a removable hard drive to transfer the corporate Web site file system between your workstation and the Web server.

❍ b. Obtain a modem and access to a local ISP. Use the new communication link to interact with the Web server.

❍ c. Use an FTP program to transfer the Web folder structure from your workstation to the Web server.

❍ d. Configure FrontPage to use the proxy services of the firewall just like all the other Internet utilities in use.

The best solution is to use a proxy server. Therefore, answer d is correct. Using a removable hard drive system is expensive and renders the Web server useless while the drive is in the workstation. Therefore, answer a is incorrect. Adding a modem and using ISP access to reach the Web server is a security breach most businesses will not tolerate. Therefore, answer b is incorrect. Using an FTP program eliminates your ability to use Server Extensions functions on the Web site and requires an FTP server to be present on the Web server. In addition, the FTP program will be using the proxy services of the firewall anyway, so why not let FrontPage use a proxy? Therefore, answer c is incorrect. Although some of these options are plausible solutions, the question asked for the best solution; therefore, we marked this as a trick question.

Question 8

Your Web site includes a repository of coding examples that are stored in text files. All these text files end in the extension .CODE. You want to be able to edit these files by double-clicking on them in FrontPage Explorer. How can you accomplish this?

- ❍ a. Define a text editor to be launched on the Configure Editors tab of the Options dialog box.
- ❍ b. Set the access permissions on the CODE files to Author through the Permissions dialog box.
- ❍ c. Associate CODE files with the text MIME type on the Web Settings dialog box.
- ❍ d. Nothing is required. FrontPage uses Notepad as the default editor for unknown file types.

Defining a text editor to be launched on the Configure Editors tab of the Options dialog box is the only way to accomplish this task. Therefore, answer a is correct. You cannot set access permissions on a file basis through FrontPage. Therefore, answer b is incorrect. You also cannot associate files with MIME types through FrontPage. Therefore, answer c is incorrect. FrontPage does not have a default editor when a file type is unknown; you are prompted to select your own editor. Therefore, answer d is incorrect.

Question 9

How can Web sites be updated? [Check all correct answers]

- ❑ a. One site at a time
- ❑ b. All files are transferred
- ❑ c. Multiple sites at a time
- ❑ d. Only changed files are transferred

FrontPage can publish Web sites to one site at a time and upload either every file every time or only those files that have changed. Therefore, answers a, b, and d are correct. FrontPage cannot publish to multiple sites simultaneously, although you may publish to multiple sites individually. Therefore, answer c is incorrect.

Question 10

When will FrontPage use FTP to publish a Web? [Check all correct answers]

- ❑ a. When selected in the Publishing Options dialog box
- ❑ b. If the Web server is too busy
- ❑ c. If the proprietary method fails
- ❑ d. When the Web server does not have Server Extensions

FrontPage will use FTP when the proprietary transfer method fails and when the Web server does not use Server Extensions. Therefore, answers c and d are correct. There is no Publishing Options dialog box. Therefore, answer a is incorrect. The load on the Web server is not a factor in selecting the transfer method to use. Therefore, answer b is also incorrect.

Need To Know More?

Lehto, Kerry A. and W. Brett Polonsky. *Official Microsoft FrontPage 98 Book*, Microsoft Press, Redmond, WA, 1997. ISBN 1-57231-629-2. Chapters 3, 4, and 5 discuss FrontPage Explorer, new Web creation, and general Web site management. Other individual topics may be found throughout this book.

Stanek, William R., et al. *Microsoft FrontPage 98 Unleashed*, Sams.net Publishing, Indianapolis, IN, 1998. ISBN 1-57521-349-4. Chapter 2 discusses FrontPage Explorer. Individual topics may be found throughout this book.

Microsoft TechNet. Useful information about the FrontPage 98 topics discussed in this chapter can be found by searching for keywords related to the topics.

www.microsoft.com/frontpage/. This is the official FrontPage Web site hosted by Microsoft. It offers overview information about the product.

4

Editing Web Pages In FrontPage Editor

Terms you'll need to understand:

- √ FrontPage Editor
- √ Templates
- √ URL
- √ HTTP

Techniques you'll need to master:

- √ Structuring Web pages
- √ Editing text
- √ Defining and formatting paragraphs
- √ Adding line breaks and hard rules
- √ Creating hypertext links
- √ Setting text styles
- √ Adding lists
- √ Using Web page templates to create pages
- √ Creating your own Web page templates
- √ Previewing a Web page in a browser
- √ Saving pages
- √ Printing pages

In the previous chapter, you learned how to use FrontPage Explorer to work with a Web site. In this chapter, you'll learn about the other major application of Microsoft FrontPage 98: FrontPage Editor. With FrontPage Editor, you can put together the individual pages that will form your Web site.

The FrontPage Explorer Display Window

When you're working in FrontPage Explorer, if you double-click on one of the icons representing a page of your Web site, FrontPage Editor opens that page. Another more direct method of opening FrontPage Editor is to click on the Tools drop-down menu from FrontPage Explorer and select Show FrontPage Editor. You can also click on the FrontPage Editor icon in the FrontPage Explorer toolbar. (See Figure 4.1.)

Because FrontPage Explorer and FrontPage Editor are so closely tied in the interface, distinguishing between the two is sometimes difficult. However, you should understand that FrontPage Explorer is used for working with the Web site as a whole, whereas FrontPage Editor focuses on the creation and modification of individual Web pages.

Once you've launched FrontPage Editor, you'll see the display window shown in Figure 4.2.

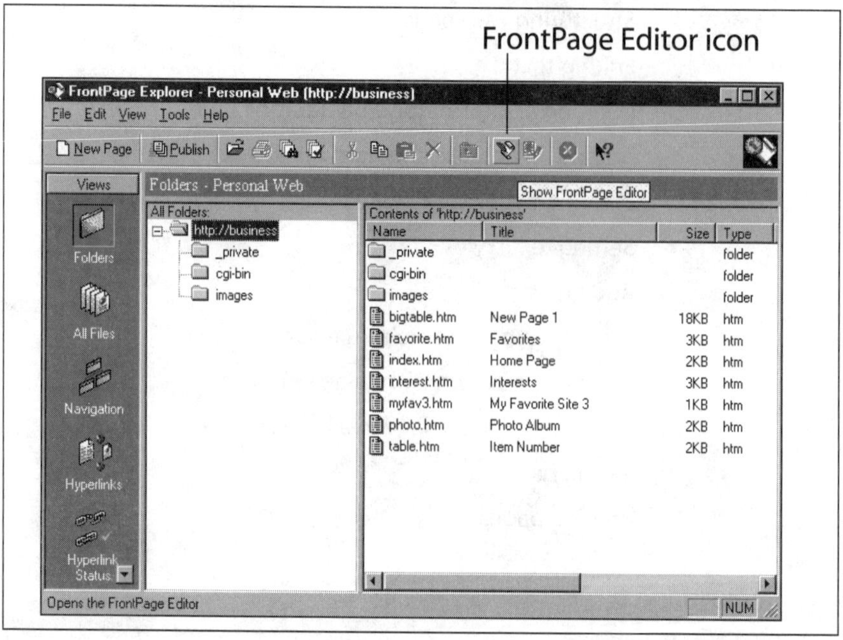

Figure 4.1 The FrontPage Editor icon in the FrontPage Explorer toolbar.

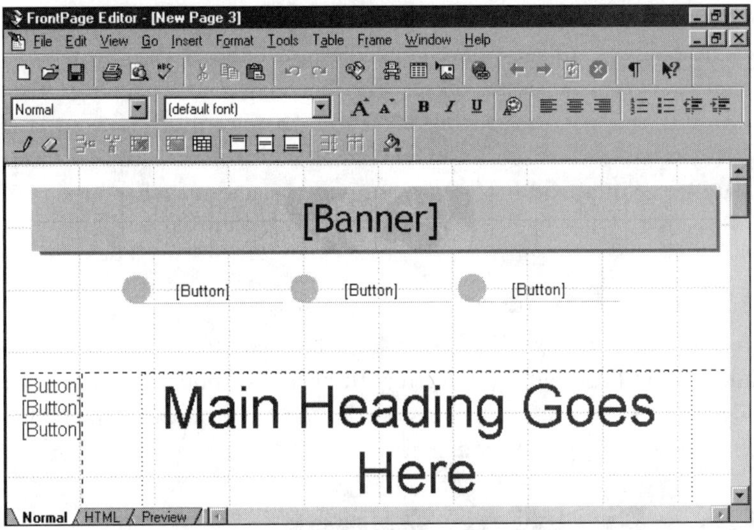

Figure 4.2 The FrontPage Editor display window.

The display window consists of the normal Windows components: a title bar, menu bar, standard toolbar, scrollbars, and status bar. The display window also has a formatting toolbar that's similar to those found in word processors such as Microsoft Word. Some of the most unique and useful items on the FrontPage display window are the View tabs, which allow you to see Web pages in different formats: Normal, HTML, and Preview. The Normal View allows you to use the FrontPage editing window to cut, paste, create, and modify Web page objects. The HTML View allows you to view and edit the HTML code that generates the page. The Preview View allows you to see the page as it would be displayed by a Web browser.

> *Note: FrontPage Editor is not the only application that can edit Web pages. If you right-click on a Web page in Internet Explorer (IE), you can choose View Source to modify the HTML code directly. You can then save that page to your own Web server. You can also open HTM and HTML files with Notepad, WordPad, or other text editors. These applications can be used to modify your Web pages.*

Standard Toolbar

The standard toolbar is similar to the type of toolbar you find in Microsoft Word. It has common options such as Open, New, Save, and Print, which allow you to open existing pages, create new pages, save pages, and print pages, respectively. However, other options are included that are not commonly found in a standard word processing toolbar—for example, Preview In Browser, which allows you to look at the page you've opened or created in a Web browser so that you can see what your users will see when viewing your Web page. Also, the Show In FrontPage Explorer icon shows you where your page fits into the overall Web site via FrontPage Explorer. Other buttons allow you to insert tables, create hyperlinks, add FrontPage components, and refresh a page. (See Figure 4.3.)

Formatting Toolbar

The formatting toolbar, shown in Figure 4.4, allows you to change font style, type, color, size, and formatting. Creating numbered or bulleted lists can be done easily via their respective buttons on the toolbar. You can also modify paragraph style, alignment, and indentation.

Editing Existing Pages

As previously stated, you can open an existing Web page for editing in FrontPage Editor by double-clicking on the object representing that page from the FrontPage Explorer. If you're already in FrontPage Editor and would like to edit a page, you can select File|Open to open an existing page or use the Open

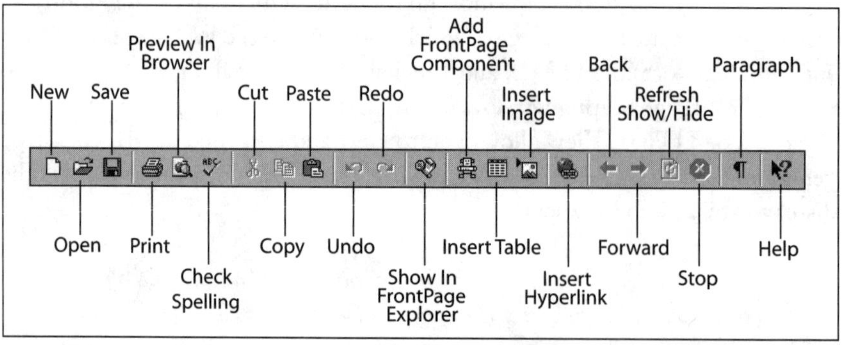

Figure 4.3 The standard toolbar.

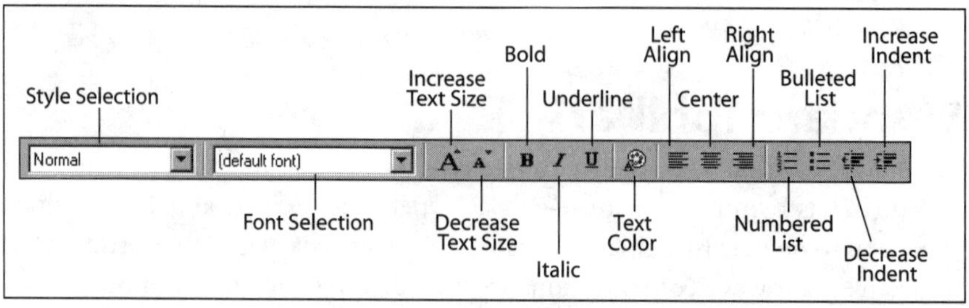

Figure 4.4 The formatting toolbar.

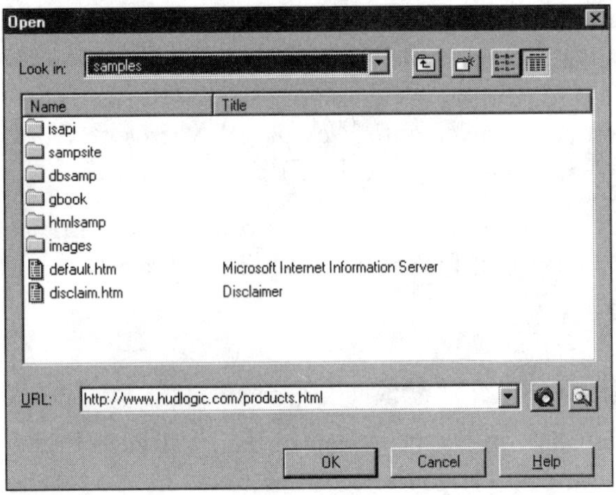

Figure 4.5 The Open dialog box.

icon from the toolbar. All these methods launch the Open dialog box, shown in Figure 4.5.

At first glance, this Open dialog box looks deceptively like the ones found in other Windows applications. However, a few tricky inconsistencies exist between this box and similar ones found in Microsoft Word and other common Windows 95 and 98 or Windows NT applications. For instance, the Look In selection box at the top of this dialog box starts with "http:". This means you must enter an HTTP (Hypertext Transfer Protocol) address (also referred to as a URL). You can type in a Uniform Resource Locator (URL) in the box below to search a particular Web location. This feature allows you to connect to your local Web site or any site on the World Wide Web (WWW) that's accessible to you.

> *Note: Pages on the WWW are referred to by their URLs. URLs are usually prefixed by the type of communication protocol they use. For example, Web communications take place over the HTTP protocol. When you open a page from the WWW, a copy of the page is created in FrontPage Editor and the original page remains unchanged. Therefore, you'll have to copy over the changes to the Web location once you've finished making your modifications.*

If you're interested in opening pages that are not yet part of a Web site, you must change this dialog box. Because you can't edit the drop-down selection box directly, you must use one of the buttons on the lower-right side of the dialog box. The icon of the globe and magnifying glass represents access to files on the Internet; the icon of the folder and magnifying glass represents access to files on your local computer or local network.

If you choose the folder and magnifying glass icon, the Select File dialog box appears. This dialog box allows you to explore your local computer and local network for the file you want to edit; the file does not have to be a Web page. FrontPage Editor can open (and convert into Web pages) Microsoft Word, Microsoft Excel, Lotus 1-2-3, rich text format (RTF), and text files.

Once you've selected the file you want to edit, the page is loaded into FrontPage Editor. You can then use FrontPage Editor to view, modify, and save the page to your Web site.

Creating New Pages

To create a new Web page, click on the New icon in the FrontPage Editor toolbar to open a new blank page. If you select New from the File menu (Ctrl+N), the New dialog box appears (see Figure 4.6). Notice that this dialog box contains a list of Web page templates you can select from on the Page tab. Also, the Frames tab allows you to create Web page frames.

> *Note: Web page frames (or just frames) are multipaned windowed Web pages that create the effect of viewing multiple Web pages at once. The topic of frames is covered in greater detail in Chapter 7.*

With the exception of the Normal template, the templates listed in the New dialog box contain placeholder text (and quite often placeholder graphics). The

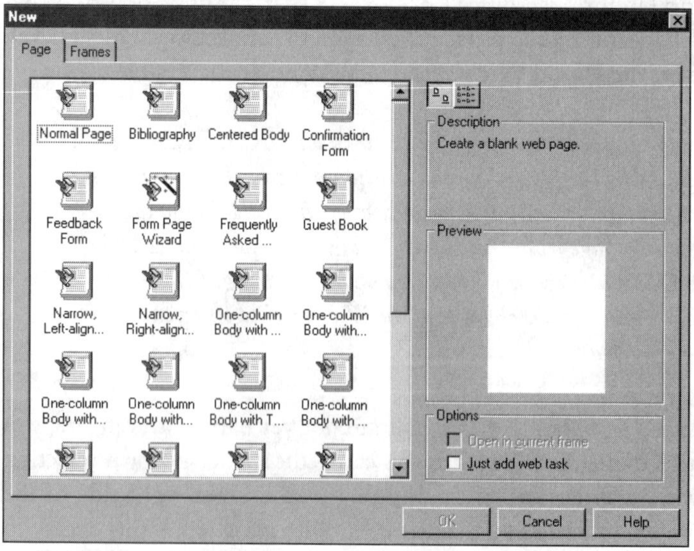

Figure 4.6 The New dialog box.

Normal template simply creates an empty page, for those who want to start with a clean slate. Before selecting a template, you can read a brief description about each template and see a small preview for the layout of that page style. You can also add the item as a task. (Tasks are discussed in Chapter 5.)

Setting Up Document Structure

When you are creating a new document, its structure and appearance are usually defined in the selected template. Once you've chosen to create the new file from an existing template, you can easily work inside the template by modifying the text, graphics, and other objects to suit your needs. For example, if you choose the three-column body template, a page with headings, subheadings, and three columns of replaceable text appear in the FrontPage Editor display window. You can simply replace the headings and text with your own words and then save it to your Web site.

The templates available include a number of different body styles and alignments: centered, two columns, three columns, with or without sidebars, and so on. In addition, you can select specialized templates such as Search Page, User Registration, Table Of Contents, Bibliography, Feedback Form, and Guest Book. The specialized templates contain FrontPage components and scripting that allow users to interact with FrontPage Web services. You can view the properties of these scripted objects by right-clicking on and selecting Front Page Component Properties or Form Field Properties, as applicable. Some objects, such as the Search object, allow you to configure settings through the object properties. Others must be modified directly through the HTML code. Additional information on these templates is presented in Chapter 5.

> *Note: When working with FrontPage Web pages, you should set everything up using a normal (640-by-480) screen resolution. This allows you to see your Web pages as they're likely to be viewed by your clients. If you use 800-by-600 resolution, your clients using 640-by-480 resolution might not see your pages as you intend.*

Editing Text

FrontPage Editor allows you to modify and create your Web pages as if you were working in a word processor; tasks such as cutting, pasting, and dragging and dropping text and objects can be completed using methods identical to those of a word processor. However, as you make changes, FrontPage automatically modifies the HTML code, which allows you to quickly save your changes as an HTML file when you're finished.

Note: If you try to rename or change a Web page title, you have to do so through FrontPage Explorer by right-clicking on the icon that represents the page. Choose Rename to change the title of the page. This change can then be seen in FrontPage Editor once you click on Refresh.

Making FrontPage Editor even more like a word processor, a spellchecker and thesaurus are built in. You can open the spellchecker via the standard toolbar by clicking on the Check Spelling button (or you can go through the Tools drop-down menu and choose Spelling). The thesaurus can be accessed through the Tools drop-down menu by selecting Thesaurus. Both of these utilities help to ensure that your Web pages have a professional appearance by reducing the number of spelling errors and helping you to vary your word usage.

You can also use the Find and Replace utilities in FrontPage, which allow you to locate words or phrases, and if you wish, replace them automatically with other words or phrases. For example, if you were editing a Web page and realized that the acronym DNS (Domain Name Service) was consistently misspelled as DMS, you might want to use the Replace utility. In this case, you would open the Edit menu, select Replace, and type "DMS" in the Find What dialog box. Then, you would type "DNS" in the Replace With dialog box and click on one of the following: Find Next, Replace, or Replace All. Choosing Find Next allows you to control the replacement, item by item, by subsequently clicking on the Replace button so that you can find and selectively replace text. However, if you want to replace every instance of DMS with DNS, you would just select Replace All.

You should also be aware of the Match Whole Word Only and Match Case checkboxes in the Find And Replace dialog box. For example, if you select to replace the word "not" with the phrase "should not," be sure to check the Match Whole Word Only checkbox; otherwise, words that include "not" will also be selected for replacement, such as "knot" and "cannot." You could therefore end up with words such as "kshould not" and "canshould not." If you want to change or match text case, you should choose Match Case.

STUDY ALERT

Find and Replace utilities through FrontPage Editor only work on the active page. If you want to find and/or replace text and phrases on your entire Web site, you should use the Find and Replace utilities through FrontPage Explorer via the Tools menu.

Defining And Formatting Paragraphs

Paragraphs are as easy to define and format in Microsoft FrontPage Editor as they are in a word processor. Of course, this is a very simple matter when you're creating a new page and select a predefined template—in a template, the paragraph styles are already defined for you.

When you're editing an existing document or template, you might want to modify the format of a paragraph. This can be done through the Format drop-down menu by selecting Paragraph. Once you've opened the Paragraph Properties dialog box, you can choose from one of many predefined paragraph styles. You can also modify the alignment via the Paragraph Alignment selection box. If you want to modify one of the predefined paragraph style sheets, you can click on the Style button. The Style button leads to a Style dialog box, where you can choose from the following modification settings: Class, Alignment, Borders, Font, and Text.

To learn more about your options, select the desired tab (Class, Alignment, Borders, and so on) and click on the Help button on the Style dialog box. These options are very similar to those of a modern word processor.

Adding Line Breaks And Horizontal Lines

When you finish with one paragraph or section and would like to set your next section apart from the previous, you may want to use a line break or horizontal line. Both options can be found under the Insert menu by choosing Line Break or Horizontal Line.

Inserting a horizontal line is a fairly straightforward process. The horizontal line divides the page from margin to margin after insertion. The line is dropped into the location where you had your cursor positioned on the page at the time of insertion. The HTML code used to generate the line is a simple <HR> tag.

If you want to change the width, height, alignment, or color of the line, you must select the horizontal line on the page. You then right-click and choose Horizontal Line properties, which loads the Horizontal Line Properties dialog box. This allows you to change all those features or modify the style of the line altogether.

> ***Note:** If you're using a specific theme, you can only change the alignment of the line. You'll learn more about themes in Chapter 12.*

Inserting a line break has a few more options, but it is fairly simple. When you choose Line Break from the Insert menu, you immediately see the Line Break dialog box. This gives you several choices: Normal Line Break, Clear Left Margin, Clear Right Margin, and Clear Both Margins. A normal line break only separates text—it does not move graphics files. If you use one of the Clear Margin options, a graphics file will be moved to the next lower line if it occupies the margin (left, right, or both) that you've selected.

The Line Break option inserts the HTML tag **
**, which signifies white-space. This is necessary because browsers do not separate lines unless they have a specific line break embedded. Therefore, if you find, when previewing your page through the Web browser, that sentences or lines of text you intended to be separate are running together on a single line, you'll want to insert a line break.

Linking Pages With Hyperlinks

One of the best things that Web pages and HTML have to offer is the ability to use links to other pages. This is how information is linked from location to location. If you want to create a hypertext link from page to page, you need only select the Insert drop-down menu and choose Hyperlink.

Hyperlinks are added through the Create Hyperlink dialog box, which allows you to select a URL, a file from the local computer, or an email address, or you can even create a new page. These options are available as icons just below the selection window. (See Figure 4.7.)

The Bookmark field on the Create Hyperlink dialog box allows you to specify an exact location in a document. *Bookmarks* are links to a specific location within a page, and the link jumps directly to that location. In HTML code, bookmarks are identified with the pound sign (#). The following HTML code illustrates a hyperlink bookmark command:

```
<a href="#Book1">The First Book</a>
```

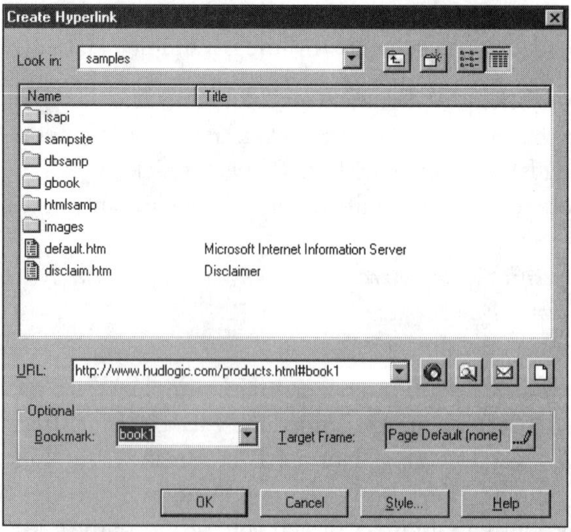

Figure 4.7 The Create Hyperlink dialog box.

The preceding code produces the text "The First Book", which, when clicked, initiates a jump inside the document. There must be a corresponding location in the document for the link to jump to. This location is represented by the same name:

```
<a name="book1">
```

When the link is clicked on, the page is scrolled through until the name **<a name="book1">** is found. You can also type a complete or partial page URL with your bookmark reference. For example, the following is an acceptable hypertext link to the bookmark "book1" on the page **www.hudlogic.com/products.html**:

```
<a href="http://www.hudlogic.com/products.htm#book1">
```

> *Note: The preceding hyperlink code can be created through the Create Hyperlink dialog box as displayed in Figure 4.7. When the name "book" is entered into the Bookmark location,* ***#book*** *is automatically added to the end of the URL in the URL field.*

The benefit of using named bookmarks is that users can click on a link that takes them to the exact location in a document that has the information they want, instead of just to the page that contains the information they seek.

On the Create Hyperlink dialog box, the option Target Frame is also available. This option is used when you're creating a link to a Web page that uses frames. Framed pages are explained in Chapter 7.

Setting Text Styles

By default, the first option on Microsoft FrontPage Editor's formatting toolbar is the Change Style selection box. This is the quickest way to change the style of your text or text selection. The *style* is a definition that includes the size, color, font, font characteristics (bold, italicized, underlined), and alignment of your text. Of course, you can change all these attributes individually through the other options on the format toolbar. In addition, these formatting options for your Web page text are located under the Format menu's Font selection.

Specifying Font Characteristics

The Font dialog box (Format|Font) has two tabs. The first is Font, which allows you to modify the text options described in the previous section. The second tab is Special Styles, which allows you to insert special types of HTML-coded text. Options include Citation, Sample, Definition, Blink, Code, Variable,

Bold, Italic, and Keyboard. Probably the best way to experience these items is to test them on your pages. You can highlight the text you want to modify and then check the special style that you want to configure and click on OK. You should then see the text appear in FrontPage Editor. You can also check the HTML code to verify that the appropriate HTML tags were added before and after the specified text.

> *Note: The context-sensitive Help button on this dialog box contains complete descriptions of each of these fonts.*

Including Lists

Lists are easy to create with FrontPage Editor. You only need to click on one of the preset list buttons on the formatting toolbar, or you can use the Format menu and select Bullets And Numbering. Selecting the Bullets And Numbering option opens the Bullets And Numbering dialog box, where you can modify the type of bullets or numbers that will be used in your list.

You have two bullet options: image bullets and plain bullets. *Image bullets* are usually tiny graphics files (such as circles, spheres, squares, triangles, and so on) that you can use as a bullet. This could literally be any graphic you want to use to indicate a bulleted item. The Specify Image selection box allows you to select the image of your choice. By default, the Use Image From The Current Theme option is selected. If no theme is selected, this option defaults to a plain bullet.

> *Note: The Enabling Collapsible Outlines checkbox allows users who have Web browsers that support Dynamic HTML (such as IE 4) to expand or collapse your bulleted lists if they are in outline form.*

Defining Page Properties

One of the most significant dialog boxes in FrontPage Editor is the Page Properties dialog box, which allows you to set the following items:

- Title
- Base location
- Background sound
- Background color
- Background image
- Hyperlink colors

- Page margins
- Page language
- Custom attributes

You can open this dialog box by clicking on the File menu and selecting Page Properties, or you can right-click on a blank space on the open page and select Page Properties from the resulting context menu.

The Page Properties dialog box is an important configuration dialog box in Microsoft FrontPage Editor.

The General tab, shown in Figure 4.8, allows you to set a title for your page. This title usually appears at the top of a Web browser window when someone downloads the page. You can also set a base location for your page. The *base location* is the absolute or base URL for that page. This could also be called the *complete address* of the page, as opposed to the *relative address* of the page.

Pages that link to one another in the same directory normally use relative links. For example, if the page PRODLIST.HTML is in the same directory as AMAZON.HTML, and the PRODLIST.HTML page contains a hyperlink to AMAZON.HTML, the link would probably look like this:

```
<a href="amazon.html">
```

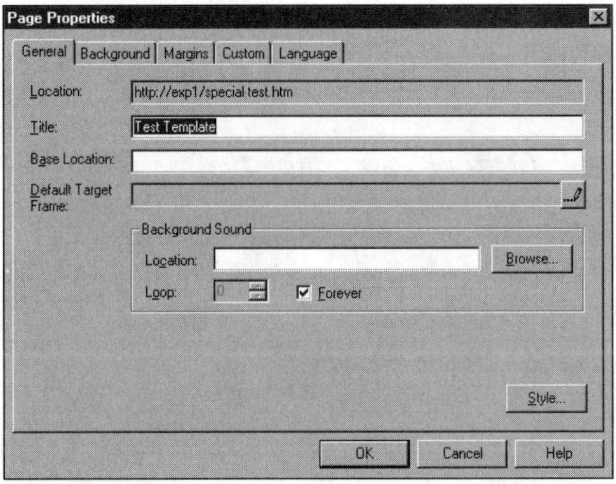

Figure 4.8 The General tab of the Page Properties dialog box.

Notice that the link does not reference the protocol, directory, server, domain name, and so on. It simply lists the file name and nothing more. However, a link to the same page from another server on the Internet would look like this:

```
http://www.hudlogic.com/prodlist.html
```

This full address, which can be used from a browser to access the page on the network or the Internet, is also known as an *absolute URL* or *base location.*

Also, on the General tab, an option is available to specify a background sound.

> ***Note:*** *As of this writing, IE users are the only ones who can hear the background sound. Therefore, you should be sure that the background sound is not of critical importance for someone viewing your site, because users of Netscape Navigator and other popular Web browsers will not be able to hear it.*

The Background tab on the Page Properties dialog box allows you to set the background image or color, default text color, and hyperlink colors.

The Margins tab allows you to configure the amount of offset (open space) that separates the text from the edge of the browser window. These margin settings only affect pages that are viewed by IE (as of this writing).

The Custom tab allows you to configure <META> tags, which are used by many search engines when indexing your pages. The <META> tags themselves do not appear when a Web browser is viewing the page; instead, they are used for informational purposes. The title that's configured on the General tab is also considered a <META> tag and is one of the major pieces of information used by search engines when indexing your Web site and Web pages.

> ***Note:*** *You can list your site for free with most search engines by visiting and registering with each individually. You can also pay a third party to list your site with multiple search engines. If you're interested in getting your Web site listed and indexed, some places to start are:*
>
> - *www.yahoo.com*
> - *www.homecom.com/global/pointers.html*
> - *www.lycos.com*
> - *www.hotbot.com*
> - *www.infoseek.com*
> - *searchenginewatch.com*

Saving Pages

Once you're finished creating or editing a Web page, saving it is a simple process. In Microsoft FrontPage Editor, click on the File menu and select Save or Save As. The Save button automatically overwrites any previously saved version of the document. The Save As option allows you to save the document under the name and location of your choice. The first time you save a given document, both the Save and Save As options lead to the same dialog box. Figure 4.9 shows the Save As dialog box.

The Save As dialog box is very similar to the Open dialog box presented earlier in this chapter, but with three notable exceptions. First, the Save As dialog box writes information to a file instead of opening a file. Second, the Save As dialog box includes a Title text box, which allows you to set or rename the page title before saving it. Finally, the As Template button at the bottom of this dialog box allows you to make the current Web page a template for creating other pages.

Clicking on the As Template button leads to the Save As Template dialog box. In the Save As Template dialog box, you enter a title, name, and description for the template. Once you've saved your template, it will appear in the list of templates in the New dialog box when you choose the option to create a new Web page.

On the File menu in FrontPage Editor, the option to Save All appears. This option lets you save the page and all embedded objects. This option is available because the normal Save and Save As options may also result in a Save Embedded Files dialog box. Anytime you've embedded objects in a Web page,

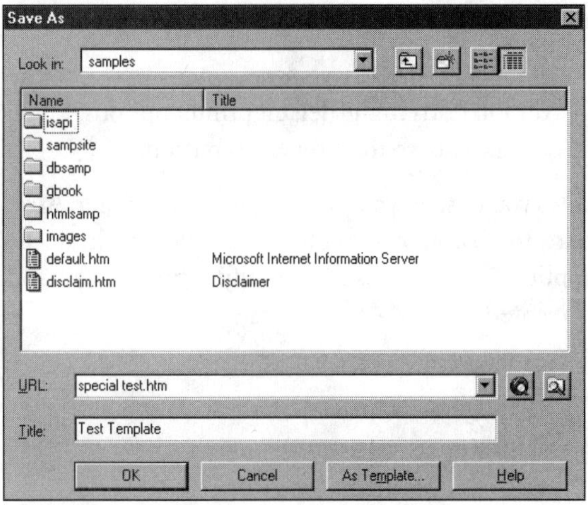

Figure 4.9 The Save As dialog box.

you'll be asked if you want to save these objects before the Save operation is complete. If you know beforehand that you want to save the page and all embedded objects, you can save time by selecting the Save All option from the File menu.

Before you're finished with your Web page, you should see what it looks like in a Web browser. To preview your Web page in a Web browser, you can click on FrontPage Editor's Edit menu and choose Preview In Browser. This action opens the Preview In Browser dialog box, where you can choose the browser you want to use and set the window size and resolution. Another option, Automatically Save Page, saves the Web page you're about to view before it's opened in the browser.

Note: IE versions 3.02 and above support the Preview In Browser option.

Printing

Three options are available on the File menu that allow you to prepare and print your Web pages: Page Setup, Print Preview, and Print.

The Page Setup selection opens the Printer Page Setup dialog box. The options on this dialog box allow you to set header, footer, and margin information before printing. These options apply to all pages printed through FrontPage Editor, not just the currently open page (active page).

By default, the Header dialog box is set to **&T**, which automatically substitutes the page title for the header when printing. The Footer dialog box is set to **Page &P**, which automatically inserts the word "Page", followed by the actual page number. Margins are set to half an inch on all sides. Any of these settings are modifiable through the Printer Page Setup dialog box.

The Print Preview selection allows you to verify your document layout before sending it to the printer. This option leads to the default printer options. If you want to change the default settings, choose the Properties button.

Finally, the Print option allows you to send your document to the printer. Also, a printer icon on the standard toolbar allows you to print your current document. Through the Print option, you'll be able to specify a print range and number of copies you want printed.

Practice Questions

Question 1

You've been asked to add several new pages to an existing Web site on your corporate network. Several of the pages are to be used as an online employee handbook. Other items include a small online newsletter and search page.

Objectives:

a. Create an online employee handbook

b. Add a search page to the Web site

c. Add a custom image to the background of the Web site

d. Add a three-column newsletter page to the site

e. Create hyperlinks to all pages from the INDEX.HTML page

Solutions:

- Obtain a copy of the employee handbook and create Web pages for each page in the handbook
- In FrontPage Explorer, choose the Search Page template and configure it
- Add a three-column page using the three-column template of FrontPage Editor and add appropriate newsletter information
- Select all the pages in FrontPage Explorer and choose Insert; then click on Hyperlink and map each page back to INDEX.HTML

Which of the above objectives were met? [Check all correct answers]

- ❑ a. Create an online employee handbook
- ❑ b. Add a search page to the Web site
- ❑ c. Add a custom image to the background of the Web site
- ❑ d. Add a three-column newsletter page to the site
- ❑ e. Create hyperlinks to all pages from the INDEX.HTML page

The suggested solutions create an online employee handbook and creates hyperlinks from the INDEX.HTML page. Therefore, answers a and e are correct. Objective b was not accomplished because that operation is not available in FrontPage Explorer—it's in FrontPage Editor. Therefore, answer b is incorrect. Objective c was not even addressed in the solutions, so it couldn't have been completed. Therefore, answer c is incorrect. Objective d is not possible. Therefore, answer d is incorrect.

Question 2

Which of the following methods are valid for editing an existing Web page? [Check all correct answers]

❑ a. From Internet Explorer, right-click on the Web page, choose View Source, and modify the HTML code. When you're finished, save the page.

❑ b. Click on the File menu in FrontPage Editor and choose Open. Find the file you want to edit. When you're finished, save it to that same location.

❑ c. Click on the File menu in FrontPage Explorer and choose Open. Find the file you want to edit and save it to the same location when you've finished making the desired changes.

❑ d. Double-click on the page you want to edit in FrontPage Explorer. Edit the page with FrontPage Editor and save it to the desired location.

You can use all these methods to edit an existing page in FrontPage Explorer except the File|Open method. Therefore, answers a, b, and d are correct. The only Open option in the File menu of FrontPage Explorer is Open FrontPage Web, which does not allow you to edit an individual Web page. Therefore, answer c is incorrect.

Question 3

Which of the following icons will allow you to open an existing Web page that's not part of your HTTP server but is on your local file system?

❍ a. The file folder with magnifying glass icon

❍ b. The robot icon

❍ c. The globe with magnifying glass icon

❍ d. The blank page icon

❍ e. The globe with chain icon

Answer a is correct. The file folder with the magnifying glass icon allows you to browse your local directory structure. The robot icon allows you to add FrontPage elements. Therefore, answer b is incorrect. The globe with the magnifying glass icon is the one that allows you to add links from the WWW. Therefore, answer c is incorrect. The blank page icon allows you to open a new page. Therefore, answer d is incorrect. The globe with a chain link is for adding hyperlinks to documents. Therefore, answer e is incorrect.

Question 4

Which of the following protocols provides Web services?

- ❍ a. TCP
- ❍ b. UDP
- ❍ c. HTTP
- ❍ d. FTP

Answer c is correct. The Hypertext Transfer Protocol (HTTP) is the communication protocol of Web publishing (Web servers are known as *HTTP servers*). The other protocols are used with TCP/IP communications (which is the protocol suite of the Internet), but they are not exclusively used for Web services. Therefore, answers a, b, and d are incorrect.

Question 5

You want to set the default color for your Web page. How can you do it?

- ❍ a. Click on Edit and then choose Color in FrontPage Editor.
- ❍ b. Find an empty spot on the open Web page in the FrontPage Editor application. Place the mouse pointer on that location and right-click. Choose Page Properties and then click on the Background tab and select the colors of your choice.
- ❍ c. In FrontPage Explorer, right-click on the icon that represents the Web page you want to configure and click on Page Properties. Then, choose Custom and set a custom background.
- ❍ d. In FrontPage Explorer, right-click on the icon that represents the Web page you want to configure and click on Properties. Then, choose Background and configure the color.

The correct answer is b. The option presented in answer a is incorrect. The options in answers c and d read FrontPage Explorer (not Editor). Explorer is not the location to set the default color for a single Web page. Therefore, answers c and d are also incorrect.

Question 6

Which of the following icons will allow you to open a Web page on the Internet or on your local Web server via the HTTP protocol?

- ❍ a. The file folder with magnifying glass icon
- ❍ b. The robot icon
- ❍ c. The globe with magnifying glass icon
- ❍ d. The blank page icon
- ❍ e. The globe with chain icon

Answer c is correct. The globe with the magnifying glass icon allows you to open a Web page either locally or from the Internet. The file folder with the magnifying glass icon allows you to browse your local directory structure. Therefore, answer a is incorrect. The robot icon allows you to add FrontPage elements. Therefore, answer b is incorrect. The blank page icon allows you to open a new page. Therefore, answer d is incorrect. The globe with a chain link is for adding hyperlinks to documents. Therefore, answer e is incorrect.

Question 7

Trick! question

You want to replace the word "Super" with the word "Outrageous" on your entire Web site, which contains about 20 pages. Which of the following is the fastest option for completing this activity accurately?

- ❍ a. FrontPage Editor: Edit|Find And Replace|Match Whole Word Only|All Pages
- ❍ b. FrontPage Explorer: Edit|Find And Replace|Match Whole Word Only|All Pages
- ❍ c. FrontPage Editor: Tools|Find And Replace|All Pages
- ❍ d. FrontPage Explorer: Tools|Find And Replace|Match Whole Word Only|All Pages

Answer d is correct. The FrontPage Explorer Tools menu is the fastest option that has a Find And Replace feature that will scan all pages. The Find And

Replace feature is located under the Tools menu (not the Edit menu) in FrontPage Explorer. Therefore answer b is incorrect. Another option would be under the Edit menu (not the Tools menu) in FrontPage Editor, but this is not the fastest option. Therefore, answers a and c are incorrect.

Question 8

You've been asked to add several new pages to an existing Web site on your corporate network. Several of the pages are to be used as an online employee handbook. Other items include a small online newsletter and search page.

Objectives:

a. Create an online employee handbook

b. Add a search page to the Web site

c. Add a custom image to the background of the Web site

d. Add a three-column newsletter page to the site

e. Create hyperlinks to all pages from the INDEX.HTML page

Solutions:

- Obtain a copy of the employee handbook and create Web pages for each page in the handbook
- In FrontPage Editor, choose the Search page template and configure it
- Open the Page Properties sheet and configure your custom image for the desired pages

Which of the above objectives were met? [Check all correct answers]

- ❑ a. Create an online employee handbook
- ❑ b. Add a search page to the Web site
- ❑ c. Add a custom image to the background of the Web site
- ❑ d. Add a three-column newsletter page to the site
- ❑ e. Create hyperlinks to all pages from the INDEX.HTML page

Objectives a, b, and c were all addressed in the recommended solutions. Therefore, answers a, b, and c are correct. Objectives d and e were not addressed in the recommended solutions. Therefore, answers d and e are incorrect.

Question 9

If you're referencing a bookmark of "products" in a hyperlink, how will it appear in the URL dialog box?

- ❍ a. $products
- ❍ b. #products
- ❍ c. ?products
- ❍ d. @products

Answer b is correct. The tag for a bookmark is a pound sign (#). The other options are invalid. Therefore, answers a, c, and d are incorrect.

Question 10

Which of the following browsers support the FrontPage Web site background sound?

- ❍ a. IE 4
- ❍ b. Netscape Navigator
- ❍ c. AOL
- ❍ d. CompuServe

Answer a is correct. Only IE supports the FrontPage background sound at this time. None of the other browsers listed supports this feature. Therefore, answers b, c, and d are incorrect.

Question 11

Which of the following is a purpose/benefit of **<META>** tags?

- ❍ a. To display custom graphics
- ❍ b. To warn users who are minors
- ❍ c. To help classify your Web site by providing key terms
- ❍ d. To format the contents of your Web page

Answer c is correct. Search engines use the information contained in <META> tags to help classify your Web site. <META> tags do serve other purposes, such as to provide a title for your Web page; however, the other choices in this question are slightly off target and incorrect. Therefore, answers a, b, and d are incorrect.

Question 12

What does it mean when you see **&T** as the header for a Web page in the Printer Page Setup dialog box?

❍ a. The time the file printed will be listed in the header

❍ b. The type of file will be listed as the header

❍ c. The file will be spooled to the temporary folder

❍ d. The title of the page will be the header

Answer d is correct. &T is for the title of the page. It does not stand for time, type, or temporary. Therefore, answers a, b, and c are incorrect.

Need To Know More?

Tauber, Daniel A. and Brenda Kienan. *Mastering Microsoft FrontPage 98*, Sybex, Alameda, CA, 1998. ISBN 0-7821-2144-6. This is a good resource and reference book for the product. It has a lot of step-by-step instructions, which are great for the beginner; later chapters have more advanced configuration information, which is excellent for the more advanced user. Chapter 2, "Using FrontPage Editor," contains the information relevant to this chapter.

www.w3c.org is the home of the World Wide Web Consortium. Here, you can learn more about the Web, its origin, and HTTP. If you haven't already, you should visit this site. You'll find that it has a lot of good and interesting information about the Web.

Microsoft TechNet (July 98 and later) contains several articles that pertain to FrontPage Editor. By searching for the term "FrontPage Editor," you should locate over 500 documents. To narrow that search down to specific items, try a new query on Last Topics Found and use one of these terms: "Designing Pages," "Using Hyperlinks And Bookmarks," "How To Use An Editor Other Than FrontPage Editor," "Creating And Opening Pages," and "Working With Pages."

5

Working With Templates, Wizards, And Tasks

Terms you'll need to understand:

- √ Templates
- √ Wizards
- √ Tasks (linked and unlinked)

Techniques you'll need to master:

- √ Creating Web documents and sites with templates
- √ Creating Web documents and sites with wizards
- √ Using tasks to track management actions
- √ Using FrontPage to simplify Web creation and management

FrontPage 98 includes several features to streamline and simplify the task of creating Web sites and individual documents as well as to keep track of all the details involved. This chapter discusses the templates, wizards, and tasks available in FrontPage 98.

Creating Web Pages With Templates

FrontPage 98 offers templates for creating individual pages or entire Web sites. A *template* is simply a tool that creates a document or a set of documents that contains structure but not content. Adding your content is the only effort required when using templates; however, you can fully customize and change any Web site or document created from a template. Once a Web site or document is created, regardless of the process used (template, wizard, import, or from scratch), you have complete control of everything (layout, structure, navigation, color scheme, content, and so on) within that document or site.

Web Templates

A Web site template creates a multidocument Web site that includes structure and navigation, but no content. A Web site created from a template can be expanded by adding new pages or reduced by deleting existing pages. The Web site templates are accessed when you create a new Web site using FrontPage Explorer. The New FrontPage Web dialog box, shown in Figure 5.1, offers you access to the following Web site templates:

- **Customer Support Web** Creates a Web site that's used to offer customers online help or technical support.
- **Personal Web** Creates a Web site that's customized for your own personal Web site, offering information about your own interests and hobbies. You can also include photos.
- **Project Web** Creates a Web site suitable for managing project development and direction.

Note: A fourth Web template, called Empty Web, is also available; however, because this template doesn't contain any pages or structure, discussing it as a template is pointless. The Empty Web template is used to start a Web from scratch, as described in Chapter 3.

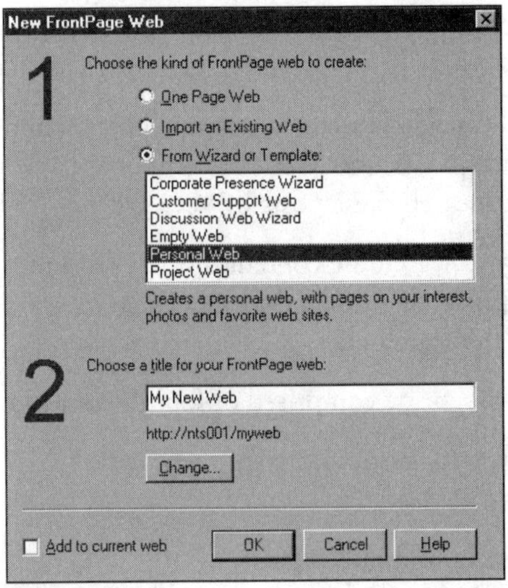

Figure 5.1 The New FrontPage Web dialog box.

The Customer Support Web template creates a Web site comprised of eight sections:

- **Welcome** The introductory document (called the *home page* and named DEFAULT.HTM) for the Web site. This document is used to introduce your organization, provide contact information, and to offer a menu of choices for other local documents. This section is comprised of a single document.
- **What's New** Details changes to the Web site so visitors can locate updated information quickly. This section is also comprised of a single document.
- **FAQ** Offers answers to commonly asked questions for the purposes of reducing customer support emails about simple or frequently discussed topics. This section is also comprised of a single document.
- **Bugs** Offers information about errors or problems as well as offers visitors the opportunity to report problems. This section is comprised of a single document that uses a WebBot component to store reports in an HTML file (BUGLIST.HTM).
- **Suggestions** Gives visitors an opportunity to give you feedback about your products, services, Web site, or whatever. This section is comprised of a single document that uses a WebBot component to store reports in an HTML file (FEEDBACK.HTM).

- **Download** Offers files for visitors to download. This section is also comprised of a single document.
- **Discussion** Offers a Web-based threaded discussion group. This section is comprised of several documents, plus it uses WebBot components to store posts in HTML files and to search these posts by keyword.
- **Search** Offers visitors the ability to search the content of the Web site by keyword. This section is comprised of a single document that uses a WebBot component to perform the search query.

The Personal Web template creates a Web site comprised of four documents:

- **Home Page** Used to introduce you to your visitors and to provide navigation to the other documents.
- **Interest** Lists your hobbies, projects, and interests.
- **Photo Album** Displays photographs that are important to you.
- **Favorites** Lists other Web sites you find interesting so that others can access them easily.

The Project Web template creates a Web site comprised of seven sections:

- **Home** Displays an overview of the project and lists all changes to the Web site. This section is comprised of a single document.
- **Members** Contains contact information about each person involved in the project. This section is also comprised of a single document.
- **Schedule** Details the schedules, events, deadlines, and priorities for the project. This section is also comprised of a single document.
- **Status** Grants access to the progress status reports for the project. This section is comprised of a single document that links to individual reports you create.
- **Archive** Provides a clearinghouse for links to project elements, such as documents, reports, graphics, software, and so on. This section is also comprised of a single document.
- **Search** Offers visitors the ability to search the content of the Web site by keyword. This section is comprised of a single document that uses a WebBot component to perform the search query.
- **Discussion** Offers a Web-based threaded discussion group. This section is comprised of several documents, plus it uses WebBot components to store posts in HTML files and to search these posts by keyword.

Note: FrontPage 98 does not include a procedure or process for creating Web site templates on your own.

Document Templates

A *document template* creates an individual document that contains structure but no real content. Document templates are accessed through FrontPage Editor. The File|New command reveals the New dialog box, shown in Figure 5.2, in which all document templates and wizards are displayed. Documents created with the Template wizard appear in FrontPage Editor, where you can customize their content and structure.

Here's a list of the document templates included with FrontPage 98:

- **Normal Page** A blank document with no structure or content.
- **Bibliography** A document used to display references to external printed resources.
- **Centered Body** A document in which all body content is centered.
- **Confirmation Form** A document used to confirm receipt of user input from a discussion, general form, or registration form.
- **Feedback Form** A document used to solicit reader feedback.
- **Frequently Asked Questions** A document used to host Q&A information regarding common topics and interests.

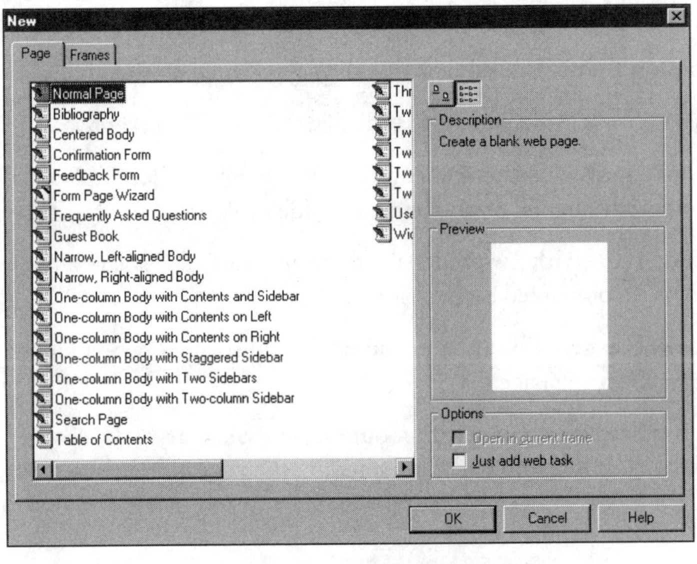

Figure 5.2 FrontPage Editor's New dialog box.

- **Guest Book** A document soliciting and listing visitors.
- **Narrow, Left-aligned Body** A document that displays an image on the right side of the page and all body text in a thin column on the left.
- **Narrow, Right-aligned Body** A document that displays an image on the left side of the page and all body text in a thin column on the right.
- **One-column Body with Contents and Sidebar** A document that displays a one-column body accompanied by a sidebar.
- **One-column Body with Contents on Left** A document that displays a one-column body on the left-hand side of the page.
- **One-column Body with Contents on Right** A document that displays a one-column body on the right-hand side of the page.
- **One-column Body with Staggered Sidebar** A document that displays a one-column body accompanied by a sidebar that is staggered on the page.
- **One-column Body with Two Sidebars** A document that displays a one-column body accompanied by two sidebars.
- **One-column Body with Two-column Sidebar** A document that displays a one-column body accompanied by a two-column sidebar.
- **Search Page** A document in which users can perform a site-wide keyword search.
- **Table of Contents** A document that displays a site's content list (that is, a list of hyperlinks to each important document within the entire Web site).
- **Three-column Body** A document that displays a three-column body.
- **Two-column Body** A document that displays a two-column body.
- **Two-column Body with Contents on Left** A document that displays a two-column body aligned on the left-hand side of the page.
- **Two-column Body with Two Sidebars** A document that displays a two-column body accompanied by two sidebars.
- **Two-column Staggered Body** A document that displays a two-column body staggered on the page.
- **Two-column Staggered Body with Contents and Sidebar** A document that displays a two-column body staggered on the page accompanied by a sidebar.

- **User Registration** A document soliciting registration information to grant access to a protected Web site.
- **Wide Body with Headings** A document with wide body text that's sectioned with subheadings.

FrontPage 98 also includes templates to create framed documents. These are accessed on the Frames tab of the New dialog box. There are 10 frame templates. Each offers two, three, or four frame areas in various configurations. You are sure to find a selection that you can customize to your exact width and layout needs. Once you select the frame template, you can alter the frame structure of the new document and define the documents to be displayed in each of the framed areas.

FrontPage 98 allows you to create your own document templates. To create a template from a document you've created from scratch or modified from another template, use the File|Save As command from FrontPage Editor while viewing the document. On the Save As dialog box, click on the As Template button. Provide a title, file name, and description. Your custom template will appear in the list of templates in the New dialog box.

Creating Web Pages With Wizards

FrontPage 98 includes wizards that aid in the creation of more complex Web sites and documents. Wizards are common elements of Windows software installation and operation; their use in FrontPage isn't much different. Once a wizard is launched, you simply follow the prompts and provide the requested information.

FrontPage uses several wizards, including the following:

- **Corporate Presence wizard** Builds a Web site suitable for a small company.
- **Discussion Web wizard** Builds a Web site suitable for hosting Web-based discussion groups.
- **Form Page wizard** Helps you create a form used to solicit visitor feedback or input. You can save the obtained information in a file (via a WebBot component). This wizard is discussed in Chapter 8.
- **Import Web wizard** Used to bring an existing Web site into FrontPage for editing and management. This wizard is discussed in Chapter 3.
- **Web Publishing wizard** Automatically appears when a Web site cannot be posted to a server due to the absence of FrontPage Server Extensions.

This wizard aids you in configuring FrontPage to use FTP to post files. This wizard is discussed in Chapter 4.

- **CDF wizard** Used to add Channel Definition Format (CDF) push information to a Web site so users can subscribe to it. This wizard is discussed in Chapter 11.
- **Database Region wizard** Used to add database interaction to Web sites via SQL queries to ODBC-compliant database systems. This wizard is discussed in Chapter 12.
- **Script wizard** Used to simplify the task of associating events with existing VBScript or JavaScript code. This wizard is discussed in Chapter 12.

Most of these wizards deal with various components of Web pages and are discussed in the chapters referenced in the preceding list. There are two wizards included with FrontPage 98 that deal solely with Web site creation; these are the Corporate Presence wizard and the Discussion Web wizard. These two wizards are accessed in the New FrontPage Web dialog box (refer to Figure 5.1). Once activated, they guide you through the creation process by offering you choices and requesting information. When this process is complete, a basic Web site based on your input is created. You can "fill out" the Web site by adding your own content. Plus, you have complete control to modify the structure as you see fit.

The Corporate Presence wizard creates simple and complex business-related Web sites. The wizard's dialog box prompts are guided by your component selections. If you choose to include every optional component within a site using this wizard, the prompts will ask for information in the following order:

- Selection of main pages/sections (What's New, Products/Services, Table Of Contents, Feedback Form, and Search Form)
- Home page topics (Introduction, Mission Statement, Company Profile, and Contact Information)
- "What's New?" topics (Web Changes, Press Releases, and Articles And Reviews)
- Number of products and number of services
- Product page elements (image, pricing, and information request form)
- Service page elements (capabilities, references, and information request form)
- Feedback form elements (full name, job title, company affiliation, mailing address, telephone number, fax number, and email address)

- Store feedback information in a tab-delimited text file or HTML format
- Table of contents options (update list automatically, show nonlinked pages [orphans], and use bullets for top-level documents)
- Page banner elements (company logo, page title, and link to main Web pages)
- Page footer elements (link to main Web pages, email address of Webmaster, copyright, and modification date)
- Use the Under Construction icon for incomplete pages
- Company info (name, one-word nickname, and street address)
- More company info (telephone number, fax number, Webmaster's email address, and general info email address)
- Use a Web theme

The Discussion Web wizard creates Web-based discussion forums. If you choose to include every optional component within a site using this wizard, the prompts will ask for information in the following order:

- Discussion forum components (table of contents, search form, threaded replies, and confirmation page)
- Discussion forum info (discussion title and name of folder to store posts)
- Discussion input fields (subject, category, comments, and product)
- Create a protected discussion
- Order to display posts (oldest or newest first)
- Set the table of contents as the home page
- Search form criteria (subject, size, data, and score)
- Set a Web theme
- Define frame use (no frames; dual, as supported by browser; contents above article; and contents beside article)

Once the selections are made and the requested information is provided, FrontPage will construct a Web site based on your input, complete with structure and navigation. Simply add your content to complete the site.

Working With Tasks

The work involved in creating and maintaining a Web site can be enormous. Keeping track of what has been completed and what items still need to be accomplished can be a difficult endeavor. You can keep up with your to-do lists via the Tasks View (see Figure 5.3). The Tasks View is just a collection of To Do items that are used to remind you of things you need to accomplish. By default, the Tasks View only lists tasks that are incomplete or in progress. Selecting Task History from the View menu displays all tasks.

A *task* is nothing more than a reminder note informing you that a specific action needs to be taken. Tasks do not perform actions automatically, nor do they act as alarms or pop-up messages.

Tasks are created in several ways:

- Using the New Task button or the command from the right-click pop-up menu from the Tasks View
- Using the Add Task command from the right-click pop-up menu from the Folders, All Files, Navigation, or Hyperlinks Views
- Using the File|New|Task menu command from any view
- Allowing the Corporate Presence wizard to create them for you

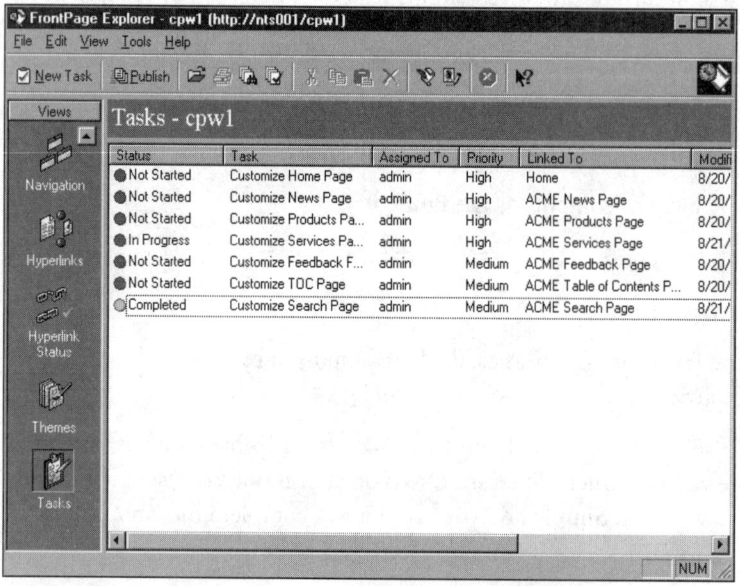

Figure 5.3 The Tasks View of FrontPage Explorer.

- Using the Edit|Add Task command from FrontPage Editor
- Selecting the Just Add Web Task checkbox on the New dialog box when creating new documents in FrontPage Editor (refer to Figure 5.2)
- Selecting the Add A Task For Each Page With Misspellings checkbox in the Spelling dialog box from FrontPage Explorer
- Dragging and dropping a file from any view to the Tasks View

Tasks are either linked or unlinked. A *linked task* is just a task that's associated with a file within your Web site. *Unlinked tasks* are not tied to a specific file but are associated with the current Web site in general. Linked tasks are notes to perform an action on the linked file. Unlinked tasks are notes to do something. Linked tasks are created by selecting a file and issuing the New Task command. Unlinked tasks are created by issuing the New Task command without selecting a file.

When a new task is created, you must provide the following information (see Figure 5.4):

- Task name
- Whom the task is assigned to
- Priority level: High, Medium, or Low
- Task description (that is, what needs to be done)

FrontPage automatically keeps track of the creator and the creation date as well as the name and date of the last user to change the task. Tasks can be viewed by opening them from the Tasks View. This displays the Task Details dialog box (which is similar to the New Task dialog box shown in Figure 5.4).

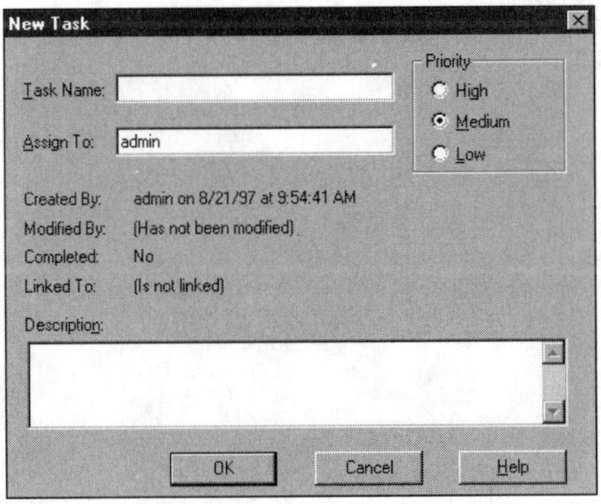

Figure 5.4 The New Task dialog box.

When viewing a task, you can change its user assignment, task name, priority, and description.

If a task is linked to a file, you can issue the Do Task command (from either the Task Details dialog box or the right-click pop-up menu from the Tasks View). The Do Task command opens the linked file in its associated editor. After you perform any modifications to the file and attempt to save or exit the editor, you'll be prompted to mark the task as complete or not complete. Selecting Yes marks the task complete, selecting No marks the task as in progress, and selecting Cancel does not change the task's status. Unlinked tasks can be marked as complete by selecting the Mark Complete command from the right-click pop-up menu when the task is highlighted (this command is also available in the Edit menu). Tasks can be deleted by selecting them and then issuing a Delete command (from the Edit menu, right-click menu, or keyboard).

Practice Questions

Question 1

Which methods of creating Web sites or individual documents through FrontPage result in a file (or files) that can be customized and edited? [Check all correct answers]

- ❑ a. Templates
- ❑ b. Wizards
- ❑ c. Import
- ❑ d. From scratch

All FrontPage Webs can be customized and edited no matter how they were originally created. Therefore, answers a, b, c, and d are correct.

Question 2

Which creation process used by FrontPage creates a new document (or documents) with structure but without content based on your input?

- ❍ a. Templates
- ❍ b. Wizards
- ❍ c. Import
- ❍ d. Tasks

A wizard creates documents with structure and without content based on your input. Therefore, answer b is correct. Templates do not request input (although they do create documents with structure and without content). Therefore, answer a is incorrect. Importing does not create new documents without content. Therefore, answer c is incorrect. Tasks are not used to create documents; they are used to remind you of actions that need to be performed on documents. Therefore, answer d is incorrect.

Question 3

Which of the following Web creation tools is best suited for creating a Web site that can offer the widest range (in types) of information to visitors about a business' products and services?

- ❍ a. Personal Web template
- ❍ b. Discussion Web wizard
- ❍ c. Project Web template
- ❍ d. Customer Support Web template

The Customer Support Web template creates a Web site that hosts sections, such as FAQ, Bugs, Feedback, Download, Discussion, and Search. Therefore, answer d is correct. The Personal Web template creates a Web site focused on an individual's interests, not a business' products. Therefore, answer a is incorrect. The Discussion Web wizard creates a Web site that hosts discussion groups but does not include any other types of informational sections. Therefore, because it doesn't have the widest range of information, answer b is incorrect. The Project Web template creates a Web site used to track and manage the progress of a project, not to distribute information about products and services. Therefore, answer c is incorrect.

Question 4

Which of the following definitions best describes a template?

- ❍ a. A tool that creates documents based on user input
- ❍ b. A tool that sets the look and feel for a Web site
- ❍ c. A tool that creates structured documents without content
- ❍ d. A tool that forces a strict set of parameters to documents

A template is a tool that creates structured documents without content. Therefore, answer c is correct. A tool that creates documents based on user input is a wizard. Therefore, answer a is incorrect. A tool that sets the look and feel for a Web site is a theme. Therefore, answer b is incorrect. A tool that forces a strict set of parameters to documents is a DTD (Document Type Definition), which is an SGML syntax list that defines how HTML functions. Therefore, answer d is incorrect.

Question 5

Which wizards incorporate the use of a WebBot component to offer support for special features that HTML alone cannot provide? [Check all correct answers]

- ❑ a. Corporate Presence wizard
- ❑ b. Discussion Web wizard
- ❑ c. Form Page wizard
- ❑ d. Import Web wizard

The Corporate Presence, Discussion Web, and Form Page wizards all use WebBot components. Therefore, answers a, b, and c are correct. The Import Web wizard does not use WebBot components because it does not create Web sites—it's used to import existing Web sites. Therefore, answer d is incorrect.

Question 6

Which of the following layout types can you create quickly and easily using a template? [Check all correct answers]

- ❑ a. A newsletter with a column of text, pictures, and images
- ❑ b. A newspaper with three columns of text
- ❑ c. A book page with sidebars
- ❑ d. An advertisement with all centered text

Trick! question

The templates included with FrontPage 98 enable you to create all these layout schemes. Therefore, answers a, b, c, and d are correct. Although you may not think of newspapers or books as information that can be disseminated via a Web page, they can be created using the templates included with FrontPage, which is why this question is labeled as a trick.

Question 7

FrontPage 98 includes processes for creating your own document and Web site wizards and templates.

❍ a. True

❍ b. False

This is a false statement. Therefore, answer b is correct. FrontPage 98 only includes a process to create your own document templates. FrontPage 98 does not include the ability to make wizards or Web site templates.

Question 8

Tasks can be assigned a deadline date so that as the deadline approaches, site administrators will receive pop-up messages prompting them to complete the defined task.

❍ a. True

❍ b. False

This is a false statement. Therefore, answer b is correct. Tasks in FrontPage do not act as alarms and do not cause pop-up reminders. Tasks only function as a manually accessible To Do list.

Question 9

Which of the following actions can result in the creation of tasks? [Check all correct answers]

❑ a. Using the Corporate Presence wizard and selecting all options

❑ b. Using the New dialog box

❑ c. Using the Spelling command and selecting all options

❑ d. Dragging and dropping files into the Tasks view

All these actions can be used to create new tasks. Therefore, answers a, b, c, and d are correct.

Question 10

Which of the following detail items of a task can be changed? [Check all correct answers]

- ❑ a. Creation date
- ❑ b. Priority
- ❑ c. Assigned user
- ❑ d. Linked file

The priority and assigned user are the task details that can be changed. Therefore, answers b and c are correct. The creation date and the linked file of a task cannot be changed. Therefore, answers a and d are incorrect.

Need To Know More?

Lehto, Kerry A. and W. Brett Polonsky. *Official Microsoft FrontPage 98 Book*, Microsoft Press, Redmond, WA, 1997. ISBN 1-57231-629-2. Chapter 4 discusses templates and wizards. Pages 54 through 58 discuss tasks. Other individual topics may be found in scattered places elsewhere in this book.

Matthews, Martin S. and Erik B. Poulsen. *FrontPage 98: The Complete Reference*, Osborne McGraw-Hill, Berkeley, CA, 1998. ISBN 0-07882-394-3. Page 61 in Chapter 2 covers task lists, Chapter 3 covers wizards, and Chapter 4 covers templates.

Stanek, William R., et al. *Microsoft FrontPage 98 Unleashed*, Sams.net Publishing, Indianapolis, IN, 1998. ISBN 1-57521-349-4. Part VI discusses templates and wizards. Individual topics may be found in scattered places elsewhere in this book.

Tauber, Daniel A. and Brenda Kienan. *Mastering Microsoft FrontPage 98*, Sybex, Alameda, CA, 1998. ISBN 0-7821-2144-6. Chapter 6 discusses tasks. Individual topics may be found in scattered places elsewhere in this book.

Microsoft TechNet. Useful information about the FrontPage 98 topics discussed in this chapter can be found by searching on keywords related to the particular topics.

www.microsoft.com/frontpage/. This is the official FrontPage Web site hosted by Microsoft. It offers overview information about FrontPage.

6

Building Tables

Terms you'll need to understand:

- ✓ Table toolbar
- ✓ Table properties
- ✓ Cell padding
- ✓ Cell spacing

Techniques you'll need to master:

- ✓ Creating tables
- ✓ Assigning table captions and headings
- ✓ Adding text and images to tables
- ✓ Setting the No Wrap option
- ✓ Modifying table size and alignment
- ✓ Adding and removing rows, columns, and cells
- ✓ Splitting cells
- ✓ Setting cell padding, spacing, and border width
- ✓ Adding colors and background images to tables
- ✓ Using proper screen resolution

In this chapter, we explore how tables can improve the look and feel of your Web pages. You'll learn how to use templates that contain tables as well as how to create tables of your own using several different methods. We also discuss working with table layout, colors, and general table editing techniques.

Creating Tables

Tables are a great way to organize data on a Web page, and they've been used for this purpose for a long time. However, many Web page designers have discovered that tables also provide a good way to organize eye-catching content and to vary the presentation of that content. Beyond just organizing text information, you can insert graphics, links, and icons into tables to create entertaining and aesthetically pleasing content.

Figure 6.1 shows how a table can be used to organize information on a Web page.

In Figure 6.2, you can see how the site at **www.hudlogic.com** uses multiple tables to enhance the look and accessibility of the site. On the left, you see a table of contents table with links to various pieces of information. On the right, you see the company's Services and Employees sections, which are part of a two-column table.

Now that you've seen a couple examples of how different tables can enhance your site and organize your content, let's investigate the methods you can use to add tables to your Web pages.

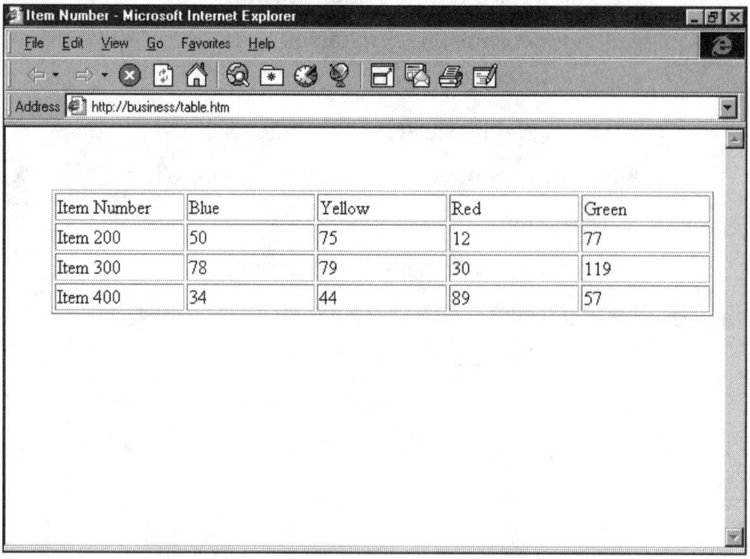

Item Number	Blue	Yellow	Red	Green
Item 200	50	75	12	77
Item 300	78	79	30	119
Item 400	34	44	89	57

Figure 6.1 Using a simple table to organize data.

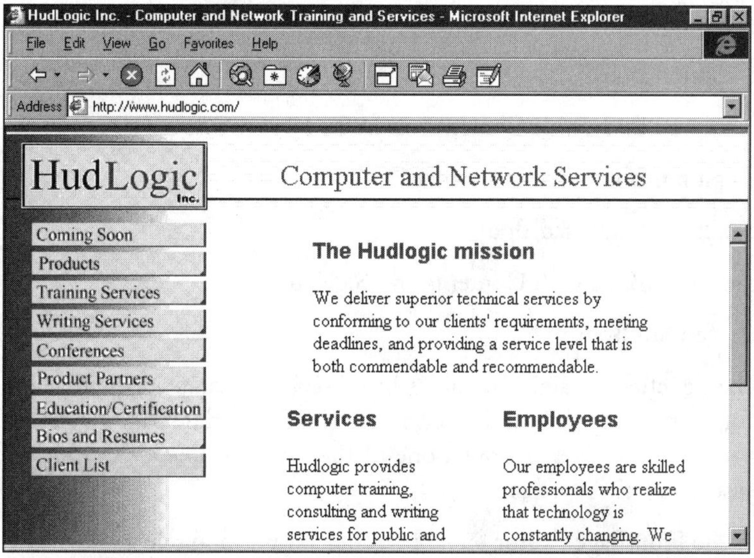

Figure 6.2 An example of a more complex table arrangement.

Inserting Tables

You can use many different methods to insert tables in your Web site. All these methods are available through FrontPage Editor. Essentially, your options are to use a template configured for tables, use the standard toolbar to insert a table, use the menu bar to insert a table, or use the table toolbar to draw a table. The following sections detail the available options for inserting tables via FrontPage Editor.

Templates

Several templates in FrontPage include tables. You can see these options when you create a new Web page through FrontPage Editor. Here's a list of all the templates that have embedded tables:

- Narrow, Left-aligned Body
- Narrow, Right-aligned Body
- One-column Body with Contents and Sidebar
- One-column Body with Contents on Left
- One-column Body with Contents on Right
- One-column Body with Staggered Sidebar
- One-column Body with Two Sidebars

- One-column Body with Two-column Sidebar
- Two-column Body
- Two-column Body with Contents on Left
- Two-column Body with Two Sidebars
- Two-column Staggered Body
- Two-column Body with Contents and Sidebar
- Three-column Body

One of the benefits of using the tables in the existing templates is that the work of formatting, aligning, and determining the appropriate page layout has already been done for you. To open one of these table-embedded pages for editing, just follow these steps:

1. From the FrontPage Editor menu bar, click on File and select New.
2. Click on a template to see a preview of its page.
3. Once you've found the template you want to use, click on OK.

You may notice that these pages include dummy text that serves as a placeholder for your own content. Depending on the page style you choose, you'll be able to replace the text, pictures, clip art, and contents with your own content.

Insert Table Button

One of the simplest and quickest methods for inserting a table is through the Insert Table button on the standard toolbar. There are two basic steps in this process:

1. On the FrontPage Editor standard toolbar, click on the Insert Table button.
2. A small table icon representation appears. Highlight the number of columns and rows you want in your table.

Initially, this option limits you to creating a table with a maximum of five columns and four rows (see the grid in Figure 6.3). However, after the table has been dropped on the page, it will dynamically expand as the mouse moves outside of the five-by-four grid. When the table is dropped onto your Web page, it's placed wherever you left the cursor on the page when you inserted the table. You're not given the chance to modify the table setup before it's pasted onto your page. If you want to modify the table, you have to do so after it has been dropped.

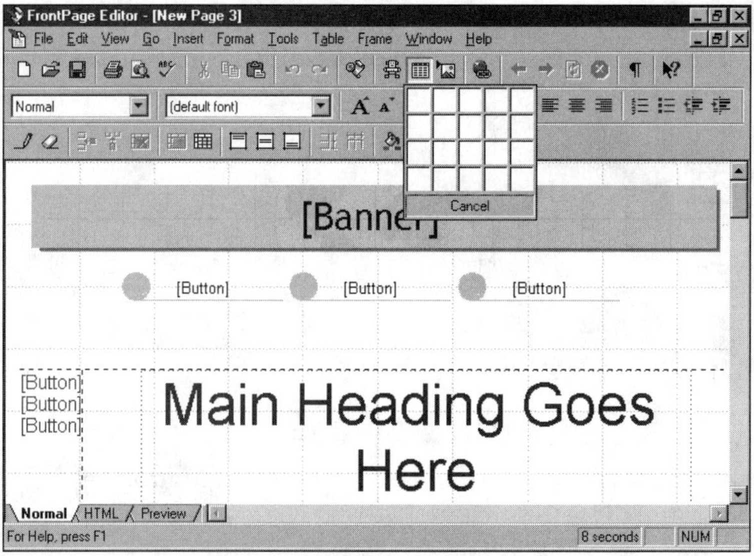

Figure 6.3 The Insert Table icon allows you to create a maximum of four rows and five columns.

Insert Table Option

If you want to have more control over the table before it's created or you just want to exceed the limitation of having only five columns and four rows, you can try the Insert Table option from FrontPage Editor.

The Insert Table option can be found in the Table menu in FrontPage Editor. The Insert Table option allows you to control the number of rows and columns as well as the layout of your new table. You can also specify a width in pixels or a percentage of the screen that the table will occupy.

To insert a table using this method, complete the following steps:

1. On the FrontPage Editor toolbar, click on the Insert option and then choose Table. This action will open the Insert Table dialog box (see Figure 6.4).
2. Configure the number of rows and columns you want in the Size section of the Insert Table dialog box.
3. Configure the alignment, border size, cell padding, and cell spacing in the Layout section of the Insert Table dialog box.
4. Specify the width of the table as a percentage of the screen or by the number of pixels.
5. Click on OK to place the table on your page.

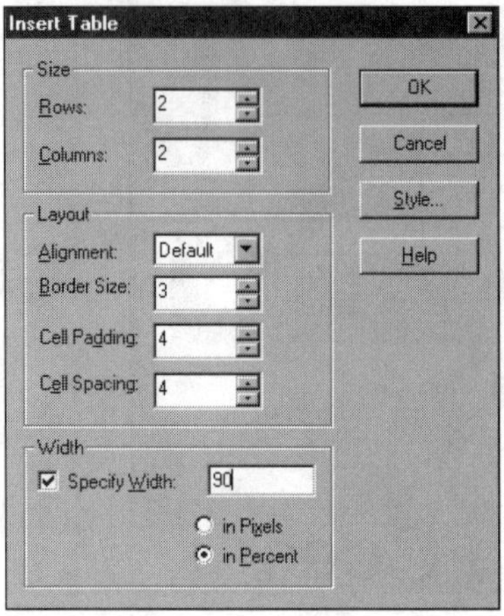

Figure 6.4 The Insert Table dialog box allows you to control the formatting of your new table.

Note: The maximum number of rows and columns you can create through the Insert Table option is 25-by-25.

Table Toolbar

The table toolbar gives you several options for creating, formatting, and editing tables that are not available on the standard toolbar in FrontPage Editor. The table toolbar, shown in Figure 6.5, is not displayed in the default FrontPage Editor display window. You have to activate the display of the table toolbar in order to see it.

To display the table toolbar, follow these steps:

1. Click on View on the FrontPage Editor menu bar.
2. Click on the Table Toolbar option to check this selection.

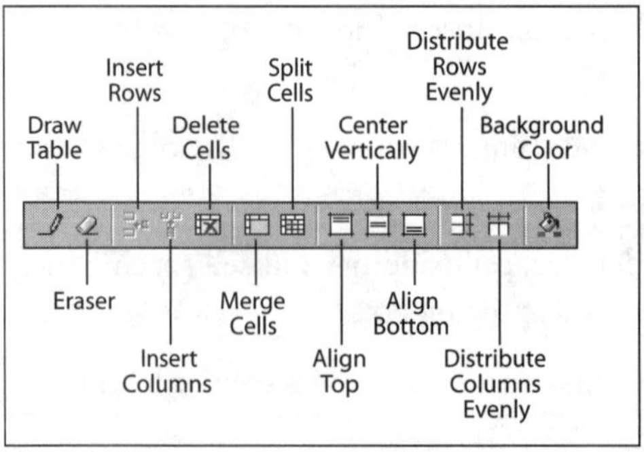

Figure 6.5 The table toolbar.

The table toolbar should be visible in FrontPage Editor just below the other toolbars.

Table 6.1 describes the options in the default table toolbar.

Drawing A Table

To draw a table, perform the following steps:

1. Click on the Draw Table button.
2. Place the pencil icon on the part of the page where you want the table to begin.
3. Click on and drag the pencil icon to create a table of whatever size you want.

   Note: You can also access the Draw Table option from the FrontPage Editor menu bar; it's located under the Table option.

Table 6.1 The table toolbar components.

Option	Description
Draw Table	Allows you to draw a table or cell wall.
Eraser	Erases the borders between cells.
Insert Rows	Inserts the specified number of rows above the selected row.
Insert Columns	Inserts the specified number of columns to the left of the selected column.
Delete Cells	Deletes the current or highlighted cell(s).
Merge Cells	Combines the selected cells into a single cell.
Split Cells	Divides the selected cell into two cells.
Align Top	Aligns the text inside the cell with the top of the cell.
Center Vertically	Places the text in the vertical center of the cell.
Align Bottom	Aligns the text inside the cell with the bottom of the cell.
Distribute Rows Evenly	Makes the space between rows uniform (even).
Distribute Columns Evenly	Makes the space between columns uniform (even).
Background Color	Opens the Color dialog box to allow the background color to be set.

Editing Table Properties

Although you have many options for configuring your table just the way you want it, there will probably be a time when you want to change the way it looks. When that time comes, you'll want to know how to edit that table. You can use FrontPage Editor to modify the tables on your Web pages.

Table Properties

Tables are objects in FrontPage Editor and, as objects, they have properties that can be configured. To access a table's properties, place your cursor on the table and right-click on it. Choose Table Properties from the resulting context menu. The Table Properties dialog box appears (see Figure 6.6).

This dialog box allows you to control the layout, size, background, and color of your table. From the options in the Layout section of the Table Properties dialog box, you can specify the Alignment, Float, Border Size, Cell Padding, and Cell Spacing settings. For a brief description of each of these terms, see Table 6.2.

Adding Rows And Columns

You can add rows and columns to your table via the table toolbar options shown earlier in Figure 6.5. If you want to insert multiple rows or columns, you might try the FrontPage Editor menu bar. To add a row or column to your table via the menu bar, follow these steps:

1. Position your cursor on a row or column that borders the spot where you want to expand the table.

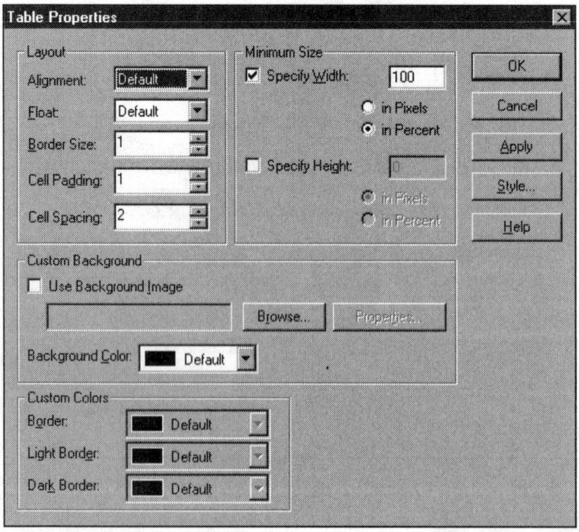

Figure 6.6 The Table Properties dialog box.

Property	Description
Alignment	The location where the table will be placed on the page. You can set this for left, right, or center.
Float	Allows you to specify how text on the page will flow outside the table (left, right, or default). The default setting does not allow text to the left or the right of the table on the page.
Border Size	The size of the table's border in pixels.
Cell Padding	The number of pixels between the cell wall and contents of the cell.
Cell Spacing	The amount of space (in pixels) between cells.

Table 6.2 Table layout options.

2. Select Table|Insert Rows Or Columns from the FrontPage Editor menu bar. This will open the Insert Rows Or Columns dialog box (see Figure 6.7).
3. If you want to insert columns, select the Columns radio button. If you want to insert rows, select the Rows radio button. Depending on the button you select, the rest of the Insert Rows Or Columns dialog box will reflect options for either a row insertion or column insertion accordingly.
4. If you select column insertion, you can set the number of columns as well as the location where you want to have them added: either to the right of your cursor or to the left of your cursor in the table. Otherwise, skip to Step 5.
5. If you select row insertion, you can set the number of rows and then set the spot where you want to have them added: either above your cursor or below your cursor in the table. Otherwise, skip to Step 6.
6. Click on OK to complete the insertion.

You can use the Insert Row and the Insert Column icons to add rows and columns to your table; however, for those options to be available, you must select a row to add a row or select a column to add a column.

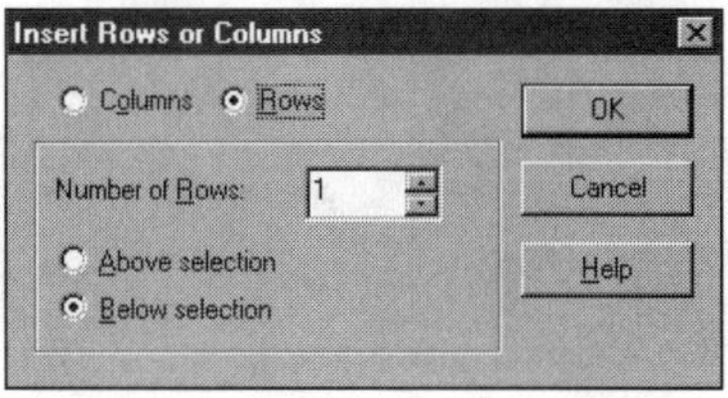

Figure 6.7 The Insert Rows Or Columns dialog box.

Cell Properties

You can use the Cell Properties dialog box to adjust the text alignment in a cell, add a custom background, and define colors. This dialog box gives you finer control over your tables.

To change the alignment of text using the Cell Properties dialog box, follow these steps:

1. Click on the cell in the table that you want to modify.
2. Right-click on this cell and select Cell Properties from the resulting context menu. This opens the Cell Properties dialog box, as shown in Figure 6.8.
3. You can choose the Horizontal Alignment and Vertical Alignment settings in the Layout section of this dialog box. The options for Horizontal Alignment are Left, Right, Center, or Default. The options for Vertical Alignment are Top, Middle, Baseline, Bottom, or Default.

> **TIP** The Baseline option allows you to set the text in a row to a common lower line (an imaginary line). If you select Baseline, the text in a cell will align itself with the rest of the text in the row so that all text appears to have been typed on the same line, regardless of actual font size.

Notice that several other options are available in the Cell Properties dialog box. Table 6.3 briefly describes these options.

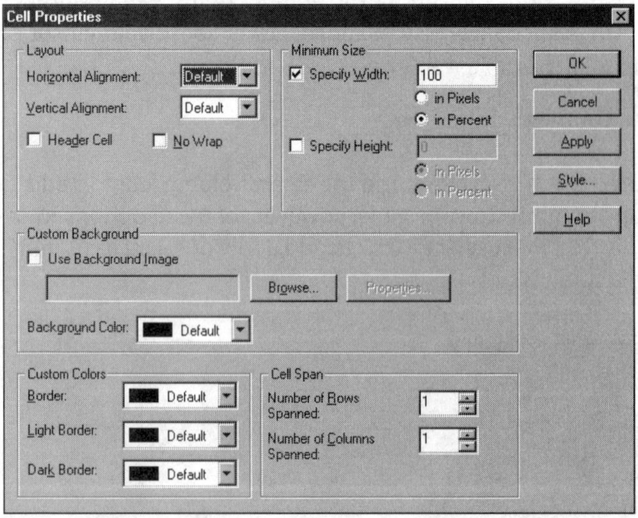

Figure 6.8 The Cell Properties dialog box.

Table 6.3 Cell Properties dialog box options.

Property	Description
Header Cell	Bolds the text in the cell to signify a header.
No Wrap	Prevents text from wrapping within the cell if the browser is resized. Otherwise, if the client resizes the browser, the cell's text might wrap inside the cell.
Specify Width	Sets the width for the contents of the cell.
Specify Height	Sets the height for the contents of the cell.
Use Background Image	Inserts a specific image into the cell. The cell can have a different background image than the table.
Background Color	Sets a specific color in the cell's background. Each cell can have a unique background color.
Border	Allows you to set a border color for the cell.
Light Border	Allows you to specify a light color for the cell border in addition to the regular border. This option produces a three-dimensional effect.
Dark Border	Allows you to specify a dark color for the cell border in addition to the regular border. This option produces a three-dimensional effect.
Number Of Rows Spanned	Sets the number of rows that the cell should span.
Number Of Columns Spanned	Sets the number of columns that the cell should span.

Splitting Cells

If you want to create additional cells within a single cell (perhaps to subdivide data or to create an artful display of text or graphics), you can use the Split Cells option. This feature allows you to create additional columns or rows within a single cell.

To split a cell, perform the following steps:

1. Click on the cell you want to split.
2. Select the Table option from the FrontPage Editor menu bar; then choose the Split Cells option. You'll see the Split Cells dialog box, as shown in Figure 6.9.
3. In the dialog box, you can either choose Split Into Columns or Split Into Rows. Then, you can select how many additional rows or columns to create.
4. Click on OK to confirm the cell division.

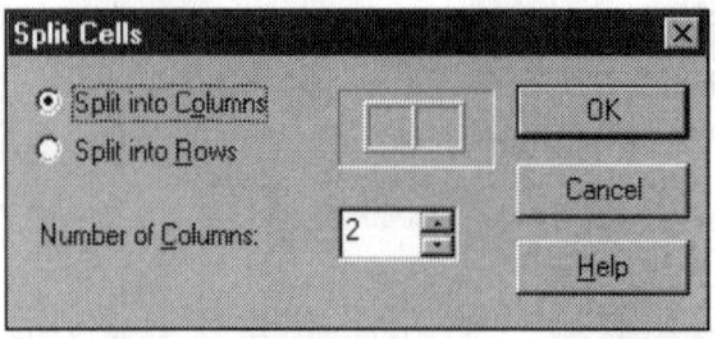

Figure 6.9 The Split Cells dialog box.

Table Headings

To make your tables easier to read and identify, you may want to add table headings within the data cells of your table. Table headings usually define the type of information that appears in the table or a particular row, column, or subsection of the table. You can place headings anywhere in the table to emphasize or designate a particular piece or set of information.

To create a table heading, follow these steps:

1. Choose the location where you want to add the heading. This can be any cell in the table; however, it's usually at the top of the table.
2. Right-click on the cell you chose in Step 1 and select Cell Properties.
3. Select the Header Cell checkbox in the Cell Properties dialog box.
4. Click on OK to confirm.

Any text you add to the cell will be bolded and centered in that cell. Any text that was already in that cell will be bolded and centered once you close the Cell Properties dialog box.

Table Captions

A table caption usually describes the contents of the table. The caption is applied as a row that spans the width of the table, breaking all cell divisions. You can place the table caption either above or below the table, but, by default, it appears at the top of the table. To insert a table caption, follow these steps:

1. Click on anywhere in the table to which you want to add a caption.
2. Click on Table from the FrontPage menu bar and select Insert Caption. The table caption will appear at the top of the table, by default.
3. You can type the caption for the table directly into the table caption cell.
4. If you want to shift the caption to the bottom of the table, select Table from the FrontPage Editor menu bar and then select Caption Properties. The Caption Properties dialog box appears, displaying two options

for the table caption position: Top Of Table and Bottom Of Table. Choose Bottom Of Table to change the caption's position.

Screen Resolution

When you're developing your Web site, you may find that using a screen resolution of 640 by 480 gives you a more accurate representation of what your clients will see when accessing your Web site. For instance, if you use a 1024-by-768 screen resolution to create a 25-by-25 table with a specified number of pixels, you may be able to see the entire table in the browser window (see Figure 6.10).

However, when your clients are viewing the table, they may only see part of the table when using the standard screen resolution of 640-by-480 (see Figure 6.11). This doesn't mean that they won't be able to get all of the data, but it does mean that your page may not have the layout that you intended people to see when they open the page.

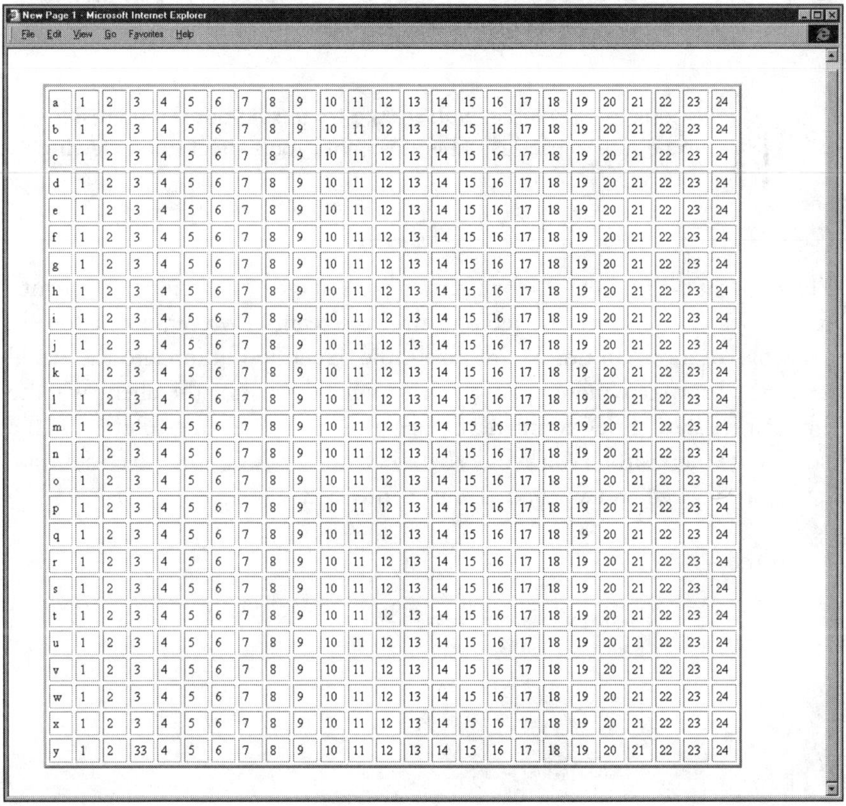

a	1	2	3	4	5	6	7	8	9	10	11	12	13	14	15	16	17	18	19	20	21	22	23	24
b	1	2	3	4	5	6	7	8	9	10	11	12	13	14	15	16	17	18	19	20	21	22	23	24
c	1	2	3	4	5	6	7	8	9	10	11	12	13	14	15	16	17	18	19	20	21	22	23	24
d	1	2	3	4	5	6	7	8	9	10	11	12	13	14	15	16	17	18	19	20	21	22	23	24
e	1	2	3	4	5	6	7	8	9	10	11	12	13	14	15	16	17	18	19	20	21	22	23	24
f	1	2	3	4	5	6	7	8	9	10	11	12	13	14	15	16	17	18	19	20	21	22	23	24
g	1	2	3	4	5	6	7	8	9	10	11	12	13	14	15	16	17	18	19	20	21	22	23	24
h	1	2	3	4	5	6	7	8	9	10	11	12	13	14	15	16	17	18	19	20	21	22	23	24
i	1	2	3	4	5	6	7	8	9	10	11	12	13	14	15	16	17	18	19	20	21	22	23	24
j	1	2	3	4	5	6	7	8	9	10	11	12	13	14	15	16	17	18	19	20	21	22	23	24
k	1	2	3	4	5	6	7	8	9	10	11	12	13	14	15	16	17	18	19	20	21	22	23	24
l	1	2	3	4	5	6	7	8	9	10	11	12	13	14	15	16	17	18	19	20	21	22	23	24
m	1	2	3	4	5	6	7	8	9	10	11	12	13	14	15	16	17	18	19	20	21	22	23	24
n	1	2	3	4	5	6	7	8	9	10	11	12	13	14	15	16	17	18	19	20	21	22	23	24
o	1	2	3	4	5	6	7	8	9	10	11	12	13	14	15	16	17	18	19	20	21	22	23	24
p	1	2	3	4	5	6	7	8	9	10	11	12	13	14	15	16	17	18	19	20	21	22	23	24
q	1	2	3	4	5	6	7	8	9	10	11	12	13	14	15	16	17	18	19	20	21	22	23	24
r	1	2	3	4	5	6	7	8	9	10	11	12	13	14	15	16	17	18	19	20	21	22	23	24
s	1	2	3	4	5	6	7	8	9	10	11	12	13	14	15	16	17	18	19	20	21	22	23	24
t	1	2	3	4	5	6	7	8	9	10	11	12	13	14	15	16	17	18	19	20	21	22	23	24
u	1	2	3	4	5	6	7	8	9	10	11	12	13	14	15	16	17	18	19	20	21	22	23	24
v	1	2	3	4	5	6	7	8	9	10	11	12	13	14	15	16	17	18	19	20	21	22	23	24
w	1	2	3	4	5	6	7	8	9	10	11	12	13	14	15	16	17	18	19	20	21	22	23	24
x	1	2	3	4	5	6	7	8	9	10	11	12	13	14	15	16	17	18	19	20	21	22	23	24
y	1	2	33	4	5	6	7	8	9	10	11	12	13	14	15	16	17	18	19	20	21	22	23	24

Figure 6.10 A 25-by-25 table created and viewed with 1024-by-768 screen resolution.

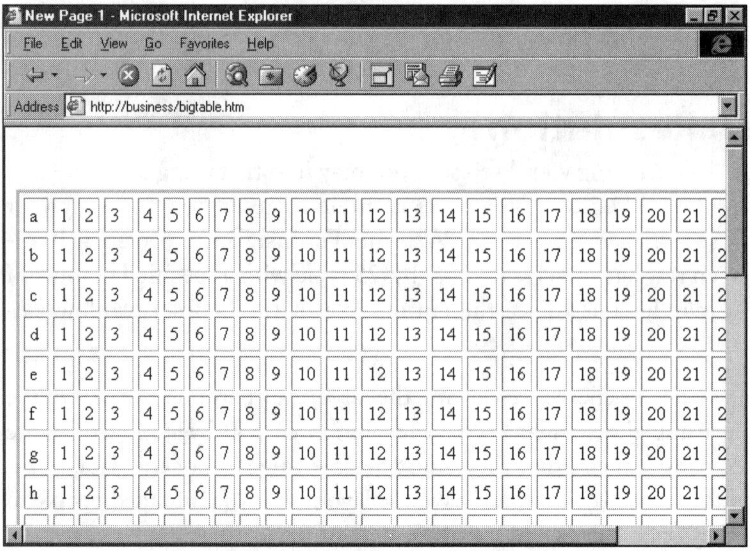

Figure 6.11 A table created with 1024-by-768 screen resolution but viewed with 640-by-480 resolution.

> **TIP** When creating tables, you should try to set your screen resolution equal to that used by the clients you expect to be viewing your site.

When you set the table width for a certain percentage of the screen, the client's browser usually modifies the table to fit the screen. However, when you set your table for a certain number of pixels, the screen resolution and the actual size of the browser window play a role in whether or not the client will see what you see during development. By using the same screen resolution as the majority of your visitors, you stand a better chance of designing a page and site that can be viewed and enjoyed as you've intended.

Practice Questions

Question 1

You've created a table that contains data on your company's financial reports. The data is organized into 15 columns and 25 rows. Some of the people in the finance department are complaining that the text is wrapping inside the table, making their calculations difficult. They would like you to correct this problem. Which of the following courses of action guarantees that the text will not wrap?

❍ a. Resetting the table properties so that the table occupies 100 percent of the screen

❍ b. Changing the font properties to ensure that the text is smaller than the cell width

❍ c. In the Cell Properties dialog box, configuring the cells not to wrap

❍ d. Decreasing the table width to ensure that the table is smaller than a full screen at 640-by-480 resolution

The correct answer is c. The No Wrap option in the Cell Properties dialog box can be checked to prevent cell text from wrapping. Table properties will not help make this distinction, nor will increasing or decreasing the font properties of the cells or table. Therefore, answers a and b are incorrect. Setting up the table to not exceed the width of a 640-by-480 screen might seem like a good idea, but this setting does not guarantee that clients will be using the full screen to view the table. Therefore, answer d is incorrect.

Question 2

Which of the following templates have embedded tables? [Check all correct answers]

❑ a. Narrow, Left-aligned Body

❑ b. Normal

❑ c. One-column Body with Contents on Right

❑ d. Guest Book

Answers a and c are correct because the Narrow, Left-aligned Body and the One-column Body with Contents on Right templates have embedded tables. The Normal and Guest Book templates do not contain tables. Therefore, answers b and d are incorrect.

Question 3

Which of the following options are valid for inserting tables into your Web pages? [Check all correct answers]

❑ a. Insert Table icon on the table toolbar

❑ b. Draw Table icon on the table toolbar

❑ c. Draw Table icon on the standard toolbar

❑ d. Insert Table icon on the standard toolbar

Answers b and d are correct. You can insert a table into a Web page by using the Draw Table icon on the table toolbar or the Insert Table icon on the standard toolbar. The Insert Table icon is on the standard toolbar, not the table toolbar. Therefore, answer a is incorrect. The Draw Table icon is on the table toolbar, not the standard toolbar. Therefore, answer c is incorrect. You must be aware of where each option is located and watch out for options listed for the wrong toolbar. That's why this is marked as a trick question.

Question 4

You would like to insert a row into your three-column table, but the option on the table toolbar is grayed out (unavailable). Which of the following statements would explain this?

❍ a. You haven't placed the cursor within the table.

❍ b. You haven't selected a column in the table.

❍ c. You haven't selected a row in the table.

❍ d. You haven't created a table with more than one column.

Answer c is the correct answer. If you're attempting to insert a row in a table using the Insert Rows icon from the table toolbar, you must first select a row. The only exception to this is when the table is one column wide; then, merely placing the icon in the table will allow you to insert rows. Merely selecting the table will not activate this option; you must select a row. Therefore, answer a is incorrect. Selecting a column will allow you to use the Insert Columns icon but not the Insert Rows icon. Therefore, answers b and d are incorrect.

Question 5

Which two locations in FrontPage Editor allow you to draw a table on your Web pages? [Check all correct answers]

❑ a. Menu bar

❑ b. Table toolbar

❑ c. Standard toolbar

❑ d. Table Properties dialog box

Answers a and b are correct. The menu bar and table toolbar are the two locations that allow you to draw a table. Neither the standard toolbar nor the Table Properties dialog box allows you to draw a table. Therefore, answers c and d are incorrect.

Question 6

Which of the following is not a selection on the Table Properties dialog box?

❍ a. Float

❍ b. Cell Padding

❍ c. Border Size

❍ d. Header Cell

❍ e. Use Background Image

Answer d is the correct selection. Only the Header Cell option does not appear on the Table Properties dialog box—it appears on the Cell Properties dialog box. All other options do appear on the Table Properties dialog box. Therefore, answers a, b, c, and e are incorrect.

Question 7

You're posting a table of average temperatures for the month. Lately, you've been receiving requests to post the high and low temperatures as well as the averages. You think you can do this in your existing table, but you'll need to subdivide the cells into three sections each. How can you accomplish this goal?

- ❍ a. Use the Split Cells option from the standard FrontPage Editor toolbar.
- ❍ b. Use the Split Cells option from the menu bar's Table selection.
- ❍ c. Use the Subdivide checkbox in the Table Properties section.
- ❍ d. Use the Subdivide checkbox in the menu bar.

Answer b is correct. A Split Cells option doesn't exist on the standard toolbar. Therefore, answer a is incorrect. The Split Cells options are available via the table toolbar, the menu bar's Table option, and by right-clicking on a cell on a table. There is no Subdivide option. Therefore, answers c and d are incorrect.

Question 8

You're creating an artful Web page that contains multiple pictures. You want to place small images in an evenly spaced format on your Web page. Which of the following options could help you accomplish this goal? [Check all correct answers]

- ❑ a. Create a table with a specific background image.
- ❑ b. Create a table and add specific cell background images.
- ❑ c. Add images into the table cells.
- ❑ d. Place images in the float area.

Answers b and c are correct. You can create a table and specify background images for cells and you can add images into table cells. If you add a background image to the table, you can only add one image. Therefore, answer a is incorrect. The float area is the area to the left or right of the table where text might reside; adding an image outside of the table does not guarantee that the images will be evenly spaced on the page. Therefore, answer d is incorrect.

Question 9

> You've developed a table using 1024-by-768 screen resolution. You set the table for 900 pixels wide, and you can see the entire table inside your browser's window. What's the most likely result that your clients will see when viewing your table using 640-by-480 screen resolution?
>
> ❍ a. The table will shrink to meet the size for the different resolution.
>
> ❍ b. The table will scroll off the edge of the browser window.
>
> ❍ c. The text in the table will be garbled.
>
> ❍ d. Any graphics in the table will be too small to view.

Answer b is correct. When you set a specified number of pixels, the table will adhere to that setting. In this case, the 640-by-480 resolution will not be able to display a table 900 pixels wide. When you set a table for a specified screen width as a percentage (instead of a set number of pixels), it will usually adapt to new resolution and browser settings. Because this question set the screen width in number of pixels instead of as a percentage, answer a is incorrect. The table text will not become garbled, just flow off screen. Therefore, answer c is incorrect. The graphics will not be affected by the screen resolution setting. Therefore, answer d is also incorrect.

Question 10

> What's the whitespace between the text in a cell and the cell wall defined as?
>
> ❍ a. Cell padding
>
> ❍ b. Cell border
>
> ❍ c. Cell spacing
>
> ❍ d. Cell wall ratio

Answer a is correct. Cell padding is the distance between the text and the cell wall. All other options are incorrect.

Question 11

What's the amount of space between cells in a table known as?

- ❍ a. Cell padding
- ❍ b. Cell border
- ❍ c. Cell spacing
- ❍ d. Cell wall ratio

Answer c is correct. Cell spacing is the distance between the cells in a table. All other options are incorrect.

Need To Know More?

Tauber, Daniel A. and Brenda Kienan. *Mastering Microsoft FrontPage 98*, Sybex, Alameda, CA, 1998. ISBN 0-7821-2144-6. This is a good resource and reference book for the FrontPage product. This book has a lot of step-by-step instructions that are great for the beginner; later chapters have more advanced configuration information that's excellent for the advanced user. Chapter 11, "Setting Tables," contains the information relevant to this chapter.

Microsoft TechNet. Useful information about the FrontPage 98 topics discussed in this chapter can be found by searching on keywords related to the topics.

www.builder.com. This site has tips on creating Web pages (including building tables).

www.w3c.org. This is the home of the World Wide Web Consortium. You can learn more about new HTML specifications that will affect the way browsers display HTML text.

7

Setting Up Frames

Terms you'll need to understand:

- √ Frame
- √ Target
- √ Frames page

Techniques you'll need to master:

- √ Understanding when frames should be used in a Web site
- √ Using frame templates
- √ Modifying frame designs
- √ Using hyperlinks with targets
- √ Creating content for nonframes visitors

A *frame* is a design method used in Web documents to divide the display window into two or more distinct sections. FrontPage 98 brings the power and versatility of frames to Web designers but removes many of the headaches associated with programming framed Web sites. This chapter discusses FrontPage 98's support of frames.

Frames Overview

Frames are used by Web authors to support unique or alternative designs or layouts. Typically, frames are used to display a company logo, common navigational aids, or some other type of content that needs to be present at all times within a Web site. Frames offer design options that tables and other HTML elements cannot. However, using frames is not a universal solution. Frames are not supported by all browsers; generally, only Netscape Navigator 2 and Microsoft Internet Explorer 3 browsers and their newer versions can display frame designs.

Frames divide the main browser display window into two or more distinct panes. Each pane displays a complete Web document, just as if each pane were an independent Web browser. The contents of each pane are completely independent of one another. Also, the use of frames does not limit the use of HTML elements or Web technologies within the document displayed inside the pane. Therefore, Java applets, CGI scripts, Active Server Pages (ASPs), dynamic HTML, tables, and even style sheets are all still valid components of any document displayed in a frame.

The most difficult concept to understand about frames is how they're created. Basically, a frames-based design is created using a frames page, which defines the size, shape, and number of panes, as well as a content page for each defined pane. The frames page contains the markup that changes the structure of the display area of the browser. It also contains pointers to each of the content pages and associates them with a pane.

If you find the concept of creating frames, frames pages, and content pages confusing, take some time to consult an HTML authoring book (several are listed in Chapter 2). Once you have a fairly decent grasp of frames, you may continue learning how FrontPage 98 handles them.

Using Frame Templates

Frames are created and manipulated through FrontPage Editor. FrontPage Editor uses frame templates to start the creation process. The New dialog box, shown in Figure 7.1, grants access to frame templates and is accessed through one of two menu commands:

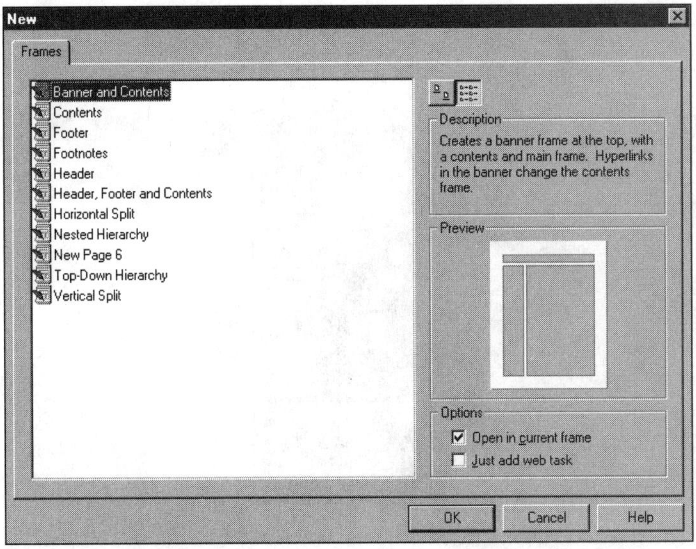

Figure 7.1 The Frames tab of the New dialog box.

- File|New; then select the Frames tab
- Frames|New Frames Page (only available when a document is being edited)

There are 10 default frame templates. Each offers a different layout of pane divisions for two, three, or four panes. These templates represent the most common layouts and divisions for framed Web sites. If a template is not offered for exactly what you want or need, you can use a similar template and modify it. Then, you can save your modifications as a template to use when creating future sites.

Once a frame template is selected, FrontPage Editor displays the frames page (see Figure 7.2). The *frames page* contains no content: It's the document used to define the structure of the panes within the browser. Notice the following five tabs at the bottom of FrontPage Editor:

- **Normal** This displays the working view of the frames page document. This tab is the primary editing interface for frames.
- **No Frames** This displays what a nonframes user will see. You can edit the information in this tab.
- **HTML** This displays the HTML used within the content pages. You can edit the information in this tab.
- **Frames Page HTML** This displays the raw HTML used to create the frames page. You can edit the information in this tab.

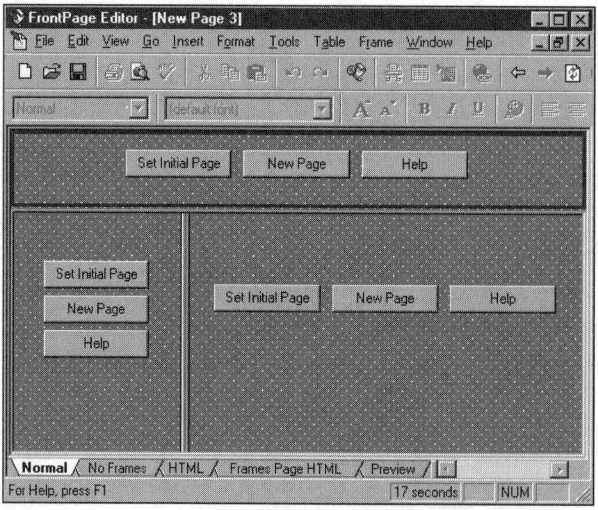

Figure 7.2 FrontPage Editor's new frames page.

- **Preview** This displays what your frame's design will actually look like in a frames-supporting browser. You cannot edit the information in this tab.

By default, no content pages are defined for a new frames page. Within each pane that does not have a defined content page, three buttons are displayed:

- **Set Initial Page** This is used to define a content page for this pane by pointing to an existing document.
- **New Page** This is used to create a new content page from scratch.
- **Help** This opens the FrontPage Help system.

You must define a content page for each pane. Otherwise, your frames page design is not only incomplete, but some browsers may not be able to display any of your content. A content page for each pane is defined by pointing to an existing page, creating a new page from scratch, or dragging and dropping a page into a pane. Content pages can be edited within a pane, or they can be edited as individual documents. Editing within a pane forces you to work within the confines of the pane.

In addition to creating the initial documents that are displayed when the frames page is loaded, you must also create all the other subsequent documents that will be displayed within a pane during a user's visit. These are typically created as standalone documents and then checked within the pane.

Once you've defined the frame layout (how to change this is discussed in the "Modifying Frames Pages" section that follows) and the initial documents, you need to save the frame design. To do this, choose either Save or Save As from the Frame menu. This opens the Save As dialog box used for frames (see Figure 7.3). This dialog box is used to save the frames page and then each initial content page. The Save As dialog box first displays a representation of the frame design, and the frames themselves are highlighted. You should provide a meaningful name for the frames page (instead of NEW_PAGE_1.HTM). Clicking on OK saves the frames page with the provided name; then the highlighted section shifts to the first pane. This allows you to save the content page for that pane with a unique name. This continues until each initial content page is saved.

Modifying Frames Pages

Frames are easily modified. Only a handful of actions are used to modify frames—moving pane borders, adding new panes, and removing panes.

You can move a pane border by clicking on the border and dragging it. Creating a new pane requires you to split an existing frame. First, select the pane to split. Next, issue the Frame|Split Frame command and then choose Split Into Columns or Split Into Rows. Now, you can move the new pane border as needed.

Removing panes allows the space used by the deleted frame to be absorbed by the most adjacent, most similar pane or panes. First, select the pane to remove. Then, issue the Frame|Delete Frame command. It's that easy.

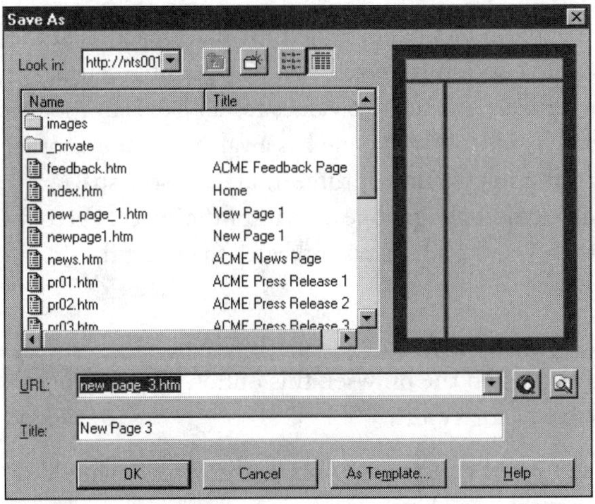

Figure 7.3 The Save As dialog box for frames.

Editing Frame Properties

Two sets of properties are associated with frames: one set for the frames page itself and the other for the pane. Both of these property sets are stored in the frames page (look at the HTML to see for yourself). To edit the frames page properties, select the Frame|Frames Page Properties command or right-click in the frame; then choose Frame Properties and click on the Frames Page button. This opens the Page Properties dialog box and selects the new Frames tab. This dialog box offers only two settings:

- **Frame Spacing** This defines the width in pixels between panes (this is also the width of the pane borders).
- **Show Borders** This checkbox instructs the browser to either display the pane edges or hide them.

The individual pane properties are manipulated in the Frame Properties dialog box (see Figure 7.4). The dialog box for a specific pane is accessed by selecting the pane and then issuing the Frame|Frame Properties command. The Frame Properties dialog box contains the following options:

- **Name** This is the name of the pane (it's also the name used to target hyperlinks to this pane).
- **Resizable In Browser** This checkbox lets you decide whether the viewer can resize the frame.
- **Show Scrollbars** This pull-down list defines whether a scrollbar is always displayed, never displayed, or displayed only when needed.
- **Width** This defines the width of a pane. When the pane reaches all the way across the browser, this option is grayed out. The possible settings are Relative, Percent, or Pixels. All relative values for all panes in the row are computed together. Therefore, if this pane has a value of 3 and another pane has a value of 1, this pane would get three-fourths of the space whereas the other pane would only get one-fourth of the space. Percent indicates a value between 1 and 100. Pixels indicates the exact fixed number of pixels.
- **Row Height** This defines the height of a pane's row. When the pane reaches all the way up and down the browser, this option is grayed out. The settings are the same as for Width.
- **Margin Width** This defines the distance in pixels the content should be offset from the left and right pane borders.

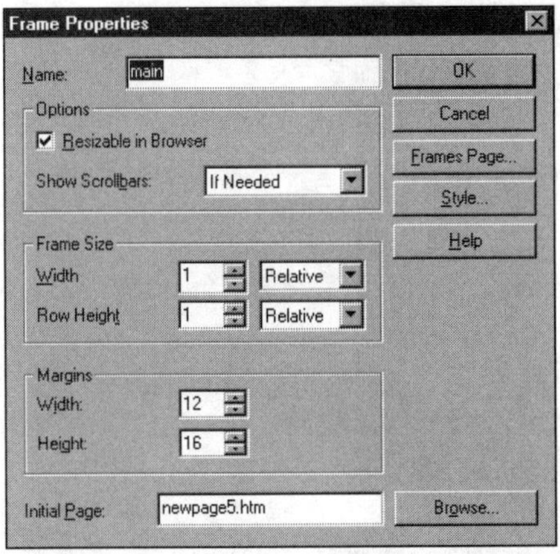

Figure 7.4 The Frame Properties dialog box.

- **Margin Height** This defines the distance in pixels the content should be offset from the top and bottom pane borders.
- **Initial Page** This displays the URL or name of the initial page for the pane.
- **Style** This button gives you quick access to the style sheet settings for the pane (see Chapter 12 for more information on style sheets).

Each pane's properties must be defined individually.

Defining Targets

Frames use names and targets to define how hyperlinks operate. Hyperlinks have an added attribute, called the *target*, that allows you to define where a resource is loaded. In other words, the target defined in a hyperlink points to the pane where the resource will be displayed. Hyperlinks are added to content pages in the same manner as any other type of Web document. However, when working with frames, you need to define one additional item—the target. Within a frameset, you can define the target using the Target Frame option located in the Edit Hyperlink dialog box (see Figure 7.5). This dialog box is accessed by adding a new hyperlink (Insert|Hyperlink) or editing an existing one (select the hyperlink and then choose Edit|Hyperlink Properties).

To change the Target Frame option, click on the button located just to the right of the Target Frame field. This reveals the Target Frame dialog box (see Figure 7.6). From this dialog box, you can select the target or destination frame by clicking on the image of the frame layout or by selecting one of the common targets from the list.

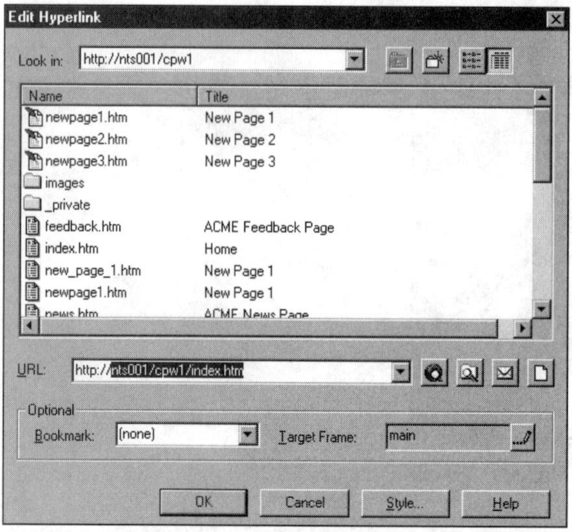

Figure 7.5 The Edit Hyperlink dialog box.

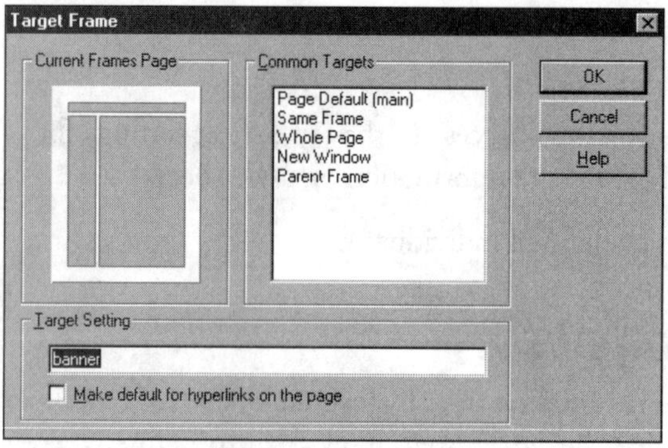

Figure 7.6 The Target Frame dialog box.

The common target settings are as follows:

- **Same Frame** Loads the resource into the same pane as the hyperlink.
- **Whole Page** Loads the resource into the entire browser window, removing the frames page and returning the browser display to "normal."
- **New Window** Loads the resource into a new, blank browser window that's separate from and independent of the original browser window.
- **Parent Frame** Loads the resource into the entire browser window, removing the frames page and returning the browser display to "normal." However, if a pane containing the hyperlink is within another frames

page, this target will load the resource into the whole pane instead of the entire browser.

- **Page Default (Main)** Loads the resource into the defined default target for all hyperlinks within the pane. A new default can be defined by selecting a pane from the graphic and then clicking on the Make Default For Hyperlinks On The Page checkbox.

For information on other hyperlink options, please see Chapter 4.

Including Information For Nonframes Users

Frames are not supported by all browsers. Actually, only a few support frames adequately enough to be worth the hassle. Although there may be a few others, the mainstream browser versions that support frames are Netscape Navigator 2 (and later) and Microsoft Internet Explorer 3 (and later). For visitors who do not have browsers that support frames or who do not wish to view frames, you can provide nonframes information.

You can have two types of nonframes information. First, you can just tell your visitors that without frames, they cannot see your content. Although this is the simplest solution, it's not the best, and it will limit your audience to frames-capable browsers only. Second, you can create a duplicate site that offers your content without the use of frames. More often than not, this second option mandates the creation of two independent Web sites.

You can create content for nonframes visitors by selecting the No Frames tab from FrontPage Editor while editing a framed document. This tab displays what nonframes users will see when they visit your site. You can see the HTML created by the nonframed section of this document on the Frames Page HTML tab. The nonframes content is contained within the **<NOFRAMES>** tags near the bottom of the frames page's HTML.

Practice Questions

Question 1

Which browsers allow you to view framed content? [Check all correct answers]

- ❑ a. Microsoft Internet Explorer 4
- ❑ b. Mosaic 1
- ❑ c. Microsoft Internet Explorer 2
- ❑ d. Netscape Navigator 3

The only browsers from this list that support frames are Internet Explorer 4 and Netscape Navigator 3. Therefore, answers a and d are correct. Mosaic 1 and Microsoft Internet Explorer 2 do not include frame support. Therefore, answers b and c are incorrect.

Question 2

Which of the following statements are true? [Check all correct answers]

- ❑ a. Each pane within a frame design can display a different content page.
- ❑ b. Frames use targeted hyperlinks to load resources into panes.
- ❑ c. A content page within a pane cannot use Java applets.
- ❑ d. Frames are supported by all browsers.

The first and second statements are true. Therefore, answers a and b are correct. A content page can contain Java applets, and frames are not supported by all browsers. Therefore, answers c and d are incorrect.

Question 3

A frame design is minimally comprised of which of the following elements? [Check all correct answers]

- ❑ a. Content page
- ❑ b. Navigation bar
- ❑ c. Frames page
- ❑ d. Background theme

A frame design only needs a content page for each pane and a frames page. Therefore, answers a and c are correct. A navigation bar and a background theme are not required within a frame design. Therefore, answers b and d are incorrect.

Question 4

How are frames typically created within FrontPage 98?

- ❍ a. With a blank page template
- ❍ b. With a frame template
- ❍ c. With the Frames wizard
- ❍ d. By importing an existing frame document

The typical method for creating frames in FrontPage 98 is to use a frame template. Therefore, answer b is correct. The blank page template cannot be used because frames typically are created using a frame template. Therefore, answer a is incorrect. There isn't a Frames wizard in FrontPage 98. Therefore, answer c is incorrect. Importing an existing frame document is a valid action, but it's not the typical way for frames to be created with FrontPage 98. Therefore, answer d is incorrect.

Question 5

When creating frames using FrontPage 98, you are limited to the layouts of panes available through the 10 default frame templates.

- ❍ a. True
- ❍ b. False

This is a false statement. Therefore, answer b is correct. You can always edit and customize frame layouts by moving pane borders, adding new panes, or removing existing panes.

Question 6

If you want to edit the HTML code that creates the document shown to a visitor using Microsoft Internet Explorer 2, which tab on FrontPage Editor must you select?

- ❍ a. Normal
- ❍ b. No Frames
- ❍ c. HTML
- ❍ d. Frames Page HTML

You need to select the Frames Page HTML tab. The visitor's browser does not support frames, so he or she will see the content within the **<NOFRAMES>** tags. The HTML for this nonframes content can be edited in this tab only. Therefore, answer d is correct. The Normal tab displays the frames page layout and its content pages. Therefore, answer a is incorrect. The No Frames tab displays the nonframes content but does not offer you direct HTML editing capabilities. This is one of the tricks to this question because the use of the **<NOFRAMES>** tag is required, which makes this a potentially confusing answer. Therefore, answer b is incorrect. The HTML tab displays the HTML code for the content pages within the layout of the frames page. This is the other trick to this question because it seems like a logical choice. Therefore, answer c is incorrect.

Question 7

When you create a frame design, you can save all the elements of the frame with a single Save/Save As command.

- ❍ a. True
- ❍ b. False

This is a true statement. Therefore, answer a is correct. Issuing a Save or a Save As command when editing a frame prompts you for file names (if they are not already defined) for each element of a frame design (the frames page and all content pages).

Question 8

How can a frames page be modified? [Check all correct answers]

- ❑ a. By moving the pane border
- ❑ b. By adding panes
- ❑ c. By changing the pane border width
- ❑ d. By deleting panes

All of these are possible modifications to a frames page. Therefore, answers a, b, c, and d are correct.

Question 9

You're using a frame layout in which your company logo and navigation bar appear in a long, thin pane across the top of the page. Which of the following pane property settings make sense for this pane? [Check all correct answers]

- ❑ a. Setting the Show Scrollbars to Never
- ❑ b. Allowing the viewer to resize the pane
- ❑ c. Setting the Row Height to an exact pixel amount
- ❑ d. Setting a large height margin

The only settings that make sense for this type of pane are to turn off scrollbars and to set the exact height of the pane. Therefore, answers a and c are correct. Allowing the viewer to resize the pane may result in difficulty of locating the navigation controls. Therefore, answer b is incorrect. Setting a large height margin forces the pane to be taller than it needs to be to accommodate the blank space. This pane should be as small as possible to allow the most viewing area for the main content. Therefore, answer d is incorrect.

Question 10

If you want a document to load into an independent browser screen when its hyperlink is activated, which of the following target definitions should you use?

- ❍ a. Same Frame
- ❍ b. Whole Page
- ❍ c. New Window
- ❍ d. Parent Frame

Loading a document into an independent browser screen requires you to use the New Window target. Therefore, answer c is correct. The Same Frame target will load the document into the pane that contains the hyperlink. Therefore, answer a is incorrect. The Whole Page target and the Parent Frame target will load the document into the entire browser window of the current browser. Therefore, answers b and d are incorrect.

Need To Know More?

Karlins, David and Stephanie Cottrell. *Teach Yourself Microsoft FrontPage 98 in a Week, Second Edition*, Sams.net Publishing, Indianapolis, IN, 1998. ISBN 1-57521-350-8. Chapter 21 discusses frames.

Lehto, Kerry A. and W. Brett Polonsky. *Official Microsoft FrontPage 98 Book*, Microsoft Press, Redmond, WA, 1997. ISBN 1-57231-629-2. Pages 160 through 170 discuss frames. Other individual topics may be found scattered throughout this book.

Matthews, Martin S. and Erik B. Poulsen. *FrontPage 98: The Complete Reference*, Osborne McGraw-Hill, Berkeley, CA, 1998. ISBN 0-07-882394-3. Chapter 8 covers frames in detail.

Stanek, William R., et al. *Microsoft FrontPage 98 Unleashed*, Sams.net Publishing, Indianapolis, IN, 1998. ISBN 1-57521-349-4. Chapter 12 discusses frames. Individual topics may be found scattered throughout this book.

Tauber, Daniel A. and Brenda Kienan. *Mastering Microsoft FrontPage 98*, Sybex, Alameda, CA, 1998. ISBN 0-7821-2144-6. Chapter 10 discusses frames. Individual topics may be found scattered throughout this book.

Microsoft TechNet. Useful information about the FrontPage 98 topics discussed in this chapter can be found by searching on keywords related to these topics.

www.microsoft.com/frontpage/. This is the official FrontPage Web site hosted by Microsoft. It offers overview information about this product.

8

Fashioning Forms

Terms you'll need to understand:

- √ Form
- √ Push button
- √ Image
- √ Validation
- √ Hidden field
- √ Confirmation
- √ WebBot
- √ Tab order

Techniques you'll need to master:

- √ Creating forms
- √ Editing form elements
- √ Using validation
- √ Creating hidden fields
- √ Providing a confirmation page

Web sites are primarily one-way communication systems. However, forms offer a versatile method for soliciting feedback, comments, and more from visitors. A *form* is just what you think it is—a document that requests information and provides input fields of some sort for the data. A Web form is not much different than a paper form. This chapter discusses the forms support included in FrontPage 98.

Forms Overview

FrontPage forms are created and managed exclusively through FrontPage Editor. FrontPage takes the guesswork out of creating HTML markup to create the form and layout you need. Form elements can be added, edited, and moved within a document in the same manner as any other HTML element. This simplifies working with forms and this ultimately allows you to focus more on the data you want to gather and less on the structure required to manipulate it.

FrontPage 98 allows you to create forms from scratch or use a wizard to create common form layouts. FrontPage also includes *WebBots*, which can manipulate form data (meaning you can save data to a file or email the data to anyone). Plus, you can have a confirmation page displayed to the user after a form is submitted.

The use of forms on a Web site is not a simple concept, especially because a form is useless without a server-side script of some type to handle the submitted data. FrontPage simplifies this and offers some prebuilt solutions. However, the more you know about forms, the more you can gain from their use. If you're confused about forms, take time to consult an HTML authoring book (several are listed in Chapter 2). Once you've grasped the concept of forms, you may continue learning about how they work within FrontPage 98.

Using The Form Page Wizard

The Form Page wizard is started from FrontPage Editor by selecting File|New and then selecting the Form Page wizard. This wizard is a multipaged guide that prompts you for needed information to construct your form. The following list provides a general walkthrough of the wizard (assuming you have selected every possible option):

1. The first page is a welcome/introductory page; click on Next.
2. The next page prompts you for a title and a URL (file name) for the form being created (see Figure 8.1).
3. The next page is used to define all the questions (visitor prompts) to be displayed by the form (see Figure 8.2). Click on the Add button.

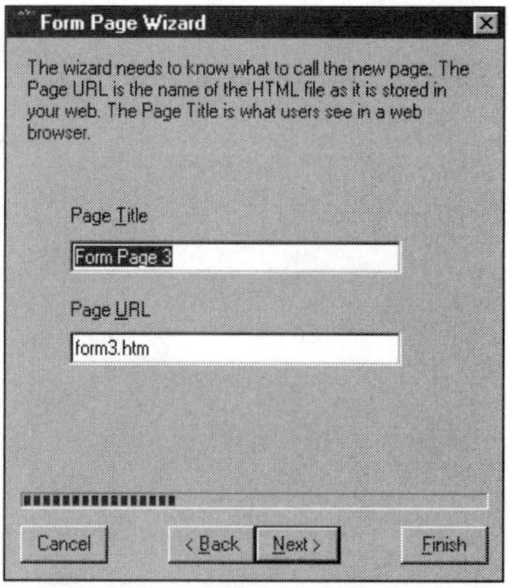

Figure 8.1 The Form Page Wizard dialog box where you are prompted for title and URL.

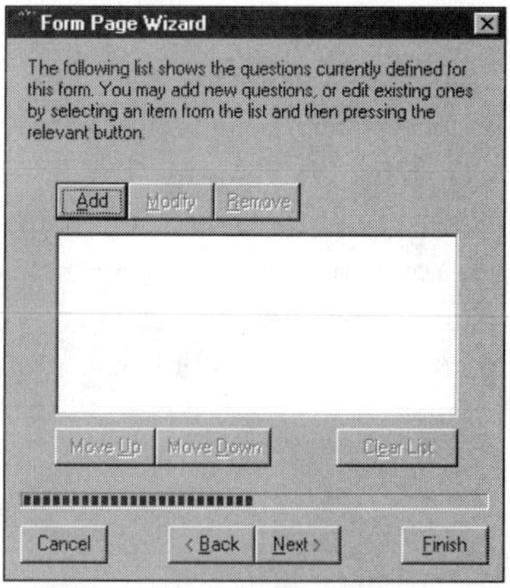

Figure 8.2 The Form Page Wizard dialog box where the questions are defined.

4. The Add button reveals a page where you can select from the 14 predefined input types (see Figure 8.3). When a type is selected, its description appears in the middle of the Form Page Wizard dialog box, and you're offered the opportunity to customize the text for the question/prompt in the lower text field.

   Note: The 14 input types include account, contact, ordering, personal, and product information, plus nonspecific inputs such as one of several, Boolean, date, number, range, string, and time.

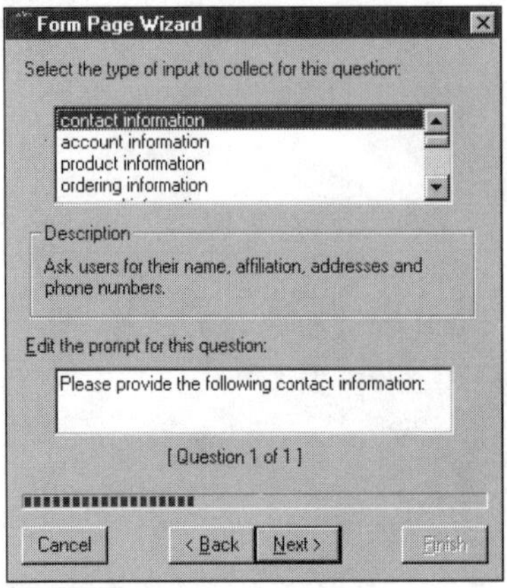

Figure 8.3 The Form Page Wizard dialog box where the input type is selected.

5. After you've selected a type and customized the question text, click on Next. You're now able to customize the input options for this input type (see Figure 8.4). The options displayed on this wizard page are different for each input type. Once you make your changes, click on the Next button. This returns you to the input type selection page, where you can add more questions using the Add button. You can also edit and remove existing questions with the Modify and Remove buttons, and you can reorder the questions using the Move Up and Move Down buttons.

6. After you've added all the questions you desire, click on Next.

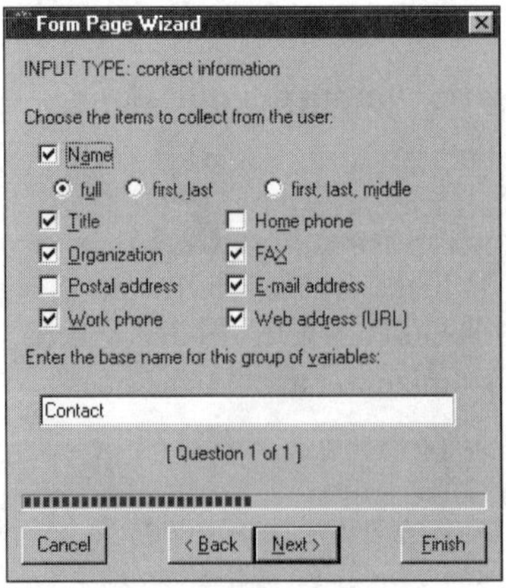

Figure 8.4 The Form Page Wizard dialog box where the input type is customized.

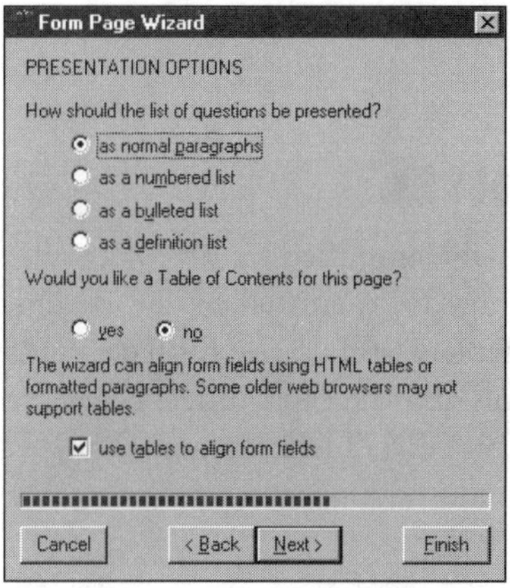

Figure 8.5 The Form Page Wizard dialog box where the presentation options are set.

7. The next wizard page, shown in Figure 8.5, allows you to select several presentation options, such as how questions are displayed (normal paragraphs, numbered list, bulleted list, or definition list), whether to display a table of contents, and whether to use tables to align fields. Click on Next.
8. The next page, shown in Figure 8.6, is where you define what is done with the acquired data. The data can be saved as an HTML file or a text file, or it can be sent to a custom CGI script. You must provide the file name if you elect to save the data. Click on Next and then click on Finish.

Your form page will be saved to the file you indicated in Step 2; then it's displayed in FrontPage Editor for you to customize and modify.

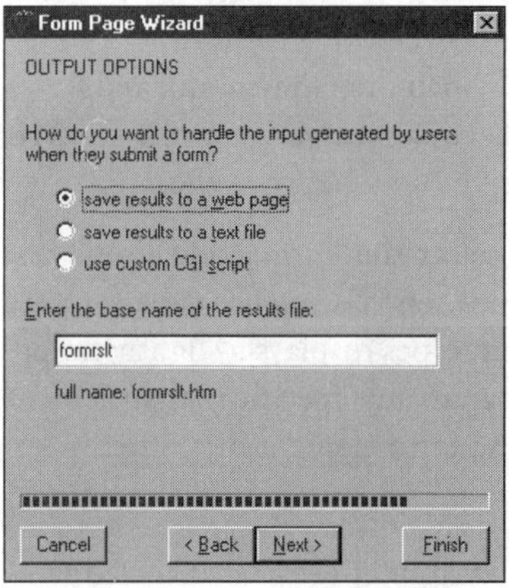

Figure 8.6 The Form Page Wizard dialog box where the output options are set.

Note: The Form Page wizard automatically adds the Submit and Reset buttons to the bottom of your form.

Editing Form Elements

Editing forms is another process that is greatly simplified by FrontPage 98. Whether you need to further customize a new form created by the wizard, have just imported a preexisting form document, or wish to add form elements to a document, FrontPage offers you the tools and the capabilities. Editing a form is really the same as editing any other type of HTML element. You can add or remove elements, move elements around on a page, or customize the elements' properties.

Adding new form elements is performed by using the Insert|Form Field command from the menu bar. Each of the eight types of form elements (one-line text box, scrolling text box, checkbox, radio button, drop-down menu, push button, image, and label) can be added from this context menu. Once an element is inserted, you can move it, customize its properties, or delete it. If you add a form element to a document that previously contained no form elements, FrontPage automatically adds the necessary HTML code for proper form markup. This includes the **<FORM>** tags as well as the Submit and Reset buttons. You can also use the Forms toolbar to add new elements. The Forms toolbar is displayed by issuing the View|Forms Toolbar command.

STUDY ALERT

An image can act as a Submit or Reset button by naming it "submit" or "reset". If you've accidentally deleted the Submit and Reset buttons or need to add them for any other reason, you can do so using the push button or image form elements.

To delete a form element, select it and issue a delete command (by pressing Delete or selecting Edit|Delete). To completely remove a form from a document, you can delete each element individually, including the Submit and Reset buttons as well as the form outline itself. Otherwise, you can view the HTML code and delete the **<FORM>** tags and everything in between them.

To edit form element properties, you must select the Form Field Properties command from the right-click pop-up menu when your mouse cursor is over the desired element. Each of the form element types displays a slightly different properties dialog box that focuses on the parameters specific to that element type. Two important common elements in the form element properties boxes are tab order and validation.

Tab order is the order in which a visitor can tab through the form elements. If you number the form elements in sequential order, visitors can jump from one element to another (in the order you define) by using the Tab key. If you do not specify the tab order, the browser automatically determines the tab order by the order in which elements are defined in the HTML code.

Validation is the establishment of limitations or rules as to what information can be submitted by a user via a form element. Validation can be as simple as requiring integers or as complex as limiting text to letters and whitespace. FrontPage generates client-side JavaScript or VBScript to handle the validation before submitting the data to the server. The type of script generated is set on the Advanced tab of the FrontPage Web Settings dialog box from FrontPage Explorer (discussed in Chapter 3). A duplicate validation script is also executed on the server to protect against Web browsers that do not support scripting.

If the data supplied by a visitor does not pass the validation test, an error message is displayed. Text box validation can be set to allow or disallow alphabetic characters, numeric characters, whitespace, or specific punctuation characters. You can also specify length requirements and numeric or text ranges (based on alphabetical order). Radio button and drop-down menu validation can require that a selection be made.

Editing Form Documents

In addition to the properties for each form element, the form page as a whole has specific properties associated with it. The Form Properties dialog box, shown in Figure 8.7, is accessed by issuing the Edit|Properties command or selecting Form Properties from the right-click pop-up menu. The selections on this dialog box include the following:

- **Send To (File name and/or Email Address)** Defines the file name and/ or email address to have the form data sent appropriately

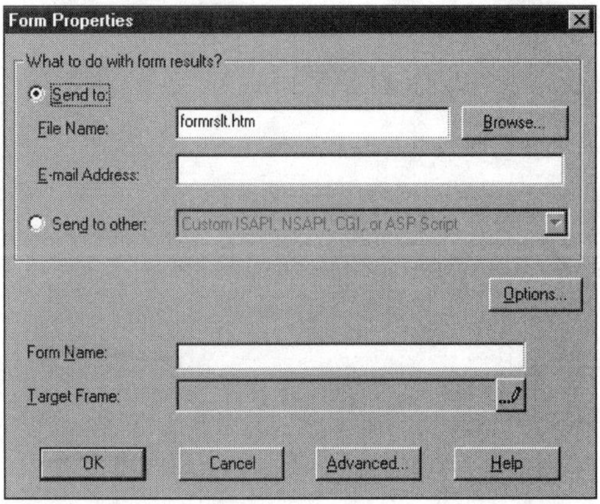

Figure 8.7 The Form Properties dialog box.

- **Send To Other** Sends the form data to a custom script or form handler
- **Form Name** Used to refer to the form by custom form handlers
- **Target Frame** Defines the pane where form results (confirmations) are displayed

When the Send To radio button is selected, clicking on the Options button reveals a four-tabbed dialog box. The Options For Saving Results Of Form dialog box allows you to set the following parameters:

- **File Results** Options include File Name, File Format, Include Field Names, and Latest Results At End. You can also define a second file for an optional format (see Figure 8.8).
- **Email Results** Here you can set the destination email address, specify its format, include field names, define a message header, and add a reply-to line (see Figure 8.9).
- **Confirmation Page** Here you can set the URL Of Confirmation Page (Optional) and the URL Of Validation Failure Page (Optional) (see Figure 8.10). The validation page is available only if validation rules have been set up in the form.
- **Saved Fields** Here you specify which form fields are written to the results file. If this area is left blank, all fields are recorded. You can also add the following information: Time, Date, Remote Computer Name, User Name, and Browser Type (see Figure 8.11).

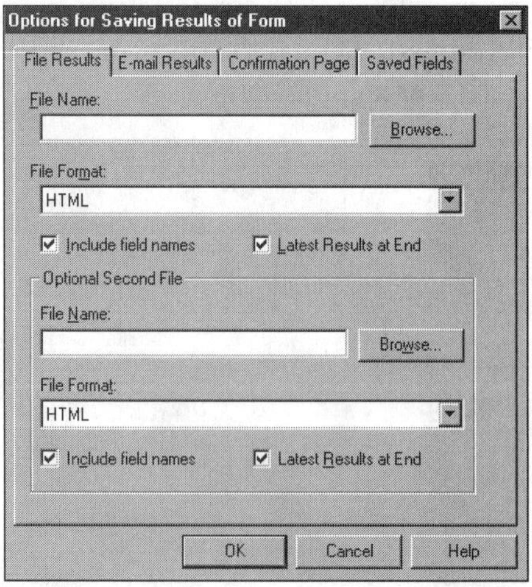

Figure 8.8 The File Results tab of the Options For Saving Results Of Form dialog box.

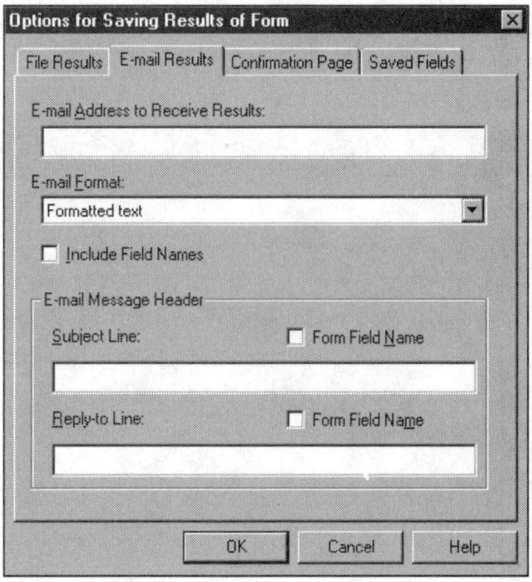

Figure 8.9 The Email Results tab of the Options For Saving Results Of Form dialog box.

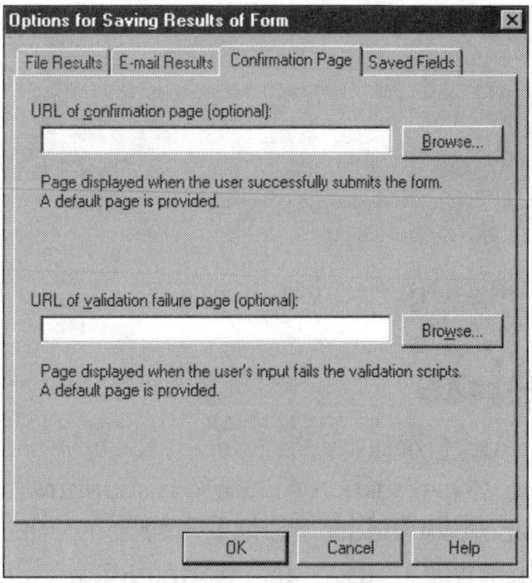

Figure 8.10 The Confirmation Page tab of the Options For Saving Results Of Form dialog box.

When the Send To Other radio button on the Form Properties dialog box (shown earlier in Figure 8.7) is selected, the Options button reveals the Options For Custom Form Handler dialog box, shown in Figure 8.12. This dialog box is used to define the Action, Method, and Encoding Type required for the custom script.

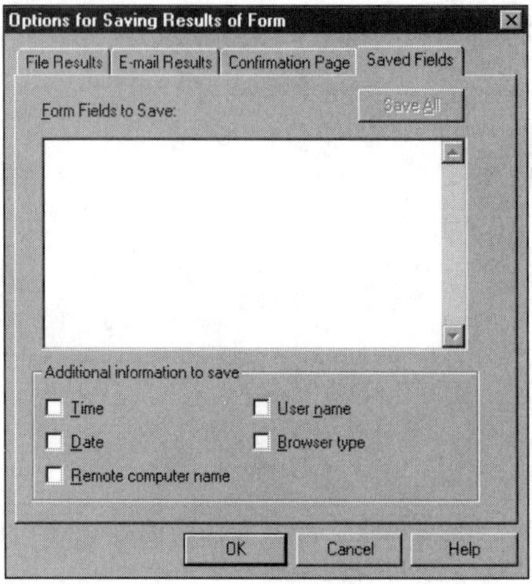

Figure 8.11 The Saved Fields tab of the Options For Saving Results Of Form dialog box.

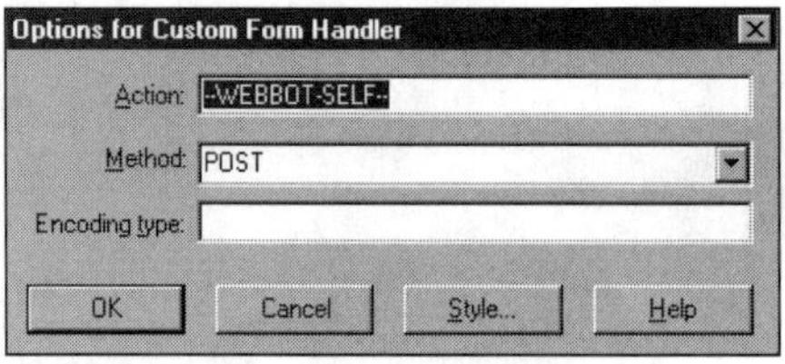

Figure 8.12 The Options For Custom Form Handler dialog box.

Using Hidden Fields

A *hidden field* is a special type of form element that isn't displayed by the browser but still transfers information back to the server when the form is submitted. FrontPage 98 includes controls and support for hidden fields. Even though the information in a hidden field is not displayed to users, its information is still contained in the data sent to your server, regardless of whether it's saved to a file, delivered in an email, or processed by a script.

Hidden fields are created through the Form Properties dialog box by clicking on the Advanced button. This reveals the Advanced Form Properties dialog box, shown in Figure 8.13. Through this interface, you can define names and their values that will be hidden from users but transmitted when the form is submitted.

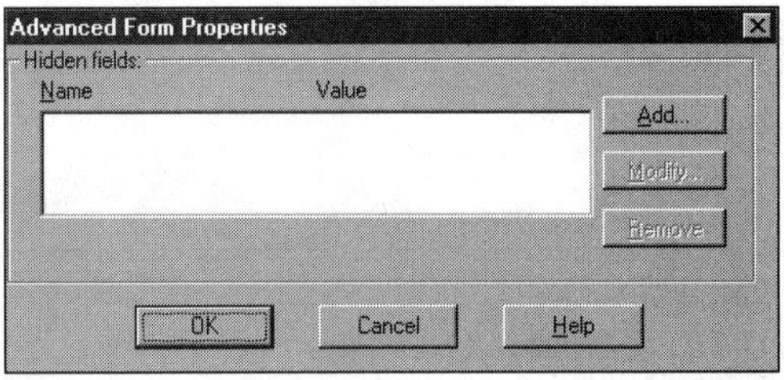

Figure 8.13 The Advanced Form Properties dialog box.

Providing Confirmation

A *confirmation* is simply a document displayed after a form is submitted. Typically, this document thanks the user for his or her input and displays some portion of the submitted data. By default, the built-in form handlers display a confirmation stating that the data was submitted as well as list all the data. You have a couple of choices for confirmation pages: You can create a static page to display or you can create a page that includes submitted form fields. The Confirmation Form template can be used as a starting point (create a new page from FrontPage Editor). The existing form fields in this template can be edited by double-clicking on them. You can also add your own confirmation fields by using the Insert|FrontPage Component command and then selecting Confirmation Field from the selection list. You'll then be prompted for the field name. Be sure to provide a valid name, because FrontPage does not automatically verify the cogency of the confirmation page with the associated form.

Once you've created a confirmation page, you must define its location on the Confirmation Page tab of the Options For Saving Results Of Form dialog box.

Practice Questions

Question 1

By which methods can form documents be added to a FrontPage Web site? [Check all correct answers]

- ❑ a. Adding form elements to an existing document
- ❑ b. Using the Form Page wizard
- ❑ c. Scanning a paper form
- ❑ d. Importing an existing form

Answers a, b, and d are correct. You can add forms to a Web site by adding form elements to an existing document, using the Form Page wizard, and importing an existing form. Scanning a paper form does not create a Web form. Therefore, answer c is incorrect.

Question 2

Which actions are offered by FrontPage to handle form data? [Check all correct answers]

- ❑ a. Save to an HTML file
- ❑ b. Send an email
- ❑ c. Save to a text file
- ❑ d. Send to custom CGI script processing

Answers a, b, c, and d are correct—all of these are actions offered by FrontPage.

Question 3

When creating a form using any method, you must always add the Submit and Reset buttons manually.

- ❍ a. True
- ❍ b. False

This is a false statement. Therefore, answer b is correct. FrontPage adds the Submit and Reset buttons automatically when a form is created.

Question 4

Which form functionality can be performed by either a push button or an image?

- ❍ a. Checkbox
- ❍ b. Drop-down list
- ❍ c. Submit button
- ❍ d. Selection list

Answer c is correct—a push button and an image can both act as a Submit button. Neither a push button nor an image can act as a checkbox, drop-down list, or a selection list. Therefore, answers a, b, and d are incorrect.

Question 5

Which parameter is used to define the sequence in which form elements are linked together?

- ❍ a. Validation
- ❍ b. Range
- ❍ c. Tab order
- ❍ d. Value name

Answer c is correct. The tab order sets the sequence in which form elements are linked, thus enabling a user to tab from one field to the next. Validation is a process by which data is checked against submission rules. Therefore, answer a is incorrect. Range is a submission rule used by validation. Therefore, answer b is incorrect. Value name is an element property not associated with sequence. Therefore, answer d is incorrect.

Question 6

Which scripting languages can be used by FrontPage to validate form data? [Check all correct answers]

- ❑ a. Perl
- ❑ b. JavaScript
- ❑ c. Java
- ❑ d. VBScript

Answers b and d are correct—only JavaScript and VBScript are used for validation.

Question 7

Which response pages can be customized through FrontPage 98? [Check all correct answers]

- ❑ a. Validation Failure
- ❑ b. Server Communication Failure
- ❑ c. Confirmation
- ❑ d. Unauthorized Access

Answers a and c are correct. Only the Validation Failure and Confirmation documents can be customized through FrontPage 98. The Server Communication Failure and Unauthorized Access documents are often customizable through the Web server itself. Therefore, answers b and d are incorrect. The trick here is to recognize where the control for a document is managed.

Question 8

By default, when form data is saved to a file, which fields are stored?

- ❍ a. All fields
- ❍ b. Only those created by the Form Page wizard
- ❍ c. Only fields with names comprised of letters
- ❍ d. None

Answer a is correct. By default, FrontPage will store all the fields of a form when saving to a file.

Question 9

Which of the following parameters can be defined for a custom form handler? [Check all correct answers]

- ❑ a. Encoding type
- ❑ b. Programming language
- ❑ c. Method
- ❑ d. Action

Answers a, c, and d are correct. A custom form handler only needs to have the encoding type, method, and action defined. These are set through the Options For Custom Form Handler dialog box. The programming language is not a parameter. Therefore, answer b is incorrect.

Question 10

Which of the following statements are true about hidden fields? [Check all correct answers]

- ❑ a. They are not displayed in a browser.
- ❑ b. They are not saved in files with other form data.
- ❑ c. They can consist of selection lists.
- ❑ d. They are passed to the server along with other form field values.

Answers a and d are correct. Hidden fields are not displayed, and they are passed to the server. Hidden fields are saved with other form data in files, and they are simple name/value combinations. Therefore, answers b and c are incorrect.

Need To Know More?

Lehto, Kerry A. and W. Brett Polonsky. *Official Microsoft FrontPage 98 Book*, Microsoft Press, Redmond, WA, 1997. ISBN 1-57231-629-2. Chapter 9 discusses forms in detail. Other individual topics related to forms may be found in scattered places elsewhere in this book.

Stanek, William R., et al. *Microsoft FrontPage 98 Unleashed*, Sams.net Publishing, Indianapolis, IN, 1998. ISBN 1-57521-349-4. Part V (Chapters 22 through 26) discusses forms.

Tauber, Daniel A. and Brenda Kienan. *Mastering Microsoft FrontPage 98*, Sybex, Alameda, CA, 1998. ISBN 0-7821-2144-6. Chapter 14 discusses forms.

Microsoft TechNet. Useful information about the FrontPage 98 topics discussed in this chapter can be found by searching on keywords related to these topics.

www.microsoft.com/frontpage/. This is the official FrontPage Web site hosted by Microsoft. It offers overview information about the FrontPage product.

9

Including Images

Terms you'll need to understand:

- √ Joint Photographic Experts Group (JPEG)
- √ Graphics Interchange Format (GIF)
- √ Audio Video Interleave (AVI)
- √ Sprite
- √ Composition
- √ Image Map
- √ Toolbox

Techniques you'll need to master:

- √ Adding images to existing Web pages
- √ Using the Image toolbar options in FrontPage Editor
- √ Creating compositions and sprites with Image Composer
- √ Using the Button wizard
- √ Making image maps

This chapter discusses how to enhance your Web pages with graphics. You'll learn how to create and edit graphics using both FrontPage Editor and Image Composer. In addition, you'll learn how to add image maps to your site to improve navigation as well as how to use the Button wizard.

Importing Images Into Web Pages

One of the best ways to enhance the appearance of your Web pages is to add graphics and animated content. The main FrontPage tools that you can use to add images and animated content to your Web site are FrontPage Editor and Image Composer.

You can use FrontPage Editor to insert images and clip art into your Web pages to improve their overall look and feel. Inserting an image is a fairly simple task performed via FrontPage Editor's menu bar. The following steps are all you need to insert an image:

1. Open FrontPage Editor.
2. Place your cursor at the location on your Web page where you want the image to appear.
3. Click on Insert on FrontPage Editor's menu bar.
4. Select Image from the resulting menu.
5. The Image dialog box appears. Click on the icon of the globe with the magnifying glass to browse for images on the Internet using your Web browser. You can click on the icon of the file folder with the magnifying glass to launch the Select File dialog box, which enables you to browse for images on your local file system or local area network.
6. Once you've found the image you want, you can insert it in the page by double-clicking on it or by selecting it and then clicking on OK.

If you want to place clip art, pictures, sounds, or videos in your Web pages, select Insert|Clip Art in FrontPage Editor, and the Microsoft Clip Gallery 3.0 dialog box opens (see Figure 9.1). The Clip Gallery allows you to choose clip art, pictures, audio, and video objects to add to your Web site.

Clip Art

You have several categories of clip art to choose from, and you can add more clip art with the Import Clips button. The Import Clips button opens the Add Clip Art To Clip Gallery dialog box, which allows you to browse your directory structure or local network for any type of image you want to add. You can click on the Insert button to add the clip art to your Web page. You can also

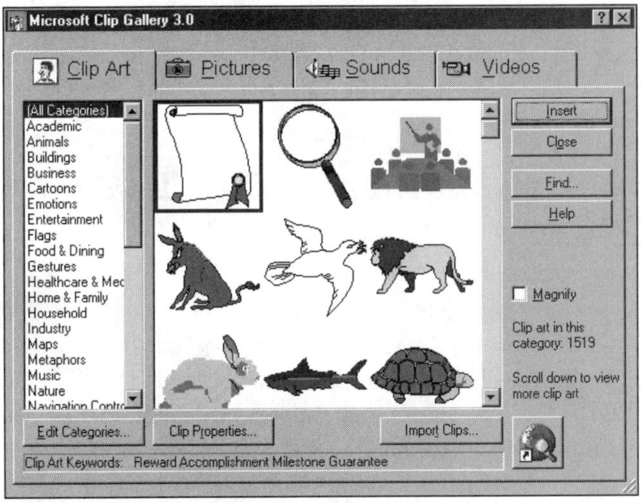

Figure 9.1 The Microsoft Clip Gallery 3.0 dialog box.

use the Find button to help you quickly locate a specific image by category, type, or keyword.

If you want to browse the Internet for clip art to use on your Web page, you can click on the icon of the globe with the magnifying glass, which launches your Web browser. By default, the Web browser opens to the Microsoft Web site's clip art section, where you can choose to download additional clip art. Only certain file types are defined as clip art; they're listed and described in Table 9.1.

Note: If you have Microsoft Office installed, the default path for the clip art files is the Clipart directory under the Microsoft Office directory.

These are the only file types that qualify as clip art; other file types are divided among the pictures, audio, and video categories. When you select Clips from

Table 9.1 Clip art file formats.

File Extension	Description
.cgm	Computer graphics metafile
.wmf	Microsoft Windows metafile
.cdr	CorelDraw's native file format
.eps	Encapsulated PostScript of Adobe
.drw	Micrografx Designer/Draw Plus format
.wpg	WordPerfect graphics metafile

the Import menu in the Clip Gallery, the clips are sorted by their file extension types, no matter which tab is selected when you start the import process. This means that all EPS files will end up under the Clip Art tab, even if they were added when the Pictures tab was selected.

Note: You can find out which type of file extensions your clips have by clicking on the Clip Properties button.

Pictures

The Pictures tab on the Microsoft Clip Gallery 3.0 dialog box allows you to add pictures to your Web site. The only real difference between the Pictures tab and the Clip Art tab is the type of files they support by default. Picture file formats and descriptions are presented in Table 9.2.

Audio Clips

You can also add an audio file to your Web page through the Sounds tab on the Microsoft Clip Gallery 3.0 dialog box. Once added, the audio file becomes the background sound for the page. By default, the audio file will be placed on a continuous background loop. If you want to modify this default behavior, you can right-click on anywhere on the page via the FrontPage Editor application

Table 9.2 Picture file formats.

File Extension	Description
.bmp	Bitmap file for Windows-based systems
.tif	Tagged Image File format (supported by most PCs and Macs)
.tiff	Another variation of the Tagged Image File format
.gif	Graphics Interchange Format (originated by CompuServe, now universally supported on the Internet)
.jpg	Joint Photographic Experts Group picture format (a universally supported, efficient picture format)
.jpeg	Another extension for the Joint Photographic Experts Group picture format
.png	Portable Network Graphics format (supports lossless, compressed images)
.pct	QuickDraw picture (one of the most commonly supported graphics formats for Macintosh computers)
.pcx	PC Paintbrush format (developed for Windows and MS-DOS computers and now widely supported by a variety of operating systems)

in Normal view and choose Page Properties. This opens the current Web page properties, and you'll be able to adjust the background sound selections. Through the Page Properties dialog box, you can modify which sound is played and how many times it will repeat.

To play audio files, you must have the appropriate drivers for that type of audio loaded on your system. Only Internet Explorer supports background audio on Web pages.

Table 9.3 describes the various audio formats you can add to your Web site.

Video

The final tab on the Microsoft Clip Gallery 3.0 dialog box is the Videos tab. Much like on the other Clip Gallery tabs, you can add files to the Clip Gallery through this interface using the Import Clip and/or the icon of the globe with the magnifying glass (which allows you to browse the Internet for video clips).

The different types of video clips are described in Table 9.4.

Table 9.3 Audio file formats.

File Extension	Description
.wav	Developed by Microsoft and supported by all Windows platforms
.mac	Macintosh sound file for Apple and other platforms
.snd	Another file extension that indicates a Macintosh sound file
.au	Sun audio files for Unix and other computers
.mid	Musical Instrument Digital Interface file (creates music on MIDI players and is universally supported by all operating systems)
.midi	Also a Musical Instrument Digital Interface file

Table 9.4 Video file formats.

File Extension	Description
.avi	Audio Video Interleave format (developed by Microsoft for Windows and Macintosh computers)
.mov	QuickTime movie format (supported by the Apple QuickTime video player, which runs on both Windows and Macintosh platforms)
.qt	Another extension for a QuickTime movie

Note: You can download the QuickTime movie player at http://quicktime.apple.com.

Editing Image Properties

After you place an image on a page, you can control that image's source, type, alternative representations, and hyperlink settings from the Image Properties dialog box. To open the Image Properties dialog box, follow these steps:

1. Open the Web page that has the image you want to configure with Microsoft FrontPage 98 Editor. Be sure to have the page open in the Normal view.
2. Select the image on the page you want to configure by single-clicking on the image on the Web page.
3. Once you've selected the image, right-click on the image and choose Image Properties from the resulting context menu. This should open the Image Properties dialog box.

General Tab

The General tab of the Image Properties dialog box is used to set an image's path, select its type, specify the image as low resolution or as text while it is being downloaded, and set it as a hyperlink.

Image Source

The first section on the General tab of the Image Properties dialog box is the Image Source text box, where you can set the path to the image file you have included (see Figure 9.2). If you click on the Browse button, the Image dialog box will appear. The Image dialog box allows you to search the local Web site, local file structure, local network, or the Internet for an image. If you click on the Edit button, either your default image editor will launch or you'll get a message telling you that no image editor is configured.

Type

The second section on the Image Properties dialog box under the General tab is the Type section. Here, you can set the image as either a GIF or JPEG file. There are also a couple of settings for each image type.

GIF images can be Interlaced and/or Transparent. Interlaced GIF images are gradually displayed by the Web browser as they are downloaded. They will be initially blurred and then slowly come into focus. If a transparent color is assigned to an image, the Transparent checkbox will be selected. You can assign

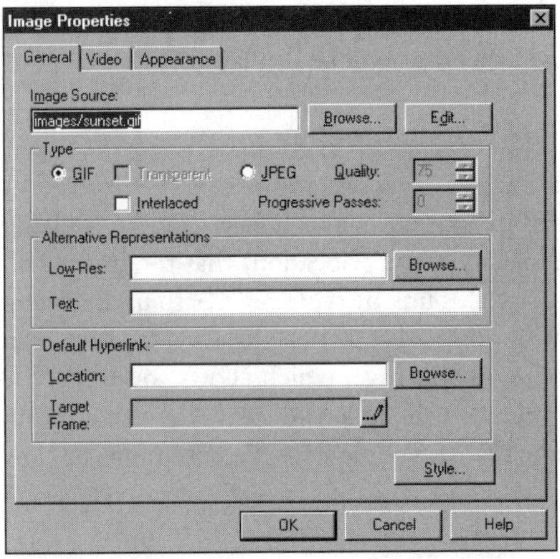

Figure 9.2 The General tab of the Image Properties dialog box.

a transparent color using the Make Transparent command on FrontPage Editor's Image toolbar (shown in Figure 9.5 later in this chapter). Clear the Transparent checkbox to turn this option off.

You can set the JPEG image's Quality and Progressive Passes options. The setting for the Quality option is an integer range from 1 to 99 (the default setting is 75). Higher-quality images will be clearer; however, the compression of images is reduced with higher quality, making the image files larger. The setting for the Progressive Passes option is similar to the GIF Interlaced setting. A progressive JPEG image will be progressively displayed in the browser window as it is downloaded. You can set the number of passes that it will take to completely display the image. If you select 0, the image will not be progressively displayed.

Alternate Representations

In the Alternate Representations section of the Image Properties dialog box's General tab, you can specify a low-resolution image and/or text to be a placeholder for the image while it's being downloaded. The Low-Res setting allows you to set a smaller image to be displayed while a larger image is being downloaded. You can add this image via the Browse button from your local Web server, file structure, or network, or from the Microsoft Clip Gallery or the Internet. You can also decide to display an alternate text-based name for your image. For instance, if your image is a picture of a sunset, you might set its alternate name to "sunset picture", which tells your client the type of image that's supposed to go there. Alternate names are useful because they're set in the page; therefore, even if the actual graphic is missing (or the client is using a text-only browser), the alternate text name will be displayed.

Default Hyperlink

Images can also be links to other images, pages, or locations on the network or the Internet. The Default Hyperlink section of the Image Properties dialog box's General tab allows you to specify a link (Location) that the image will load when it's clicked on. You can set this link by typing in a path in the dialog box or by clicking on the Browse button to discover the location for your link. You may also set the Target Frame on this page, which allows you to choose the part of a framed Web page you want the link to display. You can click on the pencil icon to select from Same Frame, Whole Page, Parent Frame, or New Window.

Video Tab

The Video tab on the Image Properties dialog box, shown in Figure 9.3, allows you to control settings for videos that you can embed in your Web page. You can use this tab to specify the video source location, whether or not the video controls are displayed in the browser, how many times the video will repeat, and how the video will start.

The video source can be any location on the local Web server, file structure, network, or the Internet. By clicking on the Browse button, you can search for the image. Otherwise, you can type the complete path to the video in the Video Source text box.

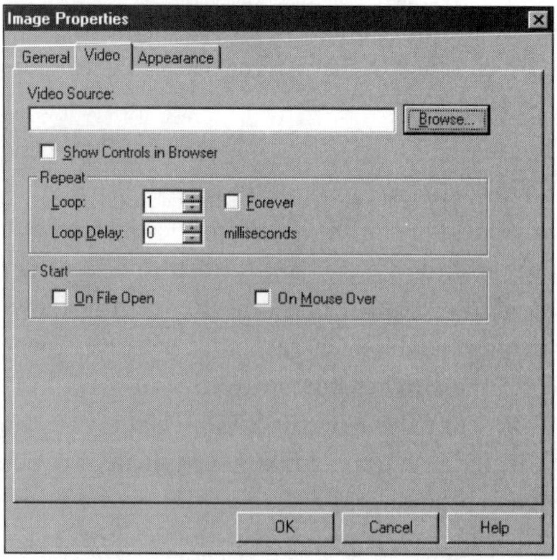

Figure 9.3 The Video tab of the Image Properties dialog box.

Just below the Video Source text box is a checkbox labeled Show Controls In Browser, which allows you to place controls on the page for the video. This enables your clients to start, stop, or replay the video.

The Repeat section allows you to specify how many times the video should be replayed in the browser window before it stops. You can configure how long the delay will be in between the replaying of the video. You can also set it to loop endlessly by clicking on the Forever checkbox.

You can set how the video will start by checking the On File Open and/or the On Mouse Over checkboxes. When the page is loaded by the client, the video will play as soon as it's downloaded if the On File Open checkbox is selected. If the On Mouse Over checkbox is selected, the video will play when the user places the mouse over the area where the video sits on the Web page.

Appearance Tab

Use the Appearance tab of the Image Properties dialog box, shown in Figure 9.4, to set and view the layout and size of an image.

The Layout section of the Appearance tab allows you to set the Alignment, Border Thickness, Horizontal Spacing, and Vertical Spacing for the image. You can choose between the types of alignments shown in Table 9.5.

The Border Thickness setting allows you to set a black border around the image by specifying its thickness. Horizontal Spacing and Vertical Spacing refer to the distance between the picture and the nearest text. The unit of measurement for all these settings is pixels. The default setting for all these options is 0.

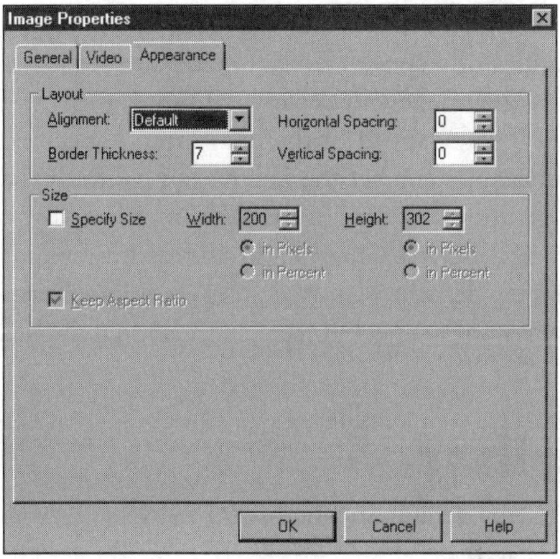

Figure 9.4 The Appearance tab of the Image Properties dialog box.

Table 9.5 Image alignment options.

Alignment	Description
Default	Sets the image to the same settings used by the Web browser
Left	Aligns the image with the left margin of the browser and wraps text to the right of the image
Right	Aligns the image with the right margin of the browser and wraps text to the left of the image
Top	Aligns the top of the image with the surrounding text
TextTop	Aligns the top of the image with the top of the tallest text in the line on which it resides
Middle	Uses the middle of the image to center it on the line
Absmiddle (Absolute Middle)	Takes into account different fonts and sets the image in the exact middle of the line
Baseline	Aligns the image with the baseline (an imaginary line that runs along the bottom of the text) of the line on which it resides
Bottom	Aligns the bottom of the image with the surrounding text
Absbottom (Absolute Bottom)	Aligns the bottom of the image with the bottom of the current line (taking into consideration different fonts)
Center	Centers the image with the surrounding text

You can set the size of the image on the Appearance tab. This allows you to make images fit within the confines of a specific area. The default setting is Keep Aspect Ratio, which means the image will occupy the same amount of space on the page as it is in size. If you want to fit the image into a specified area, click on the Specify Size checkbox and set the height and width of the image (in pixels or as a percentage of the window in the Web browser). If you choose Keep Aspect Ratio, the ratio between the height and width remains constant. Otherwise, the image may become distorted from its original proportions. For most instances, you'll want to check Keep Aspect Ratio (which is the default setting).

The Image Toolbar

The Image toolbar is not displayed, by default, in Microsoft FrontPage Editor. To view the Image toolbar, complete these steps:

1. Open FrontPage Editor.
2. Click on the View option of FrontPage Editor's menu bar.
3. Select Image Toolbar.

You should see the Image toolbar, shown in Figure 9.5, appear near the bottom of FrontPage Editor. Table 9.6 describes the options you'll find on the Image toolbar.

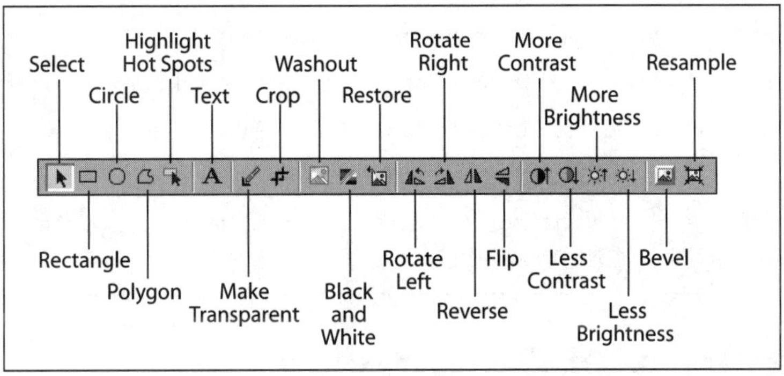

Figure 9.5 The Image toolbar.

Table 9.6 Image toolbar options.

Icon	Description
Select	Select objects
Rectangle	Insert a rectangle
Circle	Draw a circle
Polygon	Draw a polygon
Highlight Hot Spots	View hot spots (hyperlinks) on an image without viewing the image
Text	Insert text as an image or into your image
Make Transparent	Make a specific color in the selected object become the transparent color
Crop	Cut out and throw away everything that's outside of a rectangle drawn within the image
Washout	Make images less defined by removing some of the color
Black And White	Change a color image into black and white
Restore	Undo all image editing commands applied to the image

(continued)

Table 9.6 Image toolbar options *(continued)*.

Icon	Description
Rotate Left	Rotate the image to the left by 90 degrees
Rotate Right	Rotate the image to the right by 90 degrees
Reverse	Invert the image around the horizontal axis
Flip	Invert the image around the vertical axis
More Contrast	Increase the contrast between dark and light colors
Less Contrast	Decrease the contrast between dark and light colors
More Brightness	Increase the light colors and decrease the dark colors
Less Brightness	Decrease the light colors and increase the dark colors
Bevel	Add a beveled edge to the picture
Resample	After an image resizing, revise the image texture and color to fill the new space

Using Image Composer

Microsoft Image Composer is not a default component of Microsoft FrontPage 98. You have to install Image Composer separately from the main installation screen (where you first installed Microsoft FrontPage). Image Composer's main installation screen is shown in Figure 9.6.

Once you launch the installation from the main screen, the installation process is typical of most Microsoft applications. The steps for installing the product are as follows:

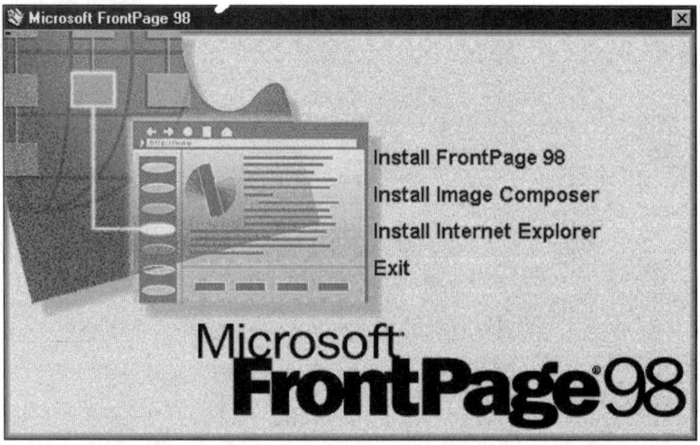

Figure 9.6 The Image Composer main installation screen.

1. From the main installation screen, choose Install Image Composer. (Note: You can get to the main installation screen by simply inserting the FrontPage 98 CD-ROM in the CD-ROM drive.)
2. Click on Continue to proceed with the installation.
3. The Name dialog box appears. Enter your name and organization. Click on OK to continue and then on OK again to confirm what you have typed.
4. Your product support identification number appears. Copy the number down so you'll have it if you ever decide to call Microsoft for product support. Click on OK to proceed.
5. The Microsoft Image Composer Setup dialog box appears. You can change the installation location or just confirm the default location (C:\Program Files\Microsoft Image Composer) by clicking on OK.
6. You'll see the end-user license agreement, which you must agree to before proceeding with the installation.
7. You must choose the type of installation you want. The three choices are Typical, Complete/Custom, and Compact Install. If you want to see all the components you're adding, choose Complete/Custom.
8. Once you've selected the installation type, you have the opportunity to select the installation group. The default group is Microsoft Image Composer under the Program Files location. Make your selection and then click on OK to proceed.
9. Finally, click on OK to conclude the Image Composer Setup program.

After the Image Composer is installed, the program is closely integrated with Microsoft FrontPage 98. You can launch Image Composer by double-clicking on an image in FrontPage Editor. You can also launch Image Composer via the Programs selection on the Start menu (choose Microsoft Image Composer and select Image Composer 1.5).

Creating And Modifying Images

Before you get started, you should know a couple of terms specific to Image Composer. The objects you create in Image Composer are called *sprites*. Sprites are maintained in files called *compositions*. You can read more about Image Composer and its features by following the Introduction To Image Composer dialog box, which is started, by default, when the application is first launched.

Once Image Composer is open, you'll see that it's a fairly sophisticated image editing program. It contains two prominently displayed toolbars with a host of options that will help you to create, modify, and apply special effects to images.

On the left side of the screen is a toolbar called the *toolbox*, and at the top of the screen is the toolbar known as simply the *toolbar* (see Figure 9.7). You can select which toolbars you see via the View|Toolbars option. Table 9.7 describes the options on the toolbar and toolbox that are unique for the Image Composer application.

> *Note: Common icons, such as Save, Print, New, and Open, have been omitted from the table because they're common to most toolbars, including the other FrontPage 98 applications.*

You can do a lot with Image Composer. Much of this you can figure out by experimenting with the product. A comprehensive description of each facet of this application is beyond the scope of this chapter. The references provided at the end of this chapter provide more detailed information on Image Composer.

Adding Animation

Image Composer can be used to add animated GIF images to your Web site. Some animated GIFs are already available with Image Composer. To see the available animated GIFs, follow these steps:

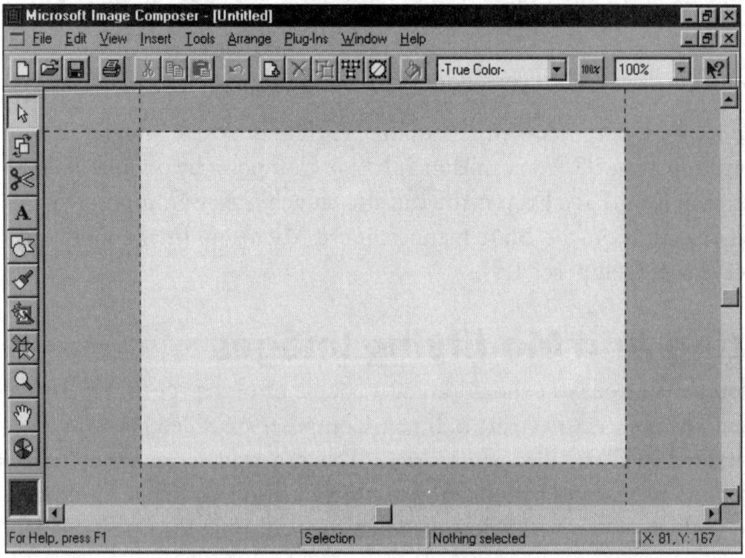

Figure 9.7 Image Composer with the toolbar and toolbox.

Table 9.7 Icons on the toolbar and toolbox of Image Composer.

Icon	Description
Insert Image File	Place an image file into the current composition
Duplicate	Duplicate an image
Select All	Select all images in the current composition
Clear Selection	Deselect objects you've selected
Color Fill	Fill in an object with a specified color
Selection	Switch to selection mode
Arrange	Move an image within a stack of images
Cutout	Cut or remove pieces of an image
Text	Create images out of text blocks
Shapes	Create images via automated shapes
Paint	Use brushes, pens, and pencils for hand drawing
Effects	Apply artistic looks, patterns, and warp enhancements to your images
Texture Transfer	Apply the properties of one image to another
Zoom	Increase or decrease magnification
Pan	Reposition items within the work area
Color Tuning	Adjust color values and brightness
Color Swatch	Choose the current color selection

1. Click on the Tools option on Image Composer's menu bar.
2. Select Microsoft GIF Animator from the resulting drop-down menu.
3. You'll see the Microsoft GIF Animator dialog box; click on the open folder icon on the toolbar in this application.
4. You should see a selection of GIF files you can open. Select one (such as IE COMINGSOON.GIF) by double-clicking on its file name.
5. The animated GIF should be loaded into Microsoft GIF Animator (see Figure 9.8).

You can use the three tabs on the Microsoft GIF Animator dialog box to control how the items appear in browser windows. You can see detailed descriptions for all of these options by clicking on the question mark on the toolbar. The question mark icon opens the help screens for Microsoft GIF Animator. There are hyperlinks that describe the options for each tab.

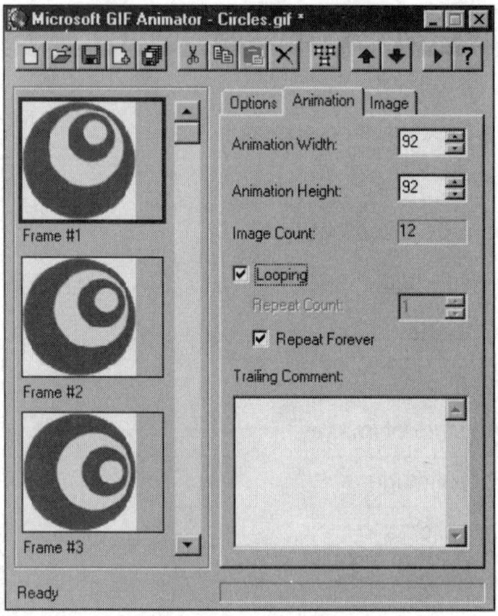

Figure 9.8 Microsoft GIF Animator.

You can actually just drag and drop GIF images into Microsoft GIF Animator to create frames. When you've added all the frames you want, you can save the image as an animated GIF. Once you have saved it, you can add it as an image via FrontPage Editor (click on Insert|Image). You can click on Browse to locate your saved image. Once it's added to the page, the image conforms to the settings you configured in Microsoft GIF Animator.

Creating Image Maps

Image maps are a great way to allow people to navigate your site. *Image maps* are essentially graphical tables of contents or indexes of your Web site or a section of your Web site. Image maps have hyperlinks that are part of the picture but not highlighted as hyperlinks. Instead, users see the image map as a single picture that has different parts that can be clicked on. A simple example of this is shown in Figure 9.9. There are four hyperlinks on this picture, even though they don't show up as highlighted hyperlinks. The images labeled Feature, Job Opportunities, and Online are hyperlinks, and so is the logo "Sony Pictures Imageworks".

You can add hyperlinks to an image via FrontPage Editor.

You can create your own image map through FrontPage Editor by importing an image and then inserting hyperlinks. The steps necessary to create an image map are as follows:

1. Locate the image you want to turn into an image map. You can create one through Image Composer or some other image editing application.

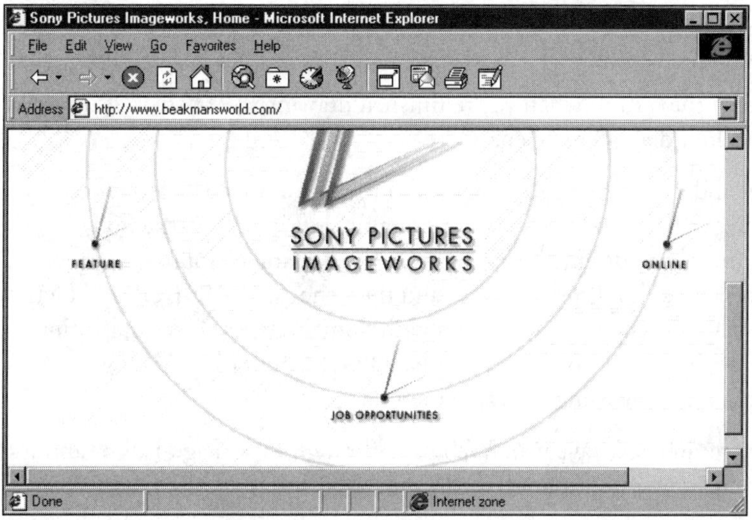

Figure 9.9 An image map example from Sony Pictures.

Save that image as a JPEG or GIF file. Or you can just locate a JPEG or GIF file that you want to use.

2. You must also decide which Web page on your site should contain the image map. You may even want to create a new Web page to hold the image map. Once you're ready, using the page and the picture (JPEG or GIF), open the Web page with FrontPage Editor.

3. Once the Web page is open inside FrontPage Explorer, click on Insert from the menu bar and select Image. The Image dialog box appears.

4. From the Image dialog box, locate and select the image you chose in Step 1 to use for your image map. Click on the globe with the magnifying glass icon to browse the Internet or click on the file with the magnifying glass icon to browse your local file structure or network. Once you've located and selected the image, click on OK to proceed.

5. After clicking on OK in the Image dialog box, you're returned to the FrontPage Editor main window with your newly inserted image.

6. Single-click on the image you just added to FrontPage Editor. (Be sure not to double-click on it; otherwise, Image Composer may open. You want to remain in the FrontPage Editor application.) The Image toolbar (see Figure 9.5 earlier in this chapter) should be displayed in FrontPage Editor.

7. Click on one of the shapes from the Image toolbar (either the circle, rectangle, or polygon). The shape you choose will be the shape of the hyperlink you create in the next step.

8. Using your mouse, draw that shape onto the image you've selected in FrontPage Editor. To draw, click on and hold the left mouse button.
9. Release the button when you're finished drawing. Next, the Create Hyperlink dialog box opens.
10. Find and select the page, image, or object you want to be referenced by the hyperlink. Click on OK. For example, in Figure 9.9, the Sony Pictures Web administrator might draw a rectangle around the check-mark labeled Job Opportunities and then choose the JOBOPS.HTML file, which lists job opportunities with Sony Pictures. You can continue to draw hyperlinks on your picture and associate specific Web pages or other objects by using the same method.

Once you're finished, save your Web page through FrontPage Editor and test it with your browser by connecting to your Web site.

You can only use GIF or JPEG images for your image map.

The Button Wizard

Another way you can represent a hyperlink is by using a button. Buttons are very common on Web sites. Literally any image can become a hyperlink, and the term *button* is just a word used to describe a certain type of image that's used specifically as a hyperlink. Because buttons are so popular, Image Composer actually has a Button wizard so that you can quickly and easily create a variety of buttons. To create a button with the Button wizard, follow these steps:

1. Open Image Composer.
2. On Image Composer's menu bar, select Insert and then choose Button. The Button Wizard dialog box opens (see Figure 9.10).

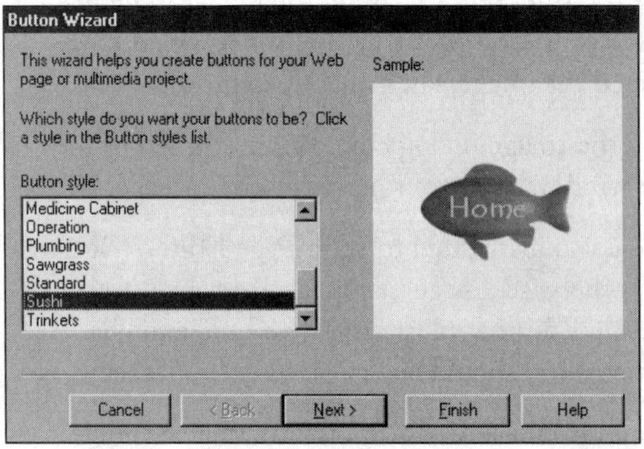

Figure 9.10 The Button wizard in Image Composer.

3. Select a button style from the Button Style selection box. You'll see a preview of each style as you click on the different titles.
4. Click on the Next button to proceed.
5. Enter the number of buttons of this particular style that you want to create. You'll have the opportunity to customize each button as the wizard proceeds.
6. You can enter text to appear in each button. You can also choose to embed an image within the button. This gives you the opportunity to select a GIF or JPEG file (which must be smaller than 320 pixels high and 240 pixels wide) to place inside the button. Otherwise, you'll just have text within the button.
7. If you've decided to create more than one button, repeat Step 6 until all your buttons are finished. Click on the Next button to proceed.
8. The next screen allows you to set the buttons for "best fit", which means they'll conform to the size of the embedded text and pictures you inserted. You can also set all the buttons to be the same size by clicking on the Same Size For All Buttons selection. If you set them all to the same size, you can use Size Preview to see how the buttons will look.
9. Click on the Next button to advance to the final screen of the Button wizard and then click on Finish to drop the button(s) onto your new composition.

You can paste these buttons as images into your Web pages and turn them into hyperlinks for your site.

Practice Questions

Question 1

You want to create an image map. Which of the following applications allows you to add hyperlinks to your image?

❍ a. Image Composer

❍ b. FrontPage Editor

❍ c. FrontPage Explorer

❍ d. Paint

The correct answer is b. FrontPage Editor allows you to add hyperlinks to an image via its Image toolbar. You can create images with Image Composer, but you don't use it to add hyperlinks to an image. Therefore, answer a is incorrect. FrontPage Explorer and Paint cannot be used to add hyperlinks to a picture either. Therefore, answers c and d are also incorrect.

Question 2

If you've installed all the components on the Microsoft FrontPage CD-ROM, what happens when you double-click on an image inside the Microsoft FrontPage Editor window?

❍ a. The Image toolbar appears.

❍ b. FrontPage Explorer opens.

❍ c. Image Composer opens.

❍ d. MS Paint opens.

Answer c is correct. If you install all the components from the MS FrontPage CD-ROM, Image Composer will be added. Once Image Composer is added, it is tightly integrated into the FrontPage system, and when you double-click on an image in FrontPage Editor, the image is opened inside of Image Composer. The Image toolbar is part of FrontPage Editor and does not open when an image is double-clicked on. Therefore, answer a is incorrect. FrontPage Explorer and MS Paint are not configured as image editors through FrontPage, by default. Therefore, answers b and d are also incorrect.

Question 3

> Which of the following image types can you add to a Web page via the Microsoft Clip Gallery 3.0 dialog box? [Check all correct answers]
>
> ❑ a. Clip art
>
> ❑ b. Pictures
>
> ❑ c. Audio clips
>
> ❑ d. Video
>
> ❑ e. Streaming

Answers a, b, c, and d are correct. The Microsoft Clip Gallery 3.0 has four tabs: Clip Art, Pictures, Sounds, and Videos. There is no option for streaming. Therefore, answer e is incorrect.

Question 4

> Which of the following is a Microsoft video format?
>
> ❍ a. AVI
>
> ❍ b. GIF
>
> ❍ c. JPEG
>
> ❍ d. MIDI

Answer a is correct. Files with the .avi extension are Audio Video Interleaves—a method for integrating audio and video from Microsoft. GIF and JPEG are graphics standards. Therefore, answers b and c are incorrect. MIDI stands for Musical Instrument Digital Interface and is a method for creating music via a musical instrument command language. Therefore, answer d is incorrect.

Question 5

You've been asked to create an image map for your company linking all the departments to a central directory. The image map is supposed to contain an image with hyperlinks to the various departments. Each department has its own unique Web page, and an overview of all the departments exists on the page DEPTOVER.HTM.

You've been asked to accomplish these specific tasks:

a. Create a map that includes all departments.

b. Place the image on a Web page as an image map.

c. Link each department's hyperlink to a page specific to the represented department.

d. Create a central link that overviews all the departments.

You take a digital picture of the building directory, which includes a map of the building (every department office is represented). You import the image into Image Composer and label each department on the directory map. Then, you import the image into FrontPage Editor and insert rectangular hyperlinks for each department and map them to DEPTOVER.HTM.

Which of the following goals have you accomplished? [Check all correct answers]

- ❑ a. Create a map that includes all departments.
- ❑ b. Place the image on a Web page as an image map.
- ❑ c. Link each department's hyperlink to a page specific to the represented department.
- ❑ d. Create a central link that overviews all the departments.

Answers a and b are the only correct selections. Even though importing the image to a single Web page was not specifically mentioned, the solution did say that you drew rectangular links over the image. In order to draw rectangular hyperlinks on the image, it must be imported into a Web page with FrontPage Editor. Therefore, answer b was actually accomplished. All the links were mapped to DEPTOVER.HTM, which is not specific to each department and fails to meet answer c. A central link was not created or mentioned in the solution. Therefore, answer d was not met either.

Question 6

Which of the following is identified as clip art in the Microsoft Clip Art Gallery?

- ❍ a. JPEG
- ❍ b. BMP
- ❍ c. GIF
- ❍ d. SND
- ❍ e. WMF

Answer e is correct. WMF is a Windows metafile and the only item that's identified as clip art in the Microsoft Clip Art Gallery. JPEG, BMP, and GIF are all identified as picture file formats. Therefore, answers a, b, and c are incorrect. SND is a Macintosh sound file. Therefore, answer d is incorrect.

Question 7

Which of the following cannot be used as an image map? [Check all correct answers]

- ❑ a. GIF
- ❑ b. JPEG
- ❑ c. AVI
- ❑ d. .JPG

Answer c is correct. The only item in the selection that cannot be used as an image map is an AVI (Audio Video Interleave). GIF and JPEG images can be used as image maps (the .JPG extension indicates JPEG). Therefore, answers a, b, and d are incorrect.

Question 8

Several users have called to complain that they cannot hear the background sound on your home page; however, some of their friends are able to get it. What are some possible reasons for this? [Check all correct answers]

- ❑ a. The users who cannot hear the background music are not using Internet Explorer.
- ❑ b. The users who cannot hear the background music have their speakers' volume turned off.
- ❑ c. The users who cannot hear the background music do not have sound cards.
- ❑ d. The users who cannot hear the background music are restricted from hearing it via the FrontPage server.

Answers a, b, and c are correct. If the users do not have Internet Explorer and a sound card, they will not be able to hear the background music. In addition, having the volume turned all the way down is something that should be checked. However, because FrontPage cannot restrict the background music to specific individuals, answer d is incorrect.

Question 9

Which of the following formats is not a Windows-based or Microsoft operating system-based format?

- ❍ a. BMP
- ❍ b. AVI
- ❍ c. WMF
- ❍ d. WAV
- ❍ e. AU

Answer e is correct. AU is an audio file associated with Sun and Unix (even though AU players exist for Windows clients). The other specifications are closely related to Microsoft and Windows. BMP is a Windows bitmap. Therefore, answer a is incorrect. AVI is the Microsoft Audio Video Interleave. Therefore, answer b is incorrect. WMF is the Windows metafile. Therefore, answer c is incorrect. Finally, answer d is incorrect because WAV is a Microsoft-specific audio file.

Question 10

You've been asked to create an image map for your company linking all the departments to a central directory. The image map is supposed to contain an image with hyperlinks to the various departments. Each department has its own unique Web page, and an overview of all departments exists on the page DEPTOVER.HTM.

You've been asked to accomplish these specific items:

a. Create a map that includes all departments.

b. Place the image on a Web page as an image map.

c. Link each department's hyperlink to a page specific to the represented department.

d. Create a central link that overviews all the departments.

You take a digital picture of the building directory, which includes a map of the building (every department office is represented). You import the image into Image Composer and label each department on the directory map. In addition, you place a tiny button labeled Overview in the middle of the directory. Then, you import the image into FrontPage Editor and insert rectangular hyperlinks for each department and map them to the specific Web pages that describe each department. You map the Overview button to the DEPTOVER.HTM Web page. You save the entire image map and supporting files to your Web site and create appropriate links from the home page.

Which of the following goals have you accomplished? [Check all correct answers]

- ❏ a. Create a map that includes all departments.
- ❏ b. Place the image on the Web page as an image map.
- ❏ c. Link each department's hyperlink to a page specific to the represented department.
- ❏ d. Create a central link that overviews all the departments.

All options were met and all answers are correct. Item a was met when you took the digital picture of the building directory, which included a map of the building that represents every department office. Therefore, answer a is correct. When you placed a tiny button labeled Overview in the middle of the directory and linked it to DEPTOVER.HTM, item d was accomplished. Therefore, answer d is correct. When the image was imported into FrontPage

Editor and rectangular hyperlinks for each department were inserted in department-specific Web pages, items b and c were accomplished. Therefore, answer b and c are correct. Because of the complexity of this question, and the careful reading required, we've marked this as a trick question.

Need To Know More?

Tauber, Daniel A. and Brenda Kienan. *Mastering Microsoft FrontPage 98*, Sybex, Alameda, CA, 1998. ISBN 0-7821-2144-6. This is a good resource and reference book for the product. It has a lot of step-by-step instructions, which are great for the beginner; later chapters have more advanced configuration information, which is excellent for the more advanced user. Chapter 9 contains the information relevant to this chapter. Also, Appendix A contains information on installing Image Composer.

Microsoft TechNet (July 98 and later) contains several articles that pertain to FrontPage Editor. Search on "Microsoft Image Composer" to see articles relating to that topic. Also, try "Image toolbar" to see more information on that item.

www.w3c.org. This is the home of the World Wide Web Consortium. You can learn more about new HTML specifications that affect the way browsers will display HTML graphics.

www.landfield.com/faqs/graphics/fileformats-faq/part3/preamble.html. This is a Web site that contains information about graphics file formats.

http://pascal.fjfi.cvut.cz/~patera/pictview/import.html. This is another Web site that contains lists of graphics file extensions and their descriptions.

www.microsoft.com/frontpage/. This is Microsoft's official FrontPage site and is a complete resource for FrontPage 98.

10

FrontPage Components And Client Compatibility

Terms you'll need to understand:

- √ FrontPage components
- √ Active Elements
- √ User registration
- √ Browser compatibility

Techniques you'll need to master:

- √ Understanding the FrontPage components
- √ Understanding the FrontPage Active Elements and other building blocks
- √ Understanding how to create a registration form for a Web site
- √ Understanding which FrontPage components and features are supported by Web browsers
- √ Previewing Web documents in Web browsers

FrontPage 98 offers several add-in components to enhance your Web documents. These range from hit counters, to marquees, to timestamps. Each of these elements is covered in detail in this chapter.

FrontPage Components

Components are add-in elements that offer specialty functions to a Web document. The use of a FrontPage component relieves you of the burden of programming the special effects on your own. The Insert|FrontPage Component command issued within FrontPage Editor reveals a dialog box that lists the nine available components (see Figure 10.1). Each of these components is discussed in the following sections.

You may notice that when you insert a FrontPage component, the HTML that results is often similar to <!—**webbot bot="action" xxxx="value"**—>. This is the shorthand notation used by FrontPage during document design. Once you save your changes, these items are replaced with the full HTML markup, scripting code, or applet call to perform the defined tasks.

Comment

A *comment* is a section of text that's not displayed in the Web page itself. Basically, comments are used to store information about the Web document and the HTML used, without altering the document's display. To insert a comment, place your cursor near the area where you want the comment to be placed; then issue the Insert|FrontPage Component command and select Comment from the resulting menu. A text field dialog box appears in which you can type your comment. When this is completed, FrontPage adds the comment to the HTML of the Web document by placing the text between the <!— and —> markers. You can check this out for yourself by viewing the HTML tab.

> *Note: The comment will appear in the display on the Normal tab, but it will be properly hidden on the Preview tab and when viewed through a Web browser.*

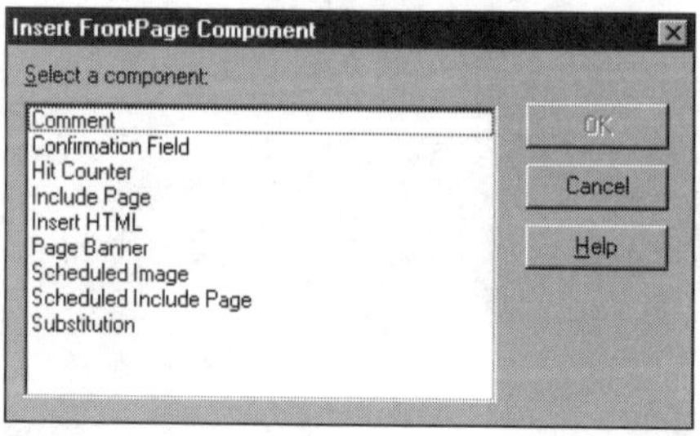

Figure 10.1 The Insert FrontPage Component dialog box.

Confirmation Field

A *confirmation field* is an element to be used in a confirmation page only. This element places information from a form value into a Web document so that it's redisplayed to the user. For example, a confirmation field can be used to display the name and email address of the user after he or she submits a feedback form. As discussed in Chapter 8, when you add a confirmation field, you must provide the exact value name. If the value name does not match a name from the submitted form, the confirmation field will not function. FrontPage does not include a validation mechanism to ensure that you properly match the confirmation fields in a confirmation page with the values from a form.

Hit Counter

A *hit counter* is an odometer that counts the number of times a document is delivered by the Web server to a browser (called a *hit*). FrontPage offers hit counters using one of five predesigned number graphics or allows you to use a custom number graphic. The Hit Counter Properties dialog box, shown in Figure 10.2, displays these graphics selections. You can specify the number of digits to display (5 is the default setting) and whether to reset the counter (to 0 or some other number). Once you make your selections, FrontPage Editor will display "[Hit Counter]" in the location where the counter will appear when viewed through a Web browser.

Include Page

The *include page* component is a trick to save time. Basically, it takes one document and inserts it into another document. Although this may not seem exciting

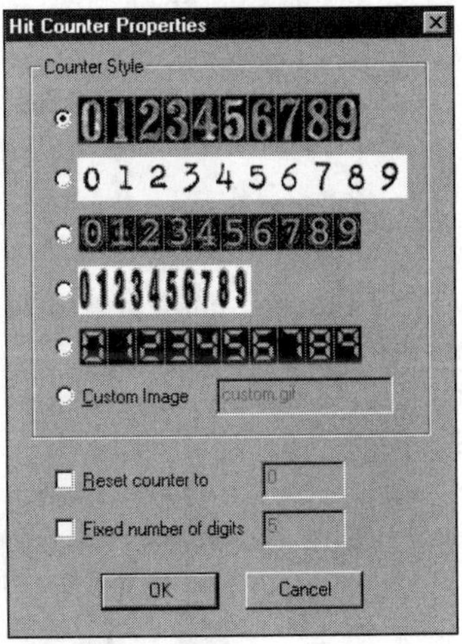

Figure 10.2 The Hit Counter Properties dialog box.

in and of itself, this little trick can save you tons of update time down the road. By creating a header or footer section (logo, name, URL, email, copyright, date, and so on) and including this in every document on your Web site, you need to edit only the included page instead of the dozens (or hundreds) of pages on the site. The included page does not need to be a full HTML document—it only has to contain the sections of HTML markup needed to create the desired content. When you select the Include Page option, you'll be prompted for the URL for that page. This can either be a local, relative URL or an absolute URL. Typically, inserted pages are pulled from the _private folder to prevent users from viewing the inserted pages outside of their parent documents.

Insert HTML

The *insert HTML* component allows you to type in HTML markup directly. The code inserted using this command is not checked, verified, or modified by FrontPage but is simply taken as-is. An HTML Markup dialog box appears where you can type in your code.

> *Note: To have your HTML verified as you type, use the HTML Tab View in FrontPage Editor.*

Page Banner

The *page banner* component is used to create a banner without using themes. A *banner* is a display element that stretches across the entire display area of the document. It can be a text or a graphics banner. By default, the text displayed is the page title (as defined within the <TITLE> tags). However, the banner text is not directly defined from the title; instead, the text displayed in the banner is the name defined on FrontPage Explorer's Navigation View. The graphic displayed by an image banner is set by the theme in use. If themes are not used, the banner reverts to a text banner.

Scheduled Image

The *scheduled image* component allows you to insert an image that will be displayed only for a specified time frame. Scheduled images are often used for drawing attention to new items, highlighting changes, or just altering the normal presence of images. The Scheduled Image Properties dialog box, shown in Figure 10.3, allows you to define the temporary image, the starting and ending date and time, plus a graphic to display in its place before and after the specified time frame.

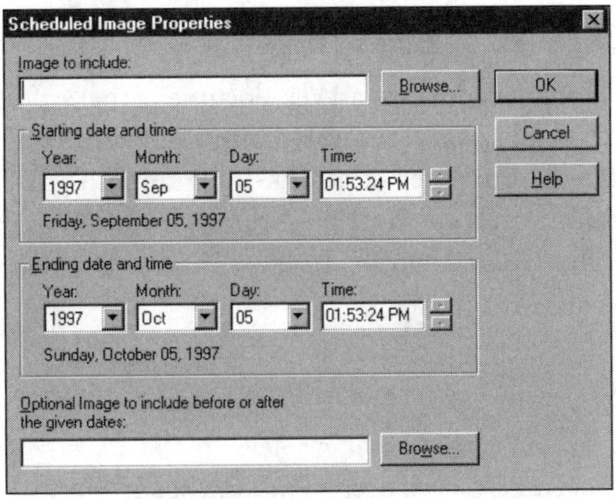

Figure 10.3 The Scheduled Image Properties dialog box.

Scheduled Include Page

A *scheduled include page* is nothing more than a combination of the scheduling feature and the include page component. This component is often used for one-time specials, displaying changed information, or showing some other type of transient text or content. The dialog box for a scheduled include page is the same as the Scheduled Image Properties dialog box. You define the page to include, the start and end times, and an alternate page to display before and after the specified time period.

Substitution

The *substitution* component allows you to include specialty information from variables defined by the Web server, the document itself, and the user's browser. The Substitution Component Properties dialog box is just a pull-down list where all known variables are listed. When you select a variable, FrontPage inserts a command to show that information in the displayed document. Here are several predefined variables:

- **Author** The name of the author who created the document
- **Modified By** The name of the author who edited the document most recently
- **Description** The title of the page
- **Page URL** The URL of the document within the Web

Note: Other variables can be defined on the FrontPage Web Settings dialog box's Parameters tab. These were discussed in Chapter 3.

FrontPage Active Elements

FrontPage *Active Elements* are elements added to a Web document that offer interaction or customization. Active Elements are created using ActiveX, Java, CGI scripts, and more. Fortunately, FrontPage takes all the programming difficulty out of using these high-tech features. FrontPage Editor's Insert|Active Elements fly-out menu offers six active elements. These are discussed in the following sections.

Hover Button

A *hover button* is an animated button created using a Java applet. A hover button activates when the mouse cursor is placed over it and/or when it's clicked on. It can change color, change size, change images, or display an effect. After you insert this Active Element, the Hover Button dialog box is displayed, as shown in Figure 10.4. The text, hyperlink, initial color, effect, and initial size are defined. The Custom button reveals another dialog box, where sounds and images can be defined.

Banner Ad Manager

The *banner ad manager* allows you to display multiple images in timed succession. You've seen this on many commercial Web sites. After you insert this item, the Banner Ad Manager dialog box is displayed (see Figure 10.5). In this dialog box, you define the size of the banner display (all images must be the same size), the transition effect, the time in seconds between transitions, the URL for the banner link, and the graphics to display. In the list of images, you can define the order in which the banners are displayed. The banner display will loop indefinitely. Unlike in other banner systems, only a single URL is used for the hyperlink created by the banner ad manager.

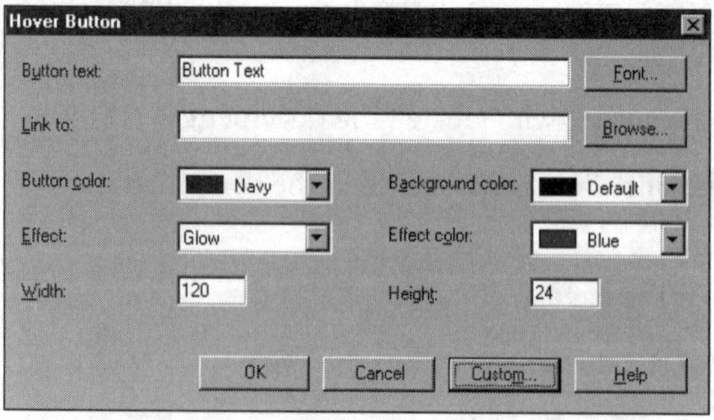

Figure 10.4 The Hover Button dialog box.

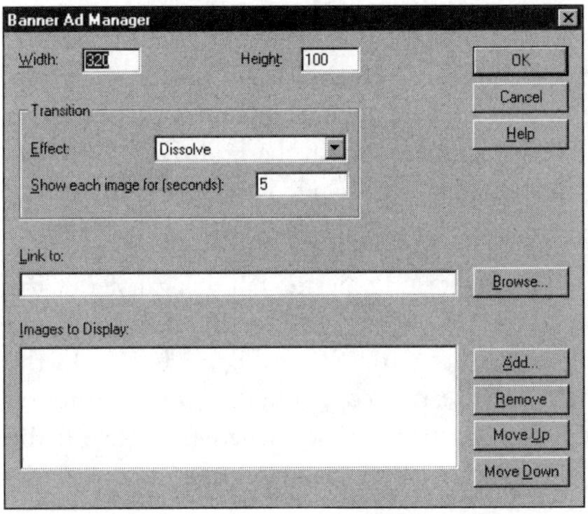

Figure 10.5 The Banner Ad Manager dialog box.

Marquee

A *marquee* is scrolling text. Marquees are often used to display stock information, provide news clips, or just attract attention to a product or service. The Marquee Properties dialog box, shown in Figure 10.6, appears when you insert this Active Element. From this dialog box, you define the text to be scrolled, as well as its direction, speed, size, and repeat times.

> *Note: Because they are implemented with proprietary HTML markup, marquees are currently only supported by Internet Explorer.*

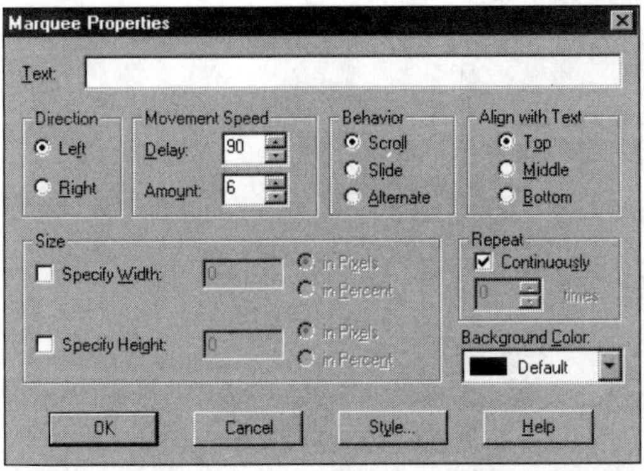

Figure 10.6 The Marquee Properties dialog box.

Search Form

FrontPage offers a simple way to add search capabilities to your Web site via the *search form* Active Element. This tool creates a simple form that interacts with a server-side WebBot. Every document within the FrontPage Web (excluding those pages in the _private folder) are included in the search.

The Search Form Properties dialog box appears when this Active Element is inserted. From this dialog box's Search Form Properties tab, you can define the search field label, the width of the search field (measured in characters), and the titles for the Start Search and Reset buttons (see Figure 10.7). On the Search Results tab, you can define the search scope (use All for the entire site or provide the name of a discussion group folder) and whether to include the closeness of match, file date, and file size on the response page.

Hit Counter

This is the same element (or component) discussed in the "FrontPage Components" section earlier in this chapter.

Video

The *video* Active Element links a video file into a Web document. This Active Element creates the proper link to the movie so that it's included in the document. Once it's inserted, you can edit the properties of the video by selecting Image Properties from the right-click pop-up menu. From the Image Properties dialog box's Video tab, shown in Figure 10.8, you can determine whether

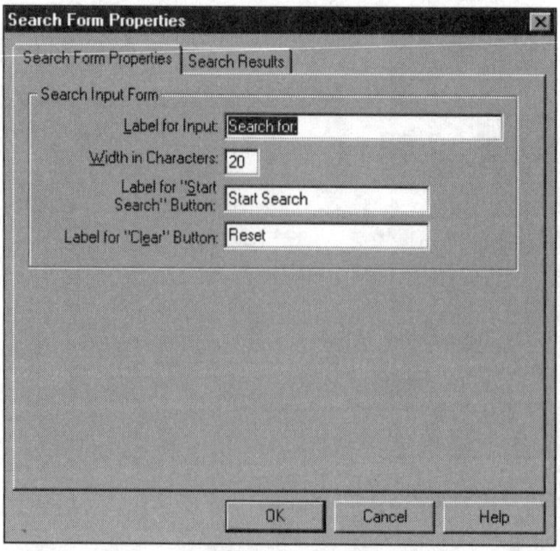

Figure 10.7 The Search Form Properties tab of the Search Form Properties dialog box.

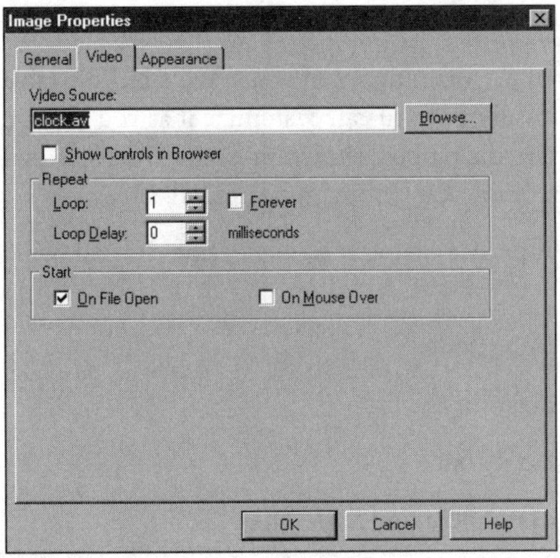

Figure 10.8 The Image Properties dialog box's Video tab.

to show video controls, how many times to play the clip, how long to wait between plays, and when to start the player (On File Open or On Mouse Over).

Other FrontPage Building Blocks

The FrontPage components and Active Elements are not the only tools available for adding special features, functions, and activities to a Web document or site. Other FrontPage building blocks are detailed in the following sections.

Timestamp

A *timestamp* is information added to a Web document that indicates the creation or modification date. The Insert|Timestamp command reveals the Timestamp Properties dialog box, shown in Figure 10.9. From this dialog box, you can set the timestamp to display creation or modification date information, as well as set the format for the date and time.

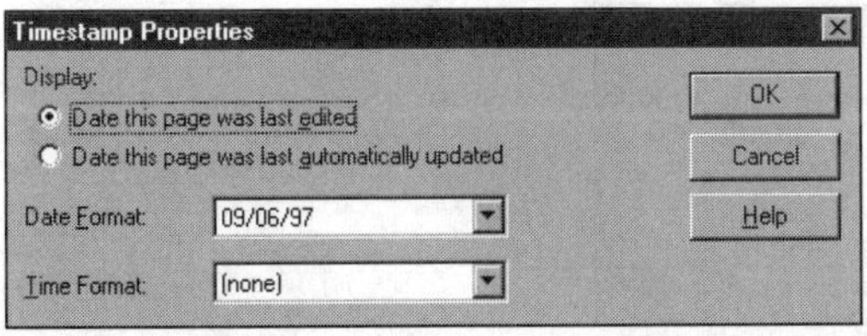

Figure 10.9 The Timestamp Properties dialog box.

Table Of Contents

A *table of contents* is a summary of the main topics of your Web site. The table of contents is generated automatically, but you can customize it as you choose. The Table Of Contents Properties dialog box, shown in Figure 10.10, is displayed when you issue the Insert|Table Of Contents command.

From the Table Of Contents Properties dialog box, you define the following items:

- The starting URL for the Web site
- The size of the first-level entries in the list
- Whether to show each page only once
- Whether to show pages with no incoming hyperlinks
- Whether to recompute the table of contents when pages are edited

Navigation Bar

A *navigation bar* is a collection of hyperlinks used to jump from the current page to another document within the Web site. The individual links of the navigation bar can be text or graphics. The Insert|Navigation Bar command reveals the Navigation Bar Properties dialog box, shown in Figure 10.11. From this dialog box, you determine which links to include as well as the orientation and appearance of the navigation bar.

> *Note: To change the labels on a navigation bar, edit the titles on the Navigation View of FrontPage Explorer.*

User Registration

User registration is a feature of FrontPage 98 that allows you to force users to register themselves before they are granted access to your Web site. This gives you the ability to track visitors to your Web site and users of your discussion forums.

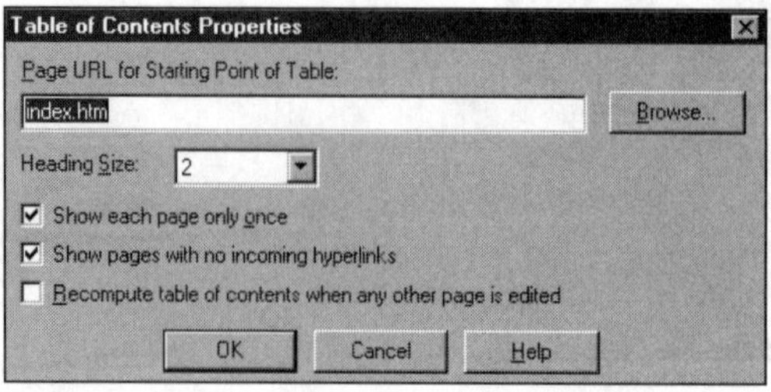

Figure 10.10 The Table Of Contents Properties dialog box.

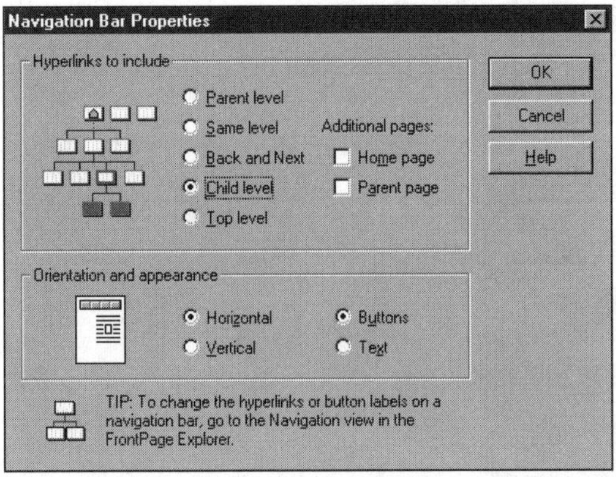

Figure 10.11 The Navigation Bar Properties dialog box.

The user registration template simplifies the process of creating a registration system. This template is accessed from FrontPage Editor's File|New command. It creates a simple registration form. However, the registration mechanism may not function with every Web server. FrontPage automatically tests the capabilities of the host Web server when the page is published. The user registration form must reside in the root of the Web. Once a user is registered, he or she is granted access to a sub-Web. The sub-Web that will be open to registered users should exist before the user registration form is created.

Once the user registration form is displayed in FrontPage Editor, scroll down to view the form area of the document. Right-click over the form area and select Form Properties from the pop-up menu. Notice that the form results are already configured to be sent to the registration form handler. Click on the Options button; this reveals the Options For Registration Form Handler dialog box.

On the Registration tab of this dialog box, shown in Figure 10.12, enter the name of the FrontPage Web site for which this registration form will grant user access. All other fields on this and the other three tabs are already set correctly for the registration form handler. If you employ a custom registration script, you may need to modify these settings. You may define a "denied access" page using the URL Of Registration Failure Page (Optional) field, but this is not required. A standard "access denied" message will be displayed otherwise. Once this change is made, click on OK on the Options and the Form Properties dialog boxes. Before you save the document, you need to change every instance of "[Other Web]" with the name of the Web site.

Once this is saved, you need to verify that the sub-Web's permissions have been set properly so that only registered users are granted access. This is done

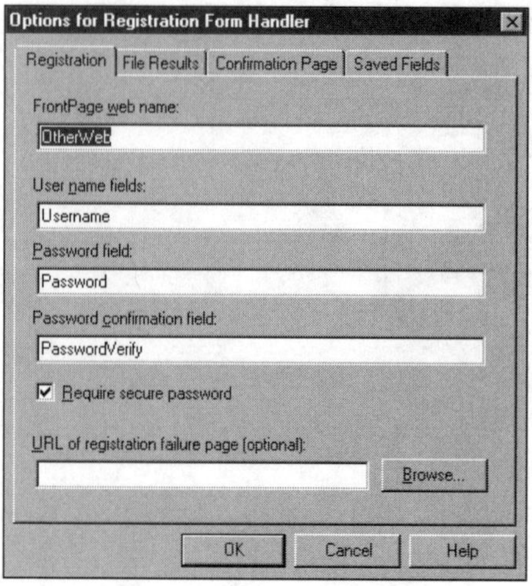

Figure 10.12 The Options For Registration Form Handler dialog box.

through FrontPage Explorer's Tools|Permissions command. You must first set the sub-Web to have unique permissions; then select the Only Registered Users Have Browse Access radio button on the Users tab.

Compatibility

Not all the functions and features that can be created through FrontPage 98 are supported by all browsers. There are different levels of advanced programming language support, proprietary markup, custom file type support, and many other variances between one browser and another. The variances are not limited to the vendor company either—each version of a browser varies greatly in its capabilities. Table 10.1 lists the features of FrontPage Webs and the browsers that support them.

If a browser does not support an element of a Web document, it's typically just ignored. Therefore, instead of displaying the animation, effect, form, applet, and so on, the browser skips the unrecognized markup as if it were a comment.

For browsers that do not support graphics (or those with the graphics display turned off) and for those users who have slow connections, providing image alternatives is important. As discussed in Chapter 9, alternate text can be supplied that's displayed in place of the image when graphics are not displayable. You should also consider creating text-only versions of your image maps and navigation controls.

FrontPage Editor offers you the ability to test a Web creation in one or more browsers. The File|Preview In Browser command reveals the Preview In Browser dialog box, shown in Figure 10.13. This dialog box lists the browsers FrontPage is aware of. You can add and remove browsers from this list using the Add and Delete buttons. You can also select the window size for the preview. Simply select a listed browser and click on Preview—FrontPage will launch the browser and load the current document. Close the browser when complete to return to FrontPage.

Table 10.1 FrontPage 98 features and browser compatibility.

Feature	AOL1	AOL3	NN1.1	NN2	NN3	NN4	IE1	IE2	IE3	IE4
ActiveX controls	N	N	N	N	N	N	N	N	Y	Y
Active Server Pages	N	N	N	N	N	N	N	N	Y	Y
Animated GIFs	N	N	N	Y	Y	Y	N	N	Y	Y
Background colors	N	Y	Y	Y	Y	Y	Y	Y	Y	Y
Background images	N	Y	Y	Y	Y	Y	Y	Y	Y	Y
Banner ad manager	N	N	N	Y	Y	Y	N	N	Y	Y
Browser plug-ins	N	N	N	Y	Y	Y	N	N	Y	Y
Channels	N	N	N	N	N	N	N	N	N	Y
Client-side scripts	N	N	N	N	Y	Y	N	N	Y	Y
Comments	Y	Y	Y	Y	Y	Y	Y	Y	Y	Y
Custom font colors	N	Y	N	Y	Y	Y	Y	Y	Y	Y
Custom font faces	N	N	N	N	Y	Y	Y	Y	Y	Y
Custom font sizes	N	Y	Y	Y	Y	Y	Y	Y	Y	Y
Dynamic HTML	N	N	N	N	N	Y	N	N	N	Y
Forms	N	Y	Y	Y	Y	Y	Y	Y	Y	Y
Frames	N	Y	N	Y	Y	Y	N	N	Y	Y
Hover buttons	N	N	N	Y	Y	Y	N	N	Y	Y
Inline video/audio	N	N	N	N	Y	Y	N	N	Y	Y
Java	N	N	N	Y	Y	Y	N	N	Y	Y
JavaScript	N	N	N	Y	Y	Y	N	N	Y	Y
Marquees	N	N	N	N	N	N	N	Y	Y	Y
Page transitions	N	N	N	N	N	N	N	N	N	Y
Style sheets	N	N	N	N	N	Y	N	N	Y	Y
Tables	N	Y	Y	Y	Y	Y	N	Y	Y	Y
VBScript	N	N	N	N	N	N	N	N	Y	Y

Note: AOL: America Online; NN: Netscape Navigator; IE: Microsoft Internet Explorer.

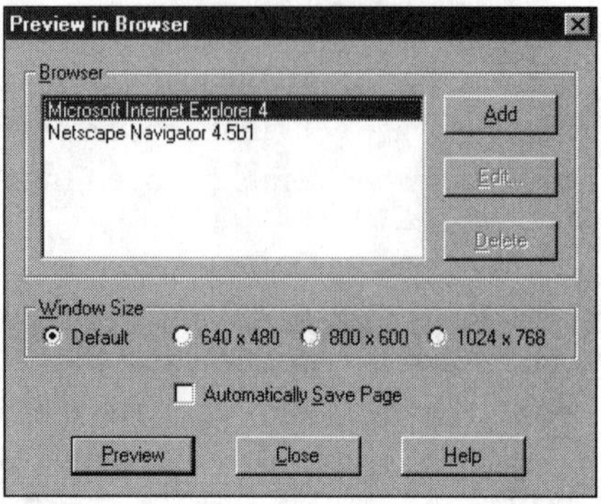

Figure 10.13 The Preview In Browser dialog box.

Practice Questions

Question 1

If elements of a Web document are transient, which features of FrontPage can be used to automate their appearance? [Check all correct answers]

- ❑ a. Include page
- ❑ b. Scheduled include page
- ❑ c. Page banner
- ❑ d. Scheduled image

The scheduled include page and scheduled image features are used to automate the appearance of transient elements within a Web document. Therefore, answers b and d are correct. Include page simplifies the editing of a common element across multiple pages, but it is not an automated feature. Therefore, answer a is incorrect. Page banner inserts a large display-wide banner showing the page's name, but it is not an automated feature. Therefore, answer c is incorrect.

Question 2

What component can you use to include custom HTML markup in a Web document and prevent FrontPage from making modifications to it?

- ❍ a. Confirmation field
- ❍ b. Comment
- ❍ c. Insert HTML
- ❍ d. Substitution

The insert HTML component allows you to insert custom HTML markup that's not modified by FrontPage. Therefore, answer c is correct. The confirmation field component is used to include details in a response page from a submitted form. Therefore, answer a is incorrect. The comment component is used to include nondisplayed information in a document; it's managed by FrontPage, and items within a comment are not processed by the browser. Therefore, answer b is incorrect. The substitution component is used to include server, document, or browser variable information in a displayed document. Therefore, answer d is incorrect.

Question 3

FrontPage does not offer a quick-and-easy method for testing your Web creations in multiple browsers. FrontPage Editor allows you to view your creations only in the Preview tab. To view documents in a real Web browser, you must manually launch the browser and load the document.

❍ a. True

❍ b. False

This is a false statement. Therefore, answer b is correct. FrontPage Editor offers you the ability to preview documents in browsers via the File|Preview In Browser command.

Question 4

Which of the following FrontPage features are supported by Internet Explorer 4 but not by Netscape Navigator 4? [Check all correct answers]

❑ a. Marquee

❑ b. Transition

❑ c. VBScript

❑ d. Java

Only IE4 supports marquee, transition, and VBScript. Therefore, answers a, b, and c are correct. Both IE4 and Netscape Navigator 4 support Java. Therefore, answer d is incorrect.

Question 5

A hover button is created in FrontPage by using which technology or technique?

❍ a. Server-side scripting

❍ b. Java

❍ c. JavaScript

❍ d. VBScript

Hover buttons are Java applets. Therefore, answer b is correct.

Question 6

You create a document that contains a style sheet that modifies the size, font, and color of text. After successfully testing the page using Internet Explorer 4, you distribute the document on the corporate intranet. Currently, the office policy requires that all clients use Netscape Navigator 3. What will the Netscape Navigator 3 users see when they view your new document?

- ❍ a. The text will be styled exactly the same as it is in IE4.
- ❍ b. No text content will be displayed at all.
- ❍ c. An error message that states that style sheets are not supported.
- ❍ d. The text will revert to the default font settings of the browser.

Netscape Navigator 3 viewers will see text that reverts back to the default font settings of the browser, because style sheets are not supported by Netscape Navigator 3. Therefore, answer d is correct. The text will not appear the same as it does in IE4, because Netscape Navigator 3 does not support style sheets. Therefore, answer a is incorrect. The text will appear, but the style sheet information will be ignored. Therefore, answer b is incorrect. Because style sheets are unknown to Netscape Navigator 3, it is not possible for it to issue a warning message stating that style sheets are not supported. Therefore, answer c is incorrect.

Question 7

A hit counter records the number of unique users to visit a document.

- ❍ a. True
- ❍ b. False

Trick! question

This is a false statement. Therefore, answer b is correct. A hit counter counts each and every time a document is delivered by the Web server to a client. Therefore, the same user can reload the same page 100 times and the counter will increment by 100. Because careful reading is required to distinguish between number of hits and number of users, we've marked this as a trick question.

Question 8

> If you want to create a Web site that's compatible with the most number of browsers, which of the following components would you choose? [Check all correct answers]
>
> ❑ a. ActiveX controls
>
> ❑ b. Background colors
>
> ❑ c. Custom font colors
>
> ❑ d. Java
>
> ❑ e. Forms

The three selections from this list that offer the widest browser compatibility are background colors, custom font colors, and forms (supported by AOL3; Netscape Navigator 2, 3, and 4; and IE1, 2, 3, and 4). Therefore, answers b, c, and e are correct. ActiveX controls are supported only by IE3 and 4. Therefore, answer a is incorrect. Java is supported only by Netscape Navigator 2, 3, and 4, and IE3 and 4. Therefore, answer d is incorrect.

Question 9

> When a browser encounters HTML markup or scripting code that it does not recognize, an error message is issued stating that unknown code has been encountered and document interpretation has been terminated.
>
> ❍ a. True
>
> ❍ b. False

This is a false statement. Therefore, answer b is correct. A browser will ignore unknown code; it will not issue a warning.

Question 10

Which of the following are true of the banner ad manager? [Check all correct answers]

- ❑ a. Each image has its own URL.
- ❑ b. Multiple images can be displayed in succession.
- ❑ c. A transition effect can be used when switching between images.
- ❑ d. The defined images will all display once before stopping.

The banner ad manager displays multiple images in succession and transition effects can be used. Therefore, answers b and c are correct. Only a single URL can be defined for all ads, and the display routine loops indefinitely. Therefore, answers a and d are incorrect.

Need To Know More?

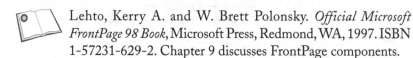

Lehto, Kerry A. and W. Brett Polonsky. *Official Microsoft FrontPage 98 Book*, Microsoft Press, Redmond, WA, 1997. ISBN 1-57231-629-2. Chapter 9 discusses FrontPage components.

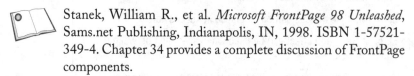

Stanek, William R., et al. *Microsoft FrontPage 98 Unleashed*, Sams.net Publishing, Indianapolis, IN, 1998. ISBN 1-57521-349-4. Chapter 34 provides a complete discussion of FrontPage components.

Tauber, Daniel A. and Brenda Kienan. *Mastering Microsoft FrontPage 98*, Sybex, Alameda, CA, 1998. ISBN 0-7821-2144-6. Chapter 15 discusses FrontPage components.

Microsoft TechNet. Useful information about the FrontPage 98 topics discussed in this chapter can be found by searching on keywords related to these topics.

www.microsoft.com/frontpage/. This is the official FrontPage Web site hosted by Microsoft. It offers overview information about this product.

11

Advanced FrontPage Tools

Terms you'll need to understand:

- √ HTML scripting
- √ ActiveX
- √ Java applets
- √ Plug-ins
- √ Channels

Techniques you'll need to master:

- √ Adding HTML code to your Web pages
- √ Inserting ActiveX controls
- √ Adding Java applets to a Web page
- √ Placing plug-ins on a page
- √ Integrating scripts into your Web pages

In this chapter, you'll learn to work with the Microsoft FrontPage Advanced toolbar. In addition, you'll learn how to add scripts, Java applets, plug-ins, and ActiveX controls to your Web pages. You'll also learn an easy technique for adding HTML code directly to a Web page. Finally, you'll be introduced to the Channel Definition Format (CDF) and explore the steps necessary to create Web channels.

The Advanced Toolbar

If you're planning to place more advanced content (such as scripts, Java applets, ActiveX controls, plug-ins, or your own HTML code) into your Web pages, the Advanced toolbar is for you. The Advanced toolbar is available in the Microsoft FrontPage Editor program. Follow these steps to activate the Advanced toolbar:

1. Open FrontPage Editor.
2. Click on the View option from the menu bar.
3. Click on the Advanced Toolbar selection.

The Advanced toolbar is fairly short. It only has five buttons: The first button allows you to add HTML code directly to your page, and the remaining buttons allow you to insert ActiveX controls, Java applets, plug-ins, and scripts, respectively (see Figure 11.1).

Where you place your cursor on the page you're modifying is important when you use the Advanced toolbar, because the code, control, applet, plug-in, or script you insert is placed where the cursor is when the insertion is executed.

Another point to remember is that in Normal View, you won't get to see your additions via the Advanced toolbar, because scripted additions are hidden from the Normal View perspective. To see your newly inserted script, either check the HTML View or use the Preview button via FrontPage Editor.

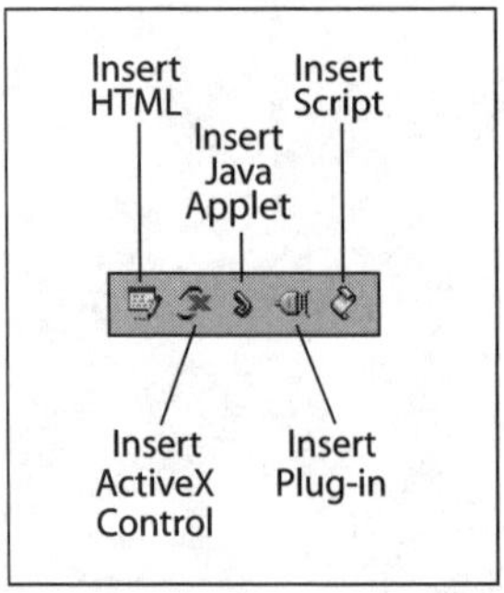

Figure 11.1 The Advanced toolbar.

Note: Although you won't see HTML or script code in Normal View, you will see an icon placeholder for Java applets, plug-ins, and ActiveX controls.

Creating Your Own HTML

The Insert HTML button on the Advanced toolbar brings up a dialog box that allows you to enter your own HTML code (see Figure 11.2).

The code you add in this dialog box must be properly formatted and is not checked for errors (as the dialog box clearly states). Also, the code you add in the dialog box does not appear in the Normal View of FrontPage Editor. Behind the scenes, FrontPage encapsulates your code with WebBot commands. For example, if you type "<I>Mother of Pearl</I>" into this dialog box, as shown in Figure 11.2, the HTML code generated by FrontPage would look like this:

```
<!--webbot bot="HTMLMarkup" startspan --><I>Mother of Pearl</I>
<!--webbot bot="HTMLMarkup" endspan -->
```

Of course, to insert properly formatted HTML code, you must know how to write HTML. HTML coding and formatting are outside the scope of this book and the Microsoft FrontPage exam; however, as you are a Web developer, it is highly recommended that you study and know at least some basic HTML coding. For example, you should know that the code **<I>Mother of Pearl</I>** would italicize the text "Mother of Pearl".

Including ActiveX Controls

ActiveX is a technology developed by Microsoft to compartmentalize application coding. Instead of writing an application from start to finish, developers can combine ActiveX controls into larger applications, called *container applications*. Microsoft's Internet Explorer application is one example of an application designed with components called *ActiveX controls*. These controls perform specific

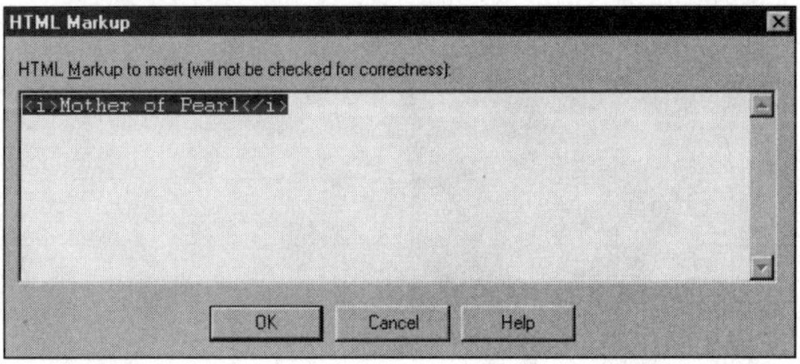

Figure 11.2 Adding HTML coding.

functions, such as displaying author information, code signing, and reading content ratings.

ActiveX controls can be used in your Web pages to enhance your content. Because many components have been developed and are available for use (usually free of charge), you can just place them in your Web pages.

> You are not required to be an ActiveX programmer to use FrontPage or pass the FrontPage 98 certification exam. However, you are expected to know how to add these components to your Web pages, as explained in the following steps. If you would like to know more about creating or obtaining additional ActiveX controls, visit **www.microsoft.com/com/activex.htm**.

To insert an ActiveX control in your Web site, follow these steps:

1. Open FrontPage Editor; then open the Web page into which you want to insert the ActiveX control.
2. Place the cursor at the location in the Web page where you want the ActiveX control to appear.
3. From the FrontPage Editor menu bar, click on Insert|Advanced and then select ActiveX Control, or click on the Insert ActiveX Control button on the Advanced toolbar (refer to Figure 11.1). Either way, you get the ActiveX Control Properties dialog box (see Figure 11.3).
4. In the Pick A Control selection box, click on the arrow to see a list of ActiveX controls installed on your computer. Then, choose the ActiveX control you want to insert. For example, if you want to insert a movie or

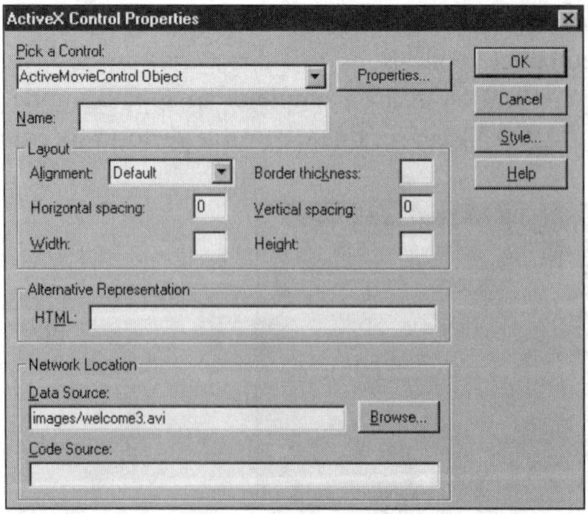

Figure 11.3 The ActiveX Control Properties dialog box.

AVI file into your Web page, you would choose the Active Movie Control (ActiveMovieControl Object) selection, as shown in Figure 11.3.

Note: You'll find that inserting an AVI or QuickTime movie is even easier as a plug-in, which is covered later in this chapter in the "Inserting Plug-Ins" section.

5. In the Name text box, type a name for your control. (Naming the control is for your reference only and is not a required step.)
6. In the Layout section of the dialog box, set Alignment, Border Thickness, Horizontal Spacing, Vertical Spacing, Width, and Height. All these settings control how your ActiveX control is placed on the page. Remember that these settings are relative to the position of the cursor on your page. To learn more about these layout settings, click on the Help button in this dialog box.
7. If the page is viewed with a browser that does not support ActiveX, you can add HTML code into the HTML text box in the Alternative Representation section. This allows you to provide an alternate option or message in place of the control. For example, maybe the ActiveX control you have selected is an animated button that links to the TRAVEL.HTM page. As an alternative, you could simply enter **<A HREF=travel.htm> Link to Travel</A>**, which would allow users with browsers that don't support ActiveX to still participate by clicking on a plain text link that reads "Link to Travel".

The HTML box allows you to enter HTML code that provides compatibility for browsers that do not support ActiveX.

8. The Network Location section has two text boxes: Data Source and Code Source. Data Source defines where the ActiveX control should obtain data or runtime parameters. For example, if you've inserted the Active Movie Control, you must configure the path to the movie file that you plan to display (refer back to Figure 11.3). The Code Source text box defines where the ActiveX control should obtain any necessary code. Click on OK.
9. Click on File|Save to save your changes.

Once you've inserted your ActiveX control, you can see what it will look like by clicking on the Preview tab at the bottom of the FrontPage Editor application. You can also look at the page and ActiveX control by selecting File|Preview In Browser from the menu bar.

Embedding Java Applets

Java applets can enhance your Web content in much the same way as ActiveX controls. You can locate and download Java applets from the Web and insert them (often for free) into your Web pages. For example, Jamie M. Hall has a free "growing text" applet at **www.ulster.net/~jamihall/java/GrowingText/1.0/GrowingText.html**. (See the "Need To Know More?" section at the end of this chapter for additional Java resources on the Internet.)

> You are not required to be a Java developer to use FrontPage or pass the FrontPage 98 certification exam. You are only expected to be able to add these components to your Web. If you would like to know more about creating or obtaining Java components, visit **www.microsoft.com/java/**. Also, check the "Need To Know More?" section at the end of this chapter for additional Internet links and resources.

Once you've obtained the Java applets you wish to use, you should place them in the folder that contains the Web site in which you plan to use them. To insert a Java applet into a specific Web page, follow these steps:

1. Open FrontPage Editor and then open the Web page in which you want to insert the Java applet.
2. Place your cursor at the location in the Web page where you want to insert the Java applet.
3. If the Advanced toolbar is visible, you can click on the Insert Java Applet icon (refer to Figure 11.1). You can also click on the Insert option on the FrontPage Editor menu bar, choose Advanced, and then click on Java Applet. The Java Applet Properties dialog box opens (see Figure 11.4). Note that when the dialog box opens, its text boxes are empty, but in the figure, they are filled in as an example.
4. In the Applet Source and Applet Base URL text boxes, enter the name of the Java applet (Applet Source) and the path where it's located (Applet Base URL). In Figure 11.4, the paths point to Jamie M. Hall's Web address where the "growing text" Java applet is located. Notice that the Java applet ends with the .CLASS file extension.
5. In the Message For Browsers Without Java Support box, type a message for those users who cannot see the Java applet. For example, you could type an error message or just substitute text for what they were supposed to see.

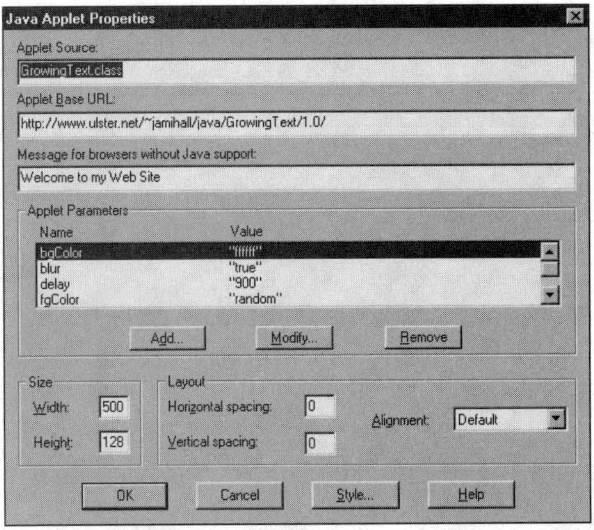

Figure 11.4 The Java Applet Properties dialog box.

STUDY ALERT: To accommodate users with browsers that do not support Java, you can configure a message under the Message For Browsers Without Java Support text box.

6. Use the Add, Modify, and Remove buttons to add, modify, and remove parameters. Applet parameters are used to configure the Java applet. For example, the growing text that has been configured in Figure 11.4 has many parameters available that define the properties that can be configured (such as the text to be displayed). The developer of the applet should provide the information concerning the configurable parameters.
7. Use the Size and Layout sections to place your applet on the Web page. In the Width and Height text boxes, set the viewable area for the applet on the page. You set the width and height of the viewable areas in pixels, and set the alignment of the area to the left, right, or center (default).
8. Once you've finished configuring the applet, click on OK to drop the applet onto your Web page.
9. Be sure to save the changes by clicking on File|Save.
10. Test your modifications by clicking on File|Preview In Browser. Figure 11.5 illustrates the "growing text" Java applet as displayed on the default INDEX.HTM page.

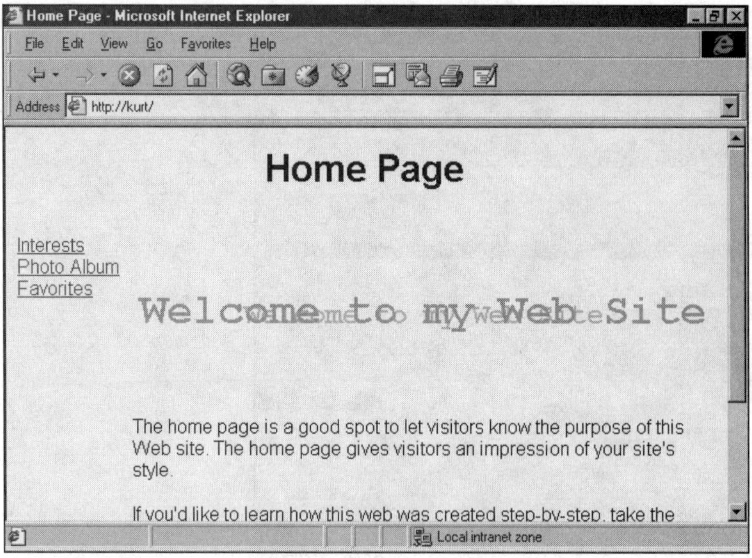

Figure 11.5 The "growing text" Java applet.

If you want to change some of the parameters on your Java applet after you've placed it on the page, double-click on the J icon that appears in the FrontPage Editor window under the Normal View. The J icon on the page represents your Java applet script, and double-clicking on it opens the Java Applet Properties dialog box.

STUDY ALERT: If you find that your Java applet is not properly displayed on the Web page and appears to be cut off on one side, increase the width or height through the Java Applet Properties dialog box.

Inserting Plug-Ins

If you want to place an AVI or QuickTime video (.QT or .MOV) in your Web page, embedding a plug-in is a great way to do it. *Plug-ins* are platform-specific components; only Netscape Navigator and Internet Explorer are able to view these video plug-ins. To insert a plug-in, follow these steps:

1. Open the page in which you want to add the plug-in with FrontPage Editor.
2. Place the cursor at the location on the page where you want to add the plug-in.
3. Click on the Insert Plug-in icon from the Advanced toolbar (refer to Figure 11.1), or click on Insert from the FrontPage menu bar, select

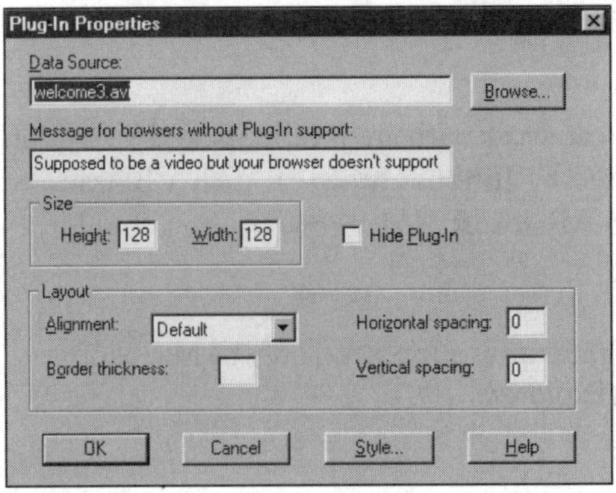

Figure 11.6 The Plug-In Properties dialog box.

Advanced, and then click on Insert Plug-in. The Plug-in Properties dialog box appears (see Figure 11.6).

4. In the Data Source text box, enter the path and file name of the plug-in.
5. In the Message For Browsers Without Plug-in Support text box, enter a message that explains that the client browser does not support video and/or plug-ins.

To accommodate users with browsers that do not support plug-ins, be sure to configure a message in the Message For Browsers Without Plug-in Support text box.

6. Set the alignment, border thickness, horizontal and vertical spacing, and size for the plug-in in the Size and Layout sections of the dialog box. Notice that you can also choose to hide the plug-in if it is meant to be run but not seen by the user. For more information on the Size and Layout configurations, click on the Help button on this dialog box.
7. Once you've properly configured the plug-in properties, click on OK to place the plug-in on the Web page. You should see a large square box appear on the Web page. This represents the plug-in.
8. To check the proper operation of the plug-in, select File|Preview In Browser from the menu bar.

Including Scripts

Inserting a script into a Web page is not that much different than inserting an ActiveX control, Java applet, or plug-in. However, one major difference is that you have to see the script you're inserting; you even have to cut and paste it or write it yourself.

The two basic types of scripts you can work with are JavaScript and VBScript. JavaScript is more widely supported by Internet browsers than VBScript; to maximize compatibility with non-Microsoft Web browsers, you should use JavaScript.

Currently, client-side VBScript is supported only by Microsoft clients using Internet Explorer.

Even though you have to insert the script into your Web page, you don't necessarily have to be a developer to use scripts. Plenty of free VBScripts and JavaScripts are available on the Internet. Check out **www.developer.com** for links to free code.

Once you've copied or created your script, you can insert it by following this simple procedure:

1. Open the page in which you want to add the script with FrontPage Editor.
2. Place the cursor at the location on the page where you want to add the script.
3. Click on the Insert Script icon from the Advanced toolbar (refer to Figure 11.1), or click on Insert in the FrontPage menu bar, select Advanced, and then click on Insert Script. The Script dialog box appears (see Figure 11.7).
4. Select a script type: VBScript, JavaScript, or Other. If you choose Other, you're expected to define which type of script you're planning to configure. If you select VBScript, you can choose to run the script on the server. Running the script on the server prevents the client from having to download the file over the Internet. Instead, the client sees the results of the script only.

VBScript can be configured to run on the server; JavaScript cannot. The result of VBScript run on the server is that it can be used by any Web client (client-side VBScript is supported only by Internet Explorer), because the server-side VBScript sends HTML to the browser, not VBScript.

5. Place your script in the Script window. If you want, you can use the Script wizard to help you write an event-driven script. Click on the

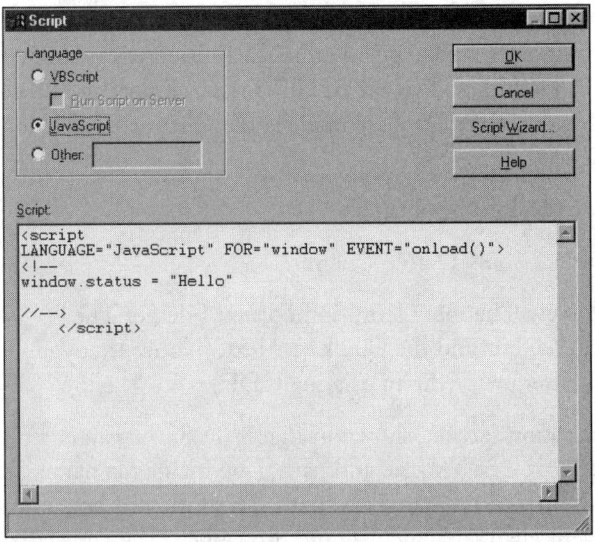

Figure 11.7 The Script dialog box.

button labeled Script Wizard; then on click Help to learn more about it. The script shown in Figure 11.7 was created with the Script wizard.

6. Once you've finished configuring your script, click on OK to place your code in the Web page.
7. To test the script for proper operation, click on File|Preview In Browser from the menu bar.

Creating Channels

If you want people to visit your site frequently (and you're willing to update and change it frequently), you should consider creating a *channel.* Channels are a relatively new concept for the Web, and they support a push technology paradigm for Web content. Channels notify users when content has been changed on your Web site (which is essentially pushing information to them). This is different than the concept of "pull technology," in which users must decide to visit your site to see the latest news.

One of the earliest, and still very popular, push technologies is email update notification. When the Web site is revised, an email message is sent to notify users of the change. Today, other push technologies are available, including channels, screen savers, and desktop components.

> *Note: For more information on the various types of push technologies, visit www.strom.com/imc/4ta.html.*

Microsoft FrontPage 98 has the ability to help you make your site into a channel via its Channel Definition wizard. The Channel Definition wizard allows you to create a Channel Definition Format (CDF) file via FrontPage 98 to publish your site as a channel. To create a channel via the Channel Definition wizard, follow these steps:

1. Open the FrontPage Explorer application.
2. On the menu bar, select Tools|Define Channel.
3. Click the Create A New Channel Definition Format File For The Current FrontPage Web box and then click on Next. (Notice that you can use this same technique to edit an existing CDF.)
4. In the channel description section, shown in Figure 11.8, you can enter a title, abstract, introduction page name and path, logo image file name and path, and an icon image file name and path. The Title text box allows you to title your channel, which should probably be the same title as your Web site. The Abstract text box is where you include a short description of what your channel will provide; users will see this information when they subscribe. The Introduction Page is a path to the first page someone will see when your channel is opened, which is usually the same page as your site's home page. You can also decide to include an image (logo) that identifies your channel and creates an icon for your channel. For best viewing, the logo should be an 80-by-32-pixel GIF, and the icon should be a 16-by-16-pixel GIF. When you're ready to move on, click on the Next button.

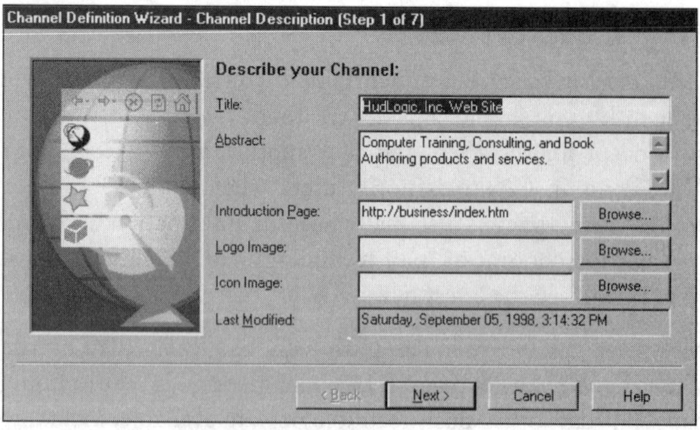

Figure 11.8 The Channel Definition Wizard Channel Description configuration dialog box.

5. In the Choose Source Folder section (under the Source Folder box), type the path for your Web content, or click on Browse, select the folder you want to use, and then click on OK. Usually, you'll set the folder that contains your Web site and click on the Include Subfolders checkbox if other files will change. When you're ready for the next step, click on the Next button.

6. On the Edit Page section, select the page(s) you do not want to include in your channel and then click on Exclude. By default, all pages are selected, but if you wish to update a few pages continuously, exclude the rest. When you're ready to move on, click on the Next button.

7. In the Channel Item Properties section, you can define several items (see Figure 11.9). In the Channel Items list, click on the item you want to customize and then set the properties for Abstract, Page Cache, and Usage, or click on the Delete button to delete an item. You can decide whether to cache a given page into the user's Web browser. The default selection is to allow the user's Web browser to decide whether to cache the page. Repeat this action for each item you want to customize. You can also select which type of notifications your users will receive. If your users are not using Active Desktop, inserting a desktop component will not work. When you're finished, click on the Next button.

8. In the Channel Scheduling section, set the start date, end date, how often you want the user's computer to check for updates, and the time schedule you want to delay connections to your site (see Figure 11.10).When you're ready to move on, click on the Next button.

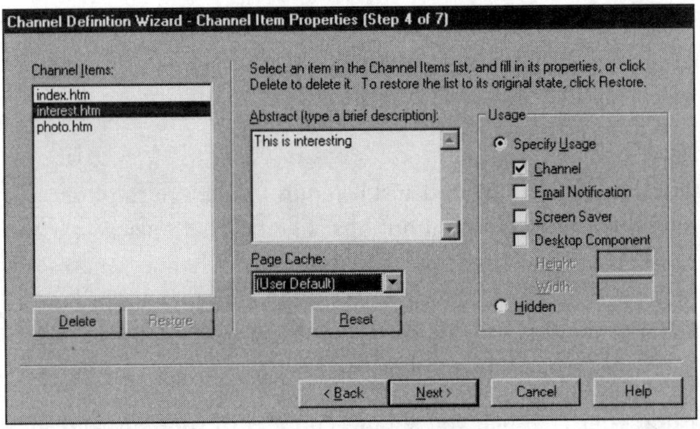

Figure 11.9 The Channel Definition Wizard Channel Item Properties configuration dialog box.

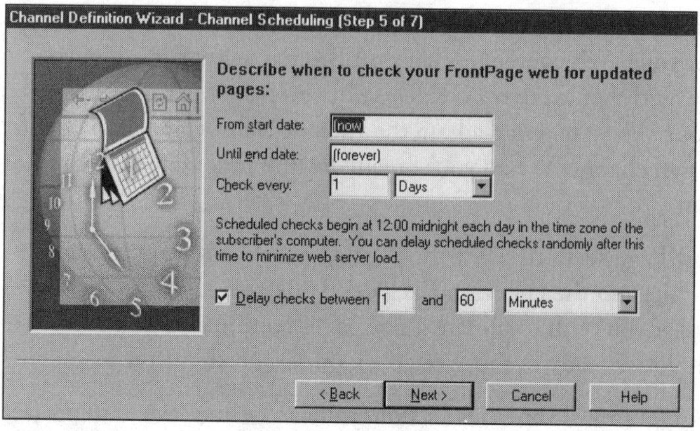

Figure 11.10 The Channel Definition Wizard Channel Scheduling configuration dialog box.

TIP You can have the channel start immediately and never end if you wish. However, you should be careful to set a schedule and time delay. If all users of your channel get their updates simultaneously, it could really slow your Web site (if you have a lot of channel participants). The time delay will randomly offset some of the updates to reduce strain on your server.

9. You can optionally decide to track access to your channel by logging. If you want to enable logging, enter the URL of the Common Gateway Interface (CGI) script you'll use to process the information in the Target URL text box, or click on Browse to locate the script. When you're ready to move on, click on the Next button.

10. Enter the name of the CDF on the final screen. You can modify where you want the CDF to be stored, but most users just accept the default location.

11. Click on Save. The CDF is created and listed in FrontPage Explorer. You can also choose two additional options: The first is to place an icon on your Web page to allow users to subscribe to your channel, and the second is to prepare your channel for publishing to another Web site. You must first get permission from the administrator of the other Web site to publish your channel on another site.

Once you've created your channel, you should connect to your site and subscribe. Remember to use Internet Explorer 4 or later. You should see that a Subscribe link has been added to your home page. If you click on it, you'll see the Add Active Channel Content dialog box (see Figure 11.11).

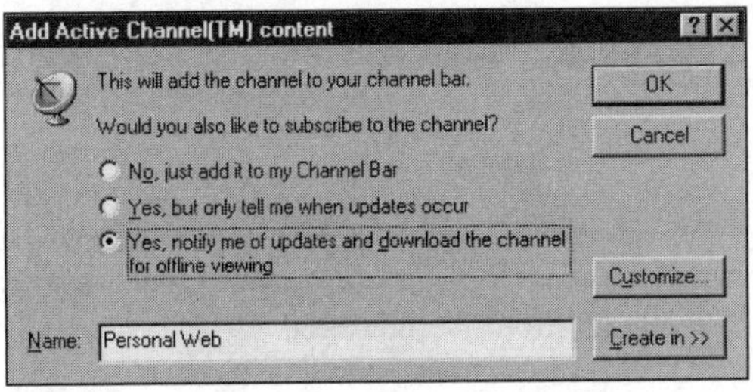

Figure 11.11 Testing the CDF on your Web site.

Note: To learn more about creating channels in general, check CDF 101 at www.microsoft.com/workshop/prog/ie4/channels/cdf1-f.htm.

Practice Questions

Question 1

Which of the following items can you add from the Advanced toolbar? [Check all correct answers]

❑ a. HTML

❑ b. Java applets

❑ c. Scripts

❑ d. ActiveX controls

❑ e. The Database Registration wizard

The Advanced toolbar allows you to insert HTML, Java applets, scripts, and ActiveX controls. Therefore, answers a, b, c, and d are correct. The Advanced toolbar does not have an option for a Database Registration wizard. Therefore, answer e is incorrect.

Question 2

You've just added HTML code using the HTML Markup dialog box in the FrontPage Editor program. Which of the following statements are true about the HTML Markup dialog box? [Check all correct answers]

❑ a. It allows you to type text directly into the box.

❑ b. It provides HTML error checking.

❑ c. The code you insert will be placed in your Web page after you click on OK.

❑ d. If you want to modify the code after you've placed it in your Web page, you must switch to the HTML View in order to modify it.

Answers a, c, and d are correct. You can type text directly into the dialog box, and you must format it properly. Therefore, answer a is correct. The HTML code is placed in your Web page after you click on OK, and you cannot edit it via the dialog box after it is placed. Instead, you must go to HTML View to edit HTML code that you've already placed in your Web page. Therefore, answers c and d are correct. The HTML Markup dialog box tells you that it will not check your code for correctness. Therefore, answer b is incorrect.

Question 3

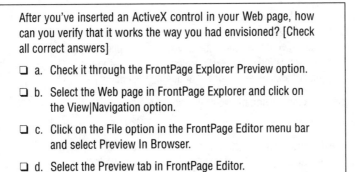

After you've inserted an ActiveX control in your Web page, how can you verify that it works the way you had envisioned? [Check all correct answers]

- ❑ a. Check it through the FrontPage Explorer Preview option.
- ❑ b. Select the Web page in FrontPage Explorer and click on the View|Navigation option.
- ❑ c. Click on the File option in the FrontPage Editor menu bar and select Preview In Browser.
- ❑ d. Select the Preview tab in FrontPage Editor.
- ❑ e. Click on the File option in FrontPage Explorer while selecting the Web page. Then select Preview In Browser.

You can use the Preview In Browser option or the Preview tab from FrontPage Editor to check your ActiveX control. Therefore, answers c and d are correct. FrontPage Explorer, as described in options a, b, and e, does not have a facility for viewing ActiveX controls. The options presented in answers a and e are not available in FrontPage Explorer (only FrontPage Editor). Therefore, answers a and e are incorrect. Clicking on View|Navigation, as described in answer b, does not allow you to verify your ActiveX control. Therefore, answer b is incorrect.

Question 4

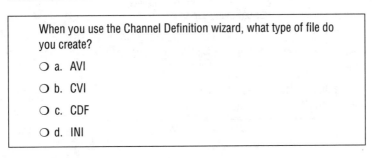

When you use the Channel Definition wizard, what type of file do you create?

- ❍ a. AVI
- ❍ b. CVI
- ❍ c. CDF
- ❍ d. INI

The Channel Definition wizard helps you to create a Channel Definition Format (CDF) file. Therefore, answer c is correct. Answers a, b, and d are incorrect because the Channel Definition wizard creates only CDF files.

Question 5

You've been asked to increase the traffic on your Web site and have decided to use channels to do so. You know that it will involve frequent updates to your Web content, but you have the people in place to make that happen. The early projections are that you'll have thousands of additional visitors after adding the channel.

You've been asked to accomplish these specific items:

- Turn your site into a channel.
- Ensure that the company's logo is displayed in the channel bar of IE4 client browsers that add your site to their channel selection.
- Ensure that a subscription link is available on your home page.
- Ensure that excessive channel updates will not occur simultaneously.

You used the Channel Definition wizard from FrontPage Explorer to define the channel; you set the channel to INDEX.HTML (your home page); and you configured the last frame of the Channel Definition wizard, as shown in the following figure.

Which of the following goals have you accomplished? [Check all correct answers]

- ❑ a. Turn your site into a channel.
- ❑ b. Ensure that the company's logo is displayed in the channel bar of IE4 clients that add your site to their channel selection. (Your company's logo has been rendered as ICON.GIF and LOGO.GIF.)
- ❑ c. Ensure that a subscription link is available on your home page.
- ❑ d. Ensure that excessive channel updates will not occur simultaneously.

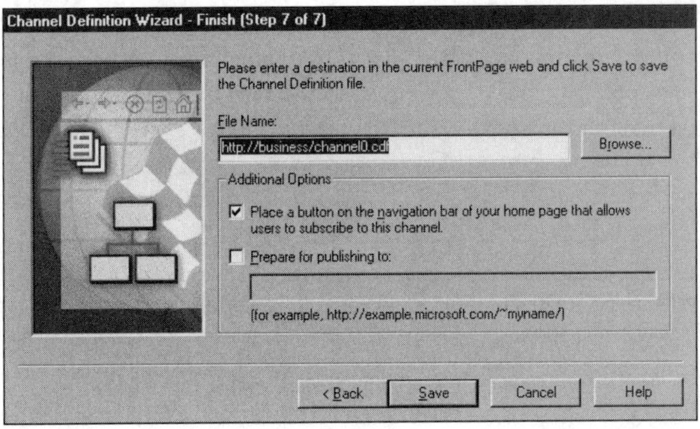

You turned your site into a channel, and the figure shows that you'll allow the Channel Definition wizard to create a link on your home page. Therefore, answers a and c are correct. There was no mention of placing a logo, and the default is not to identify a logo for the channel bar. Therefore, answer b is incorrect. Using the Channel Definition wizard does turn your site into a channel. However, in the solution, there's no mention of configuring channel scheduling to prevent too many simultaneous updates (the default is to allow everyone to update at the same time). Therefore, answer d is incorrect.

Question 6

You've configured the "growing text" Java applet on your Web page. It's supposed to read "Welcome to my Web site", but you see only the letters "come to my We" and want to fix this problem. What is the most likely solution?

- ❍ a. The applet was corrupted during development.
- ❍ b. The Java applet is missing.
- ❍ c. The parameters for the width of the applet are too small.
- ❍ d. You inserted it as an ActiveX control.
- ❍ e. FrontPage Webs are not 100 percent Java compatible.

It is very reasonable to assume that the frame for the Java applet is not large enough if you can only see part of the text you configured. Therefore, answer c is correct. If the Java applet was corrupt or missing, you wouldn't see anything when you loaded the page. Therefore, answers a and b are incorrect. You cannot insert a Java applet as an ActiveX control—they are two different things altogether. Even if you did manipulate the dialog boxes somehow, the component would still be a Java applet. Therefore, answer d is incorrect. FrontPage Webs are Java compatible. Therefore, answer e is incorrect.

Question 7

Which of the following are methods for adding Java to your Web page? [Check all correct answers]

- ❑ a. Type it directly into the page through the HTML View in FrontPage Explorer.
- ❑ b. Use the Insert Java Applet icon on FrontPage Editor's Advanced toolbar.
- ❑ c. Click on the Insert Script icon on FrontPage Editor's Advanced toolbar.
- ❑ d. Use the Insert option on the FrontPage Explorer menu bar and select Insert Script or Insert Java Applet.

Trick! question

Because Java can be added as an applet or a script, you can use either method presented in answer b or c to place a Java script into your Web page. Therefore, answers b and c are the correct selections. If you selected answer a or d, you didn't read the question carefully enough. The answers say Explorer, not Editor. You should know the differences between FrontPage Explorer and Editor, which is why we marked this as a trick question.

Question 8

An easy way to insert an AVI or a QuickTime video into your Web site with "play" and "stop" controls is to insert it as ___________.

- ❍ a. a Java applet
- ❍ b. a script
- ❍ c. a plug-in
- ❍ d. HTML code

Answer c is the best choice. Although it's possible to use Java applets, scripts, and HTML code to insert "play" and "stop" controls for an AVI or QuickTime video, they are not easier solutions than using a plug-in. Therefore, answers a, b, and d are incorrect.

Question 9

You've been asked to increase the traffic on your Web site and have decided to use channels to do so. You know that it will involve frequent updates to your Web content, but you have the people in place to make that happen. The early projections are that you'll have thousands of additional visitors after adding the channel.

You have been asked to accomplish these specific items:

- Turn your site into a channel.
- Ensure that the company's logo is displayed in the channel bar of IE4 clients that add your site to their channel selection. (Your company's logo has been rendered as ICON.GIF and LOGO.GIF.)
- Ensure that a subscription link is available on your home page.
- Ensure that excessive channel updates will not occur simultaneously.

You used the Channel Definition wizard from FrontPage Explorer to define the channel; you set the channel to INDEX.HTML (your home page); and you configured the Channel Definition wizard, as shown in the following figure. On the last frame of the Channel Definition wizard, you left the default settings to create a subscription button on your navigation bar.

Which of the following goals have you accomplished? [Check all correct answers]

- ❑ a. Turn your site into a channel.
- ❑ b. Ensure that the company's logo is displayed in the channel bar of IE4 clients that add your site to their channel selection.
- ❑ c. Ensure that a subscription link is available on your home page.
- ❑ d. Ensure that excessive channel updates will not occur simultaneously.

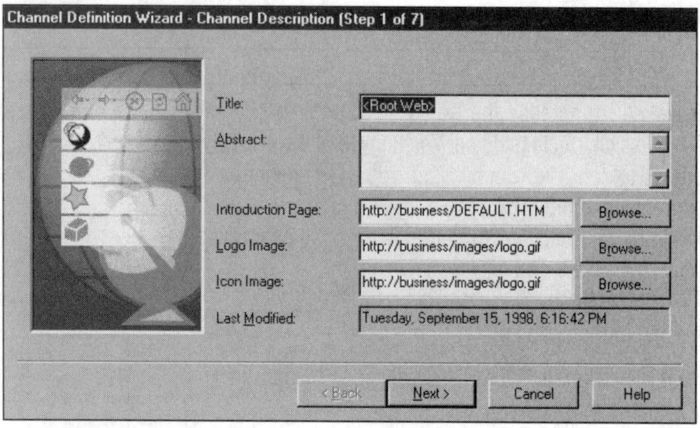

Using the Channel Definition wizard does turn your site into a channel. The graphic shows that you've configured a logo and icon for the channel using your company's LOGO.GIF and ICON.GIF files, and the default option to create a subscription link through the Channel Definition wizard adds a link to your home page. Therefore, answers a, b, and c are correct. However, in the solution, there's no mention of configuring channel scheduling to prevent too many simultaneous updates (the default is to allow everyone to update at the same time). Therefore, answer d is incorrect.

Need To Know More?

Cerami, Ethan. *Delivering Push*, Computing McGraw-Hill, New York, NY, 1998. ISBN 0-07-913693-1. This book covers channels.

Chappell, David. *Understanding ActiveX and OLE*, Microsoft Press, Redmond, WA, 1996. ISBN 1-57231-216-5. This book explains the finer details concerning ActiveX and object linking and embedding (OLE).

Denning, Adam. *ActiveX Controls Inside Out, 2nd Edition*, Microsoft Press, Redmond, WA, 1997. ISBN 1-57231-350-1. This book is about ActiveX controls.

Flanagan, David. *JavaScript: The Definitive Guide*, O'Reilly & Associates, Sebastopol, CA, 1998. ISBN 1-56592-392-8. This is a Java applet resource guide.

Tauber, Daniel A. and Brenda Kienan. *Mastering Microsoft FrontPage 98*, Sybex, Alameda, CA, 1998. ISBN 0-7821-2144-6. This is a good resource and reference book for the product. It has a lot of step-by-step instructions, which are great for the beginner; later chapters have more advanced configuration information, which is excellent for the more advanced user. In the back of the book is a section titled "Master's Reference," which covers HTML coding in great detail. In addition, Chapter 19 covers Java and ActiveX in greater detail. Chapter 8 has a section titled "Transforming Your Site into a Channel," which gives more detailed information on that topic. Also, Chapter 21 has additional information on Java and Visual Basic scripting for your Web pages. Inserting plug-ins is covered on pages 328 through 331.

Microsoft TechNet (July 98 and later) contains several articles that pertain to FrontPage Editor. Search on "ActiveX," "Java," "HTML coding," and "plug-ins" to read articles relating to those topics. In addition, read article Q174055, "How to create a Channel Definition File," for detailed information on this topic.

http://pioneer.pointcast.com/connections/webcaster/. Visit this site for more information on creating a push channel.

www.developer.com. Visit this site for more information on all types of Web programming, including Java, ActiveX, and advanced HTML.

www.microsoft.com/com/activex.htm. Visit this site for more information on ActiveX controls.

www.microsoft.com/java/. Visit this site for more information on Java scripting the Microsoft way.

www.microsoft.com/sitebuilder/. Visit this site to get the latest information on Web site building. Look for free ActiveX controls on this site under the "Tools & Samples" heading.

www.microsoft.com/standards/cdf/default.asp. Visit this site to read about Microsoft's Channel Definition Format (CDF) specification.

www.microsoft.com/frontpage/resources/howto.htm. Visit this site to find an article titled "How to create a channel definition file."

www.ulster.net/~jamihall/java/GrowingText/1.0/GrowingText.html. Visit this site to learn more about the "growing text" Java effect. This is a great sample application that you can use to experiment with adding a JavaScript to a Web page. Figure 11.5 and the Java applet configuration directions in this chapter will help you.

www.strom.com/imc/4ta.html. Visit this site for information on a wide variety of push technologies.

12

Working With Advanced Web Technologies

Terms you'll need to understand:

- √ Style sheets
- √ Dynamic HTML
- √ Database connectivity
- √ Scripting

Techniques you'll need to master:

- √ Adding style sheets to Web documents
- √ Adding DHTML to Web documents
- √ Using the Database Region wizard
- √ Adding client scripts to Web documents

FrontPage 98 includes several tools and wizards to simplify the task of creating dynamic Web pages, including those that access databases. In this chapter, we explain how to use those tools and wizards.

Adding Style Sheets To Web Pages

A *style sheet* is technically known as a Cascading Style Sheet (CSS) and is defined by the World Wide Web Consortium (W3C). The purpose of a style sheet is to simplify Web authoring and maintenance by separating presentation and style settings from the content of a Web document. Styles override the default appearance of a Web document. Style definitions may be placed in an external file or within a Web document.

External style sheet files are files that usually have the extension .CSS. External style sheets are either linked to or imported into a Web document. By referencing the same external style sheet in every Web document, you can apply a consistent set of style definitions to an entire Web site. External style definitions are overridden by *page-level style definitions*, which are styles defined inside the <STYLE>...</STYLE> tags. Page-level styles are overridden by inline style definitions. This provides enormous capability and flexibility when it comes to setting—and using—style sheets and style-related markup in Web documents.

FrontPage 98 does not have a style sheet wizard, but it does offer a tool that facilitates the manual process of creating an embedded style sheet. Inline styles can be applied easily using the Style button found on several FrontPage formatting dialog boxes.

You'll need Netscape 4 (or newer) or Internet Explorer (IE) 4 (or newer) to view your styles. Also note that although IE3 supports styles, its implementation is slightly different and doesn't fully support the capabilities of CSS.

Formatting Style Sheets

The first thing you should notice about the Format Stylesheet dialog box is its name. It consists of only one word, even though the official W3C documents always use two words to refer to a style sheet. Access this dialog box from the FrontPage Editor menu bar by using the Format|Stylesheet command. Keep in mind that using this dialog box is partly a manual process. You must know enough about HTML and style sheet syntax to know what to enter manually.

You must also specify those aspects of a document to which your style parameters apply. Let's say you want to set a wide left margin for your Web page. That means you must alter the default appearance of your entire Web page by

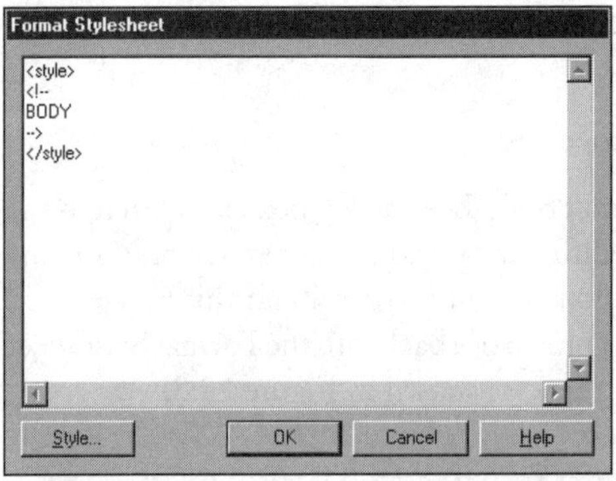

Figure 12.1 The Format Stylesheet dialog box.

using page-level styles. To do this, you must apply a style to the <BODY> tag. The Format Stylesheet dialog box, shown in Figure 12.1, sets only style properties for you. You must enter the names of the tags between the <!-- and --> tags manually.

Click on the Style button to bring up the Style dialog box to gain access to the following five style tabs:

- **Alignment** Sets properties for margins, padding, and text wrapping (see Figure 12.2).
- **Borders** Sets the style, color, and width for each of the four borders of a Web page.
- **Font** Sets the font and font size. An alternate font can be specified in case a particular client browser doesn't support the primary font. Additional alternate fonts can be specified manually.

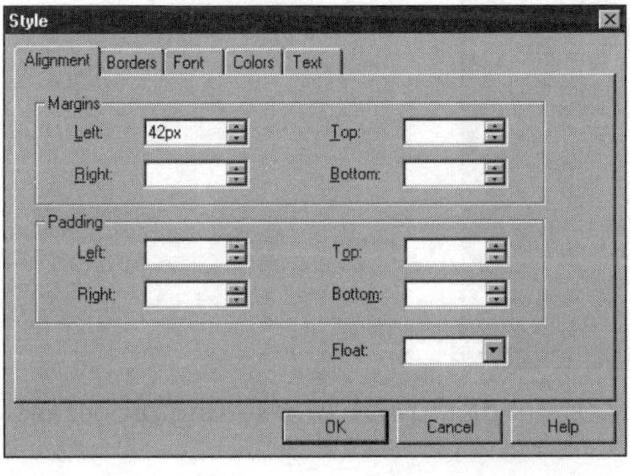

Figure 12.2 The Alignment tab of the Style dialog box.

- **Colors** Specifies background color, foreground color, and background image.
- **Text** Sets text font and text properties.

All the properties set using the Format Stylesheet dialog box are written to the same line of text. This can make it difficult to read the generated text if many properties are set. Fortunately, you don't need to worry about this because you can use the Style button to load these properties back into the Format Stylesheet dialog box to view the information there, as shown in Figure 12.3.

> *Note: If you forget to move the cursor from its default location before clicking on the Style button, you still have a second chance to place style properties between the comment tags. Just select the entire style properties string (including the curly braces), cut the text, and paste it between the comment tags, as shown in Figure 12.3.*

Style Button

The Style button is used to apply inline styles; it can be found on the Form Field Properties dialog box. It's also found on the following dialog boxes accessed from the menu bar's Format option:

- Font
- Paragraph
- Bullets And Numbering
- Animation

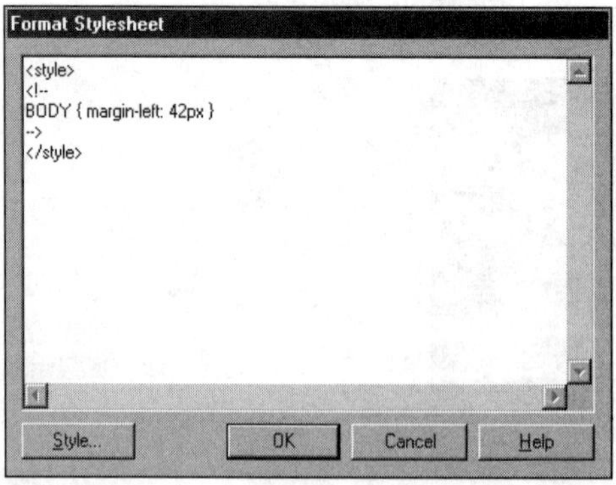

Figure 12.3 The Format Stylesheet dialog box after setting properties.

You can quickly and easily see how the Style button works by following these steps:

1. Select the text to be modified in FrontPage Editor.
2. On the menu bar, select Format|Font.
3. Click on the Style button.
4. On the Style dialog box, select the Colors tab.
5. Click on the Foreground Colors list and change the color of the text.

Themes

Themes define how Web documents look. Like a style sheet, a theme can be applied to a single document or all the documents in a Web site. Unlike style sheets, themes include graphics that are used for buttons, page headers, and backgrounds. You can choose between animated graphics and regular, static images. Each predefined theme has its own set of GIF and CSS files. The GIF files store the graphic images, and the CSS files store the rules about how text will appear and where GIF files will be applied. Figure 12.4 shows a simple Web page before a theme is applied.

STUDY ALERT

Because themes use their own style sheets, combining themes with your own style sheets and inline styles can lead to unexpected results. For this reason, Microsoft recommends against using your own styles with themes.

Using Themes

Themes are applied to a Web site in FrontPage Explorer. The Themes button is located under the Views bar. Click on this button to see the list of themes and options to choose from, as illustrated in Figure 12.5.

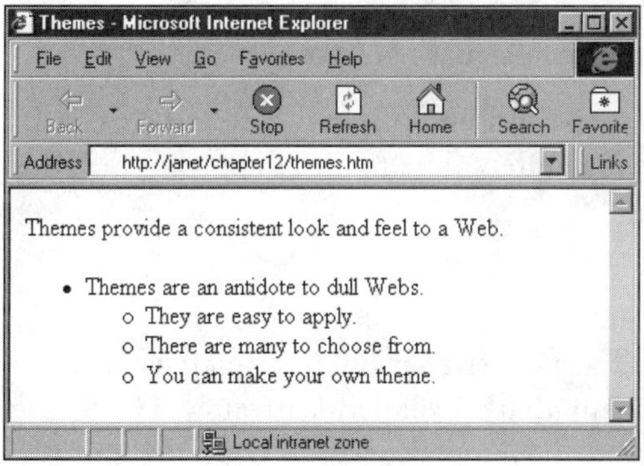

Figure 12.4 A Web page without a theme.

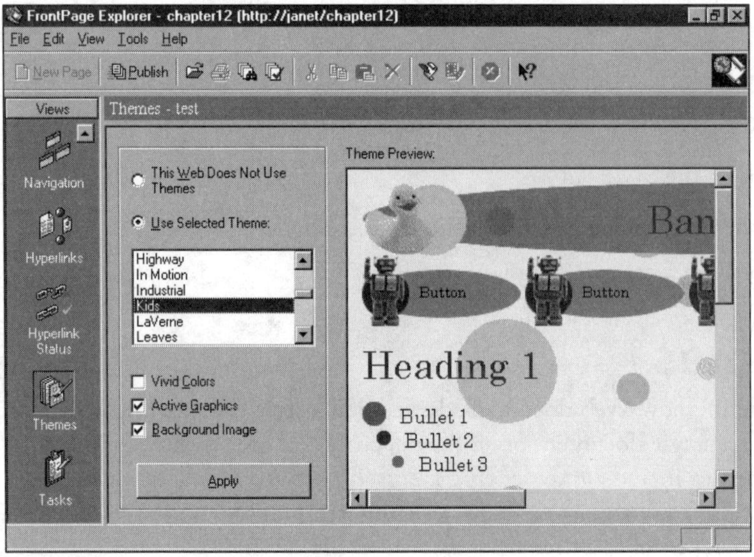

Figure 12.5 Themes and options.

In addition to the choice of themes, there are three options affecting how the theme will appear:

- **Vivid Colors** Brighter colors are used. When designing a Web site, you must consider the implications of your choices. Bright, vivid colors can convey a cheery, fun presence as well as detract from a serious, functional presence.
- **Active Graphics** Java applets are used to animate the buttons on the pages. Only Java-capable browsers are able to show the animation effect.
- **Background Image** A background graphic is used. You may want to turn this feature off if you have a lot of text to display and don't want competition from the background image. If you want to use a corporate logo as the background image, you can make your own theme.

A theme controls all background properties, and you cannot set a page's background properties while a theme is in effect. The result of applying the Kids theme is shown in Figure 12.6.

Editing Themes

It's easy to edit a theme using the Theme Designer, but first you must install it because it's an optional component that's installed separately. Go to the \SDK\Themes\Designer folder on the FrontPage 98 CD-ROM and run TDSETUP.EXE to install the Theme Designer. After installing the Theme

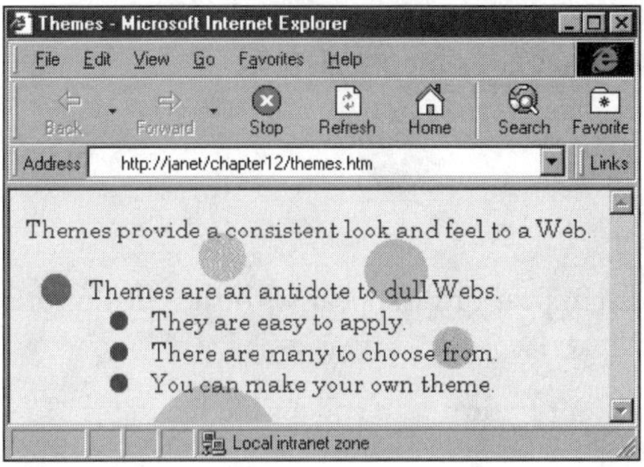

Figure 12.6 The Web page after applying a theme.

Designer, go to the menu bar in FrontPage Explorer and select Tools|Show Theme Designer to create or edit a theme. You might find it easier to edit an existing theme than to create a new one. Just be sure to rename the theme; otherwise, you'll overwrite the original theme. Online help isn't available for editing themes. For help, refer to the Word document FPDEVKIT.DOC in the \SDK folder on your FrontPage 98 CD-ROM.

Adding DHTML To Web Documents

Dynamic HTML (DHTML) is a Web technology that combines HTML, scripts, and style sheets to add animation to a Web site. You can add the following DHTML elements through FrontPage Editor:

- **Dynamic Outlining** Text items can be arranged as lists that can be made to collapse or expand at a click of the mouse. FrontPage simplifies this complex task with a single dialog box.
- **Text Animations** Selected text can be animated to spiral, fly, or zoom in. FrontPage automatically generates the complicated client scripts required for such dramatic visual effects.
- **Page Transitions** You can specify page transitions (dissolve, blend, and so on) when navigating from page to page. The results are similar to what PowerPoint users have available to transition from one slide to the next.
- **Form Field Extensions** The default tab order on a Web page can be overridden by explicitly assigning tab order numbers to a page's input fields. Alt+ key shortcuts, which are known as *access keys*, can also be created.

All the DHTML special effects you can implement with FrontPage require IE4 or later; IE3 does not support DHTML.

Dynamic Outlining

You can make items in a nested list appear or disappear with the click of the mouse by following these steps:

1. Identify the nested items you want to turn into collapsible list items.
2. Select the list item under which the nested items should appear.
3. On the menu bar, select Format|Bullets And Numbering.
4. Check Enable Collapsible Outlines.
5. Click on OK.

FrontPage generates several dozen lines of client-side JavaScript code to enable a collapsible outline. The results of this activity appear in Figure 12.7, which shows an expanded version of a collapsible outline as well as the List Properties dialog box.

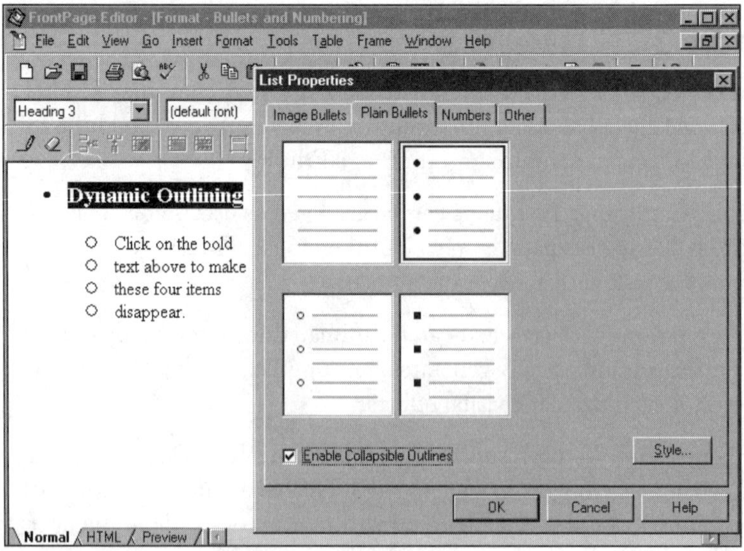

Figure 12.7 A collapsible outline example and the List Properties dialog box.

If you don't know how to make a nested outline, one way is to follow these steps in FrontPage Editor:

1. Enter a line of text; then press Enter.
2. Click on either the Numbered List or Bulleted List button.
3. Enter a line of text; then press Enter.
4. Double-click on the Increase Indent button.
5. Enter a second line of text; then press Enter.
6. Enter a third line of text; then press Enter.
7. Hit the Enter key three more times to stop the nesting, indenting, and the list itself.

Text Animations

The procedure for animating text is even easier than enabling a collapsible outline. Follow these steps:

1. Select the text you want to animate.
2. On the menu bar, select Format|Animation.
3. Choose the animation effect you want to apply to the text.

FrontPage generates several pages of client-side JavaScript code to animate the text. The code generated is somewhat generic in nature and contains instructions for processing all the FrontPage text animation effects, not just the effect you chose. The menu hierarchy for selecting an animation effect appears in Figure 12.8, where Fly From Right has been selected for the text item shown.

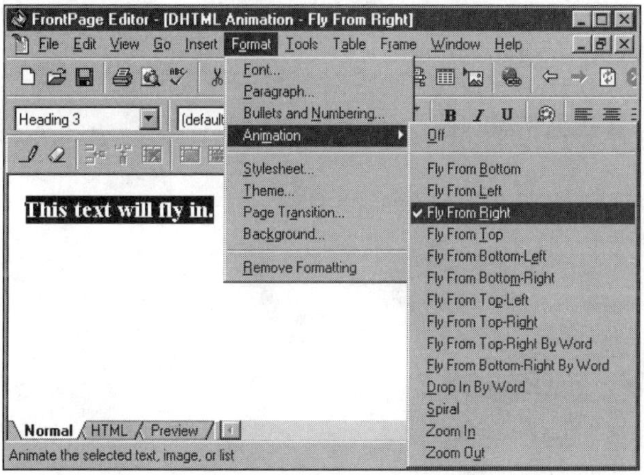

Figure 12.8 Animating selected text.

Page Transitions

Page transitions provide visual effects that will be familiar to users of Microsoft PowerPoint. Transitions can be applied at the site level or page level. The effect is seen either upon entering or exiting. For example, if the blend effect is chosen for the Page Enter event, each new page blends in for the number of seconds specified. If you anticipate the typical user will navigate through many pages on your Web site, it could be annoying to endure a page transition on every page. The solution to that problem is to apply a page transition to the Site Enter event of your Web's default Web page. You can see in Figure 12.9 a partial listing of the transition effects available through the Page Transitions dialog box.

Access to the Page Transitions dialog box is accomplished from FrontPage Editor's menu bar by selecting Format|Page Transition. You must navigate to or from a page to see a transition effect. Once the page is loaded, clicking on Refresh or reentering the URL for the page will *not* trigger the event that begins the transition.

Form Field Extensions

Form field extensions facilitate movement within a Web page by defining field tab order and creating Alt+ keyboard shortcuts. In our example, we selected a checkbox on our Web page, right-clicked on it, and chose Form Field Properties from the pop-up menu. This selection produces the Text Box Properties dialog box, shown in Figure 12.10. To specify the tab order, enter a value in the Tab Order box. If the same value is assigned to more than one field, the tab order sequence for those fields will be determined by the order in which the fields are defined, where fields defined earlier take precedence over those defined later. You can remove a field from the tab order sequence by assigning it a negative one (-1) value in the Tab Order box.

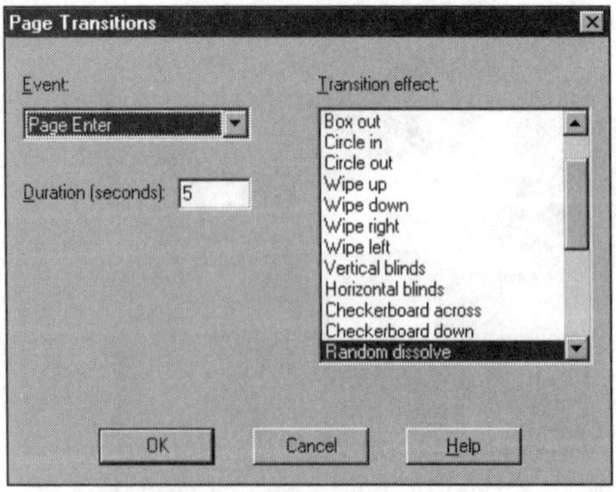

Figure 12.9 The Page Transitions dialog box.

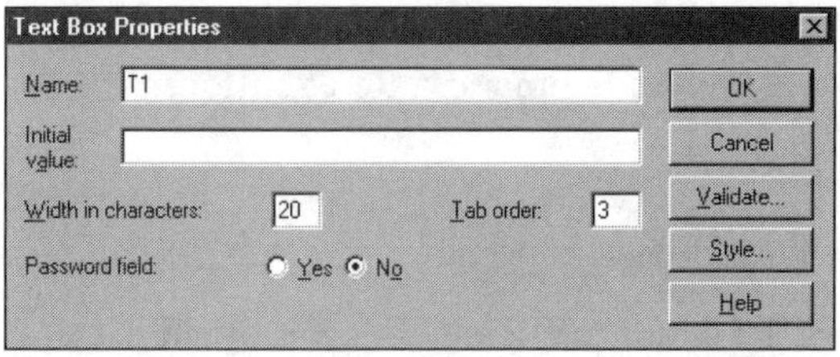

Figure 12.10 Changing the tab order using the Text Box Properties dialog box.

Using The Database Region Wizard

It's important that you understand how to use the Database Region wizard. You must know how to collect input data from a Web page and submit that data to a second Web page. On the second Web page, the Database Region wizard is used to generate database calls. Although the Database Region wizard does not require you to collect inputs from the user, we've chosen to do so because you'll have a more complete understanding, thus preparing you for differing scenarios.

The first Web page must contain a form to collect user input. In HTML, forms begin with the <FORM> tag and end with the </FORM> tag. Between those <FORM>...</FORM> tags, form fields must be defined and used to collect user input. Here are the steps you need to follow to create such an input solicitation page (the Text Box Properties dialog box used to create the **LastName** form field is shown in Figure 12.11):

1. Begin by creating a new Web page in FrontPage Editor.
2. Select File|New and then choose Normal Page.
3. Select Insert|Form Field and then choose One-Line Text Box. The <FORM>...</FORM> tags in HTML are generated automatically. The

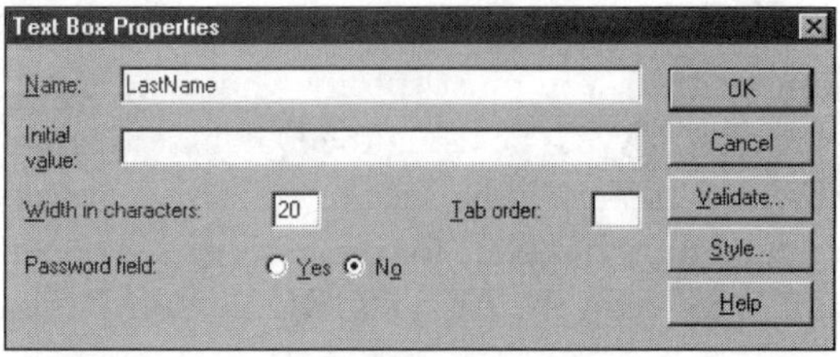

Figure 12.11 Assigning the form field properties of a one-line text box using the Text Box Properties dialog box.

form is surrounded by an outline that defines its boundaries. The form contains a one-line text box as well as Submit and Reset buttons.

4. Click on the one-line text box.
5. Right-click on and choose Form Field Properties.
6. Replace the default name of **T1** with **LastName**. This form field name will be referenced in the results page.
7. Right-click anywhere within the form's boundaries and select Form Properties.
8. Select the Send To Other radio button.
9. Click on the Options button. This brings up the Options For Custom Form Handler dialog box.
10. Enter an action for AUTHORDATA.ASP. This is the name of the Web page that the Database Region wizard will modify to display the results of the database query. Click on OK.
11. Click on OK to exit Form Properties.
12. Save your new Web page to file GETAUTHOR.HTM.

Now that you have created a text box, you can customize it to suit your needs. The following sections discuss additional text box settings.

Setting Text Box Properties

The Text Box Properties dialog box (refer to Figure 12.11) is used to assign a field name to a one-line text box. This field name is entered in the Database Region wizard to link the database query to the user's input. The Database Region wizard is discussed in detail in the "ODBC Data Source Name" section later in this chapter.

Form Properties And Options For Custom Form Handler

After you've named the form's input field, you must specify where the input will be sent and how it will be processed. We'll be using the Database Region wizard in the next step; therefore, the input will be sent to an Active Server Page (ASP) script (which is executed on the server) for processing. As shown in Figure 12.12, the ASP script will reside in the AUTHORDATA.ASP file.

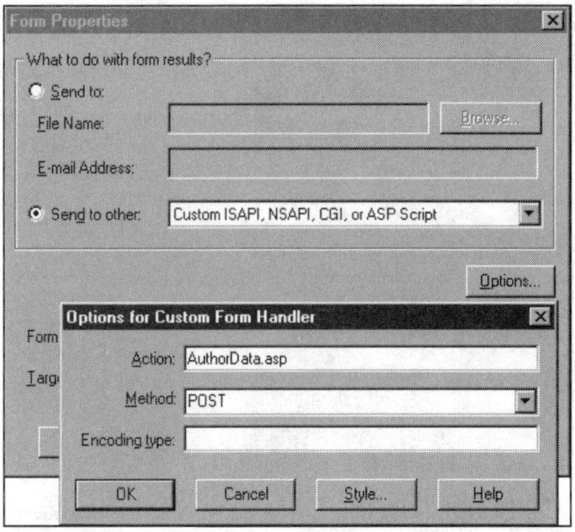

Figure 12.12 The Form Properties and Options For Custom Form Handler dialog boxes.

The author's last name is sent by means of a post to the ASP script named AUTHORDATA.ASP. Because ASP scripts are executed on the Web server, they must reside in a directory with script access turned on.

ODBC Data Source Name

The next step is to create the results page. Open up a new, normal page in FrontPage Editor. Go to the menu bar and select Insert|Database|Database Region Wizard. You must provide an ODBC data source name (DSN). Your system administrator or database administrator can provide you with this name.

An ODBC data source name is needed to link a Web page to a database.

You can also enter a database user name and password, as shown in Figure 12.13. It's good practice to password-protect a database. When you do this, users must provide a user name and password when accessing the database. The user name and password fields are not required by FrontPage or the Database Region wizard. The Database Region wizard merely provides a place for users to supply this information if it is required by the database.

You needn't concern yourself too much with database security issues. However, you do need to understand fully which inputs the Database Region wizard requires. Remember that the database itself requires a database user name and password, not

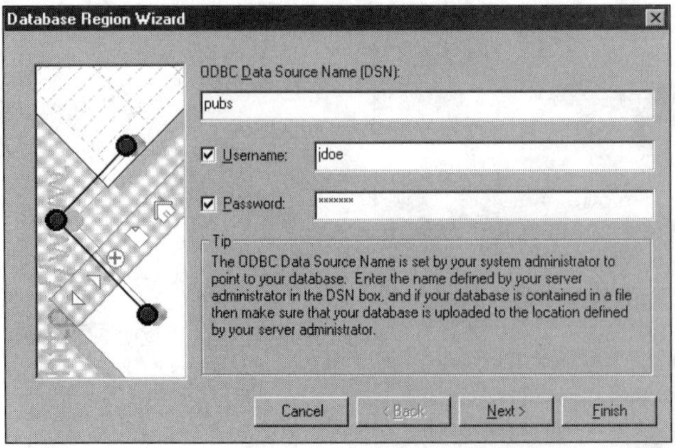

Figure 12.13 Specifying the ODBC DSN in the Database Region wizard.

the Database Region wizard in FrontPage. Experiment with the Database Region wizard to find out what happens when you fail to enter values in all the input fields.

SQL Query String

A SQL query string is a database command that can retrieve, delete, add, or modify data in a database that can handle input formulated using the Structured Query Language (SQL). A SQL query string can be entered manually, or Microsoft Access can be used to generate a SQL query string that can be copied and then pasted into the Database Region wizard.

Because the SQL query string defines the interaction with the database, it's a required input. The Database Region wizard does not require you to insert form field parameters. *Form field parameters* are used to pass user inputs into the SQL query string. Sometimes a SQL query does not have any user inputs. Because we're passing the author's last name into this query, we use the Insert Form Field Parameter dialog box. A SQL query string was entered manually in Figure 12.14 to show what such a query can look like and how much work is involved.

When comparing character data in a database to a particular value, SQL uses single quotation marks to delimit (that is, to *enclose*) the character data value. That's why the beginning single quotation mark is shown in the upper pane in Figure 12.14. The ending quotation mark is added after the Insert Form Field Parameter step. Notice the form field name entered in the Insert Form Field Parameter dialog box: It's the form field name entered on the GETAUTHOR.HTM Web page; it links the results page to the input page. The final form of the SQL query string appears in Figure 12.15.

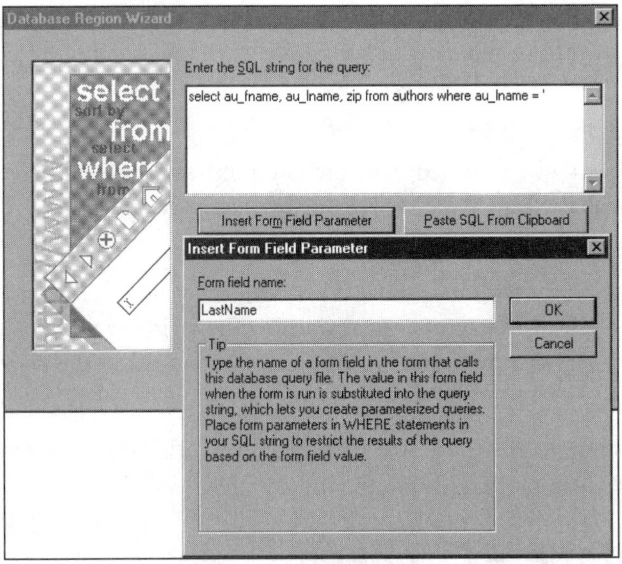

Figure 12.14 Entering the SQL query string in the Database Region wizard.

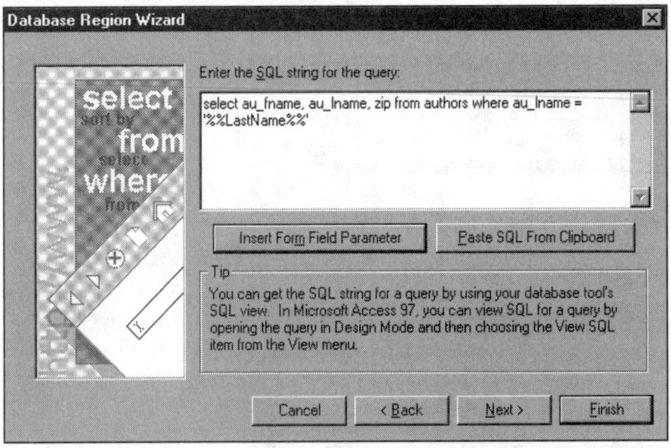

Figure 12.15 The SQL query string after the Insert Form Field Parameter step has been completed and a final closing single quotation mark has been added.

Query Field Names

The Database Region wizard added **LastName** to the SQL query string and appended **%%** at the beginning and end. The **%%** string signifies that a value will be substituted for **LastName**. In this example, the substituted value is obtained from the **LastName** field on the GETAUTHOR.HTM page. Because the **LastName** field is a character value, SQL requires it to be inside single quotation marks. That's why it's absolutely necessary for you to add the closing single quotation mark manually.

Query Field Names

To complete the process, the returned database column names (called *query field names* in the Database Region Wizard dialog box) must also be specified, as shown in Figure 12.16.

Click on OK after adding each query field. When all the query fields have been entered, click on Finish. You'll receive the warning shown in Figure 12.17, which tells you what subsequent actions will be necessary to make the code work properly.

As the warning admonishes, you must save your file with an .ASP extension in a directory with script access.

Internet Database Connector

Instead of using Active Server Pages to access an ODBC database, you can use the Internet Database Connector (IDC). This is an older technology that uses IDC files and HTML extension files (.HTX). Although FrontPage 97 provided

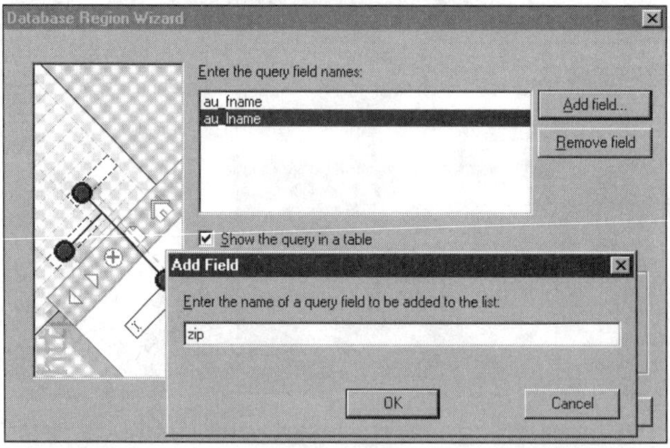

Figure 12.16 Adding query fields in the Database Region wizard.

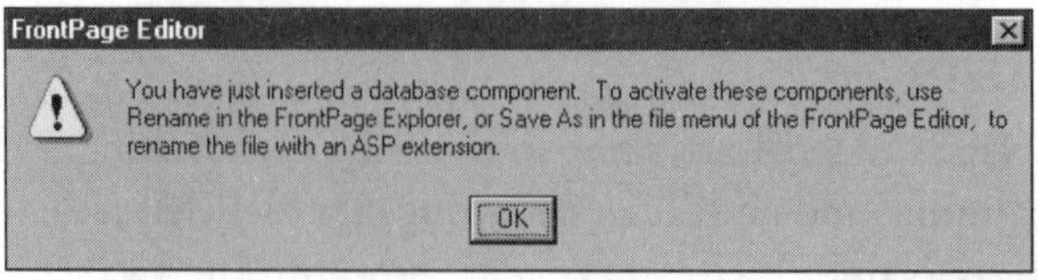

Figure 12.17 FrontPage notifies you when additional actions are required to activate database components.

templates for the IDC and HTX files, FrontPage 98 does not. The IDC file must contain entries for the ODBC DSN and the SQL query statement. Although the IDC file itself does not require a user name, if a user name is required to access the database, it must be provided in the IDC file. The final required entry in the IDC file is the name of the HTX file that serves as a template for presenting the results returned from the database query. As with ASP files, the query string input parameters are entered in a form on an ordinary Web page with an .HTM extension. As shown in Figure earlier 12.12, the Form Properties dialog box is used to send the results to a custom ISAPI script and specify a method of POST. The action is the URL of the IDC file.

How you format the results of a database query can change depending on what kind of further processing of the data, if any, is required. If your results need to be loaded into Excel or Access, you might want to consider formatting the output data with commas (CSV format).

Scripting

Client-side scripts can be used to make a Web page interact with the user. Form field inputs can be validated using client-side scripting instead of submitting the Web page to the server. Writing client-side scripts manually requires knowledge of a scripting language such as VBScript or JavaScript. Specialized knowledge is not required when using the Script wizard, which is accessed from the FrontPage Editor menu bar by using the Insert|Advanced|Script command. Click on the Script Wizard button on the Script dialog box, as shown in Figure 12.18.

Notice the language options available in the Script dialog box. You can specify VBScript, JavaScript, or Other. If you have an intranet environment where you know that all the browsers support the Perl scripting language, you could specify Perl in the Other text box. It's important that you consider browser capabilities

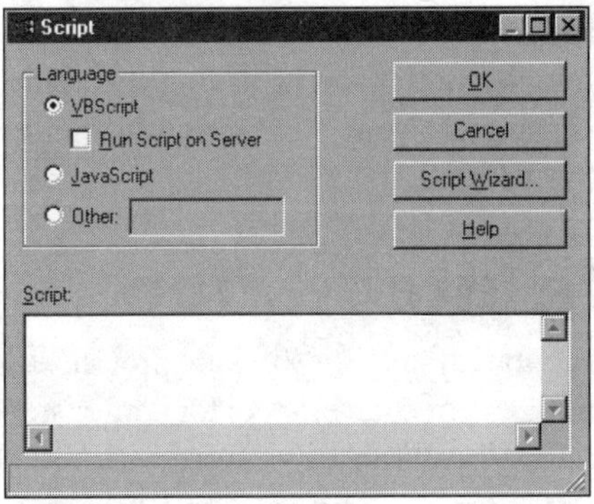

Figure 12.18 The Script dialog box.

when choosing a client scripting language. Netscape supports only JavaScript. IE3 or later supports both VBScript and JavaScript.

STUDY ALERT

Remember that FrontPage can write client-side form validation scripts for you. If you use this feature, you should know that the default scripting language for form validation scripts is JavaScript. If you change the validation script's language to VBScript, Netscape users will be unable to execute them. In FrontPage Explorer, choose Tools|Web Settings. On the Advanced tab, you can change the language for validation scripts.

Server-side scripting is independent of the browser because it's executed on the server. In other words, it's compatible with all browsers because only standard HTML is sent to the browser. By checking the Run Script On Server checkbox, you can use the Script dialog box to help you write server-side ASP scripts. The Database Region wizard writes server-side ASP scripts for you. Common Gateway Interface (CGI) scripts and ISAPI DLLs can also provide server-side processing.

The factors that determine the appropriate server-side scripting implementation are portability, performance, and programming difficulty. CGI scripts are actually executable programs that can be recompiled and ported to different operating systems. You'll find that CGI scripts are common on Unix systems. When CGI scripts are being used, each connection requires a separate process. Consequently, CGI scripts are less scalable and more demanding on system resources. ISAPI DLLs, which run only on Microsoft platforms, do not require separate processes and are a high performance solution. That's why FrontPage Server Extensions for IIS are implemented as ISAPI DLLs.

Both CGI scripts and ISAPI DLLs are highly customizable and require advanced programming skills. ASP scripts are instructions executed by an ISAPI DLL and therefore have the performance advantages of an ISAPI DLL. However, writing ASP scripts does not require a mastery of a programming language to implement the scripts. In fact, by using the Database Region wizard, you don't have to have any programming knowledge. However, having the ability to write VBScript code enables you to customize your ASP scripts, although not as much as programming custom ISAPI DLLs.

Visual SourceSafe Integration

Visual SourceSafe is Microsoft's version control system for software projects. It's similar in purpose to RCS in Unix. FrontPage is, of course, a tool for administering, authoring, and publishing Web projects. When FrontPage is used with Visual SourceSafe, version control management is greatly simplified and enhanced. FrontPage Server Extensions automate many of the SourceSafe tasks.

Practice Questions

Question 1

Your large corporate client has asked for an easily maintained Web site with a consistent and professional look and feel. What is the simplest and best way to accomplish this?

- ❍ a. Use the Format Stylesheet dialog box on every page to apply a consistent set of style rules
- ❍ b. Use the Corporate Presence Web wizard to build the site
- ❍ c. Apply a theme to the Web site
- ❍ d. Use an external, linked style sheet on every page

Answer c is correct. A theme imposes a consistent, professional look and feel to a Web site with a minimum of effort. Themes include style sheets as well as graphics and automatically apply them to all Web documents. Answers a and d are incorrect because they involve too much effort and are not easy to maintain as new pages are added to the site. Using the Corporate Presence Web wizard would accomplish the task if you applied a theme to the Web site, which is only an optional step. Additionally, this wizard may not be appropriate for your client's requirements. Therefore, answer b is incorrect.

Question 2

The Format Stylesheet wizard fully automates the creation of embedded style sheets.

Trick! question

- ❍ a. True
- ❍ b. False

Answer b is correct. This is a false statement. There is no Format Stylesheet wizard. The Format Stylesheet dialog box, on the other hand, requires manual intervention to get the style sheet to work. Because of the specific terminology used, we marked this as a trick question.

Question 3

Which of the following inputs are required for the Database Region wizard? [Check all correct answers]

- ❑ a. ODBC Data Source Name (DSN)
- ❑ b. Database user name and password
- ❑ c. The SQL string for the query
- ❑ d. Form Field parameter
- ❑ e. One or more query field names

The Database Region wizard requires a DSN, a SQL string, and one or more query field names. Therefore answers a, c, and e are correct. Although it's a good practice to require a database user name and password, these items are not required. Therefore, answer b is incorrect. Not all database queries require input. Therefore, answer d is incorrect.

Question 4

Trick! question

You are designing a Web site that will be on the Internet. You want to select a theme that is fully compatible with all IE and Netscape browsers. Which of the following allows you to do this?

- ❍ a. Make no special provisions; all themes are compatible with all browsers, provided FrontPage Server Extensions are installed.
- ❍ b. Use a conservative theme such as Downtown.
- ❍ c. Select any theme, but be sure to turn off Active Graphics.
- ❍ d. Use an ActiveX plug-in for Netscape to enable Active Graphics.

Answer c is correct. Active Graphics are Java applets and IE2 is not Java capable. (Note that the question says *all* versions of IE.) Answer a is incorrect because the FrontPage Server Extensions are on the server, not the browser. Answer b is incorrect because the individual themes differ only in appearance, not browser requirements. Answer d is incorrect because Active Graphics are not implemented with ActiveX.

Question 5

You have static text on a Web page that your client wants animated. The type of animation is not important as long as there is movement. Browser compatibility is not an issue because the Web site is part of an intranet where only IE4 or higher is used. What is the easiest way to animate the text?

- ❍ a. Replace the static text with an animated GIF.
- ❍ b. Write a Java applet.
- ❍ c. Use the Script wizard to write a JavaScript applet.
- ❍ d. Highlight the static text, go to the Format menu, and select an animation effect.

Answer d is correct. It is the easiest method of the choices given. An animated GIF provides a very portable animation effect, but requires the creation of at least two separate images to create an animation effect. Therefore, answer a is incorrect because of the effort involved. Answer b is incorrect for the same reason. There is no such thing as a JavaScript applet. Therefore, answer c is incorrect.

Question 6

Which of the following are required in the IDC file? [Check all correct answers]

- ❑ a. The name of the template HTX file
- ❑ b. ODBC Data Source Name (DSN)
- ❑ c. Database user name
- ❑ d. The SQL string for the query
- ❑ e. One or more query field names

The IDC file requires an HTX template file name, a DSN, and a SQL string. Therefore answers a, b, and d are correct. The user name is optional, making answer c incorrect. Query field names are required by the Database Region wizard, not the IDC file. Therefore, answer e is incorrect.

Question 7

What does the Database Region wizard create or insert to accomplish database access?

- ❍ a. A FrontPage WebBot
- ❍ b. Client-side VBScript
- ❍ c. Client-side JavaScript
- ❍ d. Server-side VBScript

Answer d is correct. The Database Region wizard creates an Active Server Page using VBScript. It is because this script executes on the server that the Active Server Page is compatible with all browsers. The Database Region wizard does not create or insert a FrontPage WebBot. Therefore, answer a is incorrect. All database processing occurs on the server. Therefore, answers b and c are incorrect.

Question 8

Your development server is running IIS 4 on NT 4. The production server is a Unix Apache Web server with FrontPage Server Extensions hosted by your Internet Service Provider. The development and production databases are identical ODBC-compliant third-party databases. How should you accomplish database access?

- ❍ a. Write custom CGI scripts using the Perl scripting language. Recompile the CGI scripts on the Unix server.
- ❍ b. Use the Database Region wizard to generate Active Server Pages. Use FrontPage Server Extensions to publish to the Unix server.
- ❍ c. Write custom ISAPI DLLs and recompile them on the Unix server.
- ❍ d. Create IDC and HTX files and use the Internet Database Connector on both machines.

Answer a is correct. A custom CGI script is the only cross-platform solution presented. Active Server Pages, ISAPI DLLs, and the Internet Database Connector are database access solutions for Microsoft operating systems only. Therefore, answers b, c, and d are incorrect.

Question 9

You need to validate user inputs on a Web page with both one-line and scrolling text boxes. Every input field must have a value entered. Only IE3 or newer will be used to access your Web site. You want to minimize maintenance requirements as well as user delays and inconvenience. What is the best strategy?

- ❍ a. Use server-side VBScript.
- ❍ b. Write custom client-side JavaScript.
- ❍ c. Write custom client-side VBScript.
- ❍ d. Set the Page Properties requiring all fields on the page to have a value entered.
- ❍ e. Set the Form Field Properties for each field requiring each field to have a value entered.

Answer e is correct. FrontPage automatically generates the necessary client-side script. Answer a is incorrect because server-side validation requires the user to wait for a response from the server. A client-side script would be faster and less disruptive to the user. Because only IE3 or higher will be used, either JavaScript or VBScript will work. Although using a client-side script is faster than waiting for a round-trip validation from the server, a custom client script increases maintenance requirements. Therefore, answers b and c are incorrect. Answer d is are incorrect because there is no Page Properties requiring inputs for all fields.

Question 10

Which of the following tools or features are used to prevent changes from being lost when more than one developer is working on the same project?

- ❍ a. NTFS file-level security
- ❍ b. Tasks View
- ❍ c. Microsoft Project
- ❍ d. Visual SourceSafe
- ❍ e. FrontPage Server Extensions

Answer d is correct. Only Visual SourceSafe provides source code control and ease of administration. NTFS file-level security could protect individual files, but the administrative effort would be impractical. Therefore, answer a is incorrect. The FrontPage 98 Tasks View and Microsoft Project only track tasks. They do not restrict or manage access to a particular file. Therefore, answers b and c are incorrect. FrontPage Server Extensions can selectively grant permissions to author a file, but don't prevent one author from overwriting the work of another author. Therefore, answer e is incorrect.

Question 11

You must give an extension of .ASP to a file created by the Database Region wizard. You must also assign execute access to the directory where the ASP file resides so the server can execute the Active Server script.

- ❍ a. True
- ❍ b. False

You must assign script access, not execute access, to the directories containing ASP files, which makes this statement false. Therefore, answer b is correct.

Need To Know More?

Karlins, David and Stephanie Cottrell. *Teach Yourself Microsoft FrontPage 98 in a Week, 2nd Edition*, Sams.net, Indianapolis, IN, 1998. ISBN 1-5721-350-8. More of an introductory book, this title provides decent coverage of this chapter's topics in its chapters on adding dynamic content to Web pages (Chapter 7), on designing input forms (Chapter 10), and on collecting form input (Chapter 11).

Matthews, Martin S. and Erik B. Poulsen. *FrontPage 98: The Complete Reference*, Osborne/McGraw-Hill, Berkeley, CA, 1998. ISBN 0-07-882394-3. Chapters 13 to 15 cover Web scripting languages, Active Server Pages, and working with databases, in that order—all are worth consulting on the topics covered in this chapter. For more information about Visual SourceSafe, consult Chapter 18.

Tauber, Daniel A. and Brenda Kienan. *Mastering Microsoft FrontPage98*, Sybex, Alameda, CA, 1998. ISBN 0-7821-2144-6. This is a good resource and reference book for the product. Chapter 13 covers style sheets, Chapter 14 covers forms, Chapter 20 covers database publishing and the Database Region wizard, and Chapter 21 covers scripting issues.

Microsoft TechNet. FrontPage 98 information resides in the "MS Office and Desktop Applications" section on the CD-ROM. The "FrontPage 98 Manuals," "Resource Kit," "Tips And Techniques," and "Tools And Utilities" headings all contain information germane to the contents of this chapter (especially the "Resource Kit" section).

www.microsoft.com/frontpage/. This is the official FrontPage Web site hosted by Microsoft. It offers overview information about the product and includes pointers to lots of useful information. You can use the built-in search function to search on strings such as "FrontPage 98 and DHTML," "FrontPage 98 and Database Region wizard," and so forth.

www.w3c.org/style. This page is the World Wide Web Consortium's home page for the official CSS specification. Take a look at this site to view the complete specification of this special-purpose Web technology.

Web Servers, Server Management, And Server Extensions

13

Terms you'll need to understand:

- √ HTTP server
- √ FrontPage Web server
- √ Personal Web Server
- √ Internet Information Server (IIS)
- √ Peer Web Services (PWS)
- √ FrontPage Server Extensions
- √ Port number
- √ Request For Comments (RFC)

Techniques you'll need to master:

- √ Understanding the differences between the different Web servers
- √ Installing FrontPage Server Extensions
- √ Comparing FrontPage Server Extensions capabilities by platform
- √ Administering the Web server
- √ Controlling administrative access to the FrontPage Web
- √ Setting port numbers

This chapter discusses the different Web server applications that Microsoft FrontPage supports. You'll learn about installing and configuring FrontPage Server Extensions for various Web servers in addition to the capabilities supported by them. Some significant Web site administration topics will also be presented in this chapter.

Supported Web Servers

A Web site created with Microsoft FrontPage can run on any Hypertext Transfer Protocol (HTTP) server. However, if you don't have the server-side software, called *FrontPage Server Extensions*, the Web site may not have full functionality. In this section, we describe the Microsoft Web servers supported by FrontPage 98 and list the non-Microsoft-supported Web servers.

FrontPage Personal Web Server

If you don't have a Web server installed on the system you're using to run FrontPage 98, you can choose to install FrontPage Personal Web Server during the Custom installation.

> *Note: FrontPage Personal Web Server is the same Web server that is available for use with Windows 95 and 98, and is basically a scaled-down version of Internet Information Server (IIS).*

FrontPage Personal Web Server is a very simple Web server that does not allow for significant configuration. It's essentially included to allow you to check your Web site as you develop it. FrontPage Personal Web Server does require a user name and password to allow access to the FrontPage Web site. If you want to use the FrontPage 98 Explorer application to configure the site, you're required to log onto the server (see Figure 13.1).

> *Note: FrontPage Web Server security is only enabled if FrontPage was installed when user-level security (in the Network applet in the Control Panel) was enabled.*

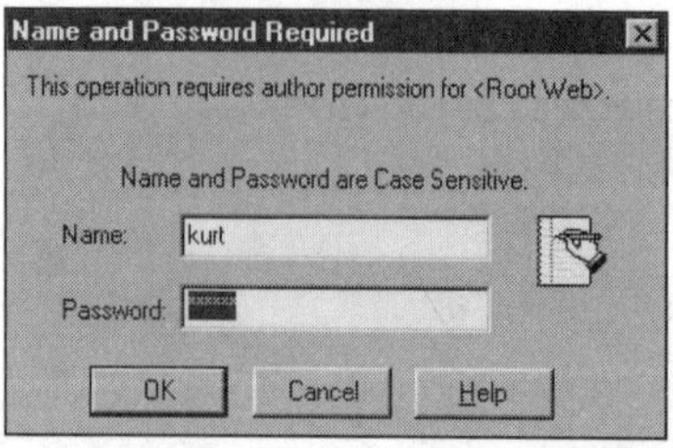

Figure 13.1 The Name And Password Required dialog box.

Other configuration parameters for FrontPage Personal Web Server are maintained in the HTTPD.CNF file in the C:\FrontPage Web\Server\Conf directory. Open this file with Notepad to see the various configuration options, including server root path, TCP port, and connection timeout settings.

Note: Several administrative tasks concerning FrontPage Personal Web Server are explained in Chapter 3.

Internet Information Server For Windows NT Server

IIS runs on the Windows NT Server operating system only. This product is able to handle moderate to heavy use on a corporate intranet or Internet Web site. IIS ships as part of the Windows NT Option Pack, which is now included with Windows NT Server 4, or it can be downloaded for free from the Microsoft Web site.

The key features of the latest version of IIS (version 4) are presented in the following list:

- **HTTP 1.1 support** Supports the latest HHTP standard (HTTP 1.1).
- **WWW service** It's a fully functional Web server.
- **FTP service** Supports File Transfer Protocol (FTP), both read and write.
- **SMTP service** Ships with support for Simple Message Transfer Protocol (SMTP) message storage and forwarding.
- **NNTP service** Has the capability to support the Network News Transfer Protocol (NNTP) and threaded discussion groups.
- **Process isolation** Applications that run on the server can be isolated, so there's less risk that an errant application will take down other applications on your Web site.
- **Active Server Pages support** Supports Active Server Page (ASP) scripting in its Web pages. ASP technology allows you to insert scripts directly into an HTML page. The code is run on the server, and the client only sees HTML.
- **Java Virtual Machine** Ships with a server-side Java Virtual Machine (JVM) to process Java code on the server.
- **Certificate Authority** Can be a Certificate Authority for Internet and intranet clients. With the Windows NT Option Pack, you can choose to install a Certificate Server that works with IIS.

- **Domain blocking** Allows you to prevent specific domains, IP addresses, and entire IP subnets from gaining access to your Web server by creating security restrictions. You can literally keep specific computers from contacting the IIS computer.
- **Posting Acceptor** Part of the HTTP 1.1 support that IIS provides is to accept files over an HTTP connection through the Posting Acceptor.
- **Index Server** Index Server ships with the Windows NT Option Pack and tightly integrates with IIS. The Index Server allows users to search your site so that they can find the information they're seeking.
- **Multiple Web sites** Has the ability to host multiple Web sites. This is done by assigning a different IP address or by using TCP port numbers.
- **ODBC logging** Has the capability to log Web access statistics to an ODBC-compliant database, such as SQL Server or Microsoft Access.

This is a brief list of IIS capabilities. This list was created so you can compare IIS to the other Microsoft Web servers as they are presented in the following sections. In the following sections of this chapter, you'll learn more about FrontPage integration with the Microsoft Web servers, including IIS.

> You are not required to be an expert on IIS to successfully complete the FrontPage exam; however, you should understand the basic IIS administrative tasks explained later in this chapter. To learn more about IIS, visit **www.microsoft.com/iis**, or purchase *MCSE IIS 4 Exam Cram* or one of many other fine publications on the subject.

Peer Web Services For Windows NT Workstation

If you're installing a Web server on a Windows NT Workstation, Microsoft provides Peer Web Services, which is a scaled-down version NT Server's IIS.

Because Peer Web Services is a scaled-down version of IIS, it does not support all the features IIS does. Here's a list of items that are not supported by Peer Web Services:

- Process isolation
- Multiple Web sites
- Domain and IP restrictions
- ODBC logging
- Index Server

Personal Web Server For Windows 95 And Windows 98

Personal Web Server is a product designed for Windows 95 and 98, and it ships on the FrontPage 98 CD-ROM under the PWS folder. You can also install this product from the Windows NT Option Pack, which contains IIS and Peer Web Services for Windows NT computers.

The Windows 95 and 98 Personal Web Server supports all the features that Windows NT Workstation Peer Web Services supports, except that it does not have integrated security. This is not so much a problem of the Web server, but rather an indication that Windows 95 and 98 do not have the ability to secure files and folders by user account.

Non-Microsoft Web Servers

Even if you develop your Microsoft FrontPage Web on a Windows 95, 98, or Windows NT computer with Microsoft software, you may wish to load your Web site to a non-Microsoft Web server. In Table 13.1, you can see the list of non-Microsoft Web servers that have the capability to support FrontPage Web sites with FrontPage Server Extensions.

Table 13.1 Non-Microsoft Web servers that can support FrontPage Webs.

Platform	Operating System	Web Server
Intel x86	Windows NT Server	Netscape Commerce Server 1.12
	Windows NT Workstation	Netscape Communications Server 1.12
	Windows 95/98	Netscape Enterprise 2 and 3 Netscape FastTrack 2 O'Reilly WebSite
Alpha	Digital Unix 3.2c, 4	Apache 1.1.3, 1.2.4, 1.2.5 CERN 3 NCSA 1.5.2 (earlier versions are not supported) Netscape Commerce Server 1.12 Netscape Communications Server 1.12 Netscape Enterprise Server 2 and 3 Netscape FastTrack 2

(continued)

Table 13.1 Non-Microsoft Web servers that can support FrontPage Webs *(continued)*.

Platform	Operating System	Web Server
Intel x86	BSD/OS 2.1	Apache 1.1.3, 1.2.4, 1.2.5
	BSD/OS 3.0	CERN 3
	Red Hat Linux 3.0.3	NCSA 1.5.2 (earlier versions are not supported)
	SCO OpenServer	Netscape Commerce Server 1.12
	SCO UnixWare 7	Netscape Communications Server 1.12 Netscape Enterprise Server 2 and 3 Netscape FastTrack 2
PA-RISC	HP/UX 9.03, 10.01	CERN 3 NCSA 1.5.2 (earlier versions are not supported) Netscape Commerce Server 1.12 Netscape Communications Server 1.12 Netscape Enterprise Server 2 and 3 Netscape FastTrack 2
RS6000	AIX 3.2.5, 4.x	CERN 3 NCSA 1.5.2 (earlier versions are not supported) Netscape Commerce Server 1.12 Netscape Communications Server 1.12 Netscape Enterprise Server 2 and 3 Netscape FastTrack 2
Silicon Graphics	IRIX 5.3, 6.2	CERN 3 NCSA 1.5.2 (earlier not supported) Netscape Commerce Server 1.12 Netscape Communications Server 1.12 Netscape Enterprise Server 2 and 3 Netscape FastTrack 2

(continued)

Table 13.1 Non-Microsoft Web servers that can support FrontPage Webs *(continued)*.

Platform	Operating System	Web Server
SPARC	Solaris 2.4, 2.5	CERN 3 NCSA 1.5.2 (earlier versions are not supported) Netscape Commerce Server 1.12 Netscape Communications Server 1.12 Netscape Enterprise Server 2 and 3 Netscape FastTrack 2
SPARC	Sun OS 4.1.3, 4.1.4	CERN 3 NCSA 1.5.2 (earlier versions are not supported) Netscape Commerce Server 1.12 Netscape Communications Server 1.12 Netscape Enterprise Server 2 and 3 Netscape FastTrack 2

Server Extensions

FrontPage uses FrontPage Server Extensions to interface with the various Web servers that FrontPage supports. Although it's possible to run a Web site created with FrontPage on Web servers without FrontPage Server Extensions installed, several features won't be supported if you don't have them. FrontPage Server Extensions provide the following:

- Multiuser authoring, which allows multiple users to work simultaneously on the same Web site
- Remote authoring via FrontPage, which allows users to connect and write directly to the Web server over the Internet
- Form handling for the custom forms that can be added via FrontPage
- Support for discussion Webs, which is closely related to multiuser authoring
- Full-text indexing, which allows users to search the Web site when the proper HTML search forms are available
- Support for FrontPage hit counters

Be sure to take notice of the support that's provided by FrontPage Server Extensions.

Installing Server Extensions

To install FrontPage Server Extensions, first install FrontPage and then open the FrontPage Server Administrator application (FPSRVWIN.EXE), which is located, by default, in the C:\Program Files\Microsoft FrontPage\Version3.0\Bin folder hierarchy.

Once you've located and opened FrontPage Server Administrator (see Figure 13.2), you can easily install the correct FrontPage Server Extensions by following these steps:

1. Click the Install button.
2. Choose the correct server type from the Configure Server Type dialog box. Click OK to continue.

From this point, the directions may vary depending on the Web server you've selected. However, in general, you confirm the Web server type, port number, and root Web document. Once you've confirmed the selections (if correct), FrontPage Server Extensions should be installed. Click OK on the dialog boxes as necessary.

Installing FrontPage Server Extensions on Unix Web servers is considerably more complex. You must use the FPSRVADM.EXE command-line utility to install the extensions on a non-Microsoft operating system. You can follow the

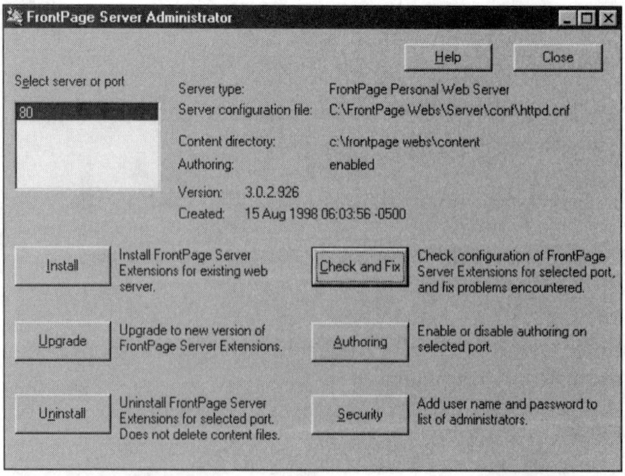

Figure 13.2 FrontPage Server Administrator.

command-line help dialog box for this application by typing "fpsrvadm -h" at the command prompt while in the C:\Program Files\Microsoft FrontPage\Version3.0\Bin directory.

Note: You can learn more about Unix Web servers and FrontPage Server Extensions by reading the Microsoft Knowledge Base article "FPUnix: Install FrontPage Extensions on Supported Unix Servers," which you can find on Microsoft TechNet or on the Microsoft Web site (search for article number Q185541).

Uninstalling Server Extensions

Removing FrontPage Server Extensions is a simple task. The option to uninstall is available through FrontPage Server Administrator. To uninstall FrontPage Server Extensions, follow these steps:

1. Open the FrontPage Server Administrator (FPSRVWIN.EXE) via the C:\Program Files\Microsoft FrontPage folder.
2. Select the TCP port number where your Web server is installed in the Select Port Number window (usually port 80). Then, click the Uninstall button.

You'll see a confirmation dialog box when the FrontPage Server Extensions are successfully removed.

Web Server Administration

FrontPage Sever Administrator (refer to Figure 13.2) is clearly one of the most important advanced graphical administrative configuration utilities for FrontPage 98. In addition, another administrative tool is available that performs the same functions as FrontPage Server Administrator, but it's not graphical. The command-line administrative tool for FrontPage 98 is FPSRVADM.EXE, and it is located in the C:\Program Files\Microsoft FrontPage\Version3.0\Bin folder. You can see the features this command-line utility supports by typing "fpsrvadmin -h" from the Bin directory (see Figure 13.3).

Setting Port Numbers

Internet and Web communications are conducted over the Transmission Control Protocol/Internet Protocol (TCP/IP) suite of protocols. TCP uses port numbers to handle communications. Servers on TCP/IP networks listen to certain port numbers for incoming communications. When these services receive a message on or for the port they are monitoring, the service responds.

Figure 13.3 The FrontPage command-line administration tool.

There are 65,535 ports available. Ports 1 to 1023 are called *well-known ports* and are reserved for specific uses. For example, FTP servers typically receive client calls on TCP port 21. This is a well-known port number, so Internet clients rely on the FTP server to be listening to TCP port 21. Typically, Web (HTTP) servers conduct their business on TCP port 80.

However, if you want to limit access to your server on the network or Internet, you could start by switching its default TCP port number to something different, such as 1025. This means that clients must know to contact your Web server on that port number, instead of the default. In the address line of their Web browsers, they would only need to add ":1025" to the end of their address to connect to your server. For example, if your Web server has the Internet address **http://www.hudlogic.com**, they would enter "http://www.hudlogic.com:1025" to contact your server on TCP port 1025.

> *Note: You can visit the Internet Network Information Center (InterNIC)—the organization responsible for registering domain names on the Internet—at **www.internic.net** to learn more about TCP and well-known port numbers via the Internet directives, called Request For Comments (RFC) documents. Look at RFC 1700 to see the list of well-known port numbers. Also, a good description of TCP and ports can be found online at **www.sockets.com/services.htm**. (See the "Need To Know More?" section at the end of this chapter for additional references.)*

If you decide to change your Web server default port number, your clients must also modify all their other Web-enabled applications to contact your Web server on the new port. This includes changing the default port used by Microsoft FrontPage 98. If FrontPage Server Extensions have been previously installed on your Web server, follow these steps to change the default TCP port number:

1. Shut down the Web server.
   - On a FrontPage Personal Web Server, close the MS FrontPage Web Server dialog box and all the FrontPage applications.
   - On a Windows 95 Personal Web Server, open the Control Panel and double-click the Personal Web Server icon. Click the Startup tab and then click the Stop button in the Web Server State section.
   - On a Windows NT PWS or IIS computer, open the Internet Service Manager through the Start menu. Locate and right-click the WWW or Web Service icon and select Stop.
2. Start FrontPage Server Administrator. You can launch the executable (FPSRVWIN.EXE) from C:\Program Files\Microsoft FrontPage\Version3.0\Bin.
3. Select the TCP port displayed in the Select Server Or Port window on the Server Administrator dialog box.
4. Click the Uninstall button to remove Server Extensions from the port. This action removes the _Vti_Bin directory, which contains the Server Extensions files, and it also removes the _Vti_Txt directory, which contains the index for the FrontPage Web. It does not remove the contents of your Web site.
5. Change the port number for your Web server.
   - On a FrontPage Personal Web Server, open HTTPD.CNF in the C:\FrontPage Web\Server\Conf directory. Modify the number (80) on the Port line in this file.
   - On a Windows 95 Personal Web Server, you must edit the Windows 95 Registry path (HKEY_LOCAL_MACHINE\System\CurrentControlSet\control\ServiceProvider\ServiceTypes\W3Svc) and modify the TcpPort value using the hex numeric equivalent of the decimal port number you want your Web server to monitor.

Note: This procedure is outlined more precisely in Microsoft TechNet or in Support Online article number Q173663, "How to Use Microsoft Personal Web Server on a Different Port."

- On a Windows NT PWS or IIS computer, open the Internet Service Manager through the Start menu. Locate and right-click the WWW or Web Service icon and select Properties. This should open the World Wide Web Publishing Service Properties dialog box. The first tab should have an option to change the TCP port of the Web server. Make the change and click OK.

6. Once you've completed the change, reinstall FrontPage Server Extensions. In Server Administrator, click the Install button to reinstall Server Extensions. The installation automatically adapts to the new port number.
7. Restart the server.

Enabling And Disabling Authoring

If you want to prevent people from changing your Web site via FrontPage, you can disable authoring on your Web site. Once authoring is disabled, the FrontPage Explorer and Editor applications are not able to access the Web site.

You can use the graphical or the command-line FrontPage Server Administrator to enable or disable authoring. Through the graphical utility (FPSRVWIN.EXE), click the Authoring button. You'll see the Enable/Disable Authoring dialog box, as shown in Figure 13.4.

To enable or disable authoring through the command-line utility (FPSRVADM.EXE), open a command prompt and go to the C:\Program Files\Microsoft FrontPage\Version3.0\Bin directory and type "fpsrvadm". From the list of options, you can type "5" to enable authoring or "6" to disable authoring. Press Enter. Next, you must choose the TCP port (normally 80) on which this command will be executed. Press Enter.

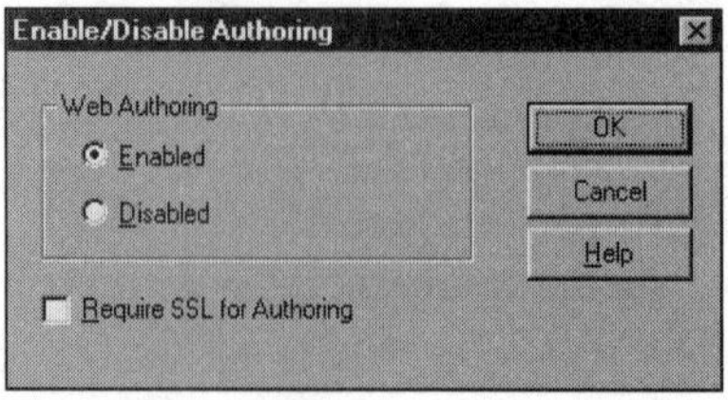

Figure 13.4 The Enable/Disable Authoring dialog box.

Encrypting FrontPage Administration

You can also set your Web server to require Secure Sockets Layer (SSL) encryption between the FrontPage applications and the Web server. When SSL is required, all communication between the administration program and FrontPage is encrypted. When the SSL option is set through FrontPage Administrator, FrontPage Explorer must also have SSL configured. The following steps show you how to configure SSL through FrontPage Explorer:

1. Open FrontPage Explorer.
2. In the Getting Started dialog box, click the More Webs button.
3. In the Open FrontPage Web dialog box, click the List Webs button and then select the name of the Web server you want to open (see Figure 13.5).
4. Click the Secure Connection Required (SSL) checkbox.
5. Click OK.

These changes apply to the root Web and all sub-Webs. The Web server must already be configured to support SSL; otherwise, subsequent authoring attempts will fail.

STUDY ALERT

When enabling SSL security between your FrontPage Web server and FrontPage Explorer, you must be sure that both applications are configured to support SSL encryption; in addition, you must ensure that the Web server you're using supports SSL encryption.

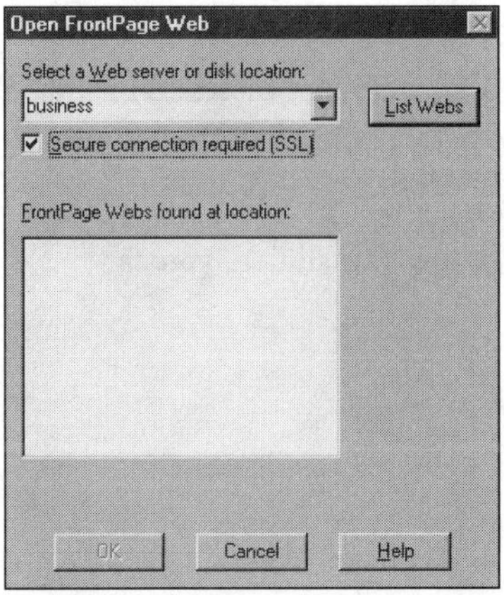

Figure 13.5 The Open FrontPage Web dialog box.

Upgrading FrontPage Extensions

The Upgrade button in the FrontPage Server Administrator can be used to upgrade your FrontPage Server Extensions, if updated versions have been placed on the server. This option upgrades the root Web and all sub-Webs. To run it, follow these steps:

1. Open the FrontPage Server Administrator (C:\Program Files\Microsoft FrontPage\Version3.0\Bin\FPSRVWIN.EXE).
2. Select the correct port for your Web server in the Select Server Or Port option dialog box.
3. Click the Upgrade button and then click OK.
4. Click OK again when the upgrade is complete.

Upgrading Your Web Server

If you decide to upgrade your Web server, you'll have to uninstall and reinstall FrontPage Server Extensions for the new Web server. For example, if you install FrontPage on a Windows 95 computer that does not have a Web server, FrontPage automatically adds the FrontPage Personal Web Server and related extensions. If you upgrade to the Windows 95 Personal Web Server later, you'll get an error message when you attempt to launch FrontPage Explorer (see Figure 13.6).

To correct this problem, follow these steps:

1. Open the FrontPage Server Administrator (FPSRVWIN.EXE) via the C:\Program Files\Microsoft FrontPage folder.
2. Select the TCP port number where your Web server is installed in the Select Port Number window (usually port 80). Then, click the Uninstall button.
3. Once the old FrontPage Server Extensions are uninstalled, you can install the new ones. Click the Install button.

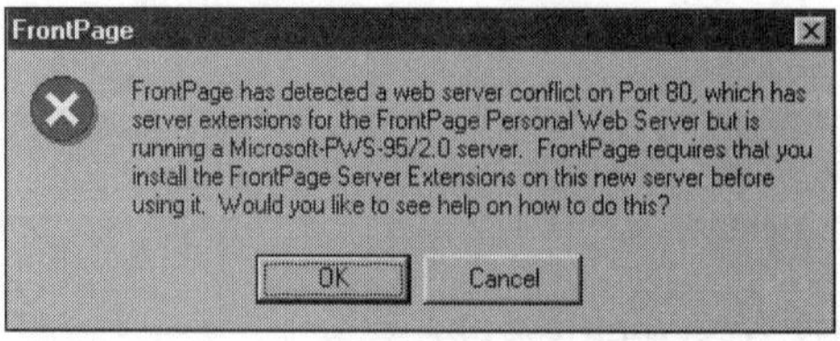

Figure 13.6 The error message that's displayed when FrontPage Server Extensions do not match the Web server.

4. Choose the correct server type from the Configure Server Type dialog box. Click OK to continue.

From this point, the directions may vary, depending on the Web server you've selected. However, in general, you'll confirm the Web Server type, port number, and root Web document. Once you've confirmed the selections (if correct), FrontPage Server Extensions should be installed. Click OK in the dialog boxes as necessary.

By uninstalling and then reinstalling FrontPage Server Extensions, FrontPage is essentially configured to interface properly with the new Web server.

Security

The FrontPage Server Administrator allows you to add to the list of site administrators via the Security button in the dialog box. After clicking the button, you see the Administrator Name And Password dialog box in which you can configure the Web location and the administrator name and password to be added.

> ***Note:*** *You will not be asked to provide a password when using a Windows 95 Personal Web Server or IIS because the password is taken from the system list of accounts.*

Practice Questions

Question 1

You want to remotely administer your FrontPage Web site using MS FrontPage utilities. Which of the following would you require?

- ❍ a. Pentium II processor
- ❍ b. FrontPage Server Extensions
- ❍ c. Alpha Server
- ❍ d. Modem

Trick! question

The correct answer is b. FrontPage Server Extensions are required for remote access. There is no requirement for a Pentium II processor or an Alpha server. These items are personal preferences, not necessities. Therefore, answers a and c are incorrect. You might have been tempted to choose d because a modem is often associated with remote connections. However, such a need is not explicitly mentioned in the question; you could just as well be connecting from another network that's connected to the Internet via a router. Therefore, answer d is incorrect.

Question 2

You've just changed the TCP port of your Web server from 80 to 8080. Before you run FrontPage Explorer, what must you do?

- ❍ a. Close all open applications
- ❍ b. Reinstall FrontPage
- ❍ c. Reinstall FrontPage Server Extensions
- ❍ d. Reload your Web page

The best choice is to reinstall FrontPage Server Extensions. Therefore, answer c is correct. Closing and opening all applications or reloading a Web page is not enough to modify the TCP port number that FrontPage uses to connect to your Web server. Therefore, answers a and d are incorrect. There is no need to reinstall the entire FrontPage application, and it would do you no good to reinstall everything else until FrontPage Server Extensions are installed. Therefore, answer b is incorrect.

Question 3

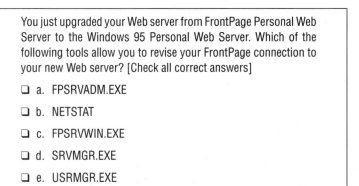

You just upgraded your Web server from FrontPage Personal Web Server to the Windows 95 Personal Web Server. Which of the following tools allow you to revise your FrontPage connection to your new Web server? [Check all correct answers]

- ❑ a. FPSRVADM.EXE
- ❑ b. NETSTAT
- ❑ c. FPSRVWIN.EXE
- ❑ d. SRVMGR.EXE
- ❑ e. USRMGR.EXE

The FrontPage Server Administrator utility is used to remove the old FrontPage Server Extension and install the new ones. This utility has both a command-line (FPSRVADM.EXE) and Windows (FPSRVWIN.EXE) version. Therefore, answers a and c are correct. You cannot use NETSTAT because it's used to check the status of your network connection (but it does not allow you to reset the communication software between FrontPage and your Web server). Therefore, answer b is incorrect. SRVMGR.EXE and USRMGR.EXE are both Windows NT administration utilities that will not modify your FrontPage-to-Web server communications. Therefore, answers d and e are incorrect.

Question 4

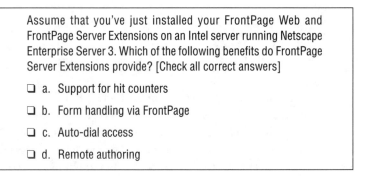

Assume that you've just installed your FrontPage Web and FrontPage Server Extensions on an Intel server running Netscape Enterprise Server 3. Which of the following benefits do FrontPage Server Extensions provide? [Check all correct answers]

- ❑ a. Support for hit counters
- ❑ b. Form handling via FrontPage
- ❑ c. Auto-dial access
- ❑ d. Remote authoring

FrontPage Server Extensions provide support for hit counters, form handling, and remote authoring. Therefore, answers a, b, and d are correct. However, they do not provide auto-dial access. Therefore, answer c is incorrect.

Question 5

Which of the following Web servers work with Windows 95? [Check all correct answers]

- ❑ a. Internet Information Server
- ❑ b. Peer Web Services
- ❑ c. FrontPage Personal Web Server
- ❑ d. Personal Web Server

Both FrontPage Personal Web Server and the Personal Web Server work on Windows 95. Therefore, answers c and d are correct. The Personal Web Server is also known as the Windows 95 Personal Web Server, because it was designed to work with Windows 95. Answer a is incorrect because Internet Information Server was designed for Windows NT Server. Answer b is incorrect because Peer Web Services is used only on Windows NT Workstation.

Question 6

You would like to change the TCP port of your FrontPage Personal Web Server from TCP port 80 to TCP port 8000. Where do you make this change?

- ❍ a. SYSTEM.INI
- ❍ b. HTTPD.CNF
- ❍ c. WIN.INI
- ❍ d. FrontPage Explorer
- ❍ e. Internet Service Manager

The FrontPage Personal Web Server configuration file is HTTPD.CNF, which is located in the C:\FrontPage Web\Server\Conf directory. For this question, you would locate the Port line and change the number that follows it from 80 to 8000. Therefore, answer b is correct. Answers a and c are incorrect because those files do not contain settings for the Web server—they are Windows configuration files. FrontPage Explorer does not have a configuration dialog box for modifying the port of the FrontPage Personal Web Server. Therefore, answer d is incorrect. The Internet Service Manager does allow you to modify the port number of a Web server, however it's used for Internet Information Server or Peer Web Services, not for the FrontPage Personal Web Server. Therefore, answer e is incorrect.

Question 7

> You've just finished configuring your FrontPage Web site and you do not want anyone to be able to modify your site via FrontPage; however, you still want other users to be able to read the content on your Web site through their Web browsers. What is the best solution for this situation?
>
> ❍ a. Change your password
>
> ❍ b. Disable authoring
>
> ❍ c. Change the TCP port number of the Web server
>
> ❍ d. Place a warning message on the INDEX.HTML page

If you disable authoring, people cannot make changes to your Web site via FrontPage. Therefore, answer b is correct. Changing your password does not prevent people from getting in if they have their own account. Therefore, answer a is incorrect. Changing the TCP port number of the Web server might work, but without any further action, it would keep anyone else from accessing your Web site via Web browsers. Therefore, answer c is incorrect. Placing a warning message on the INDEX.HTML page does not, by itself, prevent others from making changes to your Web site from Microsoft FrontPage. Therefore, answer d is incorrect.

Question 8

> You must change the TCP port number on your Peer Web Services Web server. You've looked in the Control Panel for the Peer Web Services icon, but you don't see where to change the TCP port number. Where is this configuration setting?
>
> ❍ a. Internet Service Manger
>
> ❍ b. The PWS icon in the Control Panel
>
> ❍ c. The Services icon in the Control Panel
>
> ❍ d. The HTTPD.CNF file

Internet Information Server and Peer Web Services are both configured through the Internet Service Manager. Therefore, answer a is correct. You will not find a PWS icon in the Control Panel, and the Services icon does not allow you to change the port number. Therefore, answers b and c are incorrect. The HTTPD.CNF file is correct for changing the TCP port number on FrontPage Personal Web Server, but is not correct for Peer Web Services. Therefore, answer d is incorrect.

Question 9

You've decided to change the TCP port number of your Web server, but you must avoid the preassigned numbers for known Internet services. Which of the following options represent invalid selections? [Check all correct answers]

- ❑ a. 75000
- ❑ b. 10200
- ❑ c. 21
- ❑ d. 25
- ❑ e. 8080

Answer a, c, and d are the correct selections. There are 65,535 ports available; therefore, answer a at 75000 is impossible. Answers c and d are part of the well-known port numbers (RFC 1700). Specifically, answer c invades the default FTP port number (21), and d invades the SMTP port number (25). The other options are available because 10200 and 8080 are outside of the well-known port range (1 to 1023) and within the number of valid ranges 1024 to 65535. Therefore, answers b and e are incorrect. However, port 8080 is used as an alternate for port 80, which is the well-known port address for HTTP and Web services, so you should avoid using it. But, for the purposes of this question, it is a valid port.

Question 10

You've been given an NT Server machine to configure as a Web server. You've been asked to configure the NT Server machine with a Web server that will support Microsoft FrontPage. In addition, the Web server is expected to allow you to isolate processes to increase the stability of the applications running on the Web server. Which of the following Web servers should you use?

- ❍ a. Peer Web Services
- ❍ b. FrontPage Personal Web Server
- ❍ c. Internet Information Server
- ❍ d. Personal Web Server

Answer c is the only correct selection. IIS does provide for process isolation and it runs on NT Server. Peer Web Services (for Windows NT Workstation) and the Personal Web Server (for Windows 95) are not used with Windows NT Server. Therefore, a and d are incorrect. The FrontPage Personal Web Server does not provide for process isolation. Therefore, answer b is incorrect.

Need To Know More?

Tauber, Daniel A. and Brenda Kienan. *Mastering Microsoft FrontPage 98*, Sybex, Alameda, CA, 1998. ISBN 0-7821-2144-6. This is a good resource and reference book for FrontPage. It has a lot of step-by-step instructions, which are great for the beginner; later chapters have more advanced configuration information, which is excellent for the more advanced user. Chapter 8 has some information on FrontPage Server Extensions. You can find Web site administrative information in Chapter 17. Appendix B has information on setting up Microsoft Web servers. It also covers the Windows 95 Personal Web Server and the Windows NT Workstation Peer Web Services products. Appendix C has a few additional pages on the FrontPage Server Extensions.

Microsoft TechNet (July 98 and later) contains several articles that pertain to FrontPage administration. Search on "How to Install FrontPage Server Extensions for IIS," "Installing the FrontPage Server Extensions on Unix," "Netscape Web Server," "Web Administration," and "MS FrontPage: A Technical Overview" to see articles relating to the subjects presented in this chapter. Also, see TechNet Article Q143101, "Using FrontPage without the Server Extensions," for more information on what you can and cannot do on a server without the FrontPage Server Extensions.

www.microsoft.com/frontpage/wpp/exts.htm. Visit this Web site to learn more about FrontPage Server Extensions. You can also download the FrontPage Server Extensions from this site.

www.internic.net. Visit this site to learn more about Internet standards, especially for the technical documents maintained there. For more on well-known port numbers, check RFC 1700; for more information on TCP, check RFC 793.

www.microsoft.com/frontpage/hosting/hosting_faqs.htm. Visit this site to see an FAQ sheet on FrontPage Server Extensions.

www.microsoft.com/frontpage/wpp/platforms.htm. Visit this site to see the Microsoft list of supported platforms for FrontPage Server Extensions.

www.microsoft.com/iis. Visit this site to learn more about IIS, Peer Web Services, and Personal Web Server.

www.netscape.com. Visit this site to learn more about the Netscape Web server.

www.sockets.com/services.htm. Visit this site to learn more about TCP ports and services. This site has some good, straightforward explanations.

14

Site Analysis, Design, And Maintenance

Terms you'll need to understand:

- √ Intranet
- √ Extranet
- √ Primary/target audience
- √ Secondary audience
- √ Internet connectivity
- √ Information flow
- √ Look and feel

Techniques you'll need to master:

- √ Identifying the Web site's purpose, goals, and required capabilities
- √ Establishing the Web site's security and performance requirements
- √ Designing a Web site that suits your needs and information
- √ Creating a good user interface and a useful navigation system for your Web site
- √ Identifying the Web site's maintenance requirements
- √ Establishing and following a maintenance plan

The tools and techniques you use to build a Web site play an important role in the overall quality and success of the site. However, you shouldn't even begin to code the first Web page without first performing a careful analysis of your site's requirements. You'll need to assess your site's goals and motivations, understand your site's audience, identify the information your site is designed to contain, and outline what you must do to keep your site functional. This chapter provides an overview of the different skills you need to plan, design, deploy, and maintain your Web site.

Analyzing Your Web Site Requirements

Unless you're just experimenting with HTML and Web site development tools such as FrontPage, you have an important reason for developing a Web site. It's this reason that drives your site and influences everything about it—from the color scheme you use to the way your pages link together. Before you start developing your Web site, however, you should examine why you're developing the site and what you need it to do. This analysis will provide you with the following important information:

- The site's purpose and what you plan to achieve by developing it
- Who your audience is and what its needs are
- What type of capabilities (searching, interactive pages, and so on) you need to include on the site
- What type of security you need to implement on the site
- How the site should perform
- What it will take to manage and maintain the site

Analyzing your Web site's requirements involves an examination of this information. If you overlook even one of these key areas in your initial analysis of your site's requirements, you may find yourself facing a total redesign of the site halfway through its initial development, which is a waste of time and resources. You may even end up with a Web site that falls short of meeting its requirements.

STUDY ALERT

Analyzing the requirements for all aspects of your Web site—including purpose, technology and security requirements; performance issues; and how it should be integrated with existing sites and technologies—is a significant part of developing a FrontPage Web site.

Site Purpose And Goals

When you first sit down to analyze a Web site, ask yourself these two questions:

- **What is the purpose of this site?** Your site may be an informative site for a new product, the primary Web site for an entire organization, or a sub-Web. The number and types of purposes are varied and endless, but it's important that you know the purpose of your Web site.
- **What are my goals for the site?** You may want to promote a product as well as provide technical support and downloads of new versions and related products. You may want to provide easy access to information stored in a database or other non-Web format. You may have several goals for the site, and you should identify each one.

The purpose of the Web site provides you with a broad description of the reason for the site's existence. *Goals* are highly focused statements of specific objectives the site should meet. For example, the purpose of the Microsoft SiteBuilder Web site at **www.microsoft.com/sitebuilder/** is to provide a collection of online resources for members of Microsoft's SiteBuilder Network (SBN). The objectives for the SBN site include the following:

- Provides membership information to current and potential members of SBN
- Creates an online community for SBN members
- Provides tools and online resources for Web site development to SBN members

Although these are only three of the many goals the SBN Web site is designed to achieve, the site's overall look and feel, as well as the way its information flows, clearly reflect these goals. The SBN home page, shown in Figure 14.1, provides links to different areas of the site that meet these goals, including the Member Community, Workshop, and SBN Magazine sections.

Once you've identified your site's purpose and goals, you should have the beginnings of an outline of the type of information you want to include in your site, how it should flow, and what type of design will work best for you. Although this is a major step in developing your site, it's just the first of many. The users who will be visiting the site and utilizing its resources are just as important as the purpose and goals of the site.

Your Audience And Its Needs

When telling a story, you should always keep your audience in mind. And the same is true of the Web. Your audience will have a profound effect on the way

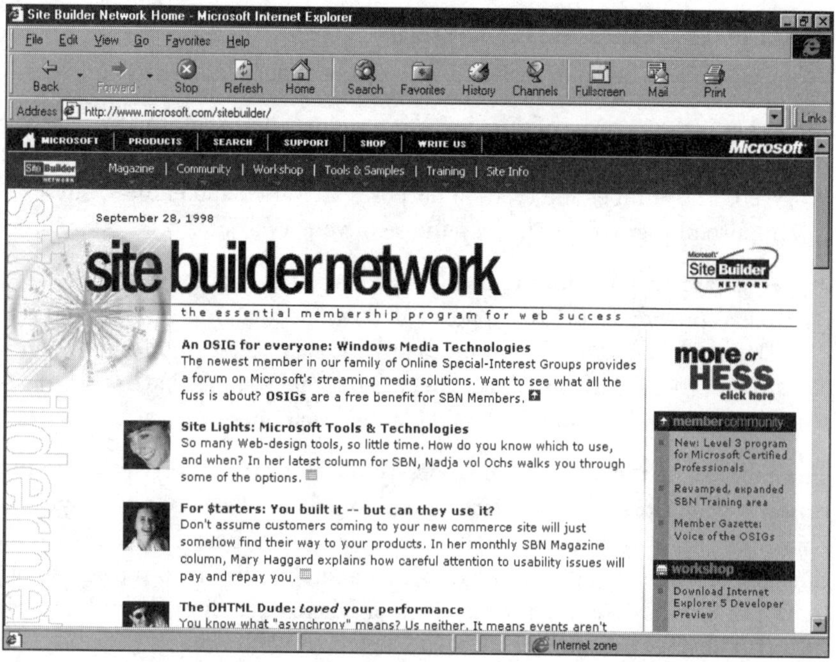

Figure 14.1 The SBN Web site's general purpose and specific goals are reflected in the site's design.

you develop and manage your site. When thinking about the users who will visit your site, ask yourself the following questions:

- **Who are they?** Answers to this question can include coworkers accessing an intranet, strategic partners accessing an extranet, product users seeking technical support, or the Internet community in general. You may also find that you have a primary audience—strategic partners, for example—as well as a secondary audience—potential customers. Although the majority of your efforts will be designed to make your site as attractive and useful to your primary audience as possible, you'll want to be aware of each of these audiences.
- **What Web browsers and operating systems do they use?** The more answers you have to this question, the more difficult your site development will be. Client software and the hardware on which it runs are the two wild cards that give every Web designer nightmares. You should ensure cross-browser and cross-platform compatibility as much as you can. This factor may limit the number and type of technologies you can include in your site.

- **What kind of Internet connectivity do they have?** If your average user has a slow Internet connection, you'll need to be concerned with bandwidth issues. If the majority of your target audience is using 28.8Kbps or 33.6Kbps modems to access your site, you'll want to keep the number of images and multimedia components to a minimum. If, however, your users are connecting to an intranet over a corporate network, you'll have more latitude in the type of high-bandwidth elements you can include on your pages. The type of connectivity your users have may also lead you to create a site with multiple versions of the same information for low-bandwidth and high-bandwidth users.
- **How often will they connect to the site and for how long?** The less time users have to spend at your site, the more important it is that the information they need is readily available. People who visit it every day usually have only a few hours a day to spend on the Web and often have only one phone line for both data and phone transmissions. If your primary audience is made up of this type of user, you'll want to make sure you include a site map or search engine that makes finding information on your site easy. In addition, you might want to create a "What's New" section to highlight new information to help users avoid digging through outdated or previously viewed information in search of the latest and most useful information.
- **What do they know?** The level of knowledge your users have will greatly influence the kind of navigation and help tools you build into your site as well as the kind and frequency of instructions you include on your Web pages.
- **How do they think?** The Web tends to make us forget that there's a person behind every Web page hit (barring search engines, of course) and every piece of email exchanged over the Internet. Do not lose sight of the fact that your users are real people with opinions, jobs, lifestyles, and prejudices. Always ask yourself, "What will my audience think about this?"

What you know about your audience, as well as its technology, connectivity, knowledge, and personality, will drive the overall design and management of your site as much as the purpose and the goals of the site do. You want to design a site that's optimized for your target audience but that also works well with your secondary audience and does not completely prevent other users (outside of these two groups) from accessing the materials on your site. After all, you never know when someone will become part of your primary or secondary audience.

The SBN Workshop Web site is obviously designed for Web developers who use Microsoft Web development tools. Most of the articles and resources provide solutions that focus on or directly involve a variety of Microsoft technologies. This approach is completely consistent with the purpose and goals of the site as well as the site's primary audience. The site even looks its best when viewed with Internet Explorer (IE) 4 on a PC running a Windows operating system (see Figure 14.2).

However, the SBN Workshop site also includes many articles and resources that are useful to all Web developers, regardless of the tools they use to develop and serve their Web sites. The creators of SBN are obviously aware that visitors to their site may one day choose to use a Microsoft solution. Therefore, they don't want to alienate those visitors and violate one of the key objectives of the site: to provide information to potential members of SBN. The site is just as functional when viewed by IE or Netscape Navigator on a platform and OS other than Windows, such as a Macintosh running OS 7.5 (see Figure 14.3).

Once you've identified your audience and familiarized yourself with it, you'll be prepared to evaluate the capabilities your Web site will need to include to achieve the site's various goals while still meeting your users' needs.

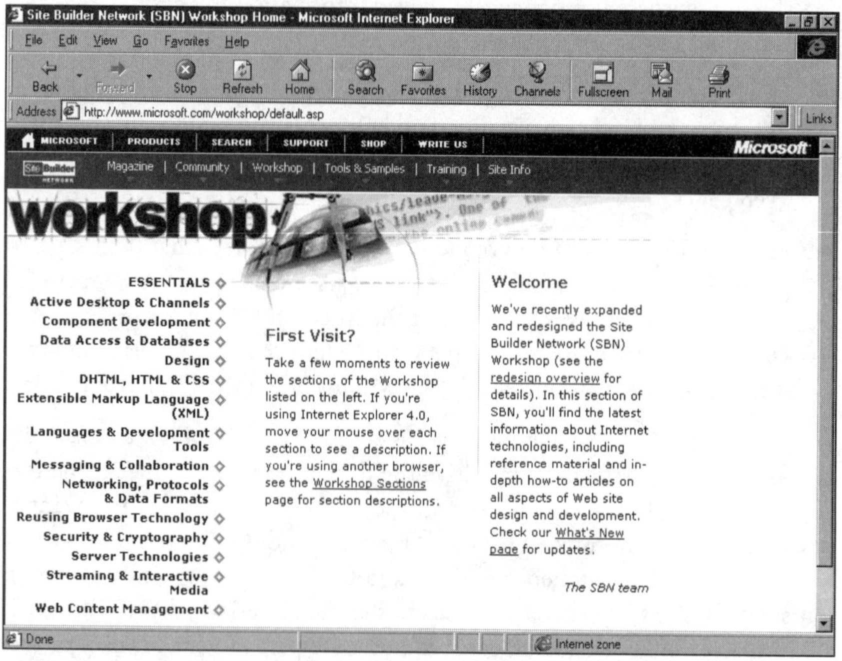

Figure 14.2 The SBN Workshop site is optimized for users viewing it with IE4 running on a Windows operating system.

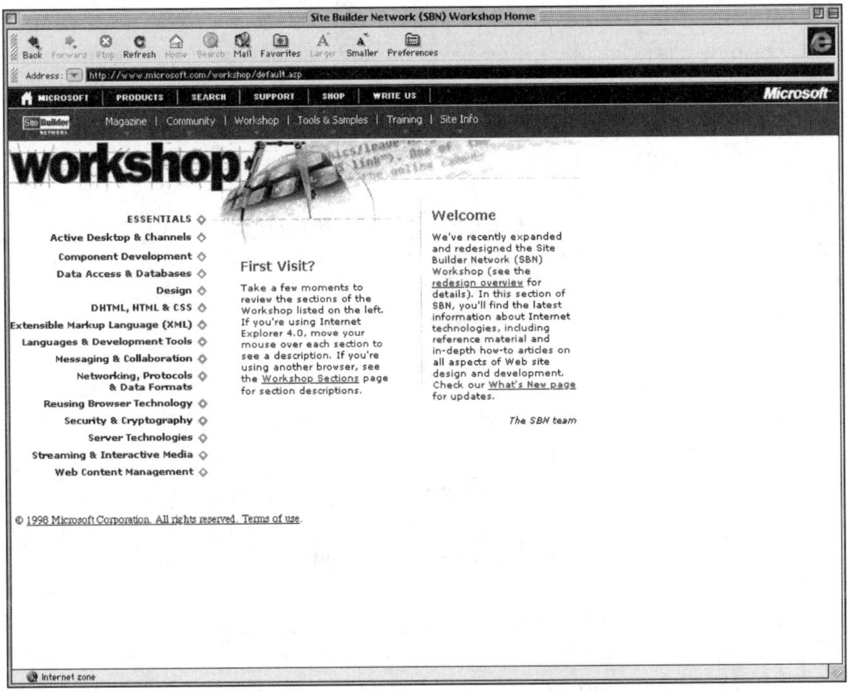

Figure 14.3 The SBN Workshop site is still accessible by users on operating systems other than Windows.

Essential Capabilities

With the myriad Web technologies available to Web developers today, it's often difficult to identify what you should and should not include in your Web site (besides text and graphics). The purpose of your Web site, its specific goals, and your users' needs and capabilities directly influence the capabilities your site will require. When deciding what to include in your site, be sure to consider the following:

- **A search engine** Search engines allow users to sift through all the content on your Web site quickly to find exactly what they need without having to navigate a long succession of pages. If your site is particularly complex or has a large number of sections and pages, a search engine can be invaluable. Implementing a search engine requires a server that supports one, and the more pages you have to catalog and search, the more power your Web server will need.

> **TIP** Be sure to review Chapter 13 for more information on choosing the right server to support your search engine and any other site capabilities that you might need.

- **Interactive forms** Forms allow you to collect data from your users, and they play a crucial role in the development of customized pages for individual users. FrontPage's support for forms (and the scripts that handle them) is extensive enough that you can make good use of forms on almost any Web site.

TIP: Be sure to review Chapter 8 when deciding whether to include forms on your site and determining what handlers you'll need on your Web server to process them.

- **Electronic commerce** If you need to conduct business on the Web, you must include support for electronic commerce on your Web site. FrontPage works directly with Site Server and Internet Information Server (IIS) to create secure Web sites for the exchange of all types of sensitive information. In addition to the programming required to set up an electronic commerce Web site, you'll need a secure server.

TIP: Different Web browsers support different types of security, and a variety of issues are associated with setting up a secure server. Revisit Chapter 3 for more information on administering a secure server using FrontPage.

- **Database access** Using Web technologies to provide a front end to a database for access over an intranet or the Internet is an everyday occurrence. If you need to include access to information stored in a database on your Web site, consider what it will take to connect your site to the database, the security issues involved, and how the constant searching and writing to and from a database via a Web site will affect your server's performance.

TIP: FrontPage is compatible with any ODBC-compliant database, and the Database Region wizard makes connecting your Web site to a database quick and easy. Take a second look at Chapter 12 to review the Database Region wizard and the issues associated with integrating database connectivity into your Web site.

For every advanced capability you include in your Web site, you'll need to consider the following:

- How will it affect your Web server?
- How will it affect the amount of time users take to access and download your Web pages?

- How difficult will it be to maintain and upgrade?
- What specific Web clients, if any, must a user have to interact with the capability?

STUDY ALERT: Your ability to judge which capabilities you need to add to your site and how they will affect your Web server and your users is key to the success of your Web site.

Security Requirements

Security is one of the most important topics any Web developer has to consider. In addition to taking steps to keep your Web server secure and free from hackers, you need to evaluate how much security you need to provide for the data you serve from the Web server. If your Web site isn't very complex and doesn't contain sensitive information that you'll have transmit, you won't need much security. If, however, any of the following statements are true of your site, security will be a major concern for you:

- There are sections on your site only certain users may access using a name and password.
- You are using Active Server Pages (ASP) that must be completely preserved.
- There's an electronic commerce section on your site that requires users to transmit confidential information, such as credit card numbers.
- Your Web site is directly linked to a database, and you need to make sure that the database is well protected against data theft or hacking.

The type and amount of security you can establish for your site is greatly influenced by the server from which you serve your site and the security options it offers. FrontPage works directly with a variety of servers that support a variety of security options.

TIP: Revisit Chapter 13 for a more detailed discussion of each of these servers and their security features.

Web Server Performance Requirements

Before your Web site goes public, you need to make sure your Web server is up to the task you're burdening it with. The choices you make about what Web server hardware and software you need to host your site successfully depends entirely on the following items:

- The site's purpose
- The capabilities you intend to include on the site
- The number of users visiting your site
- The amount and type of information you're serving

In general, the more complex your site and its content are, the bigger and faster your server's hardware and software need to be. Chapter 13 includes an overview of the different Web servers FrontPage works with that can be used to host your Web site. Once you've chosen the Web server software that supports the capabilities you need to include on your Web site, you'll need to further consider the following questions:

- **How much hard disk space do the server software and your Web site materials require?** You don't want to run out of disk space on your Web server and have to move your entire site to a new one within a matter of weeks. Instead, plan to have at least twice as much disk space on your server as you initially think you'll need. Web pages themselves are often 1 or 2K in size, but graphics, form handlers, and multimedia files can eat up disk space quickly.
- **What are the server software's CPU requirements?** You don't want to run your server on a CPU that's too slow. Generally, you should follow the vendor's recommendations for how fast your server's CPU needs to be.
- **What are the site's CPU requirements?** The number of users you expect to visit your site, as well as the amount of information you think they will be downloading, affects the speed requirements for your CPU. If your CPU is too slow, your Web server will not be able to process user requests in a timely manner and your site will slowly grind to a halt.
- **What are the server's RAM requirements?** RAM is an important component of any Web server—the more you have, the better. It's crucial that you have as much RAM as your server software suggests and then, to be on the safe side, try to double that amount. The more RAM you have, the more users you can serve quickly at one time.
- **How fast is the server's Internet connection?** When you're talking about Internet connectivity, faster is almost always better. You want your Web server to connect to the Internet with the fastest connection possible so it can serve data to users in a timely manner.

If you experience problems with your Web server, such as connection timeouts, extremely slow download times, and a general degradation in the service of the Web server, you'll want to revisit each of these questions and try to identify what has changed on your Web site. If you have twice as many users accessing your site, you may need a faster connection or CPU, or you may need to add more RAM to your server. If you're providing more complex data (multimedia and database content, for example) to your users, you may need more storage space, a faster CPU, or a faster Internet connection. If you've added a new section with higher security requirements, your CPU and RAM may not be able to handle the same number of requests because of the added burden of sending and receiving secure data.

The performance requirements for a Web server in any given Web site scenario are especially important to consider.

You evaluate your Web server requirements at the end of your overall analysis because they're affected by your site's purpose, goals, and audience, as well as the security and performance requirements. Remember that your server requirements grow and change with your site. Keep a close eye on your server so you can identify problems early and remedy them before they affect your users' experiences on your site.

Choosing The Right Technologies

After you've analyzed all your Web site's requirements, you need to choose the Web technologies best suited to fulfill them. The technologies you choose are influenced by the following factors:

- The technologies your Web server supports
- The technologies your users can easily access and use

FrontPage and the Web servers it works with support most of the advanced Web technologies, including Dynamic HTML (DHTML), style sheets, and scripting. Chapter 12 discusses using FrontPage to include these technologies in your Web pages. Although FrontPage and the Microsoft Web server family support advanced Web technologies, many of the reasons for including the technologies in Web pages are proprietary and often require a specially configured client (usually IE) running on a specific operating system (usually a flavor of Windows).

Before you can decide which of these technologies to use to meet your site's goals or to include a necessary capability, you should consider the following questions:

- Will the primary audience have to use a specific client or client configuration to view a Web page that makes use of a specific technology?
- How difficult will it be for the primary audience to acquire and run that client?
- What kind of bandwidth requirements does the technology have?
- How will those requirements affect the users' ability to access the site?

As a general rule, you don't want a technology on your Web pages that might prevent some portion of the site from being viewed by anyone in your target audience. If Macintosh users using IE3 or earlier are part of your target audience, you shouldn't use ActiveX or VBScript components on your site, unless you can replicate their functionality using other technologies, such as Java and JavaScript. If you include these additional technologies, remember that you'll have to maintain two separate versions of the same information and functions. This is a commitment that can significantly increase the site's maintenance requirements.

TIP Client compatibility is a key issue in the development of any Web site. Be sure to review Chapter 10 before implementing any special technologies on your site.

Designing The Web Site

After you've analyzed your site and decided which technologies to use and what effect they'll have on your users, you can finally get down to the nitty-gritty of site design. Designing a site includes assessing the information you'll include in the site and how it should flow as well as creating a set of cohesive navigation tools and a consistent look and feel.

Evaluating Information Flow

A site's information flow defines how the content on the pages is arranged and identifies the links that connect the user from one page to another. Essentially, the analysis of your information flow will give you a good picture of how the different pieces of your site fit together to provide an overall experience for the user. Your understanding of the information flow also contributes to the navigation system you build for your site.

A flow chart can often help graphically illustrate how your Web pages will flow. It's not practical to design a flow chart that shows every page on a site, especially a site that may ultimately contain thousands of pages. Instead, the flow chart should show all the major divisions in the Web site and identify how they're connected. Once you have a handle on your information flow, you can begin to design the interface for your site.

Prototyping The User Interface

A well-designed site can be rendered useless if the user interface is not well thought out or doesn't reflect the natural information flow. A *user interface* is comprised of all the graphics and layout components that affect what the users see when they visit your Web site. You want your interface to be consistent from page to page so users become familiar with the environment and know they're still on the same Web site. The interface is the window through which visitors view your content; therefore, it needs to be neat and clean, without any excess clutter to obscure the view.

TIP

Don't ever lose sight of the fact that users view your site through a variety of different screen resolutions—from 640-by-480 to 1024-by-768, or more. A layout that looks neat and uncluttered on your 17-inch monitor may be crowded and unreadable to someone with a smaller monitor. Always view your site on a variety of different monitors with different resolutions and color settings to make sure your interface is viable regardless of the user's monitor setup. Finally, remember that users can customize the browser's display of your Web pages in several different ways, including setting font sizes and colors, and disabling graphics, scripts, and other technologies. There's no way to know exactly what your pages will look like each time they're viewed, but if you create pages that work well on a variety of monitor and browser settings, you'll have fewer problems with user accessibility.

Regardless of the look of the final user interface, it should always be consistent. The Microsoft Web site contains information from corporate news to product specifics to technical support. Even though each portion of the site has a different focus, you always know that you're on the Microsoft site because the user interface is consistent from page to page.

The interface you design for your Web site will be a product of the site's information, the overall feeling you want to convey, and the way your information flows from one page to the other. If your site is an addition to or extension of an existing site (a sub-Web), many of the user interface decisions may have already been made for you. If this is the case, you'll want to make sure your interface is consistent with the interface being used on the existing site.

Once you have a prototype of your user interface, allow time to test its effectiveness on a variety of people. Solicit feedback from colleagues and peers in your organization as well as from a group of users that represents a cross-section of your client base—the people who will really be using the interface. Make sure you have access to all the browsers and operating systems your interface must support and test the interface on each one to evaluate how different clients in different environments display it. Chapter 10 includes a more in-depth discussion of testing FrontPage content on multiple browsers.

Planning Site Navigation

One of the most important components of your Web site's interface is the navigation system you create to help your users move through the site and access its information. An intuitive and easy-to-use navigation system can increase the value of a site two-fold, whereas a non-existent or ill-thought-out navigation system can render a site useless.

When you're planning the navigation for your site, try to evaluate all the different ways users may enter your site. These include the following:

- Through the site's home page
- From a search engine
- From another Web site

Because the Web isn't a linear world and people don't always enter your site through the front door, you have to design a navigation system that functions well regardless of the point of entry.

> *Note: If you employ a large number of framesets on your site, remember that users must open the page that contains the <FRAMESET>... </FRAMESET> markup to actually view it correctly. Often, when users enter your site from a search engine, they view one of several pages displayed in a frameset instead of the frameset itself. If you rely on one document in a frameset to provide navigation information for all the others, users who view a framed document independent of the frameset will not have a way to navigate your site. At the very least, always include a link to your home page or the frameset page on each page of your site designed to be viewed in a frames configuration.*

Your site may include several different navigation mechanisms, including one that points to all the major areas of the site and individual mechanisms used within individual subsections of the site. When you design a group of navigation mechanisms that will work together to provide an overall navigation system for your site, make sure they compliment each other and that they're clearly labeled so that users know exactly where they're going on your site.

FrontPage supports several different components that make adding a quality navigation system to your site quick and easy.

TIP Review Chapter 10 for more information on navigation bars, search pages, and table of contents components.

Site Overviews And Maps

Site overviews and maps are common navigation tools used on sites all over the Web to provide users with an in-depth view of a site's content. If you have a large site, it may not be practical to show all the pages in an overview, but you can include the first three or four levels of pages instead. This approach to site navigation furnishes users with quick-and-easy access to the lay of the land and enables them to jump quickly to a particular section of the site. It also provides them with a better understanding of how the site is organized.

The current trend in site overview construction is to use DHTML to create a hierarchical view of the site's documents in which the headings expand and contract to display a listing of the pages within a particular section.

TIP Review Chapter 12 for more information on how you can use FrontPage to include DHTML in your Web pages.

Text-Only Navigation

Although graphical navigation bars and DHTML-based site maps add value to Web sites, they can render a site's navigation system virtually useless to those users browsing the Web with text-only or non-script-compliant clients. To ensure that everyone—regardless of the client they use—can navigate your site, always include a text-only version of the key navigation tools on every page.

Maintaining The Web Site

Once you've planned, developed, and deployed a Web site, you need to manage and maintain it to ensure that it's always functional and up-to-date. The significant tasks involved in maintaining a Web site are as follows:

- **Link checking** 404 errors are simply not acceptable on the Web anymore. You should check your site at least once a week to root out and fix broken or changed links.

- **Content updates** A Web site is a dynamic entity that can and should change on a regular basis. How often your site changes depends entirely upon the content you include in it.
- **Adapting to client updates** New versions of Web browsers with new capabilities are released once or twice a year. As a Web developer, you should evaluate the new clients and determine how they will affect your users and the technologies you can use on your site. Just because a new client supports a particular technology doesn't mean you should immediately integrate it into your site. Your site will always need to be backward-compatible with as many clients as possible.
- **Integrating new technologies** Just as Web clients are constantly being revised and updated, new Web technologies are constantly created. It's up to you to keep up with the latest trends in Web technology and carefully evaluate if and how you should use them on your site. Once again, you'll have to be cognizant of the fact that older clients most likely will not support these technologies. Take extra steps to ensure that your site is viewable by as many users as possible, regardless of their client's ability to support evolving technologies.

Establishing A Maintenance Plan And Schedule

As soon as you launch your new site, if not before, you should create a maintenance plan and schedule that specifies the following:

- How often the site's links will be checked and who is responsible for updating broken links
- How often the site's content will be updated
- The process for updating site content, including assigning responsibilities for providing and verifying new content as well as converting the content to HTML
- The process for evaluating new client and Web technologies and determining if and when they should be integrated into the Web site

Of these, the most important to implement immediately are the link checking and content update schedules. Creating a plan for both ensures that the site functions well and that its content does not become stale. Other processes for evaluating new technologies will evolve over time. The more people there are involved in the development and maintenance of the site, the more necessary it becomes for these processes to be formalized into specific procedures.

TIP FrontPage includes a variety of tools and components for maintaining a Web site. Review Chapters 3 and 5 for more information on updating and maintaining Web sites using FrontPage.

A Web site can be a crucial part of any organization's information-management solution. It is often the first look a potential customer or client has at an organization, or it can be a key part of interorganizational communications. For the site to live up to its potential and meet the needs demanded of it, you need to plan it carefully, develop it well, and administer it diligently.

Practice Questions

Question 1

Which of the following should you consider when analyzing your Web site's requirements? [Check all correct answers]

- ❑ a. The browser or browsers used by the site's primary audience
- ❑ b. The purpose and goals of the Web site
- ❑ c. The technologies you should use to build the site
- ❑ d. The level of security the site will need

The correct answers to this question are a, b, and d. Browser issues, the purpose and goals of a site, and its security needs are all part of a Web site's requirements. Answer c is incorrect because you choose to use specific technologies on your site as a direct result of the site's requirements.

Question 2

When you are identifying the appropriate server software to use for your Web site, which of the following should you consider? [Check all correct answers]

- ❑ a. The site's security requirements
- ❑ b. The speed of the server's connection to the Internet
- ❑ c. The server software's CPU and RAM requirements
- ❑ d. How much hard disk space you have available on your server

Trick! question

The correct answers to this question are a, c, and d. The server software you choose must be able to meet your site's security requirements, and your server hardware must meet the CPU, RAM, and hard disk space requirements of the server software. Answer b is incorrect because the speed of your server's connection to the Internet does not directly impact the server software you choose, but it does affect the overall performance of your Web server, which is why we've marked this as a trick question.

Question 3

Which of the following Web site capabilities does not require special security considerations to implement?

- ❍ a. Active Server Pages (ASP)
- ❍ b. Database access
- ❍ c. A search engine
- ❍ d. Electronic commerce

The correct answer to this question is c. There are no special security requirements for including a search engine on your Web site. Answers a, b, and d are incorrect because ASP, database access, and electronic commerce capabilities all require some level of security.

Question 4

You're redesigning your company intranet—which is currently accessed by PC users running IE4—to accommodate a newly acquired Macintosh-based production division. Which of the following technologies currently used on your site will have to be changed, updated, or supplemented by another technology for information delivery?

- ❍ a. ActiveX controls
- ❍ b. JavaScript
- ❍ c. VBScript
- ❍ d. Standard HTML

The correct answer is a. Only ActiveX has unique implementation problems when accessed with a Macintosh Web client. IE4.01 is available for the Macintosh, and it supports both JavaScript and VBScript. Therefore, answers b and c are incorrect. Answer d is incorrect because standard HTML is accessible by all Web clients regardless of platform, even if the display is a bit different from client to client.

Question 5

As a newly hired Web developer for a small software distribution company, you have been asked by your manager to create a plan for the development and management of a new company Web site whose capabilities will include database access and electronic commerce. The proposal you present to your manager includes the following items:

- An analysis of the purpose and goals of the site
- An overview of the site's potential visitors and their technology capabilities
- A description of the technologies you would use to develop the site
- A prototype for the site's user interface and navigation systems

Which site development and management objectives does your plan meet? [Check all correct answers]

- ❑ a. An analysis of the technologies available for use on the site based on the audience
- ❑ b. An analysis of the site's scope and requirements based on the site's goals and needs
- ❑ c. An analysis of the security requirements for the capabilities required by the site
- ❑ d. An analysis of an appropriate interface for the site
- ❑ e. An analysis of the site's performance requirements

The correct answers to this question are a, b, and d. The proposal includes analysis of the site's audience, goals, needs, and interface. Answers c and e are incorrect because the proposal does not address the critical security issues associated with implementing electronic commerce or database access, and it does not address the important issue of meeting the site's performance requirements.

Question 6

Which of the following directly affect the performance of a Web server? [Check all correct answers]

- ❑ a. The type of HTML and other code used to create Web pages
- ❑ b. The amount of RAM and hard disk space available to the server
- ❑ c. The speed of the CPU
- ❑ d. The amount of bandwidth available to the server

The correct answers to this question are b, c, and d. The amount of RAM, hard disk space, and bandwidth available to a server as well as the speed of its CPU affect the overall performance of the server. Answer a is incorrect because the type of HTML and other code used to create Web pages do not affect the server's performance but instead impact a client's ability to interpret and display Web content.

Question 7

Top Label Cat Food has just deployed a new Web site. The site is comprised of a product catalog. Each page is 8K and contains a graphic of the product, which is 22K in size. The site receives an average of 10,000 page requests per month. The product catalog contains 12 products and will be increased by 1 product every month. Furthermore, FrontPage has been used to establish a common control bar for each page. The Web server hosting the site is connected to the Internet over a 1.54Mbps T1 link. Which of the following areas pinpoints the Web site's greatest weakness?

- ❍ a. Maintenance
- ❍ b. Bandwidth
- ❍ c. Security
- ❍ d. Navigation

This question did not mention security for this site. Therefore, answer c is correct. With so few pages and a moderate increase in complexity, maintenance is simple. Therefore, answer a is incorrect. The low-high count and small page size do not require much bandwidth. Therefore, answer b is incorrect. Using a common control bar through FrontPage offers universal navigation. Therefore, answer d is incorrect.

Question 8

Acme Dog Food has deployed a Web site. It used FrontPage and SQL Server to produce its site. In addition to the product pages, Acme includes articles from magazines about canine care. The site consists of 2,000 pages and is increased by over 100 pages per month. Navigation is controlled by a standardized control bar, which is present on each page. Each page in the site is at least 32K in size. The site experiences about 400,000 hits per day. The site is hosted on a single B-channel of an ISDN line (64Kbps). The site is a standalone server that allows anonymous access to the Web areas only. All other areas are restricted to administrators. In which of the following areas is this Web site deficient?

❍ a. Maintenance

❍ b. Bandwidth

❍ c. Security

❍ d. Navigation

This site requires more bandwidth than a single B-channel of ISDN. Therefore, answer b is correct. Maintenance is simplified through the use of FrontPage and SQL Server. Therefore, answer a is incorrect. Security has been addressed. Therefore, answer c is incorrect. Because a standard control bar navigation is present, answer d is incorrect.

Need To Know More?

Haggard, Mary. *Survival Guide to Web Site Development*, Microsoft Press, Redmond, WA, 1998. ISBN 1-57231-851-1. This entire book provides good advice about the important tasks and issues associated with Web site development.

Lehto, Kerry and W. Polonsky. *Official Microsoft FrontPage Book*, Microsoft Press, Redmond, WA, 1997. ISBN 9-781572-316294. Chapters 2 and 5 of this official Microsoft publication provide good information on Web site development and management.

Tauber, Daniel and Brenda Kienan. *Mastering Microsoft FrontPage 98*, Sybex, Alameda, CA, 1998. ISBN 0-7821-2144-6. This solid FrontPage resource includes an informative section on site maintenance (see Chapter 17).

www.microsoft.com/frontpage/resources/howto.htm. The How To articles included on the FrontPage section of the Microsoft Web site contain several useful articles about site design and development. Take the time to read the articles listed under the Navigation heading for more detailed information on setting up a good navigation system, as discussed in this chapter.

www.microsoft.com/workshop/c-frame.htm#/workshop/essentials/default.asp. The Essentials section of the Microsoft SiteBuilder Network online workshop includes a number of articles on Web site development, server selection, and links to a variety of relevant resources. The articles in the For Starters section are particularly relevant to the skills discussed in this chapter.

http://msdn.microsoft.com/mastering/prodinfo/mast_wsf.asp. The Mastering Web Site Fundamentals training from the Microsoft Mastering Series provides a good introduction to basic Web site design, deployment, and maintenance. Chapters 1, 3, and 10 include information relevant to the topics in this chapter.

www.microsoft.com/security/. The section of the Microsoft Web site devoted to security includes several resources that focus on how FrontPage and the various Microsoft Web servers support and handle security issues. Be sure to check the Information By Product/Feature section for links to articles on specific products, including FrontPage.

15

Sample Test

In this chapter, we provide pointers to help you develop a successful test-taking strategy, including how to choose proper answers, how to decode ambiguity, how to work within the Microsoft testing framework, how to decide what you need to memorize, and how to prepare for the test. At the end of the chapter, we include 72 questions on subject matter pertinent to Microsoft Exam 70-055, "Designing and Implementing Web Sites with Microsoft FrontPage 98." Good luck!

Questions, Questions, Questions

There should be no doubt in your mind that you are facing a test full of specific and pointed questions. If the version of the FrontPage 98 exam that you take is fixed-length, it will include 72 questions, and you will be allotted 105 minutes to complete the exam. If it's an adaptive test (the software should tell you this as you begin the exam), it will consist of somewhere between 25 and 35 questions (on average) and take somewhere between 30 and 60 minutes.

Whichever type of test you take, for this exam, questions belong to one of five basic types:

- Multiple choice with a single answer
- Multiple choice with multiple answers
- Multipart with a single answer
- Multipart with multiple answers
- Simulations whereby you click on a GUI screen capture to simulate using the FrontPage 98 interface

Always take the time to read a question at least twice before selecting an answer, and you should always look for an Exhibit button as you examine each question. Exhibits include graphics information related to a question. An *exhibit* is usually a screen capture of program output or GUI information that you must examine to analyze the question's contents and formulate an answer. The Exhibit button brings up graphics and charts used to help explain a question, provide additional data, or illustrate page layout or program behavior.

Not every question has only one answer; many questions require multiple answers. Therefore, you should read each question carefully, determine how many answers are necessary or possible, and look for additional hints or instructions when selecting answers. Such instructions often occur in brackets, immediately following the question itself (multiple-answer questions).

Picking Proper Answers

Obviously, the only way to pass any exam is to select enough of the right answers to obtain a passing score. However, Microsoft's exams are not standardized like the SAT and GRE exams; they are far more diabolical and convoluted. In some cases, questions are strangely worded, and deciphering them can be a real challenge. In those cases, you may need to rely on answer-elimination skills. Almost always, at least one answer out of the possible choices for a question can be eliminated immediately because it matches one of these conditions:

- The answer does not apply to the situation.
- The answer describes a nonexistent issue, an invalid option, or an imaginary state.
- The answer may be eliminated because of information in the question itself.

After you eliminate all answers that are obviously wrong, you can apply your retained knowledge to eliminate further answers. Look for items that sound correct but refer to actions, commands, or features that are not present or not available in the situation that the question describes.

If you're still faced with a blind guess among two or more potentially correct answers, reread the question. Try to picture how each of the possible remaining answers would alter the situation. Be especially sensitive to terminology; sometimes the choice of words ("remove" instead of "disable") can make the difference between a right answer and a wrong one.

Only when you've exhausted your ability to eliminate answers but remain unclear about which of the remaining possibilities is correct should you guess at an answer. An unanswered question offers you no points, but guessing gives you at least some chance of getting a question right; just don't be too hasty when making a blind guess.

If you're taking a fixed-length test, you can wait until the last round of reviewing marked questions (just as you're about to run out of time or out of unanswered questions) before you start making guesses. If you're taking an adaptive test, you'll have to guess to move on to the next question if you can't figure out an answer some other way. Either way, guessing should be a last resort.

Decoding Ambiguity

Microsoft exams have a reputation for including questions that can be difficult to interpret, confusing, or ambiguous. In our experience with numerous exams, we consider this reputation to be completely justified. The Microsoft exams are tough, and they're deliberately made that way.

The only way to beat Microsoft at its own game is to be prepared. You'll discover that many exam questions test your knowledge of things that are not directly related to the issue raised by a question. This means that the answers you must choose from, even incorrect ones, are just as much a part of the skill assessment as the question itself. If you don't know something about most aspects of FrontPage 98, you may not be able to eliminate obviously wrong answers because they relate to a different area of FrontPage 98 than the one that's addressed by the question at hand. In other words, the more you know about the software, the easier it will be for you to tell right from wrong.

Questions often give away their answers, but you have to be Sherlock Holmes to see the clues. Often, subtle hints appear in the question text in such a way that they seem almost irrelevant to the situation. You must realize that each question is a test unto itself and that you need to inspect and successfully navigate each question to pass the exam. Look for small clues, such as the mention of times, group permissions and names, and configuration settings. Little things such as these can point to the right answer if properly understood; if missed, they can leave you facing a blind guess.

Another common difficulty with certification exams is vocabulary. Microsoft has an uncanny knack for naming some utilities and features entirely obviously in some cases and completely inanely in other instances. Be sure to brush up on the key terms presented at the beginning of each chapter. You may also want to read through the glossary at the end of this book the day before you take the test.

Working Within The Framework

The test questions appear in random order, and many elements or issues that receive mention in one question may also crop up in other questions. It's not uncommon to find that an incorrect answer to one question is the correct answer to another question, or vice versa. Take the time to read every answer to each question, even if you recognize the correct answer to a question immediately. That extra reading may spark a memory, or remind you about a FrontPage 98 feature or function that will help you on another question elsewhere in the exam.

If you're taking a fixed-length test, you can revisit any question as many times as you like. If you're uncertain of the answer to a question, check the box that's provided to mark it for easy return later on. You should also mark questions you think may offer information that you can use to answer other questions. On fixed-length tests, we usually mark somewhere between 25 and 50 percent of the questions on exams we've taken. The testing software is designed to let you mark every question if you choose; use this framework to your advantage. Everything you'll want to see again should be marked; the testing software can then help you return to marked questions quickly and easily.

STUDY ALERT

For fixed-length tests, we strongly recommend that you first read through the entire test quickly, before getting caught up in answering individual questions. This will help to jog your memory as you review the potential answers and can help identify questions that you want to mark for easy access to their contents. It will also let you identify and mark the tricky questions for easy return. The key is to make a quick pass over the territory to begin with—so that you know what you're up against—and then to survey that territory more thoroughly on a second pass, when you can begin to answer all questions systematically and consistently.

If you're taking an adaptive test, and you see something in a question or one of the answers that jogs your memory on a topic, or that you feel you should record if the topic appears in another question, write it down on your piece of paper. Just because you can't go back to a question in an adaptive test doesn't mean you can't take notes on what you see early in the test, in hopes that it might help you later in the test.

For adaptive tests, don't be afraid to take notes on what you see in various questions. Sometimes, what you record from one question, especially if it's not as familiar as it should be or reminds you of the name or use of some utility or interface details, can help you on other questions later on.

Deciding What To Memorize

The amount of memorization you must undertake for an exam depends on how well you remember what you've read, and how well you know the software by heart. If you're a visual thinker and can see the drop-down menus and dialog boxes in your head, you won't need to memorize as much as someone who's less visually oriented. However, the exam will stretch your abilities to memorize product features and functions, interface details, and proper Web design and maintenance approaches, and how they all relate to FrontPage 98.

At a minimum, you'll want to memorize the following kinds of information:

- The important Web- and Internet-related protocols and how they work within a Web site and within FrontPage 98
- The features and functions associated with FrontPage 98 tools such as FrontPage Editor and FrontPage Explorer, as well as when using either (or both) of them is appropriate and when it is not
- The various wizards and templates available for Web page construction within FrontPage 98, and what kinds of functions, capabilities, and HTML markup these wizards and templates can deliver
- How to perform typical Web site maintenance tasks, such as checking internal and external hyperlinks on a site, spell-checking contents, uploading files, and testing new documents and related elements to make sure everything is working properly

- How to extend Web pages beyond static HTML to include Dynamic HTML, JavaScript elements, Java applets, CGI programs, access to search engines and databases, and other ways to enhance a Web site's functionality

If you work your way through this book while sitting at a machine with FrontPage 98 installed and try to manipulate this environment's features and functions as they're discussed throughout, you should have little or no difficulty mastering this material. Also, don't forget that The Cram Sheet at the front of the book is designed to capture the material that's most important to memorize; use this to guide your studies as well.

Preparing For The Test

The best way to prepare for the test—after you've studied—is to take at least one practice exam. We've included one here in this chapter for that reason; the test questions are located in the pages that follow (and unlike the questions in the preceding chapters in this book, the answers don't follow the questions immediately; you'll have to flip to Chapter 16 to review the answers separately).

Give yourself 105 minutes to take the exam, and keep yourself on the honor system—don't look at earlier text in the book or jump ahead to the answer key. When your time is up or you've finished the questions, you can check your work in Chapter 16. Pay special attention to the explanations for the incorrect answers; these can also help to reinforce your knowledge of the material. Knowing how to recognize correct answers is good, but understanding why incorrect answers are wrong can be equally valuable.

Taking The Test

Relax. Once you're sitting in front of the testing computer, there's nothing more you can do to increase your knowledge or preparation. Take a deep breath, stretch, and start reading that first question.

You don't need to rush, either. You have plenty of time to complete each question and to return to those questions that you skip or mark for return (if you're taking a fixed-length test). If you read a question twice and remain clueless, you can mark it if you're taking a fixed-length test; if you're taking an adaptive test, you'll have to guess and move on. Both easy and difficult questions are intermixed throughout the test in random order. If you're taking a fixed-length test, don't cheat yourself by spending too much time on a hard question early on in the test, thereby depriving yourself of the time you need to answer the questions at the end of the test. If you're taking an adaptive test, don't spend more than five minutes on any single question—if it takes you that long to get nowhere, it's time to guess and move on.

On a fixed-length test, you can read through the entire test, and before returning to marked questions for a second visit, you can figure out how much time you've got per question. As you answer each question, remove its mark. Continue to review the remaining marked questions until you run out of time or complete the test.

On an adaptive test, set a maximum time limit for questions and watch your time on long or complex questions. If you hit your limit, it's time to guess and move on. Don't deprive yourself of the opportunity to see more questions by taking too long to puzzle over questions, unless you think you can figure out the answer. Otherwise, you're limiting your opportunities to pass.

That's it for pointers. Here are some questions for you to practice on.

Sample Test

Question 1

Which of the following design criteria should you consider when analyzing requirements for a Web site? [Check all correct answers]

- ❑ a. The message and communication goals that drive the Web site
- ❑ b. The browser or browsers that the site's primary audience members will use
- ❑ c. The level of security and access controls that the site will require
- ❑ d. The technologies you plan to use to build this site

Question 2

To reflect the release of a new product, you want to replace the string "Mark I" with the string "Mark II" across your entire Web site, which contains over 100 documents altogether. Of the following options, which one is the best way to complete this activity?

- ❍ a. FrontPage Editor: Edit|Find And Replace|Match Whole Word Only|All Pages
- ❍ b. FrontPage Explorer: Edit|Find And Replace|Match Whole Word Only|All Pages
- ❍ c. FrontPage Explorer: Tools|Find And Replace|All Pages
- ❍ d. FrontPage Explorer: Edit|Find And Replace|All Pages

Question 3

Once you've installed all the components from the FrontPage 98 CD-ROM, what happens if you double-click on an image from inside FrontPage Editor's main edit window?

- ❍ a. MS Paint opens with the image displayed.
- ❍ b. The Image toolbar appears.
- ❍ c. FrontPage Explorer opens.
- ❍ d. Image Composer opens with the image displayed.

Question 4

To add visual interest to a Web page, you decide to animate some static text. To keep the amount of work to a minimum, you want to use the simplest type of animation possible. Browser compatibility is not an issue because your site is private, and all users have IE4 (or higher). Of the following choices, which represents the easiest way to animate the text using FrontPage Editor?

- ❍ a. Highlight the static text, go to the Format menu, and select the desired animation effect
- ❍ b. Replace the static text with an animated GIF file
- ❍ c. Use the Script wizard to write a JavaScript-based animation
- ❍ d. Write a Java applet that animates a graphic

Question 5

Of the following Web technologies, which are directly supported in FrontPage Editor? [Check all correct answers]

- ❑ a. XML
- ❑ b. Cascading Style Sheets
- ❑ c. Client-side Java applets
- ❑ d. Dynamic HTML
- ❑ e. SGML

Question 6

Using FrontPage Editor, you create a Web document that includes a style that modifies the size, font family, and background color for certain text elements. After testing the page successfully using IE4, you distribute the document to the corporate network. However, current office policy dictates that users may run only Netscape Navigator 3 on their desktops. What will happen when those users try to view this document using that browser?

❍ a. An error message stating that style sheets are unsupported will appear.

❍ b. The text will revert to the browser's default font settings.

❍ c. No text content affected by the style sheet will display.

❍ d. The text will appear the same way that it does in IE4.

Question 7

On a Web page that displays multiple small images, you want to place the images so that they're evenly spaced across the display area. Of the following approaches, which are the most likely to help you realize this layout? [Check all correct answers]

❑ a. Create a table and place the images in the float area

❑ b. Create a table and add specific cell background images from your collection

❑ c. Create a table and place the images into the table cells

❑ d. Create a table and use an image to define a background for that table

Question 8

To increase traffic on your Web site, you've been instructed to set up a channel to deliver news items about your products, along with discount information. This means that the content will have to be updated and replaced constantly, but management is funding the manpower necessary to handle the work. Early indications from a user survey indicate that your site will experience thousands of extra visits per day once this channel becomes available.

While implementing this new channel, you've also been asked to deliver these specific items:

- Turn your site into a channel.
- Make sure that your company's logo appears in the channel bar for IE4 clients who add your site to their channel selections. (The logo is available as ICON.GIF and LOGO.GIF.)
- Create a subscription link for the channel on your home page.
- Make sure that excessive channel updates do not occur at any given time.

You decide to use the Channel Definition wizard in FrontPage Explorer to help you define the channel; you set the channel to INDEX.HTML (the file name for your home page) and configure the Channel Definition wizard, as shown in the following figure. On the last frame of the Channel Definition wizard, you leave the default settings unaltered to create a subscription button on the navigation bar.

By taking this approach, which of the following goals can you accomplish? [Check all correct answers]

- ❑ a. You've turned your site into a channel.
- ❑ b. You've made sure that the company's logo appears in the channel bar of IE4 clients who add your site to their channel selections.
- ❑ c. You've made sure that a subscription link is available on your home page.
- ❑ d. You've prevented excessive channel updates from occurring at any given time.

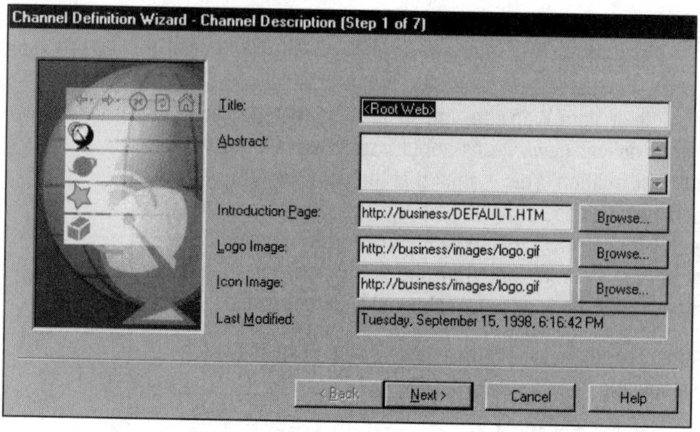

Question 9

Which of the following publishing methods can FrontPage 98 use to update Web sites? [Check all correct answers]

- ❑ a. Multiple sites at the same time
- ❑ b. Only one site at a time
- ❑ c. Copy only changed files for each site
- ❑ d. Copy all files for each site

Question 10

You've just altered the TCP port for your Web server from the default value of 80 to the hidden but reasonably well-known value of 8080. Before you run FrontPage Explorer against that site, what must you do?

- ❍ a. Reload the site's home page
- ❍ b. Reinstall FrontPage Server Extensions
- ❍ c. Reinstall FrontPage 98
- ❍ d. Close all open applications

Question 11

Of the following methods for creating Web sites or individual Web documents using FrontPage 98, which ones result in the creation of a file (or files) that can be edited and customized? [Check all correct answers]

- ❑ a. From scratch (creating raw HTML)
- ❑ b. Import
- ❑ c. Templates
- ❑ d. Wizards

Question 12

Of the following Web browsers, which can display framed content properly? [Check all correct answers]

- ❑ a. Mosaic 1
- ❑ b. Microsoft Internet Explorer 2
- ❑ c. Netscape Navigator 3
- ❑ d. Microsoft Internet Explorer 4

Question 13

Of the following actions, which ones can FrontPage 98 perform to handle collected form data when the Submit button has been clicked on (or a similar on-page function has occurred)? [Check all correct answers]

- ❑ a. Send contents via email
- ❑ b. Save contents to an HTML file
- ❑ c. Save contents to a text file
- ❑ d. Post the data to a CGI script

Question 14

You must add multiple new documents to your corporate Web site. Several of these pages are to comprise the company's travel and entertainment (T&E) policy handbook. Other elements include adding a custom background to the site, a weekly employee bulletin, and a site search facility.

Your objectives are the following:

- Create an online version of the T&E policy handbook
- Add a site search facility through a search page
- Add a custom background image for the site
- Add an employee bulletin for the site
- Add hyperlinks to all pages from the home page (INDEX.HTML)

The proposed solution is as follows:

- Obtain a copy of the T&E policy handbook and create Web pages for each of its sections
- In FrontPage Explorer, choose the Search Page template and configure it for your site
- Add an employee bulletin using the three-column template in FrontPage Editor and insert appropriate bulletin content
- Select all pages on the site in FrontPage Explorer, choose Insert|Hyperlink, and then map each page back to INDEX.HTML

Of the stated objectives, which does the proposed solution succeed in implementing?

❍ a. Creates hyperlinks from all pages to the home page

❍ b. Adds an employee bulletin to the Web site

❍ c. Adds a custom background to all pages in the Web site

❍ d. Adds a search page to the Web site

❍ e. Creates the online T&E policy handbook

Question 15

When identifying what server software to use for your Web site, which of the following criteria should you consider? [Check all correct answers]

- ❑ a. The server software's CPU and RAM requirements
- ❑ b. The site's security requirements
- ❑ c. How much hard disk space you have available on your server
- ❑ d. The speed of the server's connection to the Internet

Question 16

Which of the following file formats are Microsoft video display formats? [Check all correct answers]

- ❑ a. MPEG
- ❑ b. JPEG
- ❑ c. GIF
- ❑ d. JFIF
- ❑ e. None of the above

Question 17

A corporate client requests you to design a Web site that's easy to maintain but that delivers a consistent and professional look and feel. Of the following approaches, what is the simplest way for you to do this?

- ❍ a. Use an external, linked style sheet on every page
- ❍ b. Use the Corporate Presence Web wizard to build the site
- ❍ c. Use the Format Stylesheet tool on every page to apply a consistent set of style rules
- ❍ d. Apply a theme to the Web site

Question 18

FrontPage 98 includes a feature-rich WYSIWYG Web editor. What else does FrontPage 98 offer to Web content developers? [Check all correct answers]

- ❑ a. Database integration
- ❑ b. Push channels
- ❑ c. Personal Web hosting
- ❑ d. E-commerce templates

Question 19

If certain elements in a Web document are transient, which FrontPage 98 features may be used to automate their appearance on the document? [Check all correct answers]

- ❑ a. Page banner
- ❑ b. Include page
- ❑ c. Scheduled include page
- ❑ d. Scheduled image

Question 20

Which of the following FrontPage 98 toolbar buttons create embedded HTML tables? [Check all correct answers]

- ❑ a. The Insert Table icon on the Standard toolbar
- ❑ b. The Draw Table icon on the Standard toolbar
- ❑ c. The Insert Table icon on the Table toolbar
- ❑ d. The Draw Table icon on the Table toolbar

Question 21

Of the following items, which may be added to a Web page from FrontPage Editor's Advanced toolbar? [Check all correct answers]

- ❑ a. The Database Registration wizard
- ❑ b. Java applets
- ❑ c. ActiveX controls
- ❑ d. Scripts
- ❑ e. HTML

Question 22

When using FrontPage Explorer, which view should you use to check external hyperlinks?

- ❍ a. Hyperlinks
- ❍ b. Hyperlink Status
- ❍ c. Navigation
- ❍ d. All Files

Question 23

Of the following Web servers, which work with Windows 98? [Check all correct answers]

- ❑ a. Microsoft Personal Web Server
- ❑ b. Internet Information Server (IIS)
- ❑ c. FrontPage Personal Web Server
- ❑ d. Peer Web Services

Question 24

Of the following potential definitions, which best describes a FrontPage 98 wizard?

- ❍ a. A tool that creates structured documents without content
- ❍ b. A tool that applies a strict set of parameters to documents
- ❍ c. A tool that sets the look and feel for a Web site
- ❍ d. A tool that creates documents based on user input

Question 25

On a Web document collection that uses frames-based markup, your layout includes a company logo and a navigation bar that appear in a long, thin pane across the top of the page. Of the following pane property settings in FrontPage 98, which make sense for this particular pane? [Check all correct answers]

- ❑ a. Set the Row Height setting to an exact pixel count
- ❑ b. Set the Show Scrollbars setting to Never
- ❑ c. Allow the viewer to resize the pane
- ❑ d. Set a large height margin

Question 26

When you are building a form using FrontPage 98, which parameter is used to define the sequence according to which form elements are linked together?

- ❍ a. Value name
- ❍ b. Tab order
- ❍ c. Range
- ❍ d. Validation

Question 27

Using FrontPage 98, which of the following response pages may be customized? [Check all correct answers]

- ❑ a. Confirmation
- ❑ b. Unauthorized access
- ❑ c. Validation failure
- ❑ d. Server communication failure

Question 28

Which of the following Web site capabilities requires no special security considerations to implement?

- ❍ a. Active Server Pages
- ❍ b. A search engine
- ❍ c. Database access
- ❍ d. Electronic commerce

Question 29

Of the following explanations, which one best explains the significance of the **&T** tag in the header for a Web page in the Printer Page Setup dialog box for FrontPage Editor?

- ❍ a. The title of the page appears as the header.
- ❍ b. The time the file is printed appears in the header.
- ❍ c. The file will be spooled to a temporary folder.
- ❍ d. The type of the file will appear in the header.

Question 30

Of the following list of file formats, which is neither a Microsoft file format nor a Windows-supported file format?

- ❍ a. BMP
- ❍ b. SND
- ❍ c. AVI
- ❍ d. ZIP
- ❍ e. WAV

Question 31

Of the following FrontPage 98 tools and features, which one may be used to prevent duplication of effort or to keep changes from being lost when more than one developer is working on the same project?

- ❍ a. Microsoft Project
- ❍ b. NTFS file-level security
- ❍ c. Visual SourceSafe
- ❍ d. Tasks View

Question 32

Of the following items, which ones represent minimal requirements when installing FrontPage 98 and all its optional components on Windows NT? [Check all correct answers]

- ❑ a. Internet access
- ❑ b. Intel 486 CPU
- ❑ c. 101MB of hard drive space
- ❑ d. 32MB of RAM

Question 33

Of the following characteristics, which ones apply to the FrontPage 98 banner ad manager? [Check all correct answers]

- ❑ a. The defined images display once before stopping.
- ❑ b. A transition effect may be used to switch between images.
- ❑ c. Multiple images may be displayed in succession.
- ❑ d. Each image has its own associated URL.

Question 34

What term describes the amount of space that appears between cells in a table?

- ❍ a. Cell wall ratio
- ❍ b. Cell border
- ❍ c. Cell padding
- ❍ d. Cell spacing

Question 35

Using the HTML Markup dialog box in FrontPage Editor, you add HTML code to an existing document. Which of the following statements about the HTML Markup dialog box are true? [Check all correct answers]

- ❑ a. If you want to modify the code after it's been placed on a Web page, you must switch to the HTML View.
- ❑ b. It allows you to enter text directly into the dialog box.
- ❑ c. It performs HTML syntax and error checks.
- ❑ d. The code you insert will be placed in the Web document after you click on OK.

Question 36

Your corporate network is designed so that no traffic flows into or out of the Internet unless it passes through a firewall. You decide to use FrontPage 98 to update the corporate Web site and take advantage of its Server Extensions. Your workstation resides within the firewall, but the Web server is outside the firewall. What's the best way to complete the update under these circumstances without violating security?

❍ a. Configure FrontPage 98 to use the proxy services of the firewall just like other Internet utilities must.

❍ b. Use a removable hard drive to transfer the corporate Web site file system between your workstation and the Web server.

❍ c. Use FTP to transfer the Web folder structure from your workstation to the Web server.

❍ d. Obtain a modem and access to a local ISP; use this link to interact with the Web server and bypass the firewall.

Question 37

You're instructed to set up a Windows NT Server machine as a Web server, one that's configured to support Microsoft FrontPage 98. Also, the Web server software must be able to isolate processes to increase the stability of the applications that run on the Web server. Which of the following Web servers should you use in these circumstances?

❍ a. Internet Information Server

❍ b. Peer Web Services

❍ c. FrontPage Personal Web Server

❍ d. Personal Web Server

Question 38

Of the following detail elements, which items in a FrontPage 98 task may not be changed? [Check all correct answers]

- ❑ a. Linked file
- ❑ b. Priority
- ❑ c. Creation date
- ❑ d. Assigned user

Question 39

How are frames typically created within FrontPage 98?

- ❍ a. By importing an existing frame document
- ❍ b. Using the Frames wizard
- ❍ c. With a blank page template
- ❍ d. With a frame template

Question 40

Which of the following form elements may be handled using either a push button or an image?

- ❍ a. A selection list
- ❍ b. A drop-down list
- ❍ c. A Submit button
- ❍ d. A checkbox

Question 41

Within FrontPage Editor, which of these icons permits you to open a Web page on the Internet or on a local Web server using the HTTP protocol?

- ❍ a. The globe with chain icon
- ❍ b. The globe with magnifying glass icon
- ❍ c. The robot icon
- ❍ d. The file folder with magnifying glass icon
- ❍ e. The blank page icon

Question 42

You're redesigning a company intranet that's currently accessed by PC users who use IE4 to also accommodate Macintosh-based users. Which of the following technologies currently in use on your site must be changed, updated, or supplemented by other technologies for information delivery?

- ❍ a. VBScript
- ❍ b. ActiveX controls
- ❍ c. Standard HTML
- ❍ d. JavaScript

Question 43

Of the following Web browsers, which can support the FrontPage 98 background sound capability?

- ❍ a. AOL browser
- ❍ b. Netscape Navigator
- ❍ c. CompuServe browser
- ❍ d. Internet Explorer 4

Question 44

You've decided to create an image map for your Web site to link all departments in your organization to a central directory. This image map must contain an image with hyperlinks to each department's individual Web page, and an overview of all departments must be accessed on a page named OVERDEPT.HTML.

You must also complete these specific tasks:

- Create a map that includes all departments
- Create a central link to the departmental overview document
- Place an image map for the departments on a Web page
- Link each department's hyperlink on the overview page to the department's home page

You create a digital image of the building directory, which includes a map of the building, so that every department is represented. You import the image into Image Composer and label each department on the map. Then you import the image into FrontPage Editor and insert rectangular hyperlinks for each department name and map them to OVERDEPT.HTML.

Of the following goals, which does your work accomplish? [Check all correct answers]

❑ a. Create a central link to the departmental overview document (OVERDEPT.HTML)

❑ b. Place an image on a Web page for use as an image map

❑ c. Link each department's hyperlink to the department's home page

❑ d. Create a map that includes all departments

Question 45

In your organization, you're using Windows NT Server 4 running IIS 4 to host your Web development activities. However, the organization's production server is a Unix machine running Apache Web server software with FrontPage Server Extensions hosted at an ISP. The development and production databases are identical ODBC-compliant Oracle databases. How should you manage database access in this environment?

❍ a. Create IDC and HTX files and use the Internet Database Connector on both machines.

❍ b. Write custom CGI scripts in Perl on the NT machine. Recompile the Perl scripts on the Unix server.

❍ c. Write custom ISAPI DLLs and recompile them on the Unix server.

❍ d. Use the Database Region wizard to generate Active Server Pages. Use FrontPage Server Extensions to publish those Active Server Pages on the Unix server.

Question 46

FrontPage 98 offers more capabilities than Web site creation. Of the following software components, which ones bring additional capabilities to FrontPage 98? [Check all correct answers]

❑ a. Internet Explorer 4.01

❑ b. FrontPage Server Extensions

❑ c. Personal Web Server 1.5

❑ d. Transaction Server 2

❑ e. Index Server 2

❑ f. Image Composer 1.5

Question 47

FrontPage 98 supports hover buttons, which appear above the page when the cursor crosses over active areas on a Web page. What's the technology or programming technique that underlies this capability?

- ❍ a. Java applets
- ❍ b. VBScript code
- ❍ c. JavaScript inline with HTML
- ❍ d. Server-side scripting

Question 48

Of the following interfaces, which ones permit you to draw an HTML table on a Web page within FrontPage Editor? [Check all correct answers]

- ❑ a. Table Properties dialog box
- ❑ b. Menu bar
- ❑ c. Standard toolbar
- ❑ d. Table toolbar

Question 49

Within the FrontPage 98 environment, which of the following methods will permit you to add Java applets or scripts to a Web page? [Check all correct answers]

- ❑ a. Use the Insert option in FrontPage Explorer's menu bar and select Insert Script or Insert Java Applet
- ❑ b. Click on the Insert Script icon on FrontPage Editor's Advanced toolbar
- ❑ c. Use the Insert Java Applet icon on FrontPage Editor's Advanced toolbar
- ❑ d. Type the Java code directly into the page through the HTML View in FrontPage Explorer

Question 50

Because FrontPage 98 maintains a local compressed copy of every object published to a Web server, if you delete a Web site, you can restore it thereafter from the local copies without losing files or other data.

❍ a. True

❍ b. False

Question 51

If you wish to change the TCP port address for your FrontPage Personal Web Server from the default port address of 80 to an alternate address of 8080, how would you accomplish this task?

❍ a. Use the FrontPage Explorer Tasks View

❍ b. Use the Internet Services Manager applet in the Control Panel

❍ c. Edit the WIN.INI file

❍ d. Edit the SYSTEM.INI file

❍ e. Edit the HTTPD.CNF file

Question 52

Of the following FrontPage 98 wizards, which incorporate a WebBot component to support additional capabilities that HTML cannot provide by itself? [Check all correct answers]

❑ a. Import Web wizard

❑ b. Form Page wizard

❑ c. Discussion Web wizard

❑ d. Corporate Presence wizard

Question 53

Which of the following statements about using framed content on Web sites are true? [Check all correct answers]

- ❑ a. All browsers support frames.
- ❑ b. A content page within a forms pane cannot use Java applets.
- ❑ c. Each pane within a frame layout can display a different content page.
- ❑ d. Frames use targeted hyperlinks to load resources into panes.

Question 54

Within the FrontPage 98 environment, which of the following parameters may be defined for a custom form handler? [Check all correct answers]

- ❑ a. Method
- ❑ b. Action
- ❑ c. Programming language
- ❑ d. Encoding type

Question 55

Of the following scripting languages, which ones may be used by FrontPage 98 to validate input data from a form? [Check all correct answers]

- ❑ a. Perl
- ❑ b. Java
- ❑ c. JavaScript
- ❑ d. VBScript

Question 56

Within FrontPage Editor, which of the following icons permits you to open an existing Web page that's not part of your HTTP server but that does reside in your local file system?

- ❍ a. The globe with chain icon
- ❍ b. The robot icon
- ❍ c. The file folder with magnifying glass icon
- ❍ d. The blank page icon
- ❍ e. The globe with magnifying glass icon

Question 57

Which of the following file types may be used to create an image map? [Check all correct answers]

- ❑ a. AVI
- ❑ b. GIF
- ❑ c. JPG
- ❑ d. MPG

Question 58

The Database Region wizard in FrontPage 98 supports any custom SQL script.

- ❍ a. True
- ❍ b. False

Question 59

Your employer is a small software distribution company that has just decided to put up a Web site. You have been asked to create a plan for the development and management of the new site, whose capabilities are intended to include database access and electronic commerce. The proposal you present to your manager includes the following items:

- A description of the technologies you would use to develop the site
- A prototype for the site's user interface and navigation systems
- An analysis of the purpose and goals of the site
- An overview of the site's potential audience and its technology capabilities

Which of the following site development and management objectives does your plan satisfy? [Check all correct answers]

❑ a. An analysis of the site's scope and requirements based on the site's goals and needs

❑ b. An analysis of the technologies available for use on the site based on the audience

❑ c. An analysis of an appropriate interface for the site

❑ d. An analysis of the site's performance requirements

❑ e. An analysis of the security requirements for the capabilities required by the site

Question 60

Of the following inputs, which are required to access the Database Region wizard? [Check all correct answers]

❑ a. One or more query field names

❑ b. ODBC data source name (DSN)

❑ c. Form field parameter

❑ d. The SQL string for the query

❑ e. Database user name and password

Question 61

FrontPage 98 includes an automatic performance estimate that computes the average download time for whatever document is being edited.

❍ a. True

❍ b. False

Question 62

To create a Web site that works with the broadest possible range of Web browsers, which of the following technologies should you avoid? [Check all correct answers]

❑ a. Java

❑ b. Custom font selection

❑ c. Background colors

❑ d. ActiveX controls

❑ e. Forms

Question 63

Of the following selections listed, which appear in the Table Properties dialog box in FrontPage Editor? [Check all correct answers]

❑ a. Use Background Image

❑ b. Header Cell

❑ c. Border Size

❑ d. Cell Padding

❑ e. Float

Question 64

Which of the following techniques represents the easiest way to insert an AVI or QuickTime video into a Web page with "play" and "stop" controls?

- ❍ a. Write HTML for the controls and use a hyperlink to the resource
- ❍ b. Use a Java applet with custom controls
- ❍ c. Write a JavaScript with custom controls
- ❍ d. Use a compatible plug-in

Question 65

Of the following FrontPage 98 facilities, which is best suited for creating a Web site to deliver technical documentation and information for your company's products and services?

- ❍ a. Project Web template
- ❍ b. Discussion Web template
- ❍ c. Customer Support Web template
- ❍ d. Corporate Presence wizard

Question 66

Now that you've configured your FrontPage 98 Web site, you want to restrict others from being able to modify the site using FrontPage 98. However, ordinary users must be able to access the site's contents through their Web browsers unhindered. Of the following options, which is the best approach for realizing both aims?

- ❍ a. Place a warning message on the home page (INDEX.HTML)
- ❍ b. Disable authoring
- ❍ c. Change your password
- ❍ d. Change the TCP port number for the Web server

Question 67

FrontPage Explorer permits tasks to be associated with Web sites and Web documents. Tasks can even be assigned deadlines so that administrators will receive pop-up messages prompting them to complete assigned tasks as the deadline approaches.

❍ a. True

❍ b. False

Question 68

To cause a document to appear in an independent browser window when its hyperlink is selected, which of the following frame target definitions should you use?

❍ a. Parent Frame

❍ b. Whole Page

❍ c. Same Frame

❍ d. New Window

Question 69

Which of the following techniques does the Database Region wizard use to obtain database access?

❍ a. Client-side JavaScript

❍ b. Client-side VBScript

❍ c. FrontPage WebBot

❍ d. Server-side VBScript

Question 70

Which of the following factors affect the performance of a Web server directly? [Check all correct answers]

- ❑ a. The amount of RAM and hard disk space available to the server
- ❑ b. The speed of the CPU
- ❑ c. The kind of HTML and other code used to create Web pages
- ❑ d. The amount of bandwidth available to the server

Question 71

Which of the following items are required in the IDC file? [Check all correct answers]

- ❑ a. The name of the template HTX file
- ❑ b. ODBC data source name
- ❑ c. Database user name
- ❑ d. The SQL string for the query
- ❑ e. One or more query field names

Question 72

You must give an extension of .ASP to a file created by the Database Region wizard. You must also assign execute access to the directory where the ASP file resides so the server can execute the Active Server Page script.

- ❍ a. True
- ❍ b. False

16

Answer Key

1. a, b, c
2. c
3. d
4. a
5. b, c, d
6. b
7. b, c
8. a, b, c
9. a, c, d
10. b
11. a, b, c, d
12. c, d
13. a, b, c, d
14. e
15. a, b, c
16. e
17. d
18. a, b, c
19. c, d
20. a, d
21. b, c, d, e
22. b
23. a, c
24. d
25. a, b
26. b
27. a, c
28. b
29. a
30. b
31. c
32. b, c, d
33. b, c
34. d
35. a, b, d
36. a
37. a
38. a, c
39. d
40. c
41. b
42. b
43. d
44. b, d
45. b
46. b, c, f
47. a
48. b, d
49. b, c
50. b
51. e
52. b, c, d
53. c, d
54. a, b, d
55. c, d
56. c
57. b, c
58. a
59. a, b, c
60. a, b, d
61. a
62. a, b, d
63. a, c, d, e
64. d
65. c
66. b
67. b
68. d
69. d
70. a, b, d
71. a, b, d
72. b

Question 1

The correct answers to this question are a, b, and c. The purpose and goals that drive a site, browser issues, and the Web site's security needs and access controls all represent aspects that help to determine a Web site's requirements. Answer d is incorrect because you should choose specific technologies to build your site as a direct outcome of your analysis of a Web site's requirements, not as a part of the requirements themselves.

Question 2

Answer c is correct. FrontPage Explorer is the tool of choice for editing entire Web sites, whereas FrontPage Editor is best for editing single documents. Answer a is incorrect because it refers to the use of FrontPage Editor. Answers b and d are incorrect because they refer to the Edit menu rather than the Tools menu, which is where the Find And Replace tool is located.

Question 3

Answer d is correct. If all components from the FrontPage 98 CD-ROM are installed, this automatically includes Image Composer and creates an association between most common graphics file types and the program. Then, if an image is double-clicked on from within FrontPage Editor, the image opens within Image Composer. MS Paint and FrontPage Explorer are not configured as image editors by the FrontPage 98 setup program. Therefore, answers a and c are incorrect. The Image toolbar is part of FrontPage Editor itself and does not open when an image is double-clicked on. Therefore, answer b is also incorrect.

Question 4

Answer a is the correct answer, simply because it requires the least amount of effort. Answer b is valid, but it requires creation of at least two images to switch back and forth to create the most basic form of animation. Answers c and d are both valid, but both require programming work and additional graphics creation, and are therefore definitely not the easiest way to animate text.

Question 5

Answers b, c, and d are correct because FrontPage Editor supports CSS, client-side Java applets, and Dynamic HTML directly. Neither XML nor SGML is currently supported by FrontPage 98, making answers a and e incorrect.

Question 6

Netscape Navigator 3 does not support Cascading Style Sheets, so users will see the text, but that text will be subject to the browser's default font settings. Therefore, answer b is correct. No error message appears when unreadable markup is found in a Web document; the browser simply applies predefined defaults (as is the case here) or ignores the markup altogether. Therefore, answer a is incorrect. Navigator does display the text. Therefore, answer c is incorrect. Finally, because Navigator 3 cannot interpret style sheets, but IE4 can, the text does not appear the same as it does in IE4, making answer d incorrect as well.

Question 7

Only answers b and c result in placement of images within table cells, which is what's required to realize this design goal. Therefore, both b and c are correct. Answer b puts the images in the background so that they may be overlaid with text. Answer c puts the images in the foreground so that they alone will occupy the table cells. The float area in a table is the area around its horizontal borders where text may flow; placing images here will not produce the desired results. Therefore, answer a is incorrect. Answer d is incorrect because it uses only a single image as the background for the entire table and says nothing about arranging the individual images.

Question 8

Answers a, b, and c are correct because the solution described achieves all of the following goals:

- Using the Channel Definition wizard does indeed turn your site into a channel.
- The exhibit shows that you've configured a logo and icon for the channel, as required.
- Leaving the defaults unaltered on the last frame of the Channel Definition wizard does indeed add a subscription link to your home page.

However, none of the settings described in the solution has any effect on the size and frequency of channel updates. Therefore, answer d is incorrect (the default is to allow all users to update at the same time, in fact).

Question 9

FrontPage 98 can publish to multiple sites at the same time, and it can also upload only changed files for each site or all files for each site. Therefore, answers a, c, and d are correct. Although FrontPage 98 can update a single site at a time, it is not constrained to do so. Because answer b says "only one site at a time," this answer is incorrect.

Question 10

Whenever fundamental Web server settings change, your best bet is to reinstall FrontPage Server Extensions. Therefore, answer b is correct. Reloading the site's home page or closing all open applications will not modify the TCP port that FrontPage 98 uses to connect to your Web server. Therefore, answers a and d are incorrect. Reinstalling FrontPage 98 is not necessary and won't make any difference until FrontPage Server Extensions are installed anyway. Therefore, answer c is incorrect.

Question 11

All four of the methods described produce editable (and therefore customizable) files using FrontPage 98. Therefore, answers a, b, c, and d are all correct.

Question 12

Frames are a relatively recent HTML innovation and weren't formalized until the HTML 4 standard was finalized on December 18, 1997. Therefore, it should come as no surprise that only newer browsers, such as Netscape Navigator 3 (one of the first to support frames, even prior to the release of the 4 standard for HTML) and Internet Explorer 4, support frames. Therefore, only answers c and d are correct. The other browsers predate the development of frames markup. Therefore, answers a and b are incorrect.

Question 13

All of these actions are supported in FrontPage 98. Therefore, answers a, b, c, and d are correct. Answers a and d are customary for most forms-handling environments, and b and c are additional methods provided as a convenience to users.

Question 14

The proposed solution achieves only one of the stated objectives—namely, that of creating an online version of the T&E policy handbook. Therefore, only answer e is correct. You want to create hyperlinks from the home page to all pages, not the other way around. Therefore, answer a is incorrect. There is no three-column template in FrontPage Editor. Therefore, answer b is not possible as described. The solution makes no mention of creating a site-wide background graphic. Therefore, answer c is incorrect. The solution calls for adding a search page using FrontPage Explorer; because this may done only in FrontPage Editor, answer d is incorrect.

Question 15

The correct answers to this question are a, b, and c. Your server hardware must meet the CPU, RAM, and hard disk space requirements of your chosen server software; likewise, the server software you choose must be able to meet your site's security requirements. Answer d is incorrect because the speed of your server's connection to the Internet does not directly impact the server software you choose, even though it does affect the overall performance of your Web server.

Question 16

Of all the file formats listed, none is specific to Microsoft. Therefore, answer e is correct. MPEG is a moving image standard that originated with the Motion Picture Experts Group, not Microsoft. Therefore, answer a is incorrect. JPEG is a still-image standard that originated with the Joint Photographic Experts Group, not Microsoft. Therefore, answer b is incorrect. GIF is a widely used image format invented by CompuServe, not Microsoft. Therefore, answer c is incorrect. JFIF is the JPEG File Interchange Format and also originated with the Joint Photographic Experts Group, not Microsoft. Therefore, answer d is also incorrect.

Question 17

The easiest way to provide a professional look and feel for a Web site with a minimum amount of effort is to apply a theme to that site. Therefore, answer d is correct. Any approach that requires separate action for every page is not easy, by definition; this automatically disqualifies the approaches advocated in answers a and c. Answer b would work only if a theme were applied in addition to this wizard, so it represents an extra step. Therefore, answer b is also incorrect.

Question 18

In addition to FrontPage Editor, FrontPage 98 includes the Channel Definition wizard, which makes it easy to create and manage push channels. Likewise the Database Region wizard makes it easy to incorporate and access SQL-based databases. FrontPage 98 also supports personal Web hosting through the use of Personal Web Server. This makes answers a, b, and c correct. FrontPage 98 does not include direct support for e-commerce, and there are no e-commerce templates. Therefore, answer d is incorrect.

Question 19

In the FrontPage 98 environment, transient items must be scheduled to appear on a Web document. Therefore, answers c and d are correct. A page banner inserts a display banner that shows the page's name, but it's not automated. Therefore, answer a is incorrect. Likewise, an include page simplifies editing of common elements across multiple pages but does not provide automated capabilities. Therefore, answer b is incorrect.

Question 20

You must use either the Insert Table icon on the Standard toolbar or the Draw Table icon on the Table toolbar to insert a table into a Web page. This makes answers a and d correct. The Draw Table icon appears on the Table toolbar, not on the Standard toolbar, which makes answer b incorrect. Likewise, the Insert Table icon appears on the Standard toolbar, not on the Table toolbar, which makes answer c incorrect.

Question 21

The Advanced toolbar permits you to insert Java applets, ActiveX controls, scripts, and HTML. Therefore, answers b, c, d, and e are correct. The Advanced toolbar does not include an option for a Database Registration wizard. Therefore, answer a is incorrect.

Question 22

The only way to check external hyperlinks using FrontPage Explorer is through the Hyperlink Status View. Therefore, answer b is correct. The Hyperlinks View checks only local hyperlinks. Therefore, answer a is incorrect. Neither the Navigation nor the All Files Views check hyperlinks at all. Therefore, answers c and d are also incorrect.

Question 23

The key to answering this question lies in realizing that the same applications that work with Windows 95 also work with Windows 98. For this question, this means that answers a and c are correct, because the Microsoft Personal Web Server is included as part of Windows 98, and the FrontPage Personal Web Server is included with FrontPage 98 itself. IIS is a Windows NT product that's available for use with Windows NT Server; likewise, Peer Web Services is the name of the limited-use Web server that ships with Windows NT Workstation. Therefore, answers b and d are incorrect.

Question 24

A wizard may be best described as a tool that creates documents based on user input. Therefore, answer d is correct. A tool that creates structured documents without content is a template. Therefore, answer a is incorrect. A tool that applies a strict set of parameters to documents is a DTD, which is an SGML document definition that defines how HTML and other markup languages, such as XML, function. Therefore, answer b is incorrect. A tool that sets the look and feel for a Web site is a theme. Therefore, answer c is incorrect.

Question 25

The only settings that make sense for this kind of layout are to set the exact height for the pane and to turn off scrollbars. Therefore, answers a and b are correct. Allowing the viewer to resize the pane may limit access to the navigation bar, so this is not a good idea. Therefore, answer c is incorrect. Setting a large height margin forces a pane to be taller than needed to accommodate additional blank space. This pane should be as small as possible to maximize the content display area. Therefore, answer d is also incorrect.

Question 26

Answer b is correct. The tab order sets the sequence in which form elements are linked, which is what enables a user to tab from one frame field to the next. Value name is an element property not associated with element sequence, but rather with element identification. Therefore, answer a is incorrect. Range is a submission rule used by validation to determine whether an input value falls inside or outside a specified range of values. Therefore, answer c is incorrect. Finally, validation is a process by which input data is checked against submission rules. Therefore, answer d is incorrect as well.

Question 27

Answers a and c are correct. Only confirmation documents and the validation failure may be customized using FrontPage 98. Because the Web server catches these conditions, the unauthorized access and server communication failure documents are usually customizable only through the Web server software itself, which makes answers b and d incorrect.

Question 28

The correct answer to this question is b. There are no special security requirements when including a search engine on your Web site. Answers a, c, and d are incorrect because ASP, database access, and electronic commerce capabilities all require some level of security for proper operation and access controls.

Question 29

Answer a is correct. &T indicates that the page's title should appear in the printed header for the page as output. Although answers b, c, and d all name page properties that do (or might) start with a "T", they are incorrect.

Question 30

Of all the formats listed, only SND is a non-Windows file format (it's a Macintosh sound file format). Therefore, answer b is the only correct answer. BMP is a Windows bitmap format. Therefore, answer a is incorrect. AVI is the native Windows Audio Video Interleave format used for streaming video. Therefore, answer c is incorrect. ZIP is a compressed file format that originated on DOS but is supported by Windows. Therefore, answer d is incorrect. WAV is the native Windows file format for audio data. Therefore, answer e is also incorrect.

Question 31

Of all the options mentioned in this question, only Visual SourceSafe provides source code control and easy checkout management for source modules. Therefore, answer c is the only correct answer to this question. Microsoft Project and the FrontPage 98 Tasks View track only tasks, not access to individual files. Therefore, answers a and d are incorrect. NTFS file-level security can protect individual files but does not provide any administrative controls over or tracking of file access (both characteristics are essential when managing multiple developers who share a single set of files). Therefore, answer b is also incorrect.

Question 32

Answers b, c, and d are all correct. FrontPage 98 requires an Intel 486 CPU (or equivalent) or better, 101MB of hard drive space, and 32MB of RAM or better. Internet access is not required (only TCP/IP must be installed). Therefore, answer a is incorrect.

Question 33

The banner ad manager supports the use of transition effects between images and displays multiple images in succession. Therefore, answers b and c are correct. The display routine loops indefinitely, so images will normally display many times rather than only once. Therefore, answer a is incorrect. Only a single URL may be defined for all ads. Therefore, answer d is incorrect.

Question 34

Answer d is correct. Cell spacing describes the distance between the text and the cell wall. There is no such term as the cell wall ratio for table cells. Therefore, answer a is incorrect. The cell border describes the properties associated with the treatment of the edges of the table cell. Therefore, answer b is incorrect. Cell padding refers to the number of pixels between the sides of a cell and its contents. Therefore, answer c is incorrect.

Question 35

In this case, answers a, b, and d are correct. You must switch to the HTML View to edit HTML code that you've already placed on a Web page. You can indeed type directly into the dialog box, but it must be properly formatted. HTML code will be placed in your Web page after you click on OK, but you can't edit it using the dialog box after the HTML code has been placed. The HTML Markup dialog box includes a warning that it does not check HTML for correctness. Therefore, answer c is incorrect.

Question 36

The best solution is to use a proxy server. Therefore, answer a is correct. A removable hard drive is expensive and renders the Web server useless while the drive is in the workstation. Therefore, answer b is incorrect. Using FTP eliminates your ability to use Server Extensions functions on the Web site and requires an FTP server to reside on the same system where the Web server software resides. Therefore, answer c is incorrect. Using a modem and an ISP to bypass the firewall is a security breach that most companies will not permit. Therefore, answer d is incorrect. Although some of these other approaches are plausible, none is as convenient or secure as answer a, which is the correct answer to this question.

Question 37

Given these requirements, only answer a makes sense. IIS supports process isolation and runs well with Windows NT Server. Peer Web Services is strictly a Windows NT Workstation product and cannot support more than 10 simultaneous users. Therefore, answer b is incorrect. FrontPage Personal Web Server does not provide industrial-strength services, nor can it provide process isolation. Therefore, answer c is incorrect. Personal Web Server is a Windows 95/98 product and is not suitable for use with Windows NT Server. Therefore, answer d is incorrect.

Question 38

Neither the linked file nor the creation date details may be changed, which makes answers a and c correct. For FrontPage 98 tasks, only priority and assigned user are the details that may be changed. Therefore, answers b and d are incorrect.

Question 39

The most typical method for creating framed documents in FrontPage 98 is to use a frame template. Therefore, answer d is correct. Importing an existing frame document does work, but it's far less typical than using a frame template. Therefore, answer a is incorrect. There is no Frames wizard in FrontPage 98. Therefore, answer b is both invalid and incorrect. A blank page template may not be used because frames may only be created in FrontPage 98 using the frame template. Therefore, answer c is incorrect.

Question 40

Only a Submit button may be handled using a push button or an image element in an HTML form. Therefore, answer c is correct. A selection list requires use of the <SELECT> tag. Therefore, answer a is incorrect. The same is true of a drop-down list. Therefore, answer b is also incorrect. The type of an <INPUT> object must be a checkbox to create a checkbox. Therefore, answer d is also incorrect.

Question 41

The globe with magnifying glass icon allows you to open a Web page locally or from the Internet. Therefore, b is the correct answer. The globe with chain icon permits you to add hyperlinks to documents. Therefore, answer a is incorrect. The robot icon allows you to add only FrontPage 98 elements. Therefore, answer c is incorrect. The file folder with magnifying glass icon only supports browsing a local directory structure. Therefore, answer d is incorrect. The blank page icon only permits you to open a new page. Therefore, answer e is also incorrect.

Question 42

The correct answer is b. Only ActiveX experiences implementation problems when accessed using Macintosh Web clients. IE 4.01 is available for the Macintosh, and it supports both VBScript and JavaScript. Therefore, answers a and d are incorrect. Answer c is incorrect because standard HTML must be accessible by all Web browsers regardless of platform, even if the display varies from client to client.

Question 43

Only Microsoft's Internet Explorer 4 supports the background sound. Therefore, d is the correct answer. Neither the AOL browser, Netscape Navigator, nor the CompuServe browser support this capability. Therefore, answers a, b, and c are all incorrect.

Question 44

The correct answers for this question are b and d. You created an image that is used as an image map (answer b), and you created a map that includes all departments (answer d). What's more, all the links were mapped to OVERDEPT.HTML, not to individual departments, so you neither created a central link to the overview document, which makes answer a incorrect, nor linked each department's hyperlink to its own home, which makes answer c incorrect as well.

Question 45

The key to answering this question correctly lies in understanding which parts of the FrontPage 98 development environment can transfer from Windows NT to Unix. Only answer b is correct, because only Perl scripts can run in both environments largely unaltered. The Internet Database Connector (answer a), ISAPI DLLs (answer c), and Active Server Pages (answer d) all work only on Microsoft operating systems, not on Unix. Therefore, answers a, c, and d are all incorrect.

Question 46

Of the options listed, only FrontPage Server Extensions, Personal Web Server 1.5, and Image Composer 1.5 are part of FrontPage 98. Because each of them brings additional capabilities to FrontPage 98 beyond Web site creation, answers b, c, and f are correct. Internet Explorer 4.01 is not part of FrontPage 98 (the product includes the 3.02 version of this software). Therefore, answer a is incorrect. Transaction Server 2 and Index Server 2 are part of the Windows NT 4 Option Pack and do not ship with FrontPage 98. Therefore, answers d and e are also incorrect.

Question 47

Hover buttons are based on Java applets. Therefore, answer a is correct. Because none of the other answers represents the technology used to implement hover buttons in FrontPage 98, answers b, c, and d are incorrect.

Question 48

The menu bar and the Table toolbar are the interfaces within FrontPage Editor from which you can draw a table. Therefore, answers b and d are correct. Neither the Table Properties dialog box nor the Standard toolbar permits tables to be drawn. (Although they do allow for tables to be inserted, this is not what was asked for in the question.) Therefore, answers a and c are incorrect.

Question 49

Using FrontPage Editor, Java applets and scripts can be added to a Web page from the Advanced toolbar. Therefore, answers b and c are correct. FrontPage Explorer may not be used to place applets into individual Web documents, nor can you type Java code directly into a Web document, which is why answers a and d are incorrect.

Question 50

FrontPage 98 does not maintain a local compressed copy of Web site objects. Therefore, if you delete a Web site, it's not recoverable using only FrontPage 98 utilities. Unless you have a separate backup of these materials, the Web site could be unrecoverable after it's deleted. Therefore, answer b is correct.

Question 51

Configuration information for FrontPage Personal Web Server, including TCP port designation, resides in the HTTPD.CNF file. To change the TCP port address from its default, you must edit the **port** entry in this file and change its value to 8080. Therefore, answer e is correct. The Tasks View in FrontPage Explorer does not include a facility to change a Web server's configuration. Therefore, answer a is incorrect. The ISM applet in the Control Panel lets you modify only the port address for IIS or Peer Web Services, not for FrontPage Personal Web Server. Therefore, answer b is incorrect. Neither of the Windows configuration files mentioned in answers c and d controls the port setting for FrontPage Personal Web Server. Therefore, those answers are incorrect as well.

Question 52

Those wizards mentioned that create Web sites or Web pages—namely, the Form Page wizard, the Discussion Web wizard, and the Corporate Presence wizard—all use WebBot components. Therefore, answers b, c, and d are correct. The Import Web wizard merely converts existing content and does not create new pages or functions, so it does not use WebBot components. Therefore, answer a is incorrect.

Question 53

Because each pane with a frame layout can indeed display a different content page, and because frames use targeted hyperlinks to load resources into named panes, answers c and d are correct. Not all browsers support frames (especially older ones) nor are content pages within forms panes prohibited from using Java applets. Therefore, answers a and b are incorrect.

Question 54

A custom form handler may have the method, action, and encoding type defined. Therefore, answers a, b, and d are correct. These are set using the Options For Custom Form Handler dialog box in FrontPage Editor. Programming language appears nowhere in this dialog box. Therefore, answer c is not a valid parameter for a FrontPage 98 form.

Question 55

In FrontPage 98, only JavaScript and VBScript may be used to validate forms input. Therefore, answers c and d are correct. Answer a is incorrect because Perl is not supported. Answer b is incorrect because Java is an object-oriented programming language, not a scripting language.

Question 56

The file folder with magnifying glass icon permits you to open any Web page from your local file system within FrontPage Editor. Therefore, answer c is correct. The globe with chain icon is for adding hyperlinks to documents. Therefore, answer a is incorrect. The robot icon allows you to add FrontPage 98 elements to a site. Therefore, answer b is incorrect. The blank page icon allows you to open a new page, not an existing one. Therefore, answer d is incorrect. Finally, the globe with magnifying glass icon lets you add resources from the Internet. Therefore, answer e is also incorrect.

Question 57

Only static images may be used for image maps; both GIF and JPG are valid formats for creating image maps. Therefore, answers b and c are correct. AVI and MPG are both moving image formats and are therefore unsuitable for image maps. Therefore, answers a and d are incorrect.

Question 58

As long as a standard dialect of SQL is used, any valid custom SQL script will work with the FrontPage Database Region wizard. This gives the wizard the ability to handle database queries, updates, additions, deletions, and so forth. Therefore, answer a is correct.

Question 59

The correct answers to this question are a, b, and c. The proposal includes analysis of the site's goals and objectives, its audience and their capabilities, and its user interface. Answers d and e are incorrect because the proposal does not address the important issue of meeting the site's performance requirements, nor does it cover the critical security issues associated with implementing electronic commerce or database access.

Question 60

The Database Region wizard requires one or more query field names, a DSN, and a SQL string. Therefore, answers a, b, and d are correct. Not all database queries require user input. Therefore, answer c is incorrect. Likewise, even though good practice for database access controls dictates the use of a database user name and password, these are not required for the wizard to work. Therefore, answer e is also incorrect.

Question 61

FrontPage Editor provides this information, so the statement is true. This makes a the correct answer.

Question 62

The idea is to pick a lowest common denominator set of functions to avoid browser compatibility problems from occurring when users with older, less capable browsers visit your site. Therefore, recent or proprietary markup or browser capabilities should be avoided. For this question, this means that answers a (which works only with Navigator 2 through 4 and IE3 through 4), b (which requires CSS and works only with those same browsers), and d (which works only with Windows versions of IE3 through 4) are correct. However, background colors are widely supported in many browsers, and forms have been supported since HTML 2, so these are safe to use (even if background color is not supported, changing the background color has no other effect on the site's contents). Therefore, answers c and e are incorrect.

Question 63

The key here lies in recognizing the valid elements of HTML table markup. All the elements listed, except for answer b, represent valid attributes of HTML tables, not cells, and appear in the Table Properties dialog box. Therefore, answers a, c, d, and e are all correct. Only answer b, Header Cell, is purely a cell attribute (which is why it appears in the Cell Properties dialog box) and is therefore incorrect.

Question 64

The only technique mentioned in this question that involves no extra coding effort is described in answer d, in which a compatible plug-in will provide controls over the resource, as well as playback services. Therefore, answer d is the correct answer. Writing HTML, Java, or JavaScript code can deliver the goods but will involve considerably more work, making answers a, b, and c all incorrect.

Question 65

The Customer Support Web template is the best tool for creating a site that's meant to deliver technical documentation and customer support information. Therefore, answer c is correct. The Project Web template is too simple and unfocused to meet the needs of this site. Therefore, answer a is incorrect. The Discussion Web template is good for discussion groups but lacks facilities for publishing documentation. Therefore, answer b is incorrect. The Corporate Presence wizard is a case of overkill, because it offers numerous facilities that won't be needed for this kind of site. Therefore, answer d is incorrect as well.

Question 66

When you disable authoring, you automatically prevent FrontPage 98 users from being able to modify your site. Therefore, answer b is the correct answer. A warning message will not prevent anyone from doing anything. Therefore, answer a is incorrect. Changing the password does not prevent other users with their own FrontPage 98 accounts and valid passwords from modifying a site. Therefore, answer c is incorrect. Changing the TCP port address might do the trick, but it can also prevent ordinary users from being able to access the site, and it doesn't include any limitations on those who obtain the new port number. Therefore, answer d is also incorrect.

Question 67

Although FrontPage 98 does indeed support tasks, they do not act as alarms, and they can't issue pop-up messages for administrators. Tasks work only within the context of the to-do list, which administrators must launch manually and examine personally. Therefore, answer b is correct.

Question 68

The New Window target produces an independent browser window when it's used as the target of a hyperlink in a framed layout. Therefore, answer d is correct. Both the Parent Frame and the Whole Page targets cause the document to occupy the entire window that's currently active. Therefore, answers a and b are incorrect. The Same Frame target loads the targeted document into the frame where the target hyperlink is selected. Therefore, answer c is also incorrect.

Question 69

The key to the power and flexibility of the Database Region wizard is its use of server-side programming, which enables it to be compatible with the broadest possible range of Web browsers. Therefore, only answer d is correct. Answers a and b refer to client-side capabilities, which the Database Region wizard avoids. Therefore, they are incorrect. Likewise, the Database Region wizard does not create a FrontPage WebBot. Therefore, answer c is incorrect, as well.

Question 70

The correct answers to this question are a, b, and d. The amount of RAM, hard disk space, and bandwidth available to a server as well as the speed of its CPU affect the server's overall performance. Answer c is incorrect because the kind of HTML and other code used to create Web pages does not affect a server's performance but instead impacts a client's ability to interpret and display the related Web content.

Question 71

The IDC file requires an HTX template file name, a DSN, and a SQL string. Therefore answers a, b, and d are correct. The user name is optional, making answer c incorrect. Query field names are required by the Database Region wizard, not the IDC file. Therefore, answer e is incorrect.

Question 72

This is a false statement. You must assign script access, not execute access, to the directories containing ASP files, which makes answer b correct.

Glossary

Active Elements—Elements added to a Web document that offer interaction or customization. Active Elements are created using ActiveX, Java, and CGI scripts.

ActiveX—A technology developed by Microsoft to compartmentalize application coding.

ActiveX controls—Controls that perform specific functions, such as displaying author information, code signing, and reading content ratings.

adaptive tests—Tests that recognize when a test-taker misses a question and react by posing simpler questions on the same topic, making that topic's questions gradually more difficult until a test-taker's expertise (or lack thereof) in the category is established.

administer—The FrontPage access level that provides users with access to create, delete, and manage FrontPage Webs. It also includes author and browse access.

ASP (Active Server Page)—A Web programming technique that enriches commerce and business communications by improving script management. ASP allows you to run ActiveX scripts on the Web server. This technology was first available on IIS 3.

assessment exam—Similar to the certification exam, this type of exam gives you the opportunity to answer questions at your own pace. This type of exam also uses the same tools as the certification exam.

author—The FrontPage access level that provides users with access to create, modify, and delete pages in a FrontPage Web. It also includes browse access.

AVI (Audio Video Interleave)—A video format developed by Microsoft for Windows and Macintosh computers.

banner—A display element that stretches across the entire display area of a Web document.

browse—The FrontPage access level that provides users with access to view the Web site with a Web browser.

button—In FrontPage, as well as on the Web in general, a certain type of image that's used specifically as a hyperlink.

CDF (Channel Definition Format)—An XML vocabulary developed by Microsoft and DataChannel Inc. that lets a developer use a variety of delivery mechanisms to publish collections of information (called *channels*) from any Web server to any Internet-compatible appliance.

cell padding—In a table, the number of pixels between the cell wall and the contents of the cell.

cell spacing—In a table, the amount of space (in pixels) between cells.

CGI (Common Gateway Interface)—Executable programs that can be recompiled and ported to different operating systems.

channels—A new Web concept that supports a push technology paradigm for Web content. Channels notify users when content has been changed on your Web site (which is essentially pushing information to them).

comment—A section of text included in HTML code that's not displayed in the Web page itself.

components—Add-in elements that offer specialty functions to a Web document.

composition—The files in which sprites (objects created in Image Composer) are maintained.

confirmation—A document displayed after a form is submitted.

content page—The page contained within an individual frame.

CSS (Cascading Style Sheets)—A template that simplifies Web authoring and maintenance by separating presentation and style settings from the content of a Web document.

Customer Support Web—One of the templates available in FrontPage 98. It helps you create a Web site that's used to offer customers online help or technical support.

DHTML (Dynamic HTML)—A Web technology that combines HTML, scripts, and style sheets to add animation to a Web site.

DNS (Domain Name System)—A distributed database that provides a hierarchical naming system for identifying systems on the Internet or intranets.

document template—A template that creates an individual document that contains structure but no real content.

DSN (datasource name)—The logical name used by ODBC to point to the information (such as drive, path, and file name) that's necessary to access specific data. IIS uses this name to connect to an ODBC datasource.

extranet—All or part of an intranet in which access is granted to external users from the Internet.

form—A document that requests information and provides input fields of some sort for the data.

form element—An input field within a form.

frame—A design method used in Web documents to divide the display window into two or more distinct sections.

frames page—The document used to define the structure of the panes within the browser.

frameset—The entire collection of frames, including the frames page and the content pages.

FrontPage 98—Microsoft's Web site creation and management tool. FrontPage 98 is a full-featured WYSIWYG Web editor that may be used to either create a new Web site from scratch or modify existing Web site documents.

FrontPage Editor—One of the two main tools of FrontPage 98. FrontPage Editor focuses on the creation and modification of individual Web pages.

FrontPage Explorer—One of the two main tools of FrontPage 98. FrontPage Explorer is the primary interface to FrontPage 98, and it's also where most organizational and administrative tasks are performed.

FrontPage Server Extensions—See *Server Extensions*.

FrontPage Web Server—A very simple Web server that's shipped with FrontPage 98.

GIF (Graphics Interchange Format)—A graphics format originated by CompuServe that's now universally supported on the Internet.

hidden field—A special type of form element that isn't displayed by the browser but still transfers information back to the server when the form is submitted.

hit counter—An odometer that counts the number of times a document is delivered by the Web server to a browser (called a *hit*).

hover buttons—Java applets included with FrontPage that can animate button activity.

HTML scripting—Client-side scripts, such as scripts written in JavaScript, that are included in the markup of an HTML document.

HTTP (Hypertext Transfer Protocol)—The communication protocol of Web publishing (Web servers are known as *HTTP servers*).

hyperlink—An item on a Web page that causes an action to occur when it's clicked on. Most commonly, the action is to load another Web page, but it can also be to load an image, initiate an email, or execute a multimedia file or program.

IDC (Internet Database Connector)—Provides a communication link between ODBC-compliant databases and IIS applications.

IIS (Internet Information Server)—A Microsoft product that runs on the Windows NT Server operating system only. It's intended for moderate to heavy use on a corporate intranet or Internet Web site. IIS ships as part of the Windows NT Option Pack, which is now included with Windows NT Server 4, or it can be downloaded for free from the Microsoft Web site.

image—One of the eight types of form elements. An image used in forms is a graphic that can be used as a submit or reset button.

Image Composer—A FrontPage 98 component that's used to create and edit graphics files for Web publications.

image maps—Images that contain one or more hyperlink areas called *hotspots*.

importing—A method used to create or add to a Web site by loading content from an existing Web site.

intranet—An internal, private network that uses the same protocols and standards as the Internet.

ISAPI DLLs—Dynamic link library files for ISAPI applications.

Java—An object-oriented programming language developed by Sun Microsystems that's used for Web application development.

Java applet—A client-side platform-independent application often used on Web sites to add dynamic or interactive components.

JPEG (Joint Photographic Experts Group)—A universally supported, efficient picture format.

linked task—A task that's associated with a file within your Web site.

marquee—Scrolling text on a Web page.

MCP (Microsoft Certified Professional)—An individual who has taken and passed at least one Microsoft certification exam.

MCSD (Microsoft Certified Solution Developer)—An individual who is qualified to create and develop solutions for businesses using the Microsoft development tools, technologies, and platforms.

MCSE (Microsoft Certified Systems Engineer)—An individual who is an expert on Windows NT and the Microsoft BackOffice integrated family of server software. This individual also can plan, implement, maintain, and support information systems associated with these products.

Microsoft certification exam—A test created by Microsoft to verify a test-taker's mastery of a software product, technology, or computing topic.

Microsoft Internet Explorer (IE)—Microsoft's Web browser. Although IE3.02 was the version of this browser available at the time of FrontPage's initial release, the current version of IE (at the time this book was written) is 4.01.

Microsoft Technical Information Network (TechNet)—A Microsoft service that provides helpful information via a monthly CD-ROM. TechNet is the primary source of technical information for people who support and/or educate end users, create automated solutions, or administer networks and/or databases.

MIME (Multipurpose Internet Mail Extensions)—A protocol that allows multiple file types to be transmitted across TCP/IP networks.

navigation bar—A collection of hyperlinks used to jump from the current page to another document within the Web site.

ODBC (Open Database Connectivity)—A standard application programming interface (API) used to interact with platform/application-independent databases.

orphans—Files in a Web directory to which no link is currently attached.

pane—A divided subarea of a display or application window.

Peer Web Services—A scaled-down version of IIS used on Windows NT Workstation that allows users to publish a personal Web site from their desktops.

Perl—A programming, or scripting, language that's commonly used to write CGI scripts.

Personal Web—One of the templates available in FrontPage 98. It helps you create a Web site that contains content customized for your own personal interests, hobbies, and photos.

plug-in—A software component that's merged into a Web browser to provide a specific type of interactive multimedia capability.

port number—The TCP/IP communication port assigned to an Internet service and used by a client utility to gain access—for example, port 80 for default Web access.

primary/target audience—The group of people that represents the intended majority of viewers and consumers of your Web site.

Project Web—One of the templates available in FrontPage 98. It helps you create a Web site suitable for managing project development and direction.

proprietary markup—Scripting or HTML syntax that's nonstandard and may be supported by a limited number of clients only.

proxy server—A software product that acts as a moderator or go-between for a client and a remote host. Most proxy servers also offer content caching and firewall capabilities.

publishing—The process of moving a finished Web site to a production location.

push button—One of the eight types of form elements. A push button can be used as a Submit button.

push channel—A Web communication technique in which the content is automatically provided (pushed) to the subscriber.

PWS (Personal Web Server)—A product designed for Windows 95/98 that ships on the FrontPage 98 CD-ROM under the PWS folder. PWS is the Windows 95/98 version of the popular Internet Information Server (IIS) for Windows NT Server. PWS is a Web server that may be used to test your creations before you publish them for broader access or to host a personal Web site from your desktop.

Resource Kit—The additional documentation and software utilities distributed by Microsoft to provide information and instruction on the proper operation and modification of its software products.

RFC (Request For Comments)—TCP/IP standards that are publicly available and published.

root Web—The primary Web site on a Web server.

scripting—A type of programming language used to write custom code for Web pages.

Server Extensions—Web server add-ons that enable some of the more advanced features found in FrontPage 98.

sprites—The objects created in Image Composer.

SQL Server—A Microsoft product that supports a network-enabled relational database system.

SSL (Secure Sockets Layer)—An encryption standard used to provide secure communications between clients and servers.

style sheets—See *CSS (Cascading Style Sheets)*.

sub-Web—A self-contained Web site that exists inside a folder beneath the main root directory.

tab order—In forms, the order in which a visitor can tab through the form elements.

table properties—The features of a table, including layout, size, background, and color.

table toolbar—The FrontPage Editor toolbar that gives you several options for creating, formatting, and editing tables that are not available on the standard toolbar in FrontPage Editor.

target—In FrontPage frames, the attribute added to a hyperlink that allows you to define where a resource is loaded.

task—A reminder note that informs you that a specific action needs to be taken.

template—A tool that creates a document (or a set of documents) that contains structure but not content.

theme—A collection of graphics, background images, and color schemes used to give a Web site a consistent look and feel.

Theme Designer—An additional component of FrontPage that allows you to edit themes.

timestamp—Information added to a Web document that indicates the creation or modification date.

TWAIN devices—Devices that are TWAIN compliant (typically scanners and digital cameras).

Unix—An interactive time-sharing operating system developed in 1969 by a hacker to play games. This system developed into the most widely used industrial-strength computer operating system in the world, and it ultimately supported the birth of the Internet.

unlinked task—A task that's not tied to a specific file but is associated with the current Web site in general.

URL (Universal Resource Locator)—The addressing scheme used to identify resources on the Internet.

user registration—A feature of FrontPage 98 that allows you to force users to register themselves before they are granted access to your Web site.

validation—The establishment of limitations or rules as to what information can be submitted by a user via a form element.

VBScript—A Microsoft proprietary scripting language for HTML pages whose syntax resembles Visual Basic's. VBScript is used only in Microsoft Web products.

view—In FrontPage Explorer, a way to look at a Web site. Each view offers a different perspective and a different set of operational controls, which, when used in conjunction with one another, greatly simplify Web management tasks. The seven views available in FrontPage Explorer are Folders, All Files, Navigation, Hyperlinks, Hyperlink Status, Themes, and Tasks.

Visual SourceSafe—A Microsoft tool that's an advanced security and version control utility that uses file check-in and check-out mechanisms to manage documents, code, graphics, and other Web site components.

WebBots—The server-side executable components of FrontPage that provide special features and functions (such as searching, hit counters, user registration, and more) to Web sites hosted on FrontPage Server Extensions that support Web servers.

wizard—A "smart" tool that builds a Web site based on your input to specific prompts.

XML (Extensible Markup Language)—A new standard for describing the format of data on the Web.

Index

Bold page numbers indiciate sample exam questions.

T

U

V